Cycles of
MEANING

CO-AUTHORS

Junardi Armstrong
Cragin Elementary School
Tucson Unified School District, Arizona

Douglas Barnes
Leeds, England

Constance M. Burke
McKinley Elementary School
Normandy School District, Missouri

Kathleen Crawford
Maldonado Elementary School
Tucson Unified School District, Arizona

M. Ruth Davenport
University of Missouri-Columbia

Jean Dickinson
Cherokee Trail Elementary School
Douglas County School District, Colorado

Tonya Dix
Wren Hollow Elementary School
Parkway School District, Missouri

Lauren Freedman
Townsend Middle School
Tucson Unified School District, Arizona

Camille S. Fried
Brittany Woods Middle School
University City School District, Missouri

Carol Gilles
University of Missouri-Columbia

Janice M. Henson
University of Missouri-Columbia

Theresa Hoopingarner
Los Amigos Elementary School
Sunnyside School District, Arizona

Charlene R. Klassen
University of Arizona-Tucson

Nancy Y. Knipping
University of Missouri-Columbia

Margaret Newbold
South High School and South Middle School
Ft. Zumwalt School District, Missouri

Virginia "Gennie" Pfannenstiel
University of Missouri-Columbia

Kathryn Mitchell Pierce
University of Missouri-St. Louis

Kathy G. Short
University of Arizona-Tucson

Joan Chandler Von Dras
Wren Hollow Elementary School
Parkway School District, Missouri

Dorothy J. Watson
University of Missouri-Columbia

Cycles of
MEANING

EXPLORING THE POTENTIAL OF TALK IN LEARNING COMMUNITIES

Edited by

Kathryn Mitchell Pierce and Carol J. Gilles

in consultation with Douglas Barnes

HEINEMANN
Portsmouth, New Hampshire

Heinemann
A division of Reed Publishing (USA) Inc.
361 Hanover Street
Portsmouth, NH 03801-3912
Offices and agents throughout the world

The authors wish to thank the students and teachers whose words and
writings are quoted here for permission to reproduce them. Every effort
has been made to contact the students, their parents, and teachers for permission to reprint borrowed material. We regret any oversights that may have
occurred and would be happy to rectify them in future printings of this
work.

Acquisitions Editor: Dawn Boyer
Production Editor: Renée M. Pinard
Cover Designer: Joni Doherty

Library of Congress Cataloging-in-Publication Data

Cycles of meaning : exploring the potential of talk in learning
  communities / edited by Kathryn Mitchell Pierce and Carol J. Gilles,
  in consultation with Douglas Barnes.
      p. cm.
  Includes bibliographical references.
  ISBN 0-435-08797-5
  1. Communication in education. 2. Verbal behavior. 3. Children—
Books and reading. 4. Group work in education. 5. Interaction
analysis in education. 6. Learning. I. Pierce, Kathryn Mitchell,
1955– . II. Gilles, Carol. III. Barnes, Douglas R.
LB1033.5.C93 1993
372.6'2—dc20
                                          93-5968
                                            CIP

Printed in the United States of America on acid-free paper
98 97 96 95 94 93 EB 1 2 3 4 5 6 7 8 9

Contents

Preface

This book grew out of the explorations made in a study group of college students, teachers, and researchers interested in talk in classrooms. Our interest in talk emerged from our explorations in literature discussion groups, which led to the publication of *Talking About Books* (1988). Contributors to that book were primarily exploring responses to literature, but they were also asking how talk could enrich other classroom experiences. Studying the work of Douglas Barnes and others helped us clarify the role of talk in the classroom and recognize some of its vast potential. As we discussed Barnes's books, we found practical applications for his 1970 ideas in our 1990 classrooms. After each session we returned to our schools with clearer insights and more focused questions.

Barnes' visit to Missouri helped to answer some of our questions. He visited classrooms, listened to taped discussions of our students, and helped us to understand better the implications of the talk we had recorded. As we considered his reactions, still new questions emerged—questions that led us to write this book. At this point we approached colleagues who had not been part of our study group but who had worked and thought with us over time. They joined us in our collaborative effort to consider the potential of talk in learning communities.

CYCLES OF MEANING

As we gathered to consider talk, the concept of *cycles of meaning* helped us explain phenomena we were seeing in our classrooms. The term *cycles of meaning* was built on Barnes and Todd's (1977) notion of "cycles of utterances." Barnes and Todd suggested that meanings among people were not created in one or two utterances, but in cycles over time. Carol Gilles (1991) suggested that the cycles of meanings were more than utterances, they were the meanings and understandings that individuals and groups created over time as they transacted with one another by discussing rich texts.

As we considered these transactions, we came to some new understandings about the talk within our teacher study group as well as the talk of our students. We noted that sometimes new meanings were created quickly as group members expanded on an idea or took it in new directions. However, other topics seemed to require time. Learners thought about difficult topics both in and out of school and reintroduced those topics in discussion groups.

They also returned to topics that had produced powerful group discussions. This cycling of meaning was a metaphor to explain the ways learners created meanings as a group and over time.

When Kathryn Pierce began considering the impact of evaluation on learning, the concept of cycles of meaning that built up over time helped her explain both the evaluation of students and the professional growth cycles of teachers. Through the cycle of coming to understand what learners were accomplishing in literature discussion groups, teachers transformed their beliefs and consequently their classroom strategies. As teachers were able to "see" more, their potential to support learners increased and they discovered new questions. Some questions emerged repeatedly ("What *is* the purpose of reading? Of literature discussion groups?") but each time the questions took on new meaning. Because we had changed as a result of our learning, we revisited familiar questions that we previously thought had been answered.

Kathy Short and Carolyn Burke found the concept of cycles useful in describing the inquiry process: a regenerative search for questions and answers. Inquiry cycles develop as learners—teachers and students alike—become interested in their world, ask questions about intriguing aspects of that world, and then investigate these questions and possible solutions. Inquiry is primarily focused on exploring, rather than proving or answering questions. Each exploration reveals new and intriguing questions that will start the process anew. Contributors to this volume find significant parallels between their own professional inquiries and the inquiry cycles that help to organize their classrooms.

Dorothy Watson also used the concept of cycles as she explained the complex relationships between and among the personal knowing in which each person engages, the social knowledge that leads to and stems from that personal knowing, and the larger community meanings that are formed through our transactions with others. Watson helped us see *cycle* as a verb and understand the movement implicit in the phrase *cycling into meaning*.

Readers will find still other examples of how meanings cycle within and among participants, over time, and within the inquiry cycles of the teachers and students portrayed here.

THEMES AND INTERWOVEN MEANINGS

Although the book is divided into five major sections, certain themes weave throughout and unite the chapters. We found that each of us observed, recorded, and examined some aspect of teaching or learning. As we examined our practices and reflected on our teaching, we began to see the value of creating and sustaining community, considering literature discussion groups differently, seeing the potential of talk in other group strategies, and understanding inquiry within content areas.

Since talk is one of the best ways to help forge understanding among people, it was only natural that diversity would emerge as a theme. Our collaborative inquiries led us to confirm and expand our beliefs that:

- *Talk is important in both mainstream and "labeled" classrooms.*
  We have explored the talk in self-contained, departmentalized, LD, ESL, and "basic" classrooms.

- *Talk transcends age.*
  We have recorded and reflected upon the talk of teachers and students from kindergarten through college.

- *Talk transcends culture.*
  We have described classrooms that include African Americans, Mexican Americans, American Indians, and recent immigrants from around the world.

We are convinced that talk is an essential ingredient as we try to enlarge our understanding of the diversity in our schools.

Conversation, dialogue, and story are important aspects of the talk recorded in this book. Through conversation we learn about one another and begin to trust each other. This trust enables us to establish and sustain learning communities. Through dialogue new ideas emerge; we begin to see that knowledge is socially constructed. Story connects our lives. We use story to illustrate our own lives or to temporarily immerse ourselves in the lives of characters. Instead of approaching conversation, dialogue, and story in a linear manner, we see them woven together tightly within the life of the community. Like the fibers of a Navajo rug, conversation, dialogue, and story merge and overlap in our transactions, creating the patterns we call meaning.

PERSPECTIVES ON CYCLES OF MEANING

The organizational structure of the book is intended to highlight the various perspectives we have taken on *cycles of meaning*. The first part of the book presents the theoretical and historical contexts of our current inquiry. Watson and Barnes describe the work of those who have examined the role of talk in learning and in shaping learning communities as well as its links to our continuing inquiry. Talk is essential in establishing and sustaining communities in which learners—teachers and students alike—can effectively learn and explore, argue and disagree, and support and encourage each other as they work to outgrow their current understandings. The chapters in the second part explore the processes by which we create such learning communities within a democratic society, focusing on why we do so and how teachers can support the process.

Our interest in creating learning communities and, particularly, in the role of literature discussion groups, led naturally to our focus on talk. The chapters in the third part highlight the benefits of examining talk as a strategy for supporting learners engaged in reading and writing and in joining new learning communities.

As we continue our inquiries into literature discussion groups, we move to ever more effective small group discussions in an expanding array of contexts both in and out of school. The chapters in the fourth part provide examples of the ways we have analyzed small group discussions about books and the benefits of such analysis. One of the more significant benefits has been our enhanced professional development. We continue to learn more about the evaluation process, which influences our inquiries into the reading process and the role of talk, small groups, and collaboration in the learning process. The chapters in the fifth part present examples of the cycles of our professional development as we continually search for greater understandings and new questions about talking and learning in literature discussion groups.

The inquiry process involves continual reflection, and it is strengthened by stopping along the way to examine our current beliefs, understandings, and questions. True inquiries never really end because they lead to new questions and new perspectives on familiar experiences. In the *Afterword* Douglas Barnes, whose work significantly influenced the inquiries reflected here, compels us to consider the new questions we have discovered and the new potentials we have created for further inquiry. We offer these stories of our continuing inquiries and our new questions as invitations to continue the dialogue about talk within learning communities.

Acknowledgements

A book about talk could not have been completed without the cooperation and support of many teachers, their students, and our families. We wish to thank those whose talk we have recorded and analyzed. They have helped us grow in our understanding of the potential of talk.

We especially owe a debt of gratitude to Douglas Barnes, who graciously accepted our tentative understandings of talk and helped us move to greater understandings through his patient and gentle reading of our chapters. We also wish to thank Dorothy Barnes for her St. Louis presentations and her encouragement.

Once again Mary Bixby proved to be our *critical friend*, helping us to clarify and polish our round ideas in the manuscript, and then proofing the finished copy with us.

In addition, we would like to acknowledge:

Kathy G. Short for her insights, suggestions, and thoughtful responses throughout this project; Anita Kensler of Meramec Heights Elementary School, Arnold, Missouri, and Joel Brown, University of Arizona-Tucson, for permission to reprint their photographs; and Barbara Dorhauer for her secretarial support.

Finally, we wish to thank Dawn Boyer at Heinemann for her insights, empathy, and considerable expertise in both publishing and literacy.

Part One

CONSIDERING CONTEXTS FOR INQUIRY

Dorothy J. Watson has been instrumental in forming TAWL groups and was the first president of the Whole Language Umbrella. Her interests range from reading miscue analysis (*Reading Miscue Inventory*, 1987) to whole language classroom implications (*Ideas and Insights*, 1987) to inquiry (*Whole Language: Inquiring Voices*, 1990). Currently she is a professor at the University of Missouri-Columbia, teaching courses in reading and whole language curriculum.

Chapter 1
Community Meaning: Personal Knowing Within a Social Place

DOROTHY J. WATSON

Family gatherings, courtrooms, club houses, even coffee shops and playing fields are places where real people come together to create meaning. But of all the settings in the world, school is where people are expected to think, to explore, and in the process, to create meaning. *Talk is fundamentally connected to that creation*. It follows, therefore, that the classroom is, or should be, the most conducive and inviting setting in which to promote the human act of talking.

Cycles of Meaning is a collection of rich stories about learners—students and teachers—who have inquired, through their talk, into the meanings embedded in their literature and in their lives. As a result of their journeying together, the learners "cycled" (sometimes cautiously, sometimes with abandon) into experiences in which they shared their meaningful personal knowing and took on the responsibility for creating new, but just as meaningful, understandings.

How does talk that leads to understanding emerge? What contributes to it outside school and what facilitates it within the classroom? The paths that led to the classroom "talking-places" described in this book are as varied and unique as the school-talkers themselves. The authors here understand that it's along diverse paths that children absorb language, accept values, and take on the rules of their culture and of their many societies. It's along these paths, smooth or bumpy, that the form and substance of their utterances emerge. It's along the twists and turns that the creative minds of others contribute to the creative mind of the learner. The journey of a six-year-old may be filled with family jokes and rejoinders, "really real" questions, lengthy speeches from adults, big and little stories—in other words, with talk. Given an understanding of learners' diverse roots, the question now becomes, will they be allowed to bring their personal knowledge and personal ways of knowing (including the powerful meaning-making tool called talk) into the classroom, or will they be expected to check the depth and breadth of their lives and their powers of communication at the door? If students are welcomed whole and intact, what then constitutes the school talking-places in which they can genuinely use the fullness of their language, the metaphors and stories of their lives, and the questions in their heads to cycle once more (this time in school) into the creation of meaning? Finally, how do we as teachers interpret and encourage such phenomena? The contributors to this volume help us answer these questions and encourage further inquiry.

ORACY

When teachers refer to the power of language in the creation of meaning, their focus is often on visual language—reading and writing. Literacy demands a major part of the curriculum. Oral language—listening and speaking—is often relegated to the "assumed curriculum," which may never be actualized. This problem is not a new one. Almost thirty years ago, Andrew Wilkinson (1965) wrote that in our preoccupation with literacy, the study of oral language, whether spoken or heard, had been neglected. To help prove his point, he reminded educators that there was no term for the ability to use the oral skills of speaking and listening. There is a term to relate persons to books, *literacy*, a term to relate persons to things, *numeracy*, but not a term to relate persons to persons (one of the major functions of talk). Wilkinson (165, p. 13) found only one word, *euphasia*, coined by T.H. Pear in 1930, that might be used to label the phenomena of speaking and listening. But Wilkinson discarded the term because it described only half of oral language and because, "despite its impeccable Greek ancestry it sounds like some terrible disease" (p. 14). Instead Wilkinson proposed the term *oracy* to describe the neglected half of language education. He gave the phenomenon a name and challenged teachers to define it "in terms of particular skills and attainments, for different ages, groups, circumstances; to discover the best methods of teaching it; and to bring it into synthesis with other work, especially that designed to promote literacy" (p. 14).

In the early 1960s another researcher, Douglas Barnes, became interested in talk and the systematic way in which teachers could observe, record, and analyze their students' learning through oracy. His work with Britton and Rosen (1969), Britton and Torbe (1991) as well as his research over a professional lifetime have established a substantial and rich theoretical base that supports the practices of the writers of this volume and of teachers who espouse a whole language philosophy and who create a whole language curriculum.

ORACY AND LITERACY IN A NEW LIGHT

In *Philosophy in a New Key* (1956), Susanne Langer tells us that new ideas and insights are the result of a metaphorical light that illuminates presences which did not have form for us before the light fell on them. She argues that the truly great ideas that help us generate knowledge are born not of new answers but of new questions.

When we read Douglas Barnes' accounts of classroom discussions, we are drawn into the richness and potential of the phenomenon of oracy. Barnes calls our attention to instances of students' and teachers' creativity and courage as they work to make sense of a situation or a text. Just as important, he points out opportunities for creating meaning that, painfully, were missed by both teachers and students. Through it all, Barnes asks questions of us as critical and creative teachers and as caring humans. In so doing, he helps us "discover things that were always there." Barnes invites us to use our own classrooms as talking-places in which to ask our students and ourselves new questions. He asks us to investigate the realities of our classrooms by using inquiry in order to illuminate classroom experiences.

Theorists such as Britton (1982), Y. Goodman (1985), K. Goodman et al., (1987), Graves (1983), Emig (1971), Shaughnessey (1977), Smith (1979), and others have helped us illuminate literacy education. They have done so by turning from the static product-paradigms of reading and writing to process-paradigms that value the dynamic relationship of thought and language that results in inquiry. And they have done so without abandoning the information provided by the products of authentic literacy experiences.

Douglas Barnes' investigation of oracy paralleled the shift in literacy research. He moved us from a production/performance view of oracy to an active process one. In so doing, he has not dichotomized product and process, but instead has drawn our attention to the dialectic between speaker and speakers, speaker and the speaker's past, and speaker and text or artifact. Just as we have come to understand that teaching the sounds of letters is not teaching reading and that teaching grammar rules is not teaching writing, we now know that focusing only on production/performance speech is not promoting oracy. Barnes, his colleagues, the theorists mentioned above, and the contributors to this volume shed light on the *realities* of communication in the classroom. This new light, if focused, will illuminate a new philosophy that includes owned practices, active theories, and tested beliefs about the learning and teaching of literacy and oracy.

PERSONAL KNOWING AND SOCIAL LEARNING THROUGH TALK

In this book the authors probe the phenomenon of talk, especially what Barnes refers to as *exploratory talk*. The quality of such creative, expectant, and probing discussion should not be diminished because of the presence of typical hesitancies and silences or the use of nonstandard language forms. Utterances may be tentative, searching, and often fragmented because speakers don't always know the outcome when they speak, although they may be able to predict the responses to their talk because they have memories of previous dialogues and experiences. This remembrance of past experience is part of each learner's personal knowing.

Exploratory talk is an acceptable, even necessary way for speakers to bring their tacit knowing, or "personal knowledge" (Polanyi, 1958), to a talking-place where, through socialization, they can construct new meanings. Personal knowing *and* social learning are essential to our understanding of talk within a classroom community. Michael Polanyi, whose training in chemistry gave him first hand experience of scientific discovery, viewed personal or tacit knowledge as the dimension that allows learners to integrate the particulars of their lives with the wholes that are meaningful and important to them. "In the structure of tacit knowing, we have found a mechanism which can produce discoveries by *steps we cannot specify*" (Polanyi, 1958, p. 140, emphasis mine). (In order to move Polanyi's concept of *"personal knowledge"* to a more active meaning-making view [a new key], the term "personal *knowing*" is used here.)

Polanyi's discussion of scientific discovery enlightens our investigation of all discovery through talk, yet we can only speculate on what he means by the "steps" of tacit knowing that "we cannot specify." Could these steps help us understand the powers of the active mind that are evident in exploratory talk? I propose that such steps might include the inquiry, imagination, and creativity that precede (or accompany) understanding. I am convinced that personal knowing is more than an idiosyncratic store of facts. Personal knowing must include the processes through which learners create meaning, processes that are more valuable to learners than their "personal data banks."

The *personal knowing* any learner brings to a talking-place is constructed not in isolation but with others. In order to understand the *social* construction of knowledge, we must look at the concept in a new light. The Russian psychologist Lev Vygotsky's (1962) beliefs about the emergence of thought and language in children help to explain the personal and the social nature of meaning and talk. Vygotsky defined very young children's spontaneous talk as egocentric speech. Such speech not only provides a release of tension, but also facilitates what children are trying to do. This personal or egocentric speech helps children understand their surroundings, including all the people in it. Gradually, egocentric speech becomes a guide that determines and dominates children's actions: it directs the plans they have already conceived but have not yet acted out. As much as it may sound like a chicken and egg argument, it appears that personal speech becomes a base for social speech, just as social speech is a base for personal speech—a complex cycle of meaning making.

Vygotsky (1978) also helps us understand the phenomenon of social learning. By observing a child, we can identify when the child is able to solve problems on his or her own, without outside help. Vygotsky theorized that prior to this point there is a broad indicator of learning, called the *potential* development level. At this time the child can solve problems in collaboration with "a more capable peer or with adult guidance." The distance between a child's actual accomplishments and his or her potential accomplishments is called the "zone of proximal (next/near) development." Frank Smith provides an appealing metaphor for Vygotsky's "more capable peers." He talks about "joining the club" (1986, p. 37). He believes that "we learn from the company we keep . . . and that children grow to be like the company they keep . . . in other words, learning is social and developmental. We grow to be like the people we see ourselves as being like" (1992, p. 434). The contributors to this volume support the idea that the "club" and the "zone" must be a place in which a community of learners, both capable and less capable, can use talk in order to advance all the members' learning and knowing.

COMMUNITY MEANING

Blurring the distinction between personal knowing and social learning, inextricably combining them, leads to the concept of *community (or communal) meaning*. Community meaning is generated by and belongs to the *individual* in ways that make sense to that *individual*, and it is generated by and belongs to the *community* in ways that are meaningful to that special *collection of learners*. To understand and promote community meanings, it is essential to value personal knowing, while at the same time accepting that the base of learning is social. In large part, community meanings involve the same processes required of personal knowing: inquiry, imagination, and creativity.

Mikhail Bakhtin, considered by some to be Russia's greatest literary and cultural theorist, provides yet another view of *personal knowing, social learning,* and *community meaning.* Bakhtin redefines the relationship of individuals to *themselves* and to *others.* For Bakhtin, self and others cannot be divided or separated, they can only be distinguished or pointed out, and even then only with great difficulty, because they are so intertwined within the community. Bakhtin refers to the personal as the "inside" voice and the social as the "outside" voice(s). Both exist because of and at the expense of each other. Each exists within the other. Bakhtin believed that we respond to both "the others *without,*" and "the others *embedded within.*"

For Bakhtin, it is the tension between the personal and the social that stimulates the talk necessary for intellectual growth. It is in the tension that we hear Bakhtin's "symphony of voices." He explains the communal nature of discourse and the notion of multi-voices:

> We come into consciousness speaking a language already permeated with many voices—a social, not a private language. From the beginning, we are 'polyglot,' already in process of mastering a variety of special dialects derived from parents, clan, class, religion, country. We grow in consciousness by taking in more voices as "authoritatively persuasive" and then by learning which to accept as "internally persuasive." Finally we achieve, if we are lucky, a kind of individuality, but it is never a private or autonomous individuality in the western sense; except when we maim ourselves arbitrarily to a monologue, we always speak a chorus of languages. Anyone who has not been maimed by some imposed "ideology in the narrow sense," anyone who is not an "ideologue" respects the fact that each of us is a "we," not an "I." (Quoted in Booth, 1984, p. xxi)

CREATING TALKING-PLACES WITHIN THE CLASSROOM COMMUNITY

If the personalization of knowing and the socialization of learning are to become a way of life, it falls on teachers to create with their students a community in which meaning making is their intention, and it can't be done without talk. In a fifth-grade class, for example, six children are discussing the book *Tarantulas on the Brain* (Singer, 1982). John asks, "Are tarantulas spiders?" Without feeling any need to ask permission, Judy and Rachael go to the class resource center and choose three books on spiders. As the group explores the references chosen by the girls, Tim begins to talk about a tarantula he and his uncle found. After almost a minute in which the children are absorbed in his hesitant, but detailed information, Tim ends with, "I didn't know I knew all that!"

As Judy, Rachael, and Tim set the scene for creating meaning, the children related the new information gained from reference books, their common book, and Tim to their awakened personal information, whether it was accurate or not. It was not a matter of adding new bits of information to old; rather, it was the hesitant but dynamic process of bringing forth personal knowing in a social place. Within this setting, talk

- *Encouraged real questions* (John: "Are tarantulas spiders?").
- *Was informative and hesitant* (Tim: "Me and my uncle—we—uh found this spider—a tarantula. It was—remember when I went to Florida? G—it was—um about this big—like maybe—at least two inches—yeah. Have you ever seen one? They're neat, real hairy and—uh—two big parts and see, we don't have 'em 'round here. I think in hot places, wet maybe . . . the tropics. If you get bit I think you get real sick, maybe die. I didn't know I knew all that!").
- *Was natural* (Tina: "Tarantulas are creepy.").
- *Was a way of connecting with other texts* (Lisa: "Charlotte was a spider, she wasn't no . . .").
- *Expanded knowledge* (Judy: "Tarantulas are poisonous.").
- *Allowed a learner to emerge as a resource* (Tim: Yeah, you're right.").
- *Expanded knowing* (John: "Tarantulas are spiders, but Charlotte was a spider that wasn't a tarantula. Right?").

As these students worked, it became evident that talk in this social place was fundamental to their journey into meaning and to the strengthening of their sense of community.

INQUIRING INTO COMMUNITY MEANINGS

Perhaps the only way we can understand the complexity of the children's discussion, which is excerpted from twenty minutes of talk, is to study talking and thinking not simply as a relationship between two speakers but as a semiotic that involves the personal knowing of Tim and of all the participants, as well as how each child creates meanings within a social place. In other words, as teachers and researchers, we need to study oracy just as Berthoff (1991) suggested we study multiple literacies, "by supporting . . . ethnographic approaches to reading and writing, learning with them [colleagues] what it means to begin with meaning" (p. 281). In our investigation of multiple oracies we must describe, as ethnographers do, the origins and characteristics of learners' attitudes, customs, values, and experiences. In order to understand the theoretical interpretations of Douglas Barnes and the other whole language theorists and teachers whose stories are told in this volume, we must attend to our own classroom histories and record and reflect on the multiple voices of our students within the talking-places—the social settings—of the classroom. Histories that richly portray learners come about through the study of authentic talking experiences.

Berthoff (1991) also tells us that if we are to have a theory of the way we interpret what we see (for example, learners talking about a book they have all read), we must also have a theory about what we accept as experiences that are truly representative of learners engaged in making meaning. That is, a *theory of interpretation* requires a *theory of representation*.

An acceptable theory of representation supports wholeness and process. If students are not to be misrepresented and therefore underestimated, it is important to keep the learner whole, that is, to shun single, one-dimensional labeling, such as "learning disabled" or in the "low reading group" or the "nontalker." If students are not to be misrepresented, we must understand how learners mediate (process) the symbols of their lives; that is, how, through socialization, they have come to be the people they are. One of the most trustworthy ways of determining the multidimensions of personal knowing is not through conventional testing procedures but through experiences of talk. *Authentic representation* sets the stage for *authentic interpretation*.

In order to understand the concept of authentic interpretation I want to return to the concept of community meaning, the creation of meaning through both personal knowing and social learning. The authors of this book show that community meanings come about when students are encouraged to "be alone with their own thoughts," and to bring their lives to the lives of others through talk. Then, within the community of learners we can interpret the inquiry, imagination, and creativity involved in making meaning.

Suzanne Davis's fifth graders accepted me as a regular visitor in their classroom as I observed their literature study groups. They all generously shared their stories and projects with me. All, that is, except Gary, who, to my knowledge, had never recognized my presence, much less struck up a conversation.

I was surprised when Gary abandoned his routine of sitting through entire literature study sessions without saying more than a couple of words; one morning he arrived first at the table, spread his hands over his book, and before anyone could comment said, "I wish I could write as good as Paula Fox." His quiet statement didn't go unnoticed by the other students. Without a moment's hesitation, Alon replied, "Gary, you do write as good as Paula Fox." For the next five minutes, Gary's peers recounted, in surprising detail, pieces he had written. Cory ended the discussion with, "And Gary you draw good, too!" At the end of the day, as I was leaving, Gary spoke to me for the first time, "Here's a story I just finished writing and illustrating. *Alon* thinks you might like to read it." Through talk, these learners encouraged a friend, strengthened their community, and made each other feel a head taller.

In that same session Mynett, one of the least proficient readers in the class, got the group's attention by jabbing at the word *gargoyle* in her book, demanding, "What did you do when you came to this word?" The students immediately turned to their own books and began, sometimes hesitantly, to offer advice:

047   TOM: Well, that's really uh—just look—and say it the best way you can. It's *gar-gol-ee* I think. That's what I did.

048   ALON: And you know it means something bad because it's talking about—describing the housekeeper and you know how bad she . . .

049   CHRIS: Yeah, really mean. Just say, um, um, just say "ugLEE old dog" and go on. [Nods and smiles from the group.]

050   CORY: Or, Mynett, it was at a really exciting place and I just, just, skipped the word and went on.

051   RHONA: Yeah, the author never says it again — if she don't say it again, well . . . well

052   CHRIS: Can't be too important.

053   RHONA: Yeah, that.

054   BILLY: I didn't even *see* the word.

055   ALON: Mynett, do you want to know what it means, like . . . or what . . . how to enounce . . . *pronounce* it?

056   MYNETT: Well . . .

057   CORY: Mynett, if you want to you could look it up in the dictionary now. If you think it's an . . . an . . . interesting word.

058   MYNETT: I think I get it.

How do we interpret this oracy experience? First of all, it may come as a surprise to learn that the teacher, Suzanne Davis, was seated with the group. One of her contributions to the discussion was that she refrained from directing or taking over; instead, she was an interested listener. Suzanne did what I find few adults are able to do—she kept quiet. She did not do for students what they were quite capable of doing for themselves—create meaning within their community. This teacher understood that children learned not so much when she was talking but when they themselves were talking. She therefore made it possible for children to do what Barnes calls "shaping" the discussion. It was not that Suzanne withheld information when it could not be provided by other members but that she refused to ask all the questions (especially at the beginning of the discussion period). Paulo Freire (1973) tells us that until learners ask their own questions about things of importance to them there will never be any genuine ownership of learning. Ownership has a great deal to do with developing a social consciousness, whether with the peasants in Freire's Brazil or with this handful of eleven-year-old boys and girls. The students in this group did not think of their teacher as the only source of information, nor did they view her as the one responsible for their learning.

But how else can we interpret these two talking events?

Through talk, an authentic representation of these students' lives has been established. We can now explore, describe, and interpret *communal meaning,* that is, we can investigate the inquiry, imagination, and creativity that came about through students' talk.

Together the learners inquired into the work of another student (Gary), and they responded honestly and kindly to him when he made the genuine comment, "I wish I could write as good as Paula Fox." This is not conventional inquiry, but it indicates that the children had not only learned "content" from their experiences within their community, they had also learned how to respond truthfully and helpfully to their peers. In the second discussion, Mynett's inquiry, "What did you do when you came to this word?" was a three-tiered question: (1) How do you pronounce this word? (2) What does this word mean? and (3) What strategy did you use when you met this word? The students responded to real "problemization" (Freire, 1972) by taking the question seriously. By activating their imaginations they were able to see the similarities between Mynett's problem and those they had in their own reading. Finally, they were able to create not just one, but a collection of relevant strategies that allowed Mynett to take control of her own reading.

TEACHERS' RESPONSIBILITIES

In all his work, Barnes opens up the possibility of talk-in-the-community-of-learners as he closes down teachers' controlling routines (such as question-and-answer Ping-Pong). In the concluding chapter of *From Communication to Curriculum* (1992), Barnes specifically addresses the responsibilities of teachers for learners' creation of meaning, particularly when teachers are not present in a group setting. He suggests five ways teachers can support communal learning:

1. Provide learners with a feeling of competence. Instead of trying to guess what is in the teacher's head, students need to feel confident of their own understanding of possible solutions to real problems. Teachers must show that they value students' contributions and the language with which these contributions are made. It is equally important that the teacher "educate his pupils' sense of relevance by encouraging them to make connections between new knowledge and old" (p. 192).

2. Facilitate "common ground." Barnes suggests that shared experiences, such as investigating tangible artifacts, can provide this common currency. The authors of this volume write about learners who share a piece of literature they have personally read and may collectively return to again and again as common and public holdings. These artifacts set the stage for children's imaginations. In Barnes's words, children "can set up hypothetical ways of organizing or explaining whatever has been put before them" (p. 193).

3. Facilitate a focus for learning. Barnes cautions teachers, "it is all too easy to do the learning for our pupils, to try to by-pass the struggle to recode by dictating the adult version ready-made" (p. 194). There is the risk that teachers will focus learning too narrowly, so that students see no room for their own interests. There is also the risk that their focus will be too wide, so that the students haven't a clue about their own role in the learning experience. Barnes suggests that it is the teacher's responsibility to direct pupils' attention, while emphasizing how learners can take control of their learning by asking their own questions. Questioning is "all the more powerful as a means of learning in that it has been set up by the children themselves in a leap of imagination" (p. 194).

4. Provide suitable pacing. Pacing has to do with time—an essential element in learning. As Barnes cautions, "if the teacher thinks of pupils' language in terms of *performance* instead of in terms of *learning*, he will not give them time for the reorganization of thought to take place" (p. 195).

5. Help learners fulfill their need for a public audience. Throughout this volume there is an emphasis on exploratory talk in which learners are encouraged by their social setting to inquire, imagine, and create in whatever messy, convoluted, or logical ways group members encourage or tolerate. According to Barnes, however, learners also need "a more public discussion of the same topic." This presentational talk provides "new demands for explicitness and organization" (p. 197).

CONCLUSION

Just as individual learners can't create meaning without others, neither can a social context exist without individual learners. When students walk into our classrooms we can make diverse assumptions, from "here are empty heads for me to fill with *my knowledge*" to "here are children filled with ways of knowing that can enlighten us all." If we make the first assumption, we allow only a fraction of the learner into the classroom. We spend time and energy on "covering" a prescribed, often irrelevant, curriculum, which keeps the student standing alone at arm's distance, busy with controlled oracy and literacy activities. If we make the second assumption, we invite learners to bring their lives, their stories, their experiences, and their personal ways of knowing into the classroom. The curriculum that emerges from such invitations embraces learners, valuing and encouraging their individual and communal voices.

Watching learners engrossed in a conversation fills us with questions: "How have they learned to talk and behave this way? What was the teacher's role in all this?" Douglas Barnes and the other teacher/authors of this volume help us see relationships within the complex process of talk. They help us understand and value both personal knowing and social learning. They challenge us to make a commitment to community meanings. A starting place may be what Douglas Barnes calls "working on understanding" through the phenomenon of talk.

REFERENCES

Bakhtin, M. M. 1986. *Speech genres and other late essays.* Austin: University of Texas Press.

———. 1984. *Problems in Dostoevsky's Poetics.* Ed. and trans. by C. Emerson. Introduction by W. C. Booth. University of Minnesota Press.

———. 1981. *The dialogic imagination: Four essays by M.M. Bakhtin.* Ed. by Michael Holquist, trans. by Caryl Emerson & Michael Holquist. Austin: University of Texas Press.

Barnes, D. 1992. *From communication to curriculum.* Portsmouth, NH: Boynton/Cook.

Barnes, D., J. Britton, and H. Rosen. 1969. *Language, the learner and the school.* 1st ed. Harmondsworth: Penguin Books.

Barnes, D., J. Britton, and M. Torbe. 1991. *Language, the learner and the school.* 4th ed. Portsmouth, NH: Boynton/Cook.

Berthoff, A. 1991. "Rhetoric as hermeneutic." *College composition and communication* 42(3): 279–87.

Britton, J. 1982. *Prospect and retrospect: Selected essays of James Britton.* Ed. G. Pradl. London: Heinemann.

Emig, J. 1971. *The composing process of twelfth graders.* NCTE Research Report B. Urbana, IL: National Council of Teachers of English.

Freire, P. 1973. *Education for critical consciousness.* New York: Seabury.

———. 1972. *Pedagogy of the oppressed.* New York: Penguin.

Goodman, K., E. Brooks Smith, R. Meredith, and Y. Goodman. 1987. *Language and thinking in school: A whole-language curriculum.* 3rd ed. New York: Richard C. Owen.

Goodman, Y. 1985. "Kid watching: Observing children in the classroom." In *Observing the language learner.* Edited by A. Jaggar & M.T. Smith-Burke. Urbana, IL: National Council of Teachers of English; Newark, DE: International Reading Association.

Graves, D. 1983. *Writing: Teachers and children at work.* Portsmouth, NH: Heinemann.

Langer, S. 1956. *Philosophy in a new key.* New York: Mentor.

Polanyi, M. 1958. *Personal knowledge: Towards a post-critical philosophy.* Chicago: University of Chicago Press.

Rosenblatt, L. 1976. *Literature as exploration.* New York: Modern Language Association.

Shaughnessey, M. 1977. *Errors and expectations.* New York: Oxford University Press.

Singer, M. 1982. *Tarantulas on the brain.* New York: Scholastic.

Smith, F. 1992. "Learning to read—the never-ending debate." *The Kappan* 73 (6): 432–41.

———. 1986. *Insult to intelligence: The bureaucratic invasion of our classrooms.* Portsmouth, NH: Heinemann.

———. 1979. *Reading without nonsense.* New York: Teachers College.

Vygotsky, L. 1978. *Mind in society,* edited by M. Cole, V. John-Steiner, S. Scribner, and E. Souberman. Cambridge, MA: Harvard University Press.

———. 1962. *Thought and language.* Cambridge, MA: MIT Press.

Wilkinson, A. M, ed. 1965. *Spoken English: Educational review: Occasional publications number two.* 17(2) supplement. Edgbaston, Birmingham: University of Birmingham.

Douglas Barnes was until 1989 Reader in Education at the University of Leeds, England. Retirement has enabled him to take an active interest in the National Oracy Project, set up in the United Kingdom to help teachers take on new responsibilities for talk. His main publications have been about the role of spoken language in learning. They include *From Communication to Curriculum* (Boynton/Cook Heinemann, 1992); (with James Britton and Mike Torbe) *Language, the Learner and the School* (Boynton/Cook Heinemann, 1990); and (with Frankie Todd) *Communication and Learning in Small Groups* (Routledge and Kegan Paul, 1977). Books on other subjects include: (with Yanina Sheeran) *School Writing: Discovering the Ground Rules* (Open University Press, 1991); (with Dorothy Barnes) *Versions of English* (Heinemann, 1984); and *Practical Curriculum Study* (Routledge and Kegan Paul, 1982).

Chapter 2
Supporting Exploratory Talk for Learning

DOUGLAS BARNES

Teachers have always known that classroom language is important, but their attention has often been primarily directed to the development of children's language competences as a curricular goal. In this chapter I shall argue for the central importance of children's talk as a *means* of learning as well as a goal of learning. As Jay Lemke (1985) argues, schools are not "knowledge delivery systems" but "human social institutions in which people influence one another's lives." One implication of this idea is that teachers should give careful attention to the ways in which they and their students create shared systems of meaning through talk (Edwards and Mercer, 1987; Cazden, 1988). However, I shall go on to argue that developing children's ability to use talk as a tool of learning is an important way of developing their language abilities as a whole.

When a teacher joins a school, he or she necessarily enters a preexisting institutional subculture, which largely defines what activities, relationships, and goals are appropriate yet leaves a certain leeway for choosing particular strategies and emphases during lessons. A teacher's classroom strategy must always contain at least four elements, whether or not the teacher is conscious of them. There must be first, a sense of who the students are and what kinds of activities they are likely to be able and willing to engage in. Second, there must be conscious or tacit views about how children learn. Third, linked to these views the teacher will have a repertoire of classroom relationships and activities likely to support such learning. (For some teachers this will include ideas about the class as a community, as discussed in the chapters in Part Two.) Fourth, the course of a lesson will also be shaped by the teacher's sense of what is important for her students to experience and understand;

this is true whether teacher and students are reading a story or discussing some aspect of the physical world. This sense of relative importance will direct how she interacts with the students, what she encourages, what suggestions or new ideas she puts forward, what she makes explicit, what dead ends she directs the students away from, and so on. Here, I shall be primarily concerned with two of these: how children learn and how this relates to the teacher's sense of what is important for students to learn.

Talk as a means of learning is of great importance throughout the curriculum. Many of the contributors to this volume, however, are particularly interested in the contribution that students' talk can make to learning in the language arts through students' discussion of the works of literature they are currently reading. It so happens that my own first attempts to record and analyze young people's talk in school were also in the context of literature, though most of my published work on language and learning has been illustrated with examples from a range of subjects, including the sciences and social studies (Barnes, Britton, and Rosen 1969; Barnes and Todd 1977; Barnes 1988; Barnes 1990; Barnes, Britton, and Torbe 1991; Barnes 1992).

TALK AND RESPONSE TO LITERATURE

In the early 1960s, when portable tape recorders first became easily available, I was teaching English in a high school in the United Kingdom and it was suggested to me that it would be interesting to record my pupils talking. At that time I was particularly interested in how my high school students talked about poems when I was not there to guide them, so I recorded one or two discussions of groups of four or five fifteen-year-olds. The recordings pleased and surprised me because they showed that these older students could unaided penetrate deeply into quite difficult poems and make good sense of them. It seemed that in lessons I was not always making full use of my students' ability to make sense of the world for themselves, for they were clearly able through collaborative talk to develop their understanding of literature, supporting one another in inquiries that took them beyond where any one of them would have reached alone. Perhaps, I thought, I had been trying in my teaching to do the learning for them, which in the nature of things they could only do for themselves.

A few years later a British national project called *Children as Readers* gave me the opportunity to find out more about how older students read literature. As part of the project, a group of teachers of English from high schools in the city where I live met to study the teaching of literature. Some members said that they were puzzled at the difficulty they were having in achieving useful discussion of novels in some classes: often the students seemed to have enjoyed the novel but had little or nothing to say in class. We decided to explore the possibility that the problem lay in a mismatch between how young people "naturally" talk about a story and the ways in which teachers set up the topics and expectations in class discussions (ignoring some other possible explanations). To test this we arranged that fourteen- and fifteen-year-old students from several schools should be asked to read the novel *The Day of the Triffids* (Wyndham, 1951) and should then be tape-recorded discussing it in groups of five without the guidance of a teacher or even of set questions.

I shall illustrate these discussions of *The Day of the Triffids*, a novel which most of them had greatly enjoyed, with one group of fourteen-year-old boys and girls (noted below as B1, B2, and G1, G2 respectively). (For those who have not read the novel it is perhaps helpful to mention that it is set in England after a worldwide catastrophe in which civilization is almost destroyed. Bill, the narrator, is one of the few who are not blinded and killed.) This extract comes from near the beginning of their discussion.

13 G2: Well it was quite obvious that other countries were just in the same position as Europe . . . because they would have helped Europe if they weren't.

14 B1: Yes and if . . . you'd cast your mind back . . .

15 B2: This is what Bill said.

16 G1: Yes.

17 B1: If you'd cast your mind . . .

18 G2: Even if Bill didn't say it . . . Even if Bill didn't say it . . . it would be quite obvious, wouldn't it?

19 B1: When they found them er . . . a small party . . . that girl . . . she always depended upon the Americans that they would come and help . . . and . . .

20 G1: What, that young one?

21 B1: Yes.

22 G1: In that first party.

23 B2: But there was nothing wrong with that, surely?

24 G1: [Omission]

25 B1: He was afraid to smash a window and take something. If I'd been in his position I'd have . . . smashed the first window that I could see.

26 B2: You could see . . .

27 G2: I thought it was very true to our nature, you know, to human nature what they did the way, you know . . . The first thing you

want to do is to try to get some food and you'd do anything to get it.

28 G1: Yes, you know, I could understand Bill's situation. At first, you know, he's got a twinge of conscience . . . It wasn't really . . . He couldn't really see it was right for him to . . . because he did he had got his sight and everything like that . . .

29 B2: Yes, but as it explains in the book he has to throw . . . so many years of what we'd normally do away. All the standards and conceptions that he'd learnt all his life.

30 G1: [Inaudible]

31 B1: How did he end up in hospital? When he got . . .

32 B2: With a triffid's sting.

33 G1/2: With a sting.

34 B2: The triffids really saved his life.

35 G1: He must have built up a resistance to triffid stings. I think this was probably why he first got . . .

36 B2: Well, it's like an injection . . .

When the passage begins the group is engaged in a fairly lengthy exchange in response to one boy's criticism that the author has not told the reader explicitly that the whole world is experiencing the same catastrophe. All other members of the group had been in no doubt that this was the case, and so they were persuading the critic that this was not a valid criticism. The discussion thus was partly concerned with "sorting-out" the details of the story and partly with criticizing some aspects of the novelist's approach. In utterances 19 to 23 further checking of the story goes on to ensure that all members of the group are understanding it similarly. At 25, B1 introduces another issue: he puts himself in the place of the narrator, Bill, and says that he would have behaved differently, thus treating the events as if they were real and identifying himself with the character's experience. The other members of the group disagree; in Utterances 27 and 28, G2 and G1 argue that Bill's initial hesitation to break into a shop to get food is very lifelike. All are applying the principle of verisimilitude to their criticism of the story. B2 next (29) explains Bill's hesitation, thus moving the discussion toward a more general evaluation of the novel as artifact and enunciating one of the main themes of the earlier part of the novel. In 31 to 36 they return to explaining the character's situation at the beginning of the novel.

I quote this passage because it illustrates the kinds of response to the novel that teachers found when they met to listen to and discuss the recordings. A very large part of the talk that went on in the groups seemed to perform either of two functions, which we called "re-experiencing" and "sorting-out." The reader will recognize what constitutes "re-experiencing" if we associate it with the phrase, "You remember that bit when. . . ." The students were using the group talk as an opportunity to experience again some of the most telling episodes of the novel, as if by sharing them they were at once enjoying them again and strengthening and confirming their individual responses to them. It occurred to us that in whole-class discussions led by a teacher both the size of the class and the teacher's priorities would often prevent such sharing of recollections, even though this played a large part in the talk of the groups.

What we called "sorting-out" was an extension of this. In the course of re-experiencing parts of the novel, all of the groups spent a substantial proportion of the time confirming that they shared an understanding of the incidents, checking the order in which they occurred, and ensuring that they agreed about the causes of events and the motives of characters' actions. This sorting-out was pursued eagerly and frequently returned to; it provided a basis from which pupils made occasional leaps toward a more interpretive or evaluative discussion.

When we analyzed the recordings systematically we found what we called "four levels of talking about literature," all of them illustrated in the passage quoted above. These were

1. *Identification.* This included putting themselves into the character's situation and interpreting the events in terms of their own concerns and experiences.
2. *Verisimilitude.* This was a matter of treating the characters and events as real rather than inventions, often giving them a life outside the events of the novel, as well as criticizing the tale from the point of view of likeness to life (which is of course not always relevant).
3. *The novel as artifact.* Here the novel is treated as the creation of a particular person, an expression of the novelist's intentions, values, and visions.
4. *Virtual experience.* The novel is treated as a message that can be understood and enjoyed in its own right, separate from the author's situation and intentions. (Barnes, Churley, and Thompson, 1971)

At this point I want to consider one of the questions with which this chapter began, the kinds of talk about literature that teachers should encourage in lessons. In discussing the group talk we began to look critically at our own assumptions and eventually became less and less convinced that our metaphors of "levels," "profundity," and "maturity" could be justified. These expressions seemed to imply that re-experiencing and sorting-out, and even matching stories and poems against experience, were inferior ways of responding to literature, which teachers should not encourage. We eventually concluded that, on the contrary, the kinds of reading we had called "levels one and two" were the bedrock on which all other responses had to be built, even for adults. We concluded that our training in the conventions of adult literary criticism had led us to undervalue some of the processes that necessarily underlie response to literary works, particularly for children. The recordings persuaded us that students need to reconstruct the story, to identify themselves with the characters, to share their interpretations with their peers, and to relate the events to the world they know before they move on to more obviously "critical" responses. Upon reflection, the teachers in the group acknowledged that in their own reading they often needed to make links with their first-hand experience before they could distance themselves from the text and look at it as they had learned to do during college courses in English literature.

The teachers began to consider how they might give these basic ways of responding a central place in their lessons, though they were well aware that merely to ask students to retell a story in class would be unlikely to succeed. Perhaps this explained why some class discussions did not run smoothly: had the teachers asked "level three and four" questions when the students still needed to deal with the tale at the more basic levels? (It would certainly contrast even more strongly with the traditional approach through plot, character, and theme, though I doubt whether any members of that group were wedded to such a view of literature.) Discussion in small groups would enable students to carry out whatever retelling and checking against experience they needed. We had seen from the recordings that small group talk allows exploration of a text in different ways ("levels") to go on concurrently. Younger students in grade school should undoubtedly be given opportunities to explore whatever they are reading in the basic ways I have indicated. Many of the contributors to this volume illustrate that even very young students can support and extend their responses to stories by exploring them together, just as adults can. I still believe that class discussion led by a teacher is necessary from time to time to help students extend their strategies in reading. This is because the kinds of response that we called "levels three and four" are partly conventional—based upon "an implicit model of literary discourse" (Cazden, 1988)—so that many students will not use them without the interaction and support of an adult. This is even more clearly true in other subjects such as science. (Lemke 1985; White 1988) Empirical studies of student-led discussion of literary works in small groups are infrequent (Haught, 1972; Wilson, 1976; Barnes and Todd, 1977; Dewhirst and Wade, 1984). Their conclusions are varied, but all assert the value of such discussions, even in comparison with those led by teachers.

TALKING AND LEARNING

When I moved into university teaching, one of my tasks was to teach a group of experienced teachers from both primary and secondary schools a course called "Language in Education," and this provided an opportunity to widen my understanding of the role played by the talk of both teacher and students in school learning by applying it to areas of study other than literature. The course allowed me to involve the teacher/students in informal research in their own schools, so I asked them to tape-record selected lessons taught by colleagues in a range of curricular subjects and to analyze them according to a scheme that we developed together. The results (Barnes, Britton, and Torbe, 1991) convinced me that what I had learnt from the literature discussions about the importance of talk in learning could be applied to the whole curriculum. What both I and the teachers who were working with me found most striking was the passivity of the students in the first few weeks of secondary schooling. Most of the questions teachers asked were strictly factual and required little or no ability to sustain sequential thinking. (I was later to discover a well-established tradition of North American classroom studies that had arrived at very similar findings [Hughes, 1963; Hoetker and Ahlbrand, 1969; Westbury, 1972].) Even more discouraging was to see what effect this was having upon the students' participation in lessons: they were offering mainly single word replies, and what questions they asked were demands for reassurance rather than expressions of lively curiosity about the matter in hand. My students and I were little less than horrified at this analysis of what we acknowledged to be typical lessons: was this really the best way to support young people's learning? How can teachers set up communication in classrooms so that the students' ability to make sense of the world through talk can contribute fully to their learning in all subjects of the curriculum?

In order to see how talking can contribute to learning it is necessary to consider the processes involved in the kind of learning that goes on in schools. Although during their training all teachers study the psychology of learning, this seldom has a profound effect on their practical assumptions about learning and teaching, which are usually formed during their first few years of teaching in schools. It is worthwhile to revisit these assumptions, which can sometimes interfere with the development of a wider repertoire of teaching strategies (Schon, 1983).

Most psychologists of education, however much they disagree on other matters, nowadays accept a view of learning that can loosely be termed "constructivist." At the center of constructivist thinking is the idea that whenever learning goes beyond rote memory or the repetition of motor skills, it must involve the learner in the active construction of meaning. When a young child, for example, begins to observe that the surface of a liquid remains level even when the container is not upright, this is not merely an "addition" to knowledge, for it potentially changes a whole range of observations, understanding, and behavior. This new understanding has to be brought into relation with existing ways of seeing the world, which may then need to be changed, perhaps in quite radical ways. The child may begin to realize that when he draws a person walking up a hill he should keep the body vertical and not perpendicular to the slope. Or (to take a contrasting example) it may affect the way in which he carries containers of liquid. Now these changes in perceptions and behavior do not take place automatically: the child himself is likely to be involved in a series of readjustments and discoveries that may take some time. Learning does not take place in a moment, nor without the learner's help.

For this example I have taken a very young child, but the same principle applies throughout our lives. Some years ago I witnessed a science lesson in which a teacher passed a glass beaker of cold water through a Bunsen flame. The class of eleven-year-olds correctly observed that droplets of water appeared on the bottom of the beaker. The teacher then asked them to account for the presence of this water. Some pupils suggested that it must have spilt over the edge, others that it had condensed from the air onto the cold surface of the glass, though this appeared unlikely, since it had not been there before the beaker was passed through the flame. Other suggestions were made but none appeared to make sense. By the end of the lesson it had become clear to me that the water was in fact one of the products of the burning of town gas. As a nonscientist I found this hard to grasp, and so I am sure did many of the students. Water as a product of burning contradicted some deep-seated assumptions. To accept this new idea we had to make quite profound changes in our understanding of what burning is.

I have taken these two examples from the sciences, but the same principle applies in the arts and social studies. Learning is not a matter merely of adding new information; it requires a period of reconstruction of existing ideas in the light of the new experiences, new ideas, new ways of thinking and understanding. This process (which Piaget called "accommodation") may take time, and may even be resisted by the learner. Sometimes the new ideas are close enough to the old to be assimilated easily, but other new ideas and experiences may be so unfamiliar as to require a considerable period of time and opportunities for discussion and the consideration of different examples.

It is at this point that talk becomes an important element in learning. The process of "accommodation"—modifying existing ways of understanding in the light of new ideas and experiences—may take place in many ways, including the silence of thought. But in class, teachers cannot rely on private thought but must devise shared activities that will help and encourage students to "talk through" the new ideas. So when in a social studies lesson the teacher presents the idea of "democracy," for example, it is never enough simply to tell the class about it or to give them notes to write down about it; opportunities for talking and other activities are essential. A central skill in teaching is finding activities that challenge students to relate the ideas to their own experiences. In the "democracy" example, this might focus upon the experience of taking responsibility for making a choice, not only in electing a class spokesperson, for example, but in accepting the implications of other kinds of choices students make outside of school. It is this process of accommodation, of relating new ideas to existing understandings, that gives talk so central a role in the public arena of the classroom.

Students do not learn merely because a teacher provides them with new material or new experiences: the opportunity and the challenge to relate this new material and these new experiences to their existing expectations are essential. And this takes time, for learning of any importance seldom happens in a moment. This is why the idea of "cycles of meaning" is so important. Many years ago Jerome Bruner proposed that the curriculum should be organized on a spiral basis, so that children would revisit the same areas of knowledge many times, on each occasion at a higher level of understanding. This "spiral curriculum" was (and is) a useful idea for teachers when they plan their work. However, recordings of students talking in a group of peers show that they have their own spiral curriculum: they return again and again to the same issues whether on that occasion or some days later, building new meanings cumulatively, each time reconstructing and extending some aspect of the topic. That is why "Cycles of Meaning" is such an appropriate name for this book.

EXAMPLES OF LEARNING THROUGH TALK

One of my teacher/students once described what was going on during a small group discussion as "working upon understanding," a phrase that well characterizes what the process of "accommodation" through talk amounts to. It is easier to understand what constitutes working on understanding if we look at some examples to see how the talk contributes to the processes of interpretation and assimilation.

In the first example two twelve-year-old boys (of average academic achievement) are moving around a science room carrying out tasks and using apparatus set out by their teacher. In previous lessons the class had been given a model of the physics of air pressure; the tasks require them to apply this model of how pressure operates to a series of examples. One of the "tasks" involves sucking milk through a straw and then explaining how this is possible. At first Glyn, one of the two boys, dismisses the task easily with: "Why're you able to do this? 'Cause you make a vacuum with your . . . mouth, don't you? And then the water tries to fill the vacuum." But his friend Steve, thought by their science teacher to be the less "able" of the two, seems not to be satisfied with this explanation, and a few minutes later calls Glyn back to the question of the straw.

17   STEVE: What about this glass of milk though, Glyn?
18   GLYN: Well that's 'cause you make a vacuum in your mouth . . .
19   STEVE: When you drink the milk you see . . . you . . .
20   GLYN: Right! You you make a vacuum there, right?
21   STEVE: Yes, well, you make a vacuum in the . . . er . . . transparent straw . . .
22   GLYN: Yes.
23   STEVE: Carry on.
24   GLYN: And the, er, air pressure outside forces it down, there's no pressure inside to force it back up again, so . . .
25   STEVE: O.K.

This passage deserves close examination. Glyn's repetition (at utterance 18) of his former account does not satisfy Steve, who pushes his friend toward greater explicitness by spelling out first "When you drink the milk . . ." and who then (at 21) makes it clear that he is not satisfied with the vagueness of "a vacuum there" and specifies "in the transparent straw." He then insists that his friend carry the account further. In response Glyn spells out the essential contrast that was missing from his earlier attempts, the difference in pressure inside and outside the straw. It is particularly interesting in this case (and also in a later exchange between these two when they are dealing with another task) that it is the questioning of the apparently "less able" Steve that forces Glyn to be more explicit *to himself:* the dialogue not only benefits Steve, it presses Glyn to organize consciously what he clearly understands in part.

We have seen how during their talk students can order and clarify ideas that they have already grasped partially; now we observe three thirteen-year-olds interpreting an unfamiliar literary text, Steinbeck's tale *The Pearl* (1967).

34   DAVID: Well, I, the best part, I liked were, when when he went looking for the pearl down in the sea, did you?

35   MARIANNE: Yeah, it should have des . . . had a bit more description about the actual diving . . .

36   BARBARA: Yes, of the sea.

37   DAVID: Yeah.

38   MARIANNE: Because if if he's supposed to be a diver he hasn't spent much time . . . diving, has he?

39   DAVID: He just went down and it were there waiting for him, wan't it?

40   MARIANNE: He should have had to search for it first.

41   BARBARA: It seems a bit funny that as soon as baby gets hurt that he. . .

42   MARIANNE: That he should find the pearl.

43   BARBARA: Yeah, he found it suddenly, just like that.

45   MARIANNE: It's just typical of a story, in't it, you know.

There are several points to be made about this exchange. In looking at the verisimilitude of the tale the students are coming near to recognizing the simplifications characteristic of this kind of story, in which the symbolic weight of events is more important than their closeness to everyday experience. What they say has not been prepared: in the course of the talk they are in part exploring their responses to what they have read, but in an important sense they are also constructing them. And the constructing is being done collaboratively: the ability of Barbara and Marianne to complete one another's utterances in this case is striking. What insights they reach, both in this short extract and in their discussion as a whole, are strictly unpredictable, for they are addressing issues and arriving at formulations that none of them could have proposed in advance.

We have seen that two students working together can provoke one another to formulate explicit explanations in science, and that thirteen-year-olds can achieve a thoughtful and relevant discussion that helps them to interpret a literary text. During a visit to schools in the St. Louis area during 1991, I was impressed by the high level of discussion of stories that students even as young as grade 3 can achieve with skillful support from their teachers. (One of of these teachers, Tonya Dix, has contributed a chapter to this book.) However, teachers need the support of colleagues when they attempt radical changes in teaching methods. These North American teachers have the support of TAWL groups and others. We turn now to a British project that has given support to teachers wishing to offer their students more opportunity to learn through collaborative discussion.

THE NATIONAL ORACY PROJECT

Over the years there have been a number of attempts to establish in schools in the United Kingdom some of the teaching practices that are implicit in a constructivist view of learning and the role verbalization plays in this effort. One of the most interesting of these is the National Oracy Project (NOP), which runs from 1988 to 1993. The term "oracy" was invented by the late Andrew Wilkinson in order to give competence in spoken language a status equal to competence in written language (Wilkinson, Davies, and Berrill, 1990). During the lifetime of the project the British government has set up a compulsory National Curriculum that includes spoken language. For the first time, oracy is officially the concern of every teacher in British schools.

From the beginning, the NOP made the striking decision to identify oracy with the use of language as a means of learning. Wilkinson, who played a central part in setting up the project, had laid down the principle: "Oracy is not a subject but a condition of learning in all subjects" (Wilkinson, Davies, and Berrill, 1990; the principles underlying the project are also discussed and illustrated at length in Norman, 1992). The focus of the project was not to be a set of skills that might be taught and tested out of context. On the contrary, it was the language used by students in the course of any of their activities in or out of school that should be the central concern of teachers. Thus there was no attempt to specify in general terms the skills relevant to learning. What was important was that students should develop whatever language resources were demanded by the particular task in hand and by the social context in which it took place. One corollary of this was that the project team could not treat itself as a set of experts who would disseminate a predefined policy to schools: it was essential that serving teachers should work together to develop ways of encouraging talking for learning in their lessons, and that they should include not only primary school teachers but also high school specialists in different areas of the curriculum.

It is not easy to characterize precisely a five-year project that is still running at the time of writing, and which has involved thousands of teachers in local groups across England and Wales. Something of what these teachers have learned can be gathered from a statement issued by one of the groups.

Children who have learned to value talk in their learning:

- Are more likely to explore beyond facts, into situations, causes, and consequences.

- Know more about the language in which knowledge is expressed.
- Have a greater repertoire of learning strategies.
- Have greater insight into the relationships among bits of information.
- Have a greater understanding of how they acquire knowledge.
- Have a better understanding of the possibility of multiple solutions to problems or questions.
- Have a greater understanding of why they are working within a particular area of knowledge.

Some of these developments seem at first glance to go far beyond language, but the significance of this can be seen by reference to some research carried out by Pat Jones (1988). He showed that many thirteen-year-old students approach discussion tasks in lessons with the assumption that what they are looking for are authoritative "right answers." Such students miss the opportunity to deepen their understanding of a topic by exploring cause and effect, by testing examples and exploring those that do not fit, by considering alternative explanations and evaluating them, and in general by relating new information to what they already know and understand. It can be seen from the formalized conclusions of these teachers quoted above that the effect of engaging students in extensive discussion of their work in various subjects has been to release them from such disabling preconceptions and to enable them to take an enlightened responsibility for their own learning.

EXPLORATORY AND PRESENTATIONAL TALK

So far I have referred to "talk" as if all talk were alike, but clearly this is not so. Some students are able to make confident statements, probably because they are expressing relatively familiar ideas. The group discussing *The Pearl* for example speak with little hesitation, since what they are doing is less exploring new ideas than interrelating impressions they have brought from their individual readings. Glyn and Steve, however, struggling with the complexities of a scientific explanation, are a good deal more hesitant, though this is not always true of discussions in science. Sometimes in the struggle to formulate an unfamiliar idea, what a boy or girl says becomes hesitant, interrupted by qualifications, full of false starts and rephrasing, and may even grind to an uncompleted halt. As Gordon Wells (1986) says, "Most conversations involving young children . . . are rooted in the here and now of perception, intention, and action, and so can be inexplicit and even fragmentary, yet still be successful for the purpose at hand." It is important not to see such uncertain talk as failed attempts to communicate; the hesitations and changes of direction, as well as the use of words such as "probably," represent the student's struggle to make sense of an emerging idea. In the course of trying to formulate this idea, he or she is sorting out thoughts aloud. It will be convenient to call this kind of hesitant speech "exploratory talk" to mark the fact that its function is not simply communication but includes the reconstructive thought that is such an important part of learning.

The value of work in small groups is that it helps children to take the risks involved in thinking aloud. A small group of peers is less threatening than the full class, and the absence of the teacher temporarily releases them from the search for right answers that so often distorts their learning strategies. Every experienced teacher knows that it is often impossible to provide opportunities for exploratory talk during a discussion with a whole class. One reason is that such hesitations delay the progress of others' thinking. This is why one of the options in every teacher's repertoire should be small group discussion, though I want to make it clear that I am not recommending it as a universal remedy, but as a valuable tool among others.

I wish to contrast exploratory talk with the "presentational" talk that predominates in many whole-class discussions. Such presentational talk does not allow students enough opportunity to make the new thinking their own, since it encourages them to be less concerned about sorting out their ideas than about earning praise by giving an officially approved answer to a question. Students know that "right answers" are expected, and that teachers do not want to linger on one student's hesitations. Moreover, students often fear laughter from the others if their contribution seems misplaced or uncertain. Indeed, the common kind of questioning that teachers use to check that students are following their line of thought calls in its very nature for presentational replies, confident and brief. Schooling is often dominated by presentational talk, whereas it would benefit the students to have more opportunities for "working on understanding," that is, more opportunities for exploratory talk.

THE CONDITIONS FOR EXPLORATORY TALK

What then are the conditions under which exploratory talk will flourish? Reid, Forrestal, and Cook (1989) have developed from an earlier analysis (Barnes 1975, Appendix) a model of classroom learning activities consisting of five sequential stages:

- Engagement
- Exploration
- Transformation

- Presentation
- Reflection

What follows is my own greatly compressed summary of the authors' explanation of these stages. The Engagement stage includes both the arousal of students' interest in a topic and the providing of experience and information about it. The Exploration stage implies the kind of thinking aloud that constitutes an initial exploration of the matter in hand. In Transformation, the teacher asks the students to use or work on the material, clarifying, practicing, ordering, elaborating, and so on. Next comes the Presentation to an audience, and finally, an opportunity for Reflection, both on the content and on the process of learning that the students have been engaged in. This last stage may include writing and some form of self-evaluation.

Reid, Forrestal, and Cook go on to propose that students are likely to learn most effectively (1) if they have a clear purpose in mind; (2) if they participate actively, building on what they know; (3) if the environment is supportive, with enough time for exploration; and (4) if they are able to make some choices and (5) take responsibility for their learning. They would probably not disagree with my view that the process can at times begin with the Exploration stage in the form of a freewheeling discussion of the students' existing preconceptions about the topic, which would then be followed by the provision of detailed information or opportunities for experiences that challenge or extend. Reid, Forrestal, and Cook do not approve of presentation to the whole class but have developed a system of "home groups" and "sharing groups" to provide a more intimate audience for the Presentation. This seems to me a useful but not essential device.

The idea of a supportive environment is not easily made specific. Reid, Forrestal, and Cook suggest helpfully that there should be some challenge but also the freedom to make mistakes. At times this may imply some guiding questions to be investigated collaboratively; at other times it may be more appropriate for the students to set their own agenda, alone or with the teacher's help. Unless students' contributions to the business of the lesson are valued by the teacher, not so much by praise as by listening and replying to them, they will not perceive their own role in learning as an active one. Terry Phillips has written of the general importance in children's development of "sensitive adults, who are ready to listen carefully, to respond with interest and to be flexible in their conversational behaviour" (Phillips, 1989). Two members of the National Oracy Project, Alan Howe and Jenny Des Fountain (1992), extend this by referring to "teachers who are aware of the need to listen carefully to what pupils say, who value their ideas, and who know how to support what pupils say." They identify other ways to create a supportive environment:

- Planning for a range of talking and listening and making these demands explicit to pupils.
- Creating the expectation in the classroom that "thoughtfulness" will be valued.
- Establishing tasks that promote particular kinds of educational talk.
- Talking with pupils in a partnership, in which roles are more evenly distributed and pupils are given a greater stake in the activities.

The whole of a teacher's relationship with a class is relevant to the success of talking for learning: if students' normal expectation is that their contributions will be received with little interest, or with sharp criticism because it does not fit in with the teacher's line of thought, they will not suddenly adopt an active role when group work is announced. Indeed, the ethos set up by a teacher during everyday classwork over weeks or months is probably the most powerful influence upon the success of group work. In the following chapter Janice Henson uses the concept of classroom as community to identify aspects of a supportive ethos.

ORACY AND THE LANGUAGE ARTS

Of course, talk allows human beings to share and communicate just as it enables them consciously to inspect and reformulate (for themselves as well as for others) their understanding of the world, both social and physical. But the two—the communication and the reformulation—are not so separate as this way of putting it suggests. We learn language by using it for purposes that make sense to us in interaction with other users of that language: it is their responses, their implicit recognition that our utterances make sense, that enable us to develop the ability to mean (Halliday, 1978; Wells, 1986). Both the social context and the speaker's sense of purpose are crucial, particularly to the development of oracy. Generations of teachers have found that language exercises, in the absence of a real desire to communicate, are ineffective ways of teaching, because they affect their students' uses of language at most superficially, and often not even that. So it should not surprise us that teachers taking part in the National Oracy Project found that encouraging their students to talk through their learning tasks not only helped them to learn but also gave them opportunities to extend their uses of spoken language and to reflect upon these uses. The project was certainly not turning its back on those aspects of spoken language that have traditionally formed part of language arts.

The central task for any learner is to relate new ideas and experiences to his or her existing ways of understanding the world and acting upon it, the process that I have called "working upon understanding." We are social beings, and even most adults find it easier and more pleasant to carry out this working upon understanding through talk with friends, or at least with colleagues whose good will can be assumed. Since the most significant learning is likely to take place when young people are talking about something that matters to someone who wants to hear, it makes sense for students' talk to play a central part in all schooling. Traditional forms of instruction, based primarily upon the teacher's presentation followed by question and answer and individual written tasks, are likely to betray even the most well-intentioned teacher into discouraging students from taking an active part in learning. It is all too easy to treat students' existing knowledge as if it were irrelevant to carefully prepared curricular plans, and therefore to discount their ability to make sense of the world for themselves. This is why it is essential for all teachers, whatever the age of their students and whatever the areas of the curriculum they are responsible for, to give students' talk a central place in their lessons.

In this book, teachers whose priorities and practices differ greatly from one another testify to what their students (and they themselves) have gained from experimenting in their classes by giving wider opportunities for talking to learn. Their successes make encouraging reading.

REFERENCES

Barnes, D. 1992. *From communication to curriculum.* 2nd ed. Portsmouth, NH: Boynton/ Cook.

———. 1990. "Oral language and learning." In *Perspectives on talk and learning,* edited by Hynds, S. and D.L. Rubin. Urbana, IL: NCTE.

———. "The politics of oracy." 1988. In *Oracy matters: The development of talking and listening in education.* Edited by Maclure, M., T. Phillips, and A. Wilkinson. Milton Keynes: Open University Press.

Barnes, D., J. Britton, and H. Rosen. 1969. *Language, the learner and the school.* 1st ed. Harmondsworth: Penguin Books.

Barnes, D., J. Britton, and M. Torbe. 1991. *Language, the learner and the school.* 4th ed. Portsmouth, NH: Boynton/Cook.

Barnes, D., P. Churley, and C. Thompson. 1971. "Group talk and literary response." *English in education* 5:3.

Barnes, D. and F. Todd. 1977. *Communication and learning in small groups.* London: Routledge and Kegan Paul.

Bruner, J.S. 1960. *The process of education.* Cambridge: Harvard University Press.

Cazden, C.B. 1988. *Classroom discourse.* Portsmouth, NH: Heinemann.

Dewhirst, W. and B. Wade. 1984. "Talking and written comprehension—the primary context." *British Journal of Educational Research* 10:1.

Edwards, D. and N. Mercer. 1987. *Common knowledge: The development of understanding in the classroom.* London: Methuen.

Halliday, M.A.K. 1978. *Language as social semiotic.* London: Edward Arnold.

Haught, E. 1972. *Student patterns of thinking in teacher-led large group discussions and student-led small group discussions of literature.* Ann Arbor, MI: University Microfilms.

Hoetker, R. and W.P. Ahlbrand. 1969. "The persistence of the recitation." *American Journal of Educational Research* Vol. 6.

Howe, A. and J. Des Fountain. 1992. Unpublished private communication.

Hughes, M.M. 1963. "The Utah study of the assessment of teaching." In *Theory and Research in Teaching,* edited by A. A. Bellack. New York: Teachers College Press.

Jones, P. 1988. *Lipservice: The story of talk in schools.* Buckingham: Open University Press.

Lemke, J.L. 1985. *Using language in the classroom.* Victoria, Australia: Deakin University Press.

Norman, K., ed. 1992. *Thinking voices: The work of the National Oracy Project.* London: Hodder and Stoughton.

Phillips, T. 1989. "Beyond lip-service: Discourse development after the age of nine." In Wells and Nicholls, 1989.

Reid, J. A., P. Forrestal, and J. Cook. 1989. *Learning in the classroom.* Victoria, Australia: Chalkface Press.

Schon, D.A. 1983. *The reflective practitioner.* London: Temple Smith.

Steinbeck, J. 1967. *The Pearl.* London: Heinemann.

Wells, G. 1986. *The meaning makers: Children learning language and using language to learn.* London: Hodder and Stoughton.

Wells, G. and J. Nicholls, eds. 1989. *Language and learning—An interactional perspective.* London and Philadelphia: Falmer Press.

Westbury, I. 1972. "Conventional classrooms, open classrooms, and the technology of teaching." *J.Curriculum Studies* 5:2.

White, J. 1988. *The language of science.* London: APU/Department of Education and Science.

Wilkinson, A., A. Davies, and D. Berrill. 1990. *Spoken English illuminated.* Buckingham: Open University Press.

Wilson, M.J. 1976. "Pupils' responses to literature in small teacher-led and pupil-led groups: A study of pupils' oral and written responses during the first three years of secondary school." University of Lancaster: Unpublished M.Sc. thesis.

Wyndham, J. 1951. *The Day of the Triffids.* New York: Doubleday.

Part Two

ESTABLISHING AND SUSTAINING LEARNING COMMUNITIES

Janice Henson is a doctoral candidate at the University of Missouri-Columbia. She was a special education teacher in the public schools and has also taught at the university level. She is currently teaching both college and Adult Basic Education classes.

Chapter 3
The Tie That Binds: The Role of Talk in Defining Community

JANICE M. HENSON

A lmost all human beings have experienced community. According to Erich Fromm (1966), "the necessity to unite with other living beings, to be related to them, is an imperative need on the fulfillment of which . . . sanity depends" (p. 36). But even though we have all experienced community, defining it is difficult. The difficulty comes about because we experience many communities in a lifetime. These different communities are like sets of Venn diagrams, some overlapping and some completely autonomous. The different communities of our lives affect us in various ways. Some form simply because we share similar interests or live in the same geographical area. These groups are important parts of our lives, but they aren't the communities we turn to in times of crisis or joy (Ahrne, 1990). At those times we turn to communities of a different sort, communities that function in the way implied in the root meaning of the word *community*. These communities are places to "commune—to converse or talk together, usually with profound intensity, intimacy, etc." and share "thoughts or feelings" (*Random House Dictionary*, 1987). Unfortunately, there is no word in English to signify this type of community other than "commune," which carries with it so much baggage that to most people it implies a community which doesn't allow or encourage individuality. It is true that communities can become exclusive and stifle individuality (Greene, 1973), but this outcome isn't inevitable. An ideal community would be one in which there was a constant flow of information, both within the community itself and between the community and the outside world. In such an ideal community, members would have the security that comes from being a part of a supportive group, and yet each individual member would feel free to differ from group norms (Fromm, 1966).

Such an ideal community doesn't exist, but *approximations* do. Each of these approximate communities provides people with their greatest possibility for fulfillment. In order to differentiate between these two types of communities, I will use the term *communities* to refer to groupings that occur as the result of chance (such as most geographical communities) or as the result of similar interests (such as professional associations). I will refer to approximations of ideal communities, where people are mutually supportive but still allow for individuality, as *Communities*.

In my experience, Communities commonly have particular characteristics: they are often multi-age; they always reflect varying abilities and skill levels; they are accepting of diversity; and they relish creativity. But most of all, they are places where people communicate with each other. By communication I mean two things: People share thoughts and feelings and through this sharing they affect the thoughts and feelings of others.

By way of example, here are some of the communicative events that occurred at a "potluck" held by a Community of which I am a member (the ages of the various participants are in parentheses): Tahna (14) plays a song she composed to celebrate Mike's (30) new job and then reads a book to Emily (6); meanwhile, Ashley (3) grabs Janice's (45) hands and proceeds to tumble and flip, as three-year-olds like to do; Kaitlyn (5) discusses the ice configurations on the pond with Joel (15); Daryl (25) sings as he washes dishes; Elzan (55) shows the slide show she put together, complete with music, of her son's wedding; the newlyweds sit in the corner reading *Watership Down* (Adams, 1972); Roger (55) reads aloud his favorite passage from *Sir Gibby* (McDonald, 1983); and all around there are discussions of philosophy, books, movies, school, gardening, photography, and watermelon pickles.

All classrooms are by definition communities because they are places where groups of people interact with each other, but few classrooms ever become Communities (Bloome and Green, 1985; Bloome and Nieto, 1992). This is unfortunate, because Communities are the best possible learning environments. Classroom Community development is difficult because of institutional, societal, and bureaucratic constraints, which inhibit communication among students and between teachers and students. One effect of these inhibitions is to undermine communication, which is fundamental to the development and sustenance of Communities (Barnes, 1992; Greene, 1973).

Despite these constraints, Communities can exist within the public school system. I observed just such a Community recently. The school was in a predominately working-class neighborhood, where unemployment is becoming the norm rather than the exception. In addition, about one-third of the students at the school are bused in from the inner city. In one sixth-grade classroom students were all working on projects, either singly or in groups. One pair of students told me they were working on a "choose-your-own-adventure" book about German prisoner of war camps during World War II. When I asked them where they got the information for their book, they readily told me they used encyclopedias and other reference books, but they said they got most of the information they needed from Charlie, who at that moment was typing at the computer. They explained that Charlie wasn't part of their project, but they knew he had lots of books about World War II. They said he got the books from his mother. I talked to Charlie and found out that the books came from the library in the school where his mother was custodian. In this classroom, students talk with each other and work together collaboratively rather than competitively. The teacher and students are all learners and experts. A classroom Community like this one doesn't just happen. It requires time and a foundation of mutual trust and respect.

THE COMPLICATED ROLE OF TALK

Many teachers see a role for talk in their classrooms; it is readily apparent to them that students should enlist the help of other students when they are learning or solving problems. It is equally apparent that talking is the easiest way to collaborate. But the way in which communication enables the establishment of Communities such as the classroom I just described is not as easily recognized. Using talk to help establish learning Communities is more involved than simply providing opportunities for students to use a kind of "talking to learn" to improve their comprehension of a subject. Complications occur because of the intricate way in which social, psychological, and linguistic factors intertwine in the transmission of messages from one person to another (Gumperz, 1986).

Talk is not the only means of communication used for cultural bonding, but it is possibly the most important because it is such a common and convenient way for people to interact. For most people, talking doesn't require any external apparatus. The only requirement is that at least one other person be within earshot of the speaker. Precisely because talk is such a common form of interaction, the role of talk in creating Communities is difficult for us to envision. Talking to people in order to establish relationships is one of the parts of life that we no longer consciously think about. It is a "taken-for-granted" fact of existence, like the sun coming up in the morning (Gee, 1992; Hymes, 1972; Johnson, 1946).

Because talk is so ordinary, it is important to look at it with "new eyes." When people stop to think about why talk is an important form of communication, what usually comes to mind is that it consists of "words uttered out loud," and words communicate messages. What is not so apparent is that the messages given and received may not have to do with the words used (Gumperz, 1982, 1986).

This is true because talk at one level is not only used to supply information about things, such as the circumference of the earth, it is also used to maintain group identification among members of a Community (Gumperz, 1986). Through thousands of exchanges in which speech is used to refer to past shared experiences, Communities are formed (Gumperz, 1982). For example, when one child in a classroom tells the teacher to treat Bonnie especially nice because she is having an "Alexander Day," she means much more than the literal meaning of those words. The child is referring to the shared classroom experience of reading the book *Alexander and the Terrible, Horrible, No Good, Very Bad Day* by Judith Viorst (1982) in which nothing seems to go right for Alexander.

Talk can also become ritualized, and these rituals help to bind Communities together. Many of the noises we make (words as well as utterances such as "ow!") are intended to fill silences or to give us a pleasant sense of being alive. Information is transmitted in such cases not by the words themselves but through extraverbal means, such as tone, loudness, pauses, facial expressions, gestures, and so on. For example, the opening phrase between two farmers as they look up at a cloud-darkened sky, "Sure looks like rain," communicates nothing to either party except through these extraverbal cues. In this way, they can communicate tiredness, elation, anger, and so on (Gumperz, 1982; 1986).

A famous literary example of this use of speech is the Br'er Rabbit story about the Tar Baby. In the story, the Tar Baby fails to acknowledge the greeting, "How do?" and Br'er Rabbit gets so angry he punches him. Most of us, who are part of mainstream American culture, know (whether we realize it or not) that the purpose of "How are you?" is not to elicit information about the life status of the person to whom we are speaking. The question is asked, and answered, because it is one of the rituals of our community. "How do?" served the same purpose in Br'er Rabbit's culture, so we see why it was totally unacceptable to Br'er Rabbit for the Tar Baby to fail to respond, that is, if he expected to be part of that culture.

In this example, Br'er Rabbit's response indicates that the linguistic rituals of that community were narrowly defined. This is a sign that the community is close, but it is also a sign that the community is *closed,* in the sense that it is not very tolerant of diversity, and ritualized language can operate in this narrow fashion. However, not all ritualized language is as restrictive as in this example. As long as it does not inhibit acceptance of diversity, it can play an important role in the creation of classroom Communities. For example, in many classrooms the term *author's chair* denotes a special time when students can share their creations, whether in the form of stories, reports, poems, artistic works, or musical compositions (Harste, Short, and Burke, 1988).

Forms of contextually dependent speech, references to shared experiences, and ritualized language are important. "Societies are held together by such bonds of common reaction to sets of linguistic stimuli" (Hayakawa, 1972, p. 83). There is nothing trivial about societal glue. This is the stuff from which Communities are formed.

ALIENATION

One of the prerequisites for being part of a community is being able to communicate in a way that is accepted, whether the community is a large one, such as a religion, or a small one made up of only a few friends. For this reason, talking only enhances Community when everyone "speaks the same language" or when people from differing language communities are willing to value each other's language (Greene, 1978; Heath, 1986; Wells, 1985). In other words, in communities where the members come from diverse linguistic and cultural backgrounds Communities will form only if the members are what Adrian Peetoom (1991) calls "tolerating." By this Peetoom means that participants in a Community accept diversity within the group without having to give up what makes them unique.

Teachers who want to promote "tolerating" Communities must first ask themselves the question that Maxine Greene (1973) proposed as the central question of teaching: *What do you see when you look at a child?* (p. 48). An equally important corollary is *What do you hear when you listen to a child?* Just as children can be "rendered invisible by someone else's gaze" (p. 48), children can also be rendered silent when we don't really hear them.

Basically, every person who comes into contact with another person develops a theory, or metaphor, to explain who that person is. The word *theory* actually means "I behold" (Coles, 1989, p. 20), but since we base our theories about people on all of our sense perceptions, not just sight, a more accurate phrase might be "I perceive and interpret." These constructs about reality are very powerful. The physicist Robert Shaw said, "You don't see something until you have the right metaphor to let you perceive it" (Gleick, 1987, p. 262). Theory molds observation and observation influences theory. What you see depends on what you have seen before (Gleick, 1987; Johnson, 1946; Oliver and Gershman, 1989).

Some students are not heard in schools because the theories on which the current curriculum is based imply that these students have nothing to say. In effect, these students are silenced. Silencing goes on in schools in several different ways: when schools do not allow students to talk or when schools do not value the students' language. Either way, students who are silenced often become alienated, and students who are alienated will find it hard to become part of any learning Community in school (Giroux, 1992; Gee, 1992; Gilmore, 1992; Heath, 1986; Simon, 1992).

I remember such a student, whom I met by chance several years ago. The incident made an indelible impression on me. I had just begun working at a junior high school and walked into the first day assembly. I was a "special" teacher and had no class of my own, so I was assigned a certain section of the bleachers to monitor. I sat down next to a student in "my" section. The girl was decidedly not one of the Europe-every-summer group. Everything about her indicated, almost like a uniform, that she was from a solidly blue-collar, working-class family. As we waited for the rest of the students to get seated, I started up a conversation. I made some noncommittal statement, such as, "It sure is hot in here." She looked at me, seemingly amazed that a teacher would address such a comment to a student. She agreed that it was awful. She then went on to say that everything about school was awful. She hated school more than anything else in the world. I asked her why school was such a terrible place, and she immediately explained herself. "It's because teachers talk all the time. Talk. Talk. Talk. That's all they ever do, and kids don't ever get to say anything. Teachers don't really want to hear what we say. They'd like it a lot better if we weren't even here. Then they could just talk to the back of the wall like they do anyway, only they wouldn't have any behavior problems. School is like a prison, only it's worse than prison because in prison you at least get to talk."

This girl was expressing alienation. Patrick Shannon (1992) defines alienation as "the process of separation between people and some quality assumed to be related to them in natural circumstances" (p. 192). It isn't a coincidence that this girl associated the source of her alienation with being silenced. Human beings are innately social creatures, and a prerequisite of social behavior is communication (Peirce, 1992). Unfortunately, much of the time communication in schools could best be described as *pseudo-communication*, since it is overwhelmingly dominated by teacher-talk (Gilmore, 1992). It is no wonder, then, that most students who drop out of school say they leave school because of alienation (Williams, 1987).

RESEARCH CONCERNING TALK AND ALIENATION

The importance of dialect differences, as related to socioeconomic class and alienation from school, has been an issue of concern for many years. Basil Bernstein (1974), while teaching in England in the 1960s, investigated how this gulf between classes, which is reflected in the ways in which members of different social classes habitually use language, contributes to the lack of success of low SES (socioeconomic status) students (Wells, 1985). He reached the conclusion that schools need to be more flexible in order to accommodate all learners, regardless of dialect. Unfortunately, his suggestions about a linkage between language usage and school failure prompted some educators, such as Carl Bereiter and Siegfried Engelman, to conclude that nonstandard dialects were inferior to standard ones and needed to be remediated (Wells, 1985).

In an effort to determine empirically what the relationship between dialect and school achievement is, Gordon Wells (1985) launched a significant ten-year study of children's language development. As a result of Wells' study, we have learned a great deal about how class differences affect school achievement.

Briefly, the study tracked the day-to-day language experiences of children and their caregivers at home. The participants were chosen from socioeconomic classes ranging from the lowest to the highest. The research study began when the children were eighteen-months-old and ended when a small group of them were ten. The conclusions of the study can best be illustrated by an example: Rosie was a child in the lowest socioeconomic category. Despite Rosie's low socioeconomic status, Wells found that the linguistic interactions between Rosie and her family were not significantly different from the linguistic interactions of higher SES children and their families. Almost all of the linguistic interactions Wells documented at all SES levels were part of ongoing activities, where meaning was much more implicit than explicit. In other words, most of the time parents and children talked about what was happening at the time, instead of talking about objects and events in the abstract.

Oral language was not the differentiating factor between social classes. Wells found that the major contributing factor to school failure in lower SES students was related to their experiences with written language. By the time they first went to school, the high SES children had been exposed to written language through thousands of interactions with their parents involving books and other forms of written language. Low SES children, in contrast, had far fewer experiences involving written language. Rosie, as far as Wells could ascertain, had never been read to, had no books in her home, and had limited contact with written language activities. What resulted, according to Wells, were striking differences in school performance between low SES students and high SES students.

Wells also accounted for what seems to be a lack of language ability in lower-class children when they come to school. Rosie again is the best illustration of why low SES students appear to have trouble communicating their thoughts. On Rosie's first day of school a teacher was trying to elicit language from her by asking her to identify a picture of a Santa Claus on skis on a Christmas card. Rosie either responded with single words or did not respond at all, leaving an observer to draw the conclusion that she was not adept at using oral language. Later that same day, however, Rosie had an encounter with another teacher who, instead of trying to elicit information about a topic that was unfamiliar to Rosie, responded to Rosie's comments about life at home. The teacher's responses brought further responses from Rosie, showing this child to be a perfectly capable oral language user. The difference in the two "Rosies" reflected the way the teachers initiated conversation. In other words, Wells discovered that the secret to school success for lower-class children was not for them to learn to speak school language, but for the school to learn to respond to student language, much as parents respond to their children. Parent-child conversations tend to center on ongoing activities in which all parties are engaged. An integral part of these conversations is the natural response of parents, who acknowledge every utterance by the child as an attempt to communicate. The parent determines (as much as possible) the exact nature of the message by using all the cues available and by fine-tuning the child's attempts through a process of responding to, and elaborating on, the child's original utterances. In this way, the parent and child come closer and closer to an understanding.

Wells' conclusions about the effect of socioeconomic class on school learning are truly revolutionary because they imply that school failure for low SES students is not a result of their inability to communicate; rather, it is the result of the school's inability to listen. The research indicates that "the performance discrepancy [between low and middle class students] that is often seen as the root of learning problems may not be a matter of competence as such but rather of a context-bound response to the school situation" (Cook-Gumperz, 1986, p. 9).

Another researcher from the same era who set out to study talk in classrooms and the role that talk plays in school success was Douglas Barnes (1992). Through observation in classrooms, Barnes helped to explain the enigma of stony, silent students who become non-stop "motor-mouths" in the halls. Barnes theorized that silence in classrooms occurs because schools typically rely heavily on what he referred to as "presentational" talk. Presentational talk is polished, characterized by complete thoughts and logical conclusions with appropriate supporting details. In contrast, Barnes observed that students were more verbal and learned more when they were allowed to use more of what he calls "exploratory" talk. Exploratory talk is the type of communication that people use when they are thinking through an idea, particularly in concert with others. In exploratory talk many ideas aren't complete, interruptions are common, some threads of the talk don't go anywhere, some suggestions are far-fetched, and some things are said just for fun. Exploratory talk exemplifies most of the talk that goes on outside of school, and yet it is rarely allowed in schools. Barnes saw this as a failure on the part of schools. His observations of students "talking through" problems in school settings revealed that exploratory talk appeared to be a necessary part of problem solving and learning.

It may be that one function of exploratory talk is Community building. The importance of exploratory talk in education needs to be stressed because the tendency has been to dismiss it as frivolous, a waste of time. Barnes discovered that this type of talk is not a waste of time because it lays the groundwork for real learning.

CREATING COMMUNITY IN THE CLASSROOM

Bernstein, Wells, and Barnes are three of the many educational researchers who have investigated the connection between talk and school success. Classroom teachers must now take the next step and learn how talk can facilitate learning in their classrooms as it helps to create classroom Communities in which students no longer feel alienated.

It is possible to create classroom Communities if teachers understand how important Communities are to learning, and if they understand that talk can be part of the creation of Communities. Simply allowing students to talk will not necessarily lead to Community. The talk must involve real communication; otherwise, instead of positive effects teachers will only end up with a lot of noise. Communication involves sharing, opening up, and exploring ideas; true communication never just flows one way. Everybody, including the teacher, has to be willing to listen and consider, or communication will come to a standstill (Gumperz, 1986; Short and Burke, 1991).

There are many ways that teachers can set up classrooms to encourage Community-building talk. Whatever ways are chosen, teachers should allow for a myriad of types of talk, where talk functions for multiple purposes.

Three related and overlapping types of talk that should be part of any Community-building classroom are conversation, story, and dialogue.

Conversation

The most familiar form of talk is conversation. In many cultures it is rare for a group of people to be together for any length of time, whether they know each other or not, without starting up a conversation (unless there are constraints that keep them from talking to each other). This phenomenon is easily seen when groups of adults who, at the completion of lectures, sermons, presentations and so on, begin conversations the moment the constraints of silence are removed. For teachers, it is much easier to see that conversation is natural than that conversation is a good thing to have in classrooms. After all, kids are always wanting to talk to each other, but that just makes teaching harder.

Allowing conversation does mean giving up some control. In school we tend to substitute discussion for conversation because there is more control in a discussion; in a discussion people examine arguments and consider ideas; in a conversation people just "talk" and anything is fair game. This is not to say that discussion is a bad thing. Discussion is a good way to get students involved in learning (as long as it isn't a kind of fake discussion where the teacher asks a question for which she already has an answer in mind, and the students try to "guess what the teacher is thinking") (Barnes, 1992), but discussion doesn't have the same impact on Community development that conversation does. This means that time devoted to unstructured conversation is not wasted because of the bonding that occurs when people converse with each other.

We know about the role of conversation in Community building by observing school-age children in conversations outside of a school setting. Shirley Brice Heath (1988) has reported on research designed to discover why some students who would normally be considered "at risk" managed to succeed in school. One of the most important factors in their success appeared to be their involvement in group activities outside of school; conversation was an important part of these experiences.

Heath described the nature of these conversations as having a kind of "sense-in-chaos." They were like dust devils, constantly moving, unpredictable in their directions, constantly kicking up extraneous material, and yet, discernable. They had form even though it was nebulous. They were characterized by rapidly interactive discourse that often concentrated on "what would happen if?" explorations of multiple causations and outcomes. Talk about learning from example was common. Because the people engaged in the conversation were all part of a group they identified with, they were able to move inside a special world of information and vocabulary. Any new vocabulary pertaining to the group soon became part of their everyday language. It was through these conversations that problems were solved, Community bonds were formed, and learning took place.

The energy associated with these out-of-school conversations can be brought into the classroom. I witnessed such an event in a fifth-grade classroom, when I asked two boys to tell me about the book they were reading for literature discussion. One boy started talking excitedly. The second boy picked up on what the first one said. Pretty soon they were both talking at once. It was an example of unbounded excitement, chaotic and powerful.

Story

A second way that teachers can use talk to build Community is through telling and listening to stories. I am a firm believer in the value of telling stories, such as "Jack and the Beanstalk" and "The Ugly Duckling," to children, but in this instance I am using the word *stories* in a different way. By stories I mean the tales that we tell ourselves that let people know who we really are. These stories are "at the heart of everyday life" (Tannen, 1986, p. 91). Through stories we are able to make sense of our lives and then present these insights to others in a way that involves them (Rosen, 1984). By telling stories and listening to stories, people begin to feel connected to each other (Tannen, 1986).

The child psychiatrist Robert Coles (1989) discovered the power of this kind of story early in his career. He found that hearing people's stories is vitally important in knowing what to do for them. Coles went on to spend his life listening to the stories children tell about their hopes and fears, their triumphs and failures. What teachers can learn from this is that children's and teachers' stories should become part of the everyday life of the classroom Community because deep bonds are formed when stories are told. Shelly tells the story of how her grandmother cooks chitlins for Thanksgiving dinner, Billy tells about doing detective work to retrieve his stolen bike, and the teacher tells about the horror she felt when she fell on the subway. Everybody belongs when they have a story to tell.

Dialogue

Hope and Schooling. Bernstein, Wells, Barnes, and many others consider the question "What happens when some students are silenced?" to be vitally important because of the connection between having a say, being part of a

Community, and being a learner. The link between learning and Community occurs because human learning doesn't happen in a vacuum. Learning is greatly influenced by a multitude of psychosocial factors (Bloome and Greene, 1985; Brause, 1985; Brophy, 1983; Resnick, 1983; Wilkinson, 1985). Perhaps the most important of these factors is summed up in the word "hope" (Covington, 1983; Dweck and Bempechat, 1983; Nichols, 1983).

Learning Communities are especially important because they help learners to have hope in the future. Jules Henry (1966) states that "time, space, and objects really exist for us only when we hope. Hope . . . goes straight to the heart of organization and makes it work" (p. 396). Hope of attaining a goal is necessary for goal-oriented activity. Lack of hope the world over is usually associated with poverty, but poverty and hopelessness are not synonymous. People who leave their homelands to escape poverty or tyranny may still be impoverished but feel that a better life is possible in their adopted country, if not for them then for their children. These immigrant minorities tend to be more successful in school than indigenous minorities. Immigrants are more likely to be hopeful about the future because they bring with them the belief that anyone who is willing to work hard to overcome the temporary obstacles that all foreigners have to overcome can have some level of success, and that even a bad job in the new country is better than the abject poverty they experienced in their homelands. As a result, they often view the people in the adopted country as saviors and they try to emulate them. Since successful people are emulated, achieving success is viewed as a culturally accepted thing to do (Gibson, 1991; Ogbu, 1978, 1991).

Indigenous or caste minorities, on the other hand, are native-born citizens who have minority status. Because of their histories, they tend to have a very different perspective about success. As caste minorities they often have been slaves, or in slavelike positions. In the role of servants, they had no power except the "power" that oppressed peoples have when they passively resist the dictates of those who are over them (Brooke, 1987).

Even years after emancipation, caste minorities are typically relegated to low-status, low-wage jobs. Because caste minorities are not "foreigners" who have come from "homelands," they view success as being like the affluent citizens of their own countries. Unfortunately, except for a very few, this type of success seems impossible to obtain, no matter how hard they work. As far as they can tell, barriers to success are permanent rather than temporary. Hope for a better future seems to be illogical. In addition, successful members of the dominant society are seen, by many members of caste minorities, as oppressors rather than saviors. For this reason, being successful means "behaving like those who have oppressed [you]" (Gibson, 1991, p. 366). Tosha Whitaker, a seventeen-year-old African-American girl from West Philadelphia can testify to this attitude. When her friends see her head for the library they ask, "Why you trying to act white?" She has to decide between acceptance by her friends and success in school. She says, "You're either part of their group or you're not and it's a hard choice to make." Tosha's peer group feels that school success is a sign of disloyalty because, in their experience, the school system has treated them, and their culture, with contempt ("Good Grades," 1992).

Contempt breeds contempt, and a cycle of failure begins. Without hope the "survival self" becomes dominant. The survival self concentrates on fleeing from death and experiencing the "here and now" (Henry, 1966, pp. 397–398). When survival is paramount, learning that pertains to future goals becomes irrelevant. This emphasis on daily survival coupled with pressure not to become like the oppressors often results in minimal effort being expended in school, which leads to failure. In the eyes of some school authorities, this consistent failure is evidence that these students are inferior and incapable of learning. Some students also come to believe that they are not capable students. The cycle becomes continuous because, as the Brazilian educator Paulo Freire (1968) says, a person in such a situation lives life "divided between an identical past and present, and a future without hope. He is a person who does not perceive himself as becoming; hence he cannot have a future to be built in unity with others" (p. 174). In this condition learners don't see that it is possible to have any control over the reality that surrounds them.

A historical example provides some insight into the influence of hopefulness on learning. As slaves, African-Americans lived as if there was no economic future because they knew that "no matter how hard [they] worked, the achievement was for the master, not for [their] family[ies], not for [their] group. There was no sense of control" (Comer, 1990, p. 19). In contrast, emancipated slaves during Reconstruction felt that future success was possible and became willing and able students, often coming to the schools set up by the "New England School Marms" at all hours, begging for someone to teach them. It was only after the inception of Jim Crow laws, when African-Americans experienced "profound powerlessness" (Comer, 1990, p. 19), that lack of achievement became a problem (Noble, 1978). A similar phenomenon occurred in New Guinea. When the poor people of that country found that they weren't going to be better off economically by becoming literate, they simply "withdrew from literacy" (Heath, 1986).

Just as hopelessness can inhibit learning, a feeling of hopefulness about the future can enable immigrants who leave devastating situations in their homelands to succeed, despite economic and cultural barriers. In an effort to explain this phenomenon Caplan, Choy, and Whitmore (1992) recently studied a group of children of Vietnamese boat people who succeed in school despite poverty, language problems, and inadequate schools.

The researchers discovered that these families believed in the power of education to better their lives because the opportunities were so much greater in the United States than they were in Vietnam. Because of this belief, family life was oriented around school success. The kitchen table was used as a communal study area where older siblings taught younger siblings. The emphasis was on creating a learning Community where everyone in the family worked together.

Members of caste minorities are not usually as fortunate as these Vietnamese families. Many of them are raising children in virtual isolation, with little support from family, friends, or social organizations. As parents, they are concerned about education and work hard to try to ensure a good education for their children, but they find it difficult to be successful because of institutional and social barriers that make it almost impossible for them to believe that the future will be better than the past (Heath, 1992; Taylor and Dorsey-Gaines, 1988).

Communities of Hope. Researchers such as John Ogbu (1978, 1991) feel that there will be no real improvement in the educational status of caste minorities until the twin problems of lack of occupational opportunities and lack of respect for minority cultures are addressed. There is little doubt that this is true in terms of the society at large, but on a classroom by classroom, school by school basis we don't have to wait for major economic reforms to make a difference. This is because, as many teachers around the world are finding out, when students become part of the learning Community everyone is able to succeed.

It is the students who think there is "no way out" other than becoming disloyal to their own culture who are most in need of a learning Community; for it is through Community that they can see a way out. Unfortunately, the extreme alienation of these students, and the major cultural differences that often exist between teacher and students (Freire, 1968; Greene, 1978), make it difficult for some students to feel part of school Communities. Building a Community with students of diverse backgrounds, many of whom have histories of failure, is not easy.

Concerned teachers who attempt to bridge cultural gaps between themselves and their students by "talking to" their students are often disappointed by the lack of real communication and learning that occurs. The good intentions of these teachers come to naught because, until alienated students feel that they are part of a learning Community, they will not see themselves as capable of learning. What is needed for this transformation to occur, according to Freire (1968), is a process that involves dialogue and praxis.

Dialogue and Praxis.   For Freire, it isn't possible to separate dialogue and praxis into component parts. They constitute a never-ending *process* that is absolutely crucial to learning. Dialogue is different from mere talk. Dialogue involves looking critically at authentic problems from multiple points of view. As members of a Community engage in dialogue, they come to "extraordinarily reexperience the ordinary" (Shor, 1980, p. 93). In this way problems that seemed impossible to solve are seen from a new perspective. Constraints that were always taken for granted can be reexamined.

When people engage in dialogue they become "interdependent," each member of the Community learning from the other (William T. Grant Foundation, 1988). Interdependency is an absolute necessity for Community because it is the only way that teachers and students can come to see the world from each others' point of view. Through dialogue, teachers and students explain their own interpretation of events, and by combining their points of view, discover new solutions to old problems.

The result of dialogue, in Freire's view, should always be praxis: "the action and reflection of men upon their world in order to transform it" (Freire, 1968, p. 66), or as Maxine Greene (1978) describes it, "a thinking about and an action on reality." Once potential solutions to problems become apparent through dialogue, it is possible for members of a Community to engage in action. Sometimes the action is carried out by individuals, but more often it involves the whole Community because, to a great extent, it is only by working together that people can solve the problems that they face. The possibility of taking action has a great impact on learning because in order for them to be hopeful, people must feel they have some control over the factors that effect their lives.

But control involves more than action. After acting, the Community must reflect on what happened and reevaluate the problem in light of the results. This reflection requires dialogue and thus the entire process begins again. None of this is possible in silent classrooms or in classrooms where some students are silenced.

Many individual teachers are successfully incorporating dialogue and praxis into their classrooms in an effort to counteract alienation (Bietila and Levine, 1992; Bigelow, 1992; Sturk, 1992; Tenorio, 1992). And on a broader scale, community-wide dialogue is part of a plan for school reform developed by James Comer (Comer, 1990; Gursky, 1990). The program began with an inner-city school in New Haven, Connecticut, where teachers, parents, students, social workers, and educators from the university worked together to develop a plan to save the school. They knew that problems had to be solved—dependency, lack of hope for the future, a sense of having no control—but coming up with workable solutions to the problems required hours and hours of dialogue. All of the parties involved had to bring their own perspectives to the table and everyone's view had to be valued. The process was messy and painful, but it was also critically important.

The next step involved taking action on their decisions. But the third, and crucial, step came when they reflected on what had happened. They talked again, proposing new suggestions for further action. No part of the process was easy, and it was ongoing, never-ending; when some problems were solved new ones emerged. In the first year, all of the participants experienced anger, frustration, and a feeling that the task was impossible. But after the second year, the general consensus was that all the work was worth the effort. The participants discovered that, through dialogue, changes could be made to improve their school. The situation no longer was hopeless.

CONCLUSION

It is true that many students today do not feel part of a school Community. It may be outside forces, such as poverty or disability, or forces within the school, such as labeling or traditional teaching methods (Gilles, 1990; Meek et al., 1985), that keep students from having a voice. Whatever the reason, the situation is not irreparable. Communities can be created in classrooms when teachers recognize the way talk can bind a group of people together, when teachers create opportunities for all the learners in the classroom to converse, to tell life stories, and to engage in dialogue/praxis.

One such teacher is Anne Keiper (1987), who taught at the Missouri School for the Deaf in Fulton, Missouri. One of Anne's students, a little girl of five named Opal, spent her first day of class sobbing on the floor. She didn't understand speech because she was deaf, and no one at home had taught her to sign. She was in a limbo world, unable to communicate.

The class did everything they could to include Opal in their Community. Opal was invited to engage in all classroom activities. Wherever the class went, Opal also went. At first, nothing seemed to be working. Opal continued to be as sullen and withdrawn as before and consistently refused all of the class's invitations, until the day the class went to the library. The class had been preparing for the library trip for days by filling out applications for library cards and practicing checking out books. Anne had a tough decision to make; since Opal was still totally unresponsive it seemed fruitless to include her in the library trip, but taking all the class *except* Opal would give the child the impression that she was not a part of the Community. Anne decided to take Opal along.

Instead of being a waste of time that library trip represented a breakthrough. Opal arrived in class the day of the trip with a notepad and pencil in hand. She "wrote" on the pad for months after that. She allowed her notes to be "read," but would never let go of the precious notebook. Even though Anne was unable to read Opal's "writing," she accepted the scribbles as Opal's first attempts at communication. Gradually Anne and the rest of the class helped Opal learn to communicate through sign language. Learning to communicate opened up the world for her and confirmed to everyone that she was truly part of the Community. Anne sums up the effect: "Her face would light up when she asked for a drink of water and found that someone understood her. Her face seemed to say, 'What a wonderful thing this language is!' " (Keiper, 1987, p. 16).

Anne Keiper compares the learning that went on in her classroom to the opening of a "magic box." The magic came from the Community that developed in her classroom. Opal became a part of the Community along with all the rest of the students. The example of Opal shows us that "talk" in classrooms is something that is far deeper than "words uttered out loud." It is about the human need to communicate and the way communication binds us together. This need is so universal that even "silent" classrooms like Opal's can become places where everyone's voice is heard.

REFERENCES

Adams, R. 1972. *Watership Down*. New York: Avon.

Ahrne, G. 1990. *Agency and organization: Towards an organizational theory of society*. London: SAGE Publications.

Barnes, D. 1992. *From communication to curriculum*. 2nd ed. Portsmouth, NH: Boynton/ Cook.

Bernstein, B. 1974. *Class, codes and control*. New York: Schocken.

Bietila, S. and D. Levine. 1992. "Riverwest neighbors win a new Fratney school." In *Becoming political: Readings and writings in the politics of literacy education*, edited by P. Shannon. Portsmouth, NH: Heinemann.

Bigelow, W. 1992. "Inside the classroom: Social vision and critical pedagogy." In *Becoming political: Readings and writings in the politics of literacy education*, edited by P. Shannon. Portsmouth, NH: Heinemann.

Blau, Z. S. 1981. *Black children/White children: Competence, socialization and social structure*. New York: Free Press.

Bloome, D. and J. Greene. 1985. "Looking at reading instruction: Sociolinguistic and ethnographic approaches." In *Contexts of reading*, edited by C. Hedley & A. Baratta. Norwood, NJ: Ablex.

Bloome, D. and S. Nieto. 1992. "Children's understandings of basal readers." In *Becoming political: Readings and writings in the politics of literacy education*, edited by P. Shannon. Portsmouth, NH: Heinemann.

Brause, R. 1985. "Classroom contexts for learning." In *Contexts of reading*, edited by C. Hedley & A. Baratta. Norwood, NJ: Ablex.

Brooke, R. 1987. "Underlife and writing instruction." *College Composition and Communication* 38(2):141–52.

Brophy, J. 1983. "Fostering student learning and motivation in the elementary school classroom." In *Learning and motivation in the classroom*, edited by S. Paris, B. Olson, & H. Stevenson. Hillsdale, NJ: Lawrence Erlbaum.

Caplan, N., M. H. Choy, and J. K. Whitmore. 1992. "Indochinese refugee families and academic achievement." *Scientific American*, 266(2):36–42.

Coles, R. 1989. *The call of stories: Teaching and moral imagination*. Boston: Houghton Mifflin.

Comer, J. 1990. "Building quality relationships." In *Making schools work for underachieving minority students*, edited by J. Baine & J. Herman. New York: Greenwood.

Cook, L. 1992. "Out of the straightjacket." In *Becoming political: Readings and writings in the politics of literacy education*, edited by P. Shannon. Portsmouth, NH: Heinemann.

Cook-Gumperz, J. 1986. "Introduction: The social construction of literacy." In *The Social Construction of Literacy*, edited by J. Cook-Gumperz. Cambridge: Cambridge University Press.

Covington, M. 1983. "Motivated cognitions." In *Learning and motivation in the classroom*, edited by S. Paris, B. Olson, & H. Stevenson. Hillsdale, NJ: Lawrence Erlbaum.

Dweck, C. and J. Bempechat. 1983. "Children's theories of intelligence: Consequences for learning." In *Learning and motivation in the classroom*, edited by S. Paris, B. Olson, & H. Stevenson. Hillsdale, NJ: Lawrence Erlbaum.

Freire, P. 1968. *Pedagogy of the Oppressed*. New York: Seabury.

Fromm, E. 1966. *The Sane Society*. Greenwich, CT: Fawcett.

Gee, J. 1992. "What is literacy?" In *Becoming political: Readings and writings in the politics of literacy education*, edited by P. Shannon. Portsmouth, NH: Heinemann.

Gibson, M. 1991. "Minorities and schooling: Some implications." In *Minority status and schooling: A comparative study of immigrant and involuntary minorities*, edited by M. Gibson & J. Ogbu. New York: Garland.

Gilles, C. 1990. "Collaborative literacy strategies: 'We don't need a circle to have a group.' " In *Talking about books: Creating literate communities*, edited by K. Short & K. Pierce. Portsmouth, NH: Heinemann.

Gilmore, P. 1992. "Gimme room": School resistance, attitude and access to literacy." In *Becoming political: Readings and writings in the politics of literacy education*, edited by P. Shannon. Portsmouth, NH: Heinemann.

Giroux, H. 1992. "Critical literacy and student experience: Donald Graves' approach to literacy." In *Becoming political: Readings and writings in the politics of literacy education,* edited by P. Shannon. Portsmouth, NH: Heinemann.

Gleick, J. 1987. *Chaos: Making a new science.* New York: Viking.

Greene, M. 1978. *Landscapes of learning.* New York: Teachers College Press.

———. 1973. *Teachers as stranger: Educational philosophy for the modern age.* Belmont, CA: Wadsworth.

Gumperz, J. 1986. "Interactional sociolinguistics in the study of schooling." In *The social construction of literacy,* edited by J. Cook-Gumperz. Cambridge: Cambridge University Press.

———. 1982. *Discourse strategies.* Cambridge: Cambridge University Press.

Gursky, D. 1990. "A plan that works." *Teacher Magazine* June/July:46–54.

Harste, J. C. and K. C. Short, with C. B. Burke. 1988. *Creating classrooms for authors: The reading-writing connection.* Portsmouth, NH: Heinemann.

Hayakawa, S. I. 1972. *Language in thought and action.* New York: Harcourt Brace Jovanovich.

Heath, S. 1992. "Oral and literate traditions among Black Americans living in poverty." In *Becoming political: Readings and writings in the politics of literacy education,* edited by P. Shannon. Portsmouth, NH: Heinemann.

———. 1988. "Will the schools survive?" Speech at the National Council of Teachers of English Convention, Nov. 19. St. Louis, MO.

———. 1986. "The functions and uses of literacy." In *Literacy, society and schooling: A reader,* edited by S. de Castell, A. Luke, & K. Egan. Cambridge: Cambridge University Press.

Henry, J. 1966. "White people's time, colored people's time." In *The disadvantaged child,* edited by J. Frost. Boston: Houghton Mifflin.

Hymes, D. 1972. "Introduction." In *Functions of language in the classroom,* edited by C. Cazden, V. John, & D. Hymes. New York: Teachers College Press.

Johnson, W. 1946. *People in quandaries.* New York: Harper & Row.

Keiper, A. M. 1987. "A lesson from Opal." *Perspectives for teachers of the hearing impaired* Sept./Oct.:15–17.

McDonald, G. 1983. *The baronette's song.* Minneapolis, MN: Bethany House.

Meek, M. with S. Armstrong, V. Austerfield, J. Graham, & E. Plackett. 1985. *Achieving literacy.* London: Routledge & Kegan Paul.

Nichols, J. 1983. "Conceptions of ability and achievement motivation: A theory and its implications for education." In *Learning and motivation in the classroom,* edited by S. Pans, G. Olson, & H. Stevenson. Hillsdale, NJ: Lawrence Erlbaum.

Noble, J. 1978. *Beautiful also are the souls of my Black sisters: A history of Black woman in America.* Englewood Cliffs, NJ: Prentice-Hall.

Ogbu, J. 1991. "Immigrant and involuntary minorities in comparative perspective."

In *Minority status and schooling: A comparative study of immigrant and involuntary minorities*, edited by M. Gibson & J. Ogbu. New York: Garland.

———. 1978. *Minority education and caste.* New York: Academic Press.

Oliver, D. and K. Gershman. 1989. *Education modernity and fractured meaning: Toward a process theory of teaching and learning.* Albany, NY: State University of New York Press.

Peetoom, A. 1991. "The Bible and whole language." Presentation at the Whole Language Umbrella Conference, Aug. 4. Phoenix, AZ.

Peirce, B. 1992. "Toward a pedagogy of possibility in the teaching of English internationally: People's English in South Africa." In *Becoming political: Readings and writings in the politics of literacy education*, edited by P. Shannon. Portsmouth, NH: Heinemann.

Resnick, L. 1983. "Toward a cognitive theory of instruction." In *Learning and motivation in the classroom*, edited by S. Paris, G. Olson, & H. Stevenson. Hillsdale, NJ: Lawrence Erlbaum.

Rosen, H. 1984. *Stories and meaning.* Kittering, N. Hamptonshire, England: National Association of Teachers of English.

Shannon, P. 1992. "Reading instruction and social class." In *Becoming political: Readings and writings in the politics of literacy education*, edited by P. Shannon. Portsmouth, NH: Heinemann.

Shor, I. 1980. *Critical teaching and every day life.* Boston: South End.

Short, K. & C. Burke. 1991. *Creating curriculum: Teachers and students as a community of learners.* Portsmouth, NH: Heinemann.

Simon, R. 1992. "Empowerment as a pedagogy of possibility." In *Becoming political: Readings and writings in the politics of literacy education*, edited by P. Shannon. Portsmouth, NH: Heinemann.

Sturk, A. 1992. "Developing a community of learners inside and outside the classroom." In *Becoming political: Readings and writings in the politics of literacy education*, edited by P. Shannon. Portsmouth, NH: Heinemann.

Tannen, D. 1986. "Hearing voices in conversation, fiction and mixed genres." In *Linguistics in context: Connecting observation and understanding*, edited by D. Tannen. Norwood, NJ: Ablex.

Taylor, D. and C. Dorsey-Gaines. 1988. *Growing up literate: Learning from inner-city families.* Portsmouth, NH: Heinemann.

Tenorio, R. 1992. "A vision in two languages: Reflections on a two-way bilingual program." In *Becoming political: Readings and writings in the politics of literacy education*, edited by P. Shannon. Portsmouth, NH: Heinemann.

Viorst, J. 1982. *Alexander and the terrible, horrible, no good, very bad day.* New York: Antheneum.

Wells, G. 1985. "Preschool literacy related activities and success in school." In *Literacy, language and learning: The nature and consequences of reading and writing*, edited by D. Olson, N. Torrance, & A. Hildyard. Cambridge: Cambridge University Press.

Wilkinson, L. 1985. "Communicating in classrooms: Research on reading groups." In *Contexts of reading*, edited by C. Hedley & A. Baratta. Norwood, NJ: Ablex.

William T. Grant Foundation Commission on Work, Family and Citizenship. 1988. *The forgotten half: Non-college youth in America*. Washington: The William T. Grant Foundation Commission on Work, Family and Citizenship: 18.

Williams, S. B. 1987. "A comparative study of Black dropouts and Black high school graduates in an urban public school system." *Education and Urban Society* 19: 311–19.

Joan Von Dras currently teaches at Wren Hollow Elementary School in the Parkway School District. She has taught grades three through six. Her literature-based, writing-process oriented roots have evolved over the past few years to encompass learning through critical inquiry in the context of a democratic structure. The classroom, referred to as Space Station Earth, has a global focus, which relates what is learned to the survival of the planet.

Chapter 4
Empowerment Through Talk: Creating Democratic Communities

JOAN CHANDLER VON DRAS

My classroom has gone through another metamorphosis this year. This most recent one resulted from my reading of Douglas Barnes's *From Communication to Curriculum* (1992). Barnes's emphasis on observing talk between students opened a new dimension for me, and I began to look at my students from a new perspective. I examined how the talk they engaged in with each other helped them make discoveries and undertake new investigations. I now recognize the degree to which empowerment through talk can transform a classroom.

Talk is valued and appreciated in many different settings—among friends, in our families, or with our colleagues. It brings us together through a sharing of ideas and thoughts. It opens up alternative avenues of opinion and helps us reflect on our own. However, a sign could be hung on the doors of many classrooms across the country: "The Talk Stops Here." In their study of 80 small town schools and 119 teachers, Schmuck and Schmuck (1990) noted that two-thirds of classroom talk was teachers' talk and two-thirds of that was unidirectional lecturing. They found that the majority of classrooms were "teacher-centered, with teachers standing up in front lecturing to rows of students, with only occasional student talk as a response to teacher questions." In only ten of 119 classes did they see "student-to-student" talk that was planned by the teacher. Four times they saw students in "pairs conferring together in response to the teacher's questions, and six times saw students in small groups working together on a problem or a project" (p. 251).

The classrooms described by Schmuck and Schmuck seemed typical of many I had observed. But it wasn't until I began studying the work of Douglas Barnes that I paid specific attention to the role of talk within my own classroom. I began to examine teacher-initiated and student-initiated talk and the relationship between the two. I also looked at the opportunities I provided for students to engage in talk with one another. As Arthur Costa notes, "Not all kids, of course, but . . . so many . . . think episodically, they don't draw on past knowledge . . . they have a lack of perseverance . . . and [they have] impulsivity: they take the first thing that comes to mind, they make immediate judgments . . . they seem unable to listen to ideas and carry them forth and interact with each other; they're so busy with their own point of view that they can't get into anyone else's thinking" (Healy, 1990, p. 42). His observations may not be anything new, but they did cause me to reflect upon these behaviors.

Perhaps opportunity isn't provided, and situations aren't created to allow students to actively engage in debate and dialogue in order to foster what Costa notices is lacking. Often, when students arrive home from school, opportunity for talk gives way to the demands and icons of the 1990s: busy schedules of working parents, basketball practice and dance lessons, homework and housework. Video arcades, Nintendo, and cable TV have opened up a whole new genre of television entertainment, increasing opportunities for solitary viewing. Cullinan (1987) found that one large group of "typical" fifth graders, interviewed about the time they spent watching television, averaged 130 minutes per day of viewing (p. 11). Taking all of this into consideration, one might ask, "So when do we get genuine time to really talk with each other?"

With this in mind, educators might consider making a concerted effort to allow talk to have as credible a role in their classrooms as the traditional curriculum areas of reading, writing, social studies, and other content areas. Although an emphasis on integrating reading and writing throughout the curriculum has been a focus for many educators over the past decade, the additional integration and study of student talk largely goes unnoticed. Many educators have provided for literature-based reading and process-oriented writing programs. Others have gone a step further and taken reading and writing out of the context of traditional subject areas and successfully integrated them into their social studies, science, and mathematics agendas. Still, many classrooms have agendas—whether basal-based or literature-based—which are set by the teacher, and these agendas will remain the creation of the teacher as long as talk is not emphasized, integrated, and valued as an educational tool for growth and discovery.

So why the hesitancy to open up curriculum for such integration and opportunity? As Schmuck and Schmuck (1992) state, "True dialogue is not safe; it is unpredictable, and it makes the teacher vulnerable to negative criticism. Yet, its absence creates communication gaps between teachers and students. Communication gaps are pervasive in modern society; they are basic to generation gaps, racial gaps, gender gaps, and international gaps. They occur when language is used to conceal and veil, rather than to reveal and openly express."

Douglas Barnes (1992) looks at curriculum, not as "what teachers plan in advance for their pupils to learn," but as an enactment by teachers and pupils. He defines this enactment as a "coming together in a meaningful communication—talk, write, read books, collaborate, become angry with one another, learn what to say and do, and how to interpret what others say and do." He believes the curriculum comes to life through the "talk and gestures by which pupils and teachers exchange meanings even when they quarrel or cannot agree." Curriculum is a "form of communication" (p. 14).

Student talk needs to break away from the confines of presentations and speeches. It needs to venture beyond the isolation of the playground and lunch table. It needs to be an everyday event, so that students begin to engage in meaningful discussion generated by genuine interest and a curiosity for knowledge. It needs to be purposeful and relevant to the students' out-of-school lives.

Thomas Jefferson saw the public school system as a vehicle for preparing this nation's youth to function effectively and actively in a democratic society. But the two conditions that make democracy possible are tolerance of all forms of talk and, most important, "Freedom of Speech." All forms of talk must be allowed if our school system is to accomplish this important task, and to do so classrooms must in themselves be democratic.

TALK IS ESSENTIAL TO A DEMOCRATIC CLASSROOM SETTING

"Democratic Classrooms . . . Democratic Lives." This belief guides the Institute for Democracy in Education (IDE), and I have adopted it as my own. It is part of why I have come to value the talk in my classroom and to appreciate the essential role it plays in creating a democratic setting, a democratic environment for learning. Creating this environment doesn't come easily. Every year I have found that I need to invite students to join me in unpacking the instructional baggage of rules about their talking. Students look to me to ask the questions, to give the answers, and to solve the conflicts that exist among their peers. They have been trained to see the teacher as the primary

source of knowledge and guidance, so that the skills they possess to look elsewhere for answers have been suffocated by authoritarian role models. Didactic teaching has created student dependency. I invite my students to restructure their thinking and to be open to alternative structures: *perestroika* and *glasnost* in classroom government.

Initially, none of this can take place without building community among the members of the classroom. We accomplish this by sharing personal experiences, getting to know each other, and learning how to listen to each other. During the first week of school we each bring in a shoe box. I begin by bringing in my own on the first day. I share the contents with the class, and pretty soon they are doing the same. Within these boxes are artifacts that represent something about us: a favorite book to demonstrate love of reading, a family photograph to share the importance of family, a special keepsake or a seashell found on a family trip, or an empty container of aspirin to show what a headache we can be. Each shoe box is unique and important. We take the entire week to individually share the contents of our boxes. We begin by sitting in a big circle and giving our undivided attention to one person at a time. We talk about how each artifact represents us and pass it around so everyone can see. We ask each other questions and share common experiences. This whole process of getting to know one another lays the foundation upon which we begin to build community. It sets the tone for dialogue and interaction, serving as a model for future conversation and inquiry.

We also use interviews to get to know one another. We begin by brainstorming questions we think are interesting to investigate and then look for common bonds that unite us and differences that make us unique. We spend a great deal of time at the beginning of the year examining what conflict is and how we can create it or prevent its escalation. We look at what we say to each other and role play how our talk and actions can either create conflict or diffuse it. We learn how to work toward consensus so that all members of our community are part of a "win-win" situation. And, most important, we learn how to communicate with one another honestly, openly, and productively.

SUPPORTING DEMOCRATIC TALK

A crucial step in supporting democratic talk in my classroom was to give myself permission to become a role model for this kind of communication. I now constantly model for students how to respond to each other. I speak to them in a calm tone of voice, and I practice the art of listening. As an important part of my responsibilities as a teacher, I allow myself time to listen to each individual or group. I may say absolutely nothing or I may give students time to reflect on or add to what they have said. I don't jump in as they expect. At times I am silent so they are not.

Throughout the day, I listen to the students and write down their questions and thoughts. I just sit and listen. At first, they look at me when they are talking. Because I am not responding all the time, and I am taking notes, which limits my eye contact, students continue their dialogue without looking to me. There are times when I do contribute my "two cents' worth," but because my opinions and voice do not dominate, they value what I have to say and know they can choose to respond selectively. This modeling of interaction rubs off on the entire community. We talk and sometimes use roleplaying to examine other ways of handling situations. Eventually, students become comfortable with their own voices and with each other's in the context of a classroom setting.

When a conflict arises between individuals, I no longer take on the role of problem solver. Instead, I ask the participants to express to one another what is bothering them about a situation. I encourage them to listen carefully before responding, to look at each other and say, "It bothers me when you. . . ." No list of rules is presented by me or generated by the class identifying specific expectations and consequences. Instead, we spend our early weeks together developing respect, empathy, patience, kindness, and fairness toward one another.

When a disagreement occurs between students, or when one student is doing something that bothers another, I say to them, "Did you tell her how you felt?" This was a difficult dialogue for us to engage in until we implemented a new strategy I learned about at a professional conference: the "Peace Table." A creation of preschool teacher Do Kirk, the peace table has helped make our attempts at conflict resolution more concrete. The peace table can be formed around anything: a piece of paper, a handkerchief, or an actual table. When a student has a conflict, that student may call for a peace table with all the other students involved in the conflict. At the peace table, each student is given an opportunity to state concerns while resting one hand on the object chosen to represent the table. During this process all participants work to engage in active listening, which we have practiced before hand. The peace table conference does not end until options for solving the problem have been explored and consensus has been reached about the best option.

A peace table can be called at any time. One might occur as we come in from recess or during a collaborative project. When the designated table isn't with us, someone always thinks of something to take its place:

a book or even a soccer ball. The focus is not on the object itself, but on the symbol of negotiation it represents. Although some peace tables are private, many others include supportive spectators: fellow classmates who may contribute information or solutions. The peace table lures students away from the impulsive, often unsuccessful strategies shown on television and draws attention to solving conflicts peacefully and creatively. I, too, can be a part of a peace table when students question my actions or motives. The peace table provides an opportunity for me to state my thinking and to hear theirs. We share each other's perspectives in a nonthreatening dialogue. The opportunities created by this safe atmosphere allow us to reflect on our own behavior and thus to grow and change. It reminds us to be patient with others and to recognize and celebrate one another's growth and change.

Creating an atmosphere for talk, student choice, and mutual respect has allowed democratic values and philosophy to be experienced and internalized. Without a forum for talk, the classroom is artificial, void of true democratic principles and ideas. Without democracy, a classroom cannot be a place genuinely shared by students and teachers. Without a shared place, learning is contrived, arbitrary, and lacks true meaning and application. Without true meaning, learning has no purpose.

Ira Shor (1987) says about his changing role as a teacher, "My language counted, but so did theirs. My language changed, and so did theirs. This democracy of expression established a mutual atmosphere which encouraged the students to talk openly, not fearing ridicule or punishment for being 'stupid' " (p. 23). Providing an atmosphere where talk is valued and community is actively built empowers students to seek out knowledge and construct meaning for real purposes. Katie Mang saw it this way:

SPACE STATION EARTH

We are a little family
In our own little home
We care and reflect about wars,
Problems and the environment of our world.
We are explorers of what we can do
In reading and writing

At the end we will be part of each other
We are ones of the same color
We are Space Station Earth 1991–1992

TALK OF A GLOBAL NATURE

The study of conflict goes beyond the classroom to local, national, and international contexts. Throughout the day, but primarily during the morning work block (an integration of reading, writing, social studies, and science), we look at the political process and how it creates change. Our morning class meetings are a time for students to bring up topics of interest from the news, our lives, or our classroom inquiries. The role of the United Nations comes into play as well as its purpose. We even use it as a model for dialogue and negotiation and apply it to a variety of contexts. For example, during the Middle East peace talks we decided to engage in our own negotiations using the format of the United Nations. For several days we discussed what the nations in the Middle East should be doing to resolve their conflicts. Students discovered through these discussions that there were no easy solutions or right answers. Our interest in the complexity of the situation evolved into a decision to hold a mock peace conference to see exactly what could be worked out. A large part of our work blocks was then devoted to exploration of this conflict. This provided a perfect opportunity to explore world cultures, which was a part of my agenda for our sixth-grade curriculum that year, while remaining sensitive to the students' agenda for exploring the Middle East conflict.

Collectively, we decided which countries needed representation and which ones students wanted to represent. The students divided into individual "expert" groups representing the countries of this region—Iraq, Kuwait, Syria, Israel, Egypt, and Saudi Arabia—as well as the Palestine Liberation Organization. Each expert group gathered all of the information it could on their country as they prepared for the negotiations. Our resource plans included looking at magazines and newspapers, following news shows and documentaries, visiting libraries to look for nonfiction and traditional literature books, and perusing the UNICEF Culture Kit of Middle East Culture. We completely absorbed ourselves in inquiry, debate, discussion, and collaboration.

When the time came to begin the formal negotiation process, we reviewed the diplomacy of compromise and debate. I was amazed at how well students represented the needs of their individual countries. The passion, commitment, and knowledge with which they debated far exceeded my expectations. Students actively listened to each other, questioned one another on points brought up, and productively argued about disagreements. So heartfelt were the issues that some students would go home after school, discuss the topics with their parents, and return with new ideas to contribute, as Ben did in the following address:

Saudi Arabia is completely negotiable with all countries except Iraq. And we will negotiate with Iraq if we get a full fledged apology for the grief and sorrow and fear and destruction they caused our country during the Gulf War. We are willing to donate working service to Kuwait to help rebuild what has been destroyed.

Saudi Arabia will not take sides in the dispute between Israel and their enemies in the Middle East. Saudi Arabia's opinion still stands that any man of religion can own the land that Israel sits on. Israel has every right to be on the land. Israelis and Palestinians should live in harmony and learn to co-exist with each other.

Also, at this moment I would like to take time to thank the U.S. Government for cooperating with the Saudi Arabian Army and giving aid at a time of great need.

The Middle East has been at war with each other for too long. There has been too much bloodshed! The Middle East was the beginning of civilization and now let it be the beginning of "Peace."

Ben's engagement in "presentational talk" (Barnes, 1992) helped many of us see the importance of reaching a compromise. The statements made in his last paragraph had a significant impact and renewed our commitment to reach an agreement. On the fifth day of negotiations we began to see possibilities that might work. That night Aisha worked hard on drafting a peace treaty based on these possibilities. We were all impressed with how skillfully she had combined our ideas and stated the terms and conditions. All members were receptive and the treaty was signed. We believed our ideas to be valid and workable and sent copies of the treaty to the United Nations with additional copies to the individual countries. The most significant product for me was not the treaty itself. Instead, it was the understanding that each of us developed about the countries in the region. When the conference began, we all made assumptions about who was at fault. Those lines began to fade, however, as we learned why Palestinians felt they deserved a homeland and why Israelis felt that way, too. We began to understand the intrusion the surrounding countries felt with Israel's re-establishment, as well as why economic, religious, and territorial disputes were so heated. It gave us a new lens to evaluate national and international conflict.

I was proud of my students. They took what they had experienced in conflict resolution in the classroom and applied it on an international level. They gained perspective as to why the "win-lose" situations that have existed through hundreds of years have escalated and sustained conflict. They felt the frustration of needs that have been ignored or not met. They demonstrated empathy for the people who were affected. We came away knowing that this experience would not only shape how we looked at things for the rest of the school year, but that it would have an impact on our perspectives on world peace and global awareness for the rest of our lives. It was powerful, rewarding, and real. It was something we continued to refer back to throughout the year.

Beginning with this experience, students noticed patterns in history, examined how the past affected the present, and speculated on how the present might affect the future. This also set a course for our examination of democracy and its importance to human rights and responsibilities, rights and responsibilities that were not only important to the global community, but equally important to the members of our classroom community.

Our classroom meetings are a forum for a wide range of topics. We may be discussing the recession, the impact of Japan and other foreign interests on our economy, a chemical spill in the Mississippi River, or gun control. While some topics are as familiar as those associated with the traditional show-and-tell sessions, others are more intense and cover many subjects not generally found in elementary curriculum. Occasionally, topics raised in morning meetings are explored across several class meetings. Others, like the Middle East conflict, become the focus of full-scale inquiries during our work blocks later in the day.

One morning, Andrew posed an interesting question:

01   ANDREW: Is there space in nothing?

02   BEN: If there are no molecules, there can be nothing—not even space.

03   KATIE: But, space is something. So—if you say there is nothing, there can be no space.

04   ANDREW: But, space is made of nothing.

05   BEN: Wrong. Space has resistance. It consists.

06   LAURA: I think nothing is space.

07   KATIE: If there were space in something . . . tell me there is nothing between the stars and planets?

08   ARON: [Looking up the definition of space in *Webster's Dictionary*] It says that space is "limitless three dimensional expanse . . . the expanse in which the solar system, stars, and galaxies exist."

09   BEN: If it exists it is something. Read the definition again.

10   ARON: Space is "limitless three dimensional expanse . . . the expanse in which the solar system, stars, and galaxies exist."

11   KATIE: It says right there—the things that make up space, create space.

It was interesting to experience what had led up to this question. We had absorbed ourselves in multiple inquiries about space. Matt and Kurt visited the St. Louis Science Center to try to prove their theory that oxygen existed in space. Several other boys in the class bought David Brinn's highly technical, difficult, but brilliant futuristic novel, *Earth* (1991). They formed a literature discussion group, which met frequently to decipher the vast quantities of complex information they were discovering. They occasionally invited a colleague of mine to join the discussion group to explain such things as how a black hole could be the size of an atom yet weigh megatons. And Jessica and Sarah argued with Ben and Curtis, saying their theory, that we live in a black hole and are continually being recycled through the process, simply could not happen and was in conflict with the "black-hole" theory they were researching. "Space" was a topic that we returned to frequently throughout the year and involved exploratory discussion of complex issues and hypothetical situations: black hole-white hole debates, the role of a black hole in creation theory, the existence of parallel universes and other galaxies that might support life. I was able to see students develop their own theories through research, and revise and defend them through debate.

In another class discussion, Ben took a stand on the Haitian refugee situation that appalled the rest of the class. Ben suggested that the Haitian refugees weren't our problem and neither were the Mexican refugees. As a matter of fact, he felt the refugees should be shot if they came into this country. His defense was that "we have enough of our own problems. We don't need anyone else's." Some members of the group felt that it was our responsibility to help others who are in need. And, if the entire world had the same attitude as Ben, it would be quite a hostile planet. Still, others agreed with Ben, that we need to take care of ourselves first before we can take care of others. One point the entire class agreed upon, however, was that they didn't like Ben's idea about shooting the refugees. This topic was revisited frequently. After one such discussion, Matt went straight to his desk and expressed his feelings in his notebook.

> "Oh, say can you see, by the dawn's early night. What so proudly we held by the twilight's last gleaming. Whose broad stripes and bright stars. . . ."
>
> That was part of our National Anthem. It is something to be proud of! But, lately, some people have done some things that we're ashamed of, like Jeffrey Dahmer. Today, I was astonished by what my friend said, "Let's just shoot at the Haitians who are coming over. It'll teach them a lesson." I was ashamed of him. He is usually right on top of current events and also right a lot of times! It took up most of our current events time, but you know how stupid that is? It's like setting Jeff Dahmer loose to keep us in our house at night! There is just no reason for it! He says, "Let's take care of them, so they don't come back." We are sending them back, not gassing them or harming them at that! It's a good way until we're economically ready to house them and take care of them.

Months after this episode, Ben confessed, "The reason I took the point of view with the Haitians and took all these views that no one liked was because I wanted to debate against all of you. I didn't want to stay with the rest of you. I don't think refugees should be shot. I wanted to encourage debate."

> You taught most of us how to write, and then you gave us the courage to write what we felt. (Matt)

Topics also emerge as we share notes and observations we've recorded in our notebooks, a collection of our thoughts, inquiries, poetry, or whatever. The function of our notebooks was based on ideas of Lucy Calkins (1990, 1991). She emphasized that "we write to be moved . . . to be taken on a journey." She suggests using notebooks to collect "those strings of thought which are too short to stand on their own." Revisiting these strings creates the genius that inspires a new book or research project. She uses the term "notebook" to get away from the stereotype and confines of a journal or diary and to open the pages to a variety of forms of writing and thinking. In the example above, Matt used his notebook as a vehicle to express his opinion and diffuse his anger. The notebook becomes what the writer needs it to be. Aisha captured the function and potential of the notebooks in her opening entry:

> As I open this book, I think of all of the wonders and dreams that lie ahead. The dreams work into your mind and create the future, whereas wonders try to create illusions to trick your mind. The adventure and drama will create the suspense. The sadness and deaths will liven the character. Working all at one time, they create a special touch and work at once to make this wonderful and spectacular book.

After using notebooks to record observations and insights, the students' writing took on a new dimension. Their topics were more interesting and relevant. They began to identify information that had affected them and then to add this to their knowledge by looking for its meaning. They took their notebooks with them everywhere and pulled them out to write at any time. Some of the most interesting pieces evolved outside of class. Brooke's most significant entries occurred after school hours and included a piece about dreams written at 4:00 A.M. one Monday morning as well as a moving poem written after watching the evening news:

THE CRY OF WAR

The cry of war is sinful and a thought that boggles every man's mind
It fills the Earth with death and sorrow, harmful and unkind

Like fragile glass, people's dreams are shattered
People brutally slaughtered and battered
Young children hear the cry of death as a bomb lands on their city
Thousands die, but the few that live are filled with mourn and pity
Many died in the war with hope that one day the Earth would be filled
    with peace
But, we have yet to know—will this fighting ever cease?

Most of the entries in Brooke's journal were poetry. "The Cry of War" won a national poetry contest. Although the notebooks are open to any type of writing, it is evident that poetry plays a large role in communicating the intense thoughts and feelings of the students on a wide range of topics. During a conversation I had with a few students who were discussing the scope and breadth of the poetry produced in our classroom, Brooke commented that she never wrote anything beyond a haiku before entering our classroom. She and others wondered how they became inspired to write such wonderful poetry. During this discussion I realized that although I had never taught a unit on poetry, I had succeeded in fostering a love of poetry within them. It was simple. I shared poetry with students every day, discussed it freely with them, and gave them opportunities to share and talk about the poetry they loved. In no time we found that the poetry we discussed most of the time was our own.

Our passion for poetry escalated into publishing *The Collected Poems of Space Station Earth* for the school community. Eventually it culminated in "A Night at the Hollow: An Evening of Dramatic Poetry Reading." Since many of the activities we do in Space Station Earth are directly related to the community, we decided to use our poetic talents to raise money for the Missouri Wildlife Rescue Center. This night of poetry reading was quite exciting for us. All the poetry we read was original and the audience was impressed. One parent wrote, "This allowed us to see how creative and insightful our children could be. It made me appreciate and aware of a maturity I didn't know Jill had." We raised one hundred dollars for the rescue center and saw that we could use our talents to make a difference. We saw our talk evolve into action.

CONNECTION TO THE COMMUNITY

In *Pedagogy of the Oppressed* (1970), Paulo Freire argues that if learning is to be enlightening, students should be allowed to engage in democratic dialogue that directly relates to reality and provides opportunities for social action. It is important that what we do is meaningful, powerful, and real. It mustn't be confined within the walls of the classroom, but be expanded out into the community of which we are an integral part. Encouraging dialogue in the classroom has led to a variety of activities and pursuits. We have adopted a zoo pet, formed a schoolwide environmental club, published a globally themed newspaper, and investigated a local trash dump.

We listen to each other, contribute our opinions, and learn from each other's views. Throughout the day students work in smaller groups engaged in such dialogue, often sharing their writing or a good book they have read. Our talk provides a forum for the exploration of theories and ideas. It engages students in active learning through the examination of real issues, often leading to social action. And, as important, our talk provides multiple perspectives from which to learn and grow.

Laura used her notebook to collect items that influenced her, such as a comic strip she read one morning before school. The comic strip depicts a white police officer's comment to a black police officer on the changing labels for African-Americans, "I don't know what to call you." The black officer responds with a question, "How about 'friend'?" This comic strip and our discussions of the Rodney King trial motivated Laura to write the following:

COLORS

It doesn't matter if you're black, red or blue
What really matters is what's inside of you
Some people act like there's a color barrier that makes people quite
　　tense
The people with the barriers obviously have no common sense
While some people are trying to figure out the latest greatest
　　trends
Others are worried if their new neighbor is a color
Or a friend
God puts us on this earth for a reason which I can't figure out
But one thing's for sure—
It's not what I've been writing about!

Laura shared her notebook during the morning meeting that day and it opened up a lengthy dialogue about prejudice and injustice. This discussion, which stemmed from Laura's insights, led Aron to write the following controversial poem:

WHAT ONE IS WORTH

What one is worth no one can say
What is worth more
Night or Day
What is worth more
Rain or snow
What is worth more
White or Negro
What is worth more
Land or sea
What is worth more
You or Me

Aron's poem was well received during author's share. We thought he did a masterful job making his point. However, there was concern over the use of the term "Negro" in his poem. Again, this cycled back to the discussion on cultural labels. Aron pointed out that he only chose the word "Negro" because it rhymed and he couldn't think of any other word to use that wouldn't sacrifice the poem itself. We also discussed how labels change and speculated that if the word was acceptable for the United Negro College Fund, it was acceptable for Aron's poem.

Frequently, discussions in our class meeting address the concerns facing our communities, such as drugs and crime. Several of the students were so disturbed by America's teenage pregnancy and infant mortality rates, they began reading up on crack babies and the implications of drug use during pregnancy. Others were interested in debating gun control and the Brady Bill. Most of the students could relate to the tragedy guns can produce on a surface level. However, some students were touched personally. During the school year, Tyronica experienced the death of two friends who lived in her neighborhood. She felt quite strongly about the injustice around her and many times brought up her concern about her neighborhood and community. This concern moved her to write the following essay in her notebook:

Stop The Killing

Two little boys have been shot and killed. The boys were Christopher Harris and Maurice Neal. It doesn't make any sense. Why are people killing other people? I think that no one should have a gun that is under 30. Where do they get guns? From Mom, Dad, an aunt or uncle. You need a gun for protection, but you don't need it to kill a 9 year and 11 year old boy.

Both of the boys were smart, loved sports and school. But, was it time for them to go? Did they kill the boys because of their smartness, sportiness or because they were in school? Christopher was growing up to be somebody. Maurice was growing up to be a baseball player. Why couldn't they have a career?

All these boys and girls need to be in school. Boys need to get off the streets. Girls need to stop having babies. I want to live in a world that has peace and non-violence.

Blacks Killing Blacks
"Why?"

Martin Luther King Jr. tried to convince us to get along with the whites. It seems to me that ever since we got along with them, blacks started getting into gangs, drugs and killing. Martin asked us to love one another, not kill each other. We're not suppose to go against our own people and color.

Why are the colors Red and Blue so called Crips and Bloods? What do the colors mean? Maurice Neal had on a red shirt. They don't know if it was drug or gang related. I wear red and blue. But, I'm not in a gang. Red is my favorite color. I'm not going to stop wearing my colors because of these gang members. Should I not wear certain colors because it might cost me my life?

Tyronica's perspective helped all of us understand what she must face in her neighborhood and her concern for herself and others. Without our safe environment for talk, we never would have shared her thoughts.

One of the most powerful experiences we had this year was revising the Federal Budget for 1992. Each member of the class was a U.S. senator and referred to each other as such during our budget talks. Students were amazed when they saw how the 138 billion dollars were being spent. One of the allocations that created the most debate was the 40.7 billion dollars used to keep troops in Western Europe. Opinions differed dramatically. Some of our senators thought we should take the 40.7 billion dollars and bring the troops home to fight the war on drugs and poverty. Others thought we should slowly cut back the funding and reallocate the money to job diversification, which would help us save our environment. Still others believed we ought to keep things the same because emerging democracies can be unstable. The debates about the budget were shared at home. One parent wrote a letter to us and explained the sacrifices military families have to make. Most of us were unaware of these sacrifices or had not given them much thought. This mother's insights helped us develop more empathy toward military families and helped us be more tolerant in our budget debates about their needs.

These budget negotiations turned out to be a comprehensive way to end our year. We were able to bring all that we had learned throughout the year to bear on making a decision about what to do with the money and how to revise programs such as the Welfare and Medicare systems and work for world peace. Students studied past wars and conflicts as they worked to understand the state of the world today. They drew upon their knowledge of world cultures to help them decide what role the United States played in international politics and evaluated their knowledge as they identified which problems on our home front need to be addressed. The budget talks were the highlight of an effective global education program that stressed successful conflict resolution strategies and the empowerment of voice.

In Space Station Earth what we study is connected to our survival on the planet. We discover that we have a responsibility as Earth's caretakers and that we can make a difference individually and collectively as a community. Sarah wrote:

SPACE STATION EARTH II

Our classroom is different as you can see,
We care about the plants, the Earth, and the sea
You don't know how much we really learn,
You glance at us and then you turn.
"They won't be ready for Junior High," they say
Then the teacher pipes up high, "Yes they will, you don't know why."
"We reflect on current events you know,
Not like how to make a seed grow."
Our classroom is different you can see
And it belongs to You and Me

Sarah has captured the importance of what we do in Space Station Earth and the ownership that is such an integral part of its success.

Over pizza one day I recorded the following conversation, which captures the essence of Space Station Earth:

01   MATT: You don't have as much stress to get things done.

02   AISHA: That's because you make your own agenda. A classroom that is democratic gives you time to spend with what you want to do . . . what you like.

03   BROOKE: We talked more . . . we learned more . . . You don't forget it. You create a relationship with everybody. You have to be friends with everybody before you can get anywhere. Just respect each other.

04   BEN: You get enough time to be with everyone. You get to know them . . . what they do . . . or anything and you get to know what they're all about . . . you get to be friends with them 'cuz when you get to know someone . . . well you're not automatically friends with them, but you get to know them and they get to know you.

05   AISHA: Without getting to talk in the classroom you may look at people differently.

06   BEN: People make assumptions about others . . . without a democratic classroom you may never get to know what someone is all about. I think that most teachers are possessive with their classrooms.

> They are more afraid of what's going on in their classroom, than the real world. Most teachers have "my classroom, my rules." You don't get a say in things.

Ben has a point. Perhaps many of us are too possessive of "our classrooms." When that possession becomes a shared one it opens up a new horizon for all those who experience it. For me, this conversation reinforced the importance of actively building a democratic community. As Aisha notes, classrooms that don't provide a forum for talk may indeed lead students and teachers alike to make unfounded judgments and incorrect assumptions. This could create a classroom hierarchy that could inhibit the individual and collective potential of its members.

On a sad note, as I was concluding the writing of this chapter, I heard from a former student who is now in junior high. Her mother told me she was having difficulty in school and wanted me to see if I could discover some of her fears. What I discovered disturbed me. As always, she is getting straight A's, but her straight A's are empty ones. When I asked her what she does in school, I sensed how disempowered she had become. When I asked her about her language arts program, she told me she hadn't written anything of her own choosing. All she had been doing was diagramming sentences and identifying word parts. When asked about reading, she told me that although she could choose which book to read, she was required only to turn in book reports. The time she collaborated with her peers was limited to filling out a worksheet together. Tears came to both our eyes as she described how teacher-directed and autocratic her classes were.

It is no wonder that she hates school this year. It is no surprise that she dreads each Monday and gets sick to her stomach each week. She is "homeless" at school. She is learning how to adapt to a different definition of "community." Her voice has been stifled under a restrictive system of forty-five minute, departmentalized classes, long halls, and a sea of new faces. I hope she will draw upon the lessons she learned through her experiences in a community that empowered her in order to keep the system from crushing the "What if's" out of her.

Shor (1987) recognizes the tension that exists in a diverse classroom structure:

> I see a tension here between familiar objects and unfamiliar critical scrutiny. I see another tension between the routine curriculum of school which makes reality opaque and the critical classroom which tries to break through the official opacity. There is a third tension between the students' prior experiences of authoritarian education and the new liberatory class which proposes dialogue and self-discipline. (p. 104)

I am often asked by parents, "So, what happens next? What happens when they enter a different structure next year?" With my colleagues, I revisit these questions every year. What we come back to each time is this: We have an obligation to be reflective about what we do as teachers. We have an obligation to grow and change. We have an obligation not to acquiesce to the status quo just to make things easier on everyone. We have an obligation and a commitment to always do what is best for children. This commitment keeps us striving to meet the needs of a diverse and changing population of learners turning the page toward the twenty-first century. The bandwagon isn't coming and going anymore. Instead, it is evolving and building upon the research, experiences, and insights shared by teachers who embrace growth.

Focusing on talk has transformed not only my classroom but me as well. I now realize that talk is an integral and valid part of learning. It needn't be just teacher to student talk, for talk among students is as great, if not a greater catalyst for learning. I am not "the voice" in the room, nor am I the only one who can listen, question, differ, or respond. Our voices are individually and collectively an equal part of our classroom community. While reading Jean Craighead George's book, *The Talking Earth* (1983), I learned that the Seminole Indians listened to the sounds of the Earth and its inhabitants. It guided their decisions and beliefs about what was best for their community. I have come to realize that by listening to the inhabitants of our community, I am much the wiser. I learn so much from them, so much about them and about the direction we need to take. The conversation, debate, and dialogue that occur among students on a daily basis breathe life into our studies and build community among us.

REFERENCES

Barnes, D. 1992. *From communication to curriculum.* 2nd ed. Portsmouth, NH: Boynton/Cook.

Brinn, D. 1991. *Earth.* New York: Bantam.

Calkins, L. 1991. "Keynote address." Whole Language Umbrella Conference, Phoenix, AZ, August.

———. 1990. *Living between the lines.* Portsmouth, NH: Heinemann.

Cullinan, B. 1987. *Children's literature in the reading program.* Newark, DE: International Reading Association.

Freire, P. 1970. *Pedagogy of the oppressed.* New York: Continuum.

George, J. C. 1983. *The talking earth.* New York: Harper.

Healy, J. 1990. *Endangered minds: Why children don't think and what we can do about it.* New York: Simon & Schuster.

Kirk, D. 1992. "Helping youth resolve conflict." Conference presentation, November. St. Louis, MO.

Schmuck, R. and P. Schmuck. 1992. *Group processes in the classroom.* 6th ed. Dubuque, IA: Wm. C. Brown.

Shor, I. and P. Freire. 1987. *A pedagogy for liberation: Dialogues on transforming education.* New York: Bergin & Garvey.

Connie Burke met Judy Collier when she was working as a teacher's assistant in the Kirkwood School District. Connie is now a kindergarten teacher in the Normandy School District in St. Louis, Missouri. She is striving to build a learning environment in her own classroom like the one she observed in Judy's room. She is very grateful for the dialogue, support, and encouragement she has received from Judy Collier. Most recently, Connie has begun serving on the Editorial Advisory Board for the "Children's Books" column in *The Reading Teacher*, published by the International Reading Association.

Chapter 5
Talk Within the Kindergarten: Language Supporting a Learning Community

CONSTANCE M. BURKE

> As the form of the communication changes, so will the form
> of what is learnt. One kind of communication will encourage
> the memorizing of details, another will encourage pupils to
> reason about the evidence, and a third will head them to-
> wards the imaginative reconstruction of a way of life.
>
> Barnes, 1992

When I enter Room 111, I step into the world of the dinosaur. Judy Collier, the teacher, has just finished reading *Digging Up Dinosaurs* (Aliki, 1981), and the children are moving to different work spaces. Cody, Clint, and Charlie are poring over a very graphic dinosaur book trying to figure out whose favorite dinosaur is big enough to squash the other kids' dinosaurs. There are comments of "bigger than our van," and "Man! He'd just squash this school, I bet!," "He's 'bout a hundred of me." Cody looks in the book and reads, "The 'first' [fierce] Allosaurus was 35 feet long." The children look from one to another. What's 35 feet? At that same moment, Layla comes over, scoops up the book and starts to walk away. There are shouts of protest! Cody grabs for the book but Layla clutches it tightly and cries, "Me and Mary's writing 'bout Stegosaurus and need it!" "We're looking at it!" the boys shout. Nearby children, distracted by the loud voices, look up and cry, "Blue Chairs! Go to the blue chairs!" The arguing stops. The children walk back to the blue chairs where they will settle the problem about the book.

The dramatic play corner has been transformed into a paleontologists' dig.

Mrs. Collier is showing the children how paleontologists "dig" in the site [the sand table filled with fossils], number all specimens, use brushes to remove dirt and sand from the fossils, and identify fossils using a catalogue. "Oooooo! I've seen that one in the red book!" said Latasha. She runs to the book shelf and brings back a red book. As Latasha is flipping through the book, she tells Nick and Katy about the rocks her brother found on a family camping trip. When Latasha finds the trilobite fossil picture, Mrs. Collier says, "Yes, Latasha, that's it! Will you be the Trilobite Fossil Expert? Class, if you want to know what a trilobite looks like, or if you find a fossil and want to know if it's a trilobite, you can ask Latasha. She is our Trilobite Fossil Expert." (Journal entry, May, 1992)

On any given day, these kindergartners are asking questions, collaborating, and solving problems. They are actively constructing knowledge about how the world works and how to participate in that world. This exciting classroom belongs to Judy Collier, a full-day kindergarten teacher at Robinson School in St. Louis, Missouri.

Last year, I began working in Judy's kindergarten as a teacher's assistant. My job was to support the teacher's learning environment. However, my past experience in a transmission-type setting had not prepared me for the kinds of communication skills I would need in this classroom. While I was working to become a part of this room, I read *From Communication to Curriculum* (Barnes, 1992). It made me recall my own elementary and secondary school experience. That fall proved to be a unique instance when theory, practice, and prior experience all converged. I began to question my beliefs about teaching and learning. I started to examine the kinds of learning goals we have for our students and how we are communicating these goals to our students.

Teachers want their students to be critical thinkers and self-directed learners. We want them to be able to operate within our social system and be respectful of other people's thoughts and feelings. These goals are a combination of intellectual and social development—the written and "hidden" curriculum (Barnes, 1992; Power and Kohlberg, 1986). However, our goals for our students often contradict actual classroom practice. We tell our students what to think but expect them to be autonomous thinkers. We tell our students how to act but never allow them to interact. I believe we must move from telling to "talking" with our students because, as Barnes says, "as the form of the communication changes, so will the form of what is learnt" (p.15). It is through communication that teachers convey their beliefs about teaching, how children learn, what they value in a learner, and what learning looks like. It is through teacher communication that students learn whether they will be active or passive participants in their own social and intellectual education.

HOW CHILDREN LEARN

Judy believes that children "construct" their own knowledge and values as a result of interactions with the physical and social world (Missouri Department of Elementary and Secondary Education, 1992). Project Construct is a constructivist view of learning developed primarily from the work of Jean Piaget (1896–1980), a Swiss psychologist. (Learning, in this case, means going beyond rote memorization to incorporate new information into the way we interpret and interact with the world.) Constructivists believe that teachers cannot "pour knowledge" into students as if they were empty containers. Instead, students come to any learning situation already "filled" with past experiences and abilities, which they use to interpret new information. As children participate in authentic learning activities, they are obliged to evaluate new information in terms of any prior theories they may have formed. For example, Judy presented many scientific facts about dinosaurs. If Mary and Layla want to write a book about dinosaurs, they will have to integrate this new information with the information they have already absorbed from popular children's movies, cartoons, or their visits to the science center.

Children work through these discrepancies by thinking and reflecting on their own, or with their teacher and peers. In the end, they come to a new understanding of dinosaurs (O'Neil, 1992). The result is not simply that new information replaces old, but that children construct new relationships and new patterns. This form of learning is a process through which learners assimilate and reorganize information into their existing internal model of the world, where it is available for use in interpreting new experiences.

If learning is "a process of active construction by the learner" (Nolan and Francis, 1992), then teachers must move beyond being mere presenters of knowledge. They must become informed guides or collaborators, assisting children as they explore the relationship between what they know and new information and experiences. Teachers are challenged to develop a curriculum that includes learning activities in which students use their prior knowledge to explore, reason, and hypothesize. It also includes opportunities for teachers and peers to assist the learner in this process by discussing and exchanging information and points of view. When we interact with others we can confirm, refine, or revise our thinking. Teachers must include blocks of time within the day for students to evaluate and reflect upon their actions and hypotheses. This is more than a "hands on" curriculum. "A child can handle things without in the least finding them relevant to his purposes" (Barnes, 1992, p. 82). This is a curriculum that engages children both physically and mentally (Project Construct, 1992).

TALK SUPPORTING THE LEARNER

What are some examples of classroom talk that support children in their discovery of themselves as learners and members of the kindergarten community? The way teachers use talk in the classroom conveys to students who they are, what they can do, and how they can do it. This communication affects not only their behavior but their thinking as well. It influences how they perceive themselves as learners and how willing they are to risk themselves in the learning process. The way students use talk in the social environment influences their development of positive, cooperative relationships. In the past, teachers used praise as a way to support academic growth. However, they did not have a consistent strategy for aiding students' social learning. When personal disagreements occurred, teachers usually stepped in and settled the conflicts in ways they thought were fair. Unfortunately, neither of these strategies supported students in building a strong sense of self-esteem, engaging in autonomous thinking, or creating cooperative relationships. If we keep in mind that children need to be involved in the construction of knowledge themselves, we can modify these strategies so that they do foster academic and social growth.

Encouragement

Some teachers believe that praise is an effective way of fostering self-esteem and reinforcing appropriate learning behavior. Students are usually told that they are good, nice, or even smart. Yet comments like these do little to boost students' self-image, and they may even have a negative effect. Rowe (see Hitz and Driscoll, 1988) found that praise lowered students' confidence in their answers and reduced their willingness to respond. "The students exhibited many characteristics indicative of lower self-esteem, such as responding in doubtful tones and lack of persistence or desire to keep trying" (p. 7). The students became dependent on the teacher, frequently trying to read the teacher's eyes for approval or disapproval. In order to have a positive self-image, learners have to judge for themselves that they possess valuable knowledge and skills. Since praise is not based on students' judgment of themselves, but on the judgment of the teacher, students fail to develop their own internal valuing system. They become dependent on the teacher to tell them what is right or wrong, good or bad (Kamii, 1984). Their work becomes focused on winning adult approval and not on the rewards of a job well done. Praise also fails as an effective reinforcer because it does not provide students with specific feedback about their learning behavior (Hitz and Driscoll, 1988).

Statements such as "I like the way your numbers are nice and neat" and "John, you're a good reader!" do not provide children with the feedback they need to broaden their perception of themselves as learners.

Judy believes that learning takes place when students use their prior knowledge to explore, reason, and hypothesize about the environment. She wants to encourage this engagement. Hitz and Driscoll (1988) say that "encouragement . . . refers to a positive acknowledgment response that focuses on student efforts and/or specific attributes of work completed" (p. 10). Judy gives specific feedback to support students' continued involvement in the process of intellectual and social growth. When Judy named Latasha "Trilobite Fossil Expert," she acknowledged Latasha's contribution to the dinosaur curriculum. She supported Latasha's ability to make connections between what she knew and the present learning situation. An "I like . . ." statement would have stamped adult approval on Latasha's behavior and hindered her from drawing her own conclusions about her actions. Judy allowed her to experience the intrinsic reward of making a valuable contribution to the community.

Encouragement does not equate a student with his work—good work therefore good person. Errors in classroom work are valuable as feedback on students' thinking, but they should not be used as judgments of students' worth. Encouragement allows Judy to talk with the children about their work, and they do not have to fear that they are being judged. By removing herself as judge, Judy shifts the responsibility for acknowledging their own behaviors and achievements to the students.

Mary and Layla have never written a book together before. Today, they are writing about the fierce Stegosaurus. Judy's words acknowledge the effort they have made and the risks they have taken to write their book: "Mary and Layla, you two have been working on your book all morning! You have written a lot about the Stegosaurus. Will you read it to me when you're finished?"

Judy doesn't evaluate their work but encourages the girls to continue with their writing. She has shifted the focus of her talk from praising children's work to encouraging their continued engagement in the writing process. By supporting the decisions the students make in the learning environment, she fosters their self-confidence and self-esteem.

Conflict Resolution

Judy strongly believes that social interaction supports learning. She has incorporated cooperative learning activities into her curriculum and arranged the classroom to increase the opportunities students have to share their working and thinking. As the rate of social interaction increases, it is inevitable that personal disagreements and conflicts will also increase. This is especially true for cooperative classrooms, where there is a great deal of group work. In order for the cooperative learning atmosphere and the classroom community to be maintained, some kind of resolution strategies are essential for dealing with and resolving personal conflicts.

The personal conflicts that occur every day in the classroom provide wonderful opportunities for children to learn about social reasoning and social justice. Conflict Resolution provides a framework so that children can use language to resolve personal disagreements. In Judy's classroom, the children refer to it as the "Blue Chairs" because two blue chairs are reserved for this purpose. This conflict resolution strategy initiates young children into the thinking process adults use when they are solving problems.

Judy's "Blue Chairs" Guidelines:

1. Only the people who are part of the problem sit in the Blue Chairs.
2. No touching, yelling, or name calling.
3. One person tells his/her feelings at a time. "I feel _____, because _____." The other person must wait his/her turn. There are no interruptions.
4. The people who are part of the problem must solve the problem. Each person must be satisfied with the solution.

Initially, Judy acts as mediator, demonstrating the process and reminding children of the procedure. She emphasizes listening to the other person's point of view and responding to what has been said. If the children are having difficulty in resolving the problem, she will make suggestions. Then she withdraws and allows the children to use the "Blue Chairs" procedure independently.

The following exchange is an example of how Judy's students function within this framework. Initially, I would not have believed that kindergarten children would be able to use sophisticated strategies to solve problems.

> Cody, Clint, and Charlie are having a discussion about the pictures in a dinosaur book. Layla comes over, scoops up the book and starts to walk away. Cody grabs for the book, but Layla clutches it tightly and cries that she and Mary need to use it. The boys protest and an argument ensues. Nearby children, distracted by the loud voices, look up and shout, "Blue Chairs! Go to the Blue Chairs!" Tension leaves the four children as they walk back to the blue chairs, gathering up Mary on their way. . . . Cody, Clint, Charlie, Mary, and Layla sit together in a circle facing each other.

01 CODY: It made me mad when you took the book!

02 CLINT AND CHARLIE: Yeah . . . Yeah. We were using it!

03 LAYLA: I needed it so we could do our book . . . and . . .

04 MARY: [Interrupts] It's the only book where you kin see Stegosaurus' tail. And we need it for our picture . . . and . . .

05 LAYLA: [Interrupts] Yeah, we needed it.

06 CODY: But, we're trying to see who's got the biggest dinosaur . . . and . . . and that book . . .

07 CLINT: [Interrupts] That book's got the numbers on the bottom . . . and you kin tell . . . you kin tell who's biggest.

08 CODY: So, what're we going to do?

09 CLINT: Yeah . . . how we gonna solve it?

10 MARY: . . . well, we could . . . we could give it back to you when we're finished?

11 CLINT: No! We had it first! Go find your own book!

12 CODY: Well . . . somebody could use it for, say . . . 5 minutes, and then let the other people use it?

13 CLINT: No . . . 3 minutes!

14 CHARLIE: Yeah, 3 minutes.

15 MARY AND LAYLA: OK . . . but how we gonna tell the 3 minutes are up? And who's gonna get it first?

16 CODY: Let's roll the dice . . .

After rolling the dice, the children asked Judy if she would watch the time for them. Instead, she gave them a three-minute "hour glass" timer to use. (Journal entry, May 1992)

In this exchange the children use what Barnes (1992) calls "exploratory talk." Exploratory talk can be described as "thinking out loud" with a group. Thoughts are incomplete, interruptions are frequent, and ideas are formed collectively. Initially, children are supposed to express their feelings. Barnes says that in finding the words to express their ideas and feelings, children reflect on the situation and make it clearer in their own minds. Talk helps us clarify our thinking. Cody (01) starts the discussion by expressing his feelings. However, it is the contributions of the other children that enable the group to explore and state the problem more fully. Together, the children sort through and talk themselves into a better understanding.

"So, what are we gonna do?" Cody's question (08) stops further discussion of the problem. The children have organized the problem and now must relate it to the solution. They must also struggle with the complex issue of social justice. They begin negotiating (10–13). Mary offers a solution, but Clint rejects it and offers little in return. Cody offers a solution that appears to take both sides into consideration. Clint is resistant, but sees that a negotiated solution is coming and wants to have some input into the decision that will ultimately affect him. As a result, Clint's support is ensured because of his investment in the solution.

Are the children constructing knowledge about social reasoning? It appears so. Cody's proposal seems to offer something for both sides. Are the children constructing knowledge about social justice? The children had difficulty coming up with some fair recommendations. It appears that generating a fair solution is a far more difficult process than evaluating one. However, the children must have constructed some concept of justice, because they had no problem deciding whether Cody's proposal was a fair one. Even from an adult frame of reference, the children have come to a fair judgment, though one that is highly impractical. Since both sides share the same frame of reference regarding time, they have little trouble accepting the three-minute time limit. Judy does not impose her thinking about time upon the children's decision (the children later realized that the time limit needed adjustment). Judy will support all decisions that are acceptable to both sides and within the best interests of all concerned.

The children know that the "Blue Chairs" is a valued classroom institution, and *no one* can refuse a call to "settle a problem." This becomes doubly important for those children who are "silenced" by the school community. Henson (in this volume) states that there is a connection between having a say, being part of a Community, and being a learner. In the conflict resolution process, all of the parties involved bring their own perspectives to the dialogue, and all perspectives are considered equally valid. The "Blue Chairs" allows children more than a part in the process. It provides them with a principal role in having a say about what happens to them in the classroom.

Through engaging in dialogue, we become "interdependent," each member learning from the other. Interdependency provides opportunities to see the world from another person's point of view and to build relationships of mutual trust and respect (Henson, in this volume). Students who feel that their thoughts and feelings are valued are more likely to invest intellectually and emotionally in the classroom community. "We'll reach the individual if we care about the group. Conversely, the group will flourish if we care about the individual" (Glover and Sheppard, 1989, p. 41).

The "Blue Chairs" is a framework for resolving problems, it is not a solution. Children can talk and be a part of the procedure, but they may not come close to constructing an understanding of social reasoning and social justice. The strategy provides a framework within which children can talk themselves into a better understanding, but it requires preparation and support in order for it to be successful. Conflict resolution plays a big part in maintaining the kindergarten learning community, and Judy does not abandon it once the children have learned the procedure. Even after the children can work independently, Judy continues to monitor the situation and occasionally offers suggestions in order to extend the children's growth in talk and problem solving. Her students are able to decide for themselves when they need help, and they support each other's participation in the resolution process.

The learning community continually reaps benefits from the "Blue Chairs" procedure. Using talk to solve problems has carried over into other areas of the curriculum. In the "Blue Chairs" vignette and in later examples, the children demonstrate that they are reflecting on their thoughts before speaking. I noticed that they were selective in their choice of words and attempted to express themselves more explicitly. Since all feelings and ideas are valued in this kindergarten community, the children took more risks to express their ideas and were more willing to accept another's point of view. This enabled them to negotiate, to extend each other's thinking, and to work cooperatively on classroom projects.

TALK SUPPORTING THE PROCESS

How do we support kindergartners in becoming autonomous thinkers and life-long learners? Teachers can support kindergartners becoming autonomous thinkers and life-long learners by allowing them to take an active part in their own learning. Active engagement requires physical *and* mental interaction. Learners must go beyond physical interaction with the environment to begin to make sense of an experience, to relate it to what they already know, and to incorporate it into their perception of the world. Talk provides the means to examine what we know, to exchange information with others, and to confirm or revise our thinking. Children have always talked in the classroom, but we have not always provided opportunities for them to use the kinds of talk that develop autonomous thinking. Children need to experience authentic learning situations where they can learn and practice using talk purposefully (Edelsky and Smith, 1984). When learners can use talk to interpret information, formulate a hypothesis, and reflect on the results, they are using language to think and learn. Talk as a means of learning can be observed in Judy's classroom in three forms: demonstrations, teacher-student dialogue, and student-student dialogue.

Demonstrations

Teachers have no control over the literacy experiences children have before they enter kindergarten. Some children enter school able to read and some have had no experience with books at all. Yet every fall, kindergarten teachers begin building a learning community with this diverse group of young children. Since the children have such varied backgrounds, Judy cannot base her curriculum on common experience. She believes that her shared-literature sessions are the key to building a curriculum and a learning community in which all the children can comfortably share and contribute. Literature can offer a complete, open-ended experience that allows all the children to participate on a common basis. Having a shared knowledge of the same stories "is an important component of building a group history" (Sheppard, 1990, p. 79). This class history of stories, learning experiences, and classroom events helps build community.

In her shared-reading sessions, Judy demonstrates how readers read and how she herself feels about reading. When she reads aloud to the class, the demonstration becomes an intimate performance. She talks in a calm, conversational tone and weaves important information into her reading of the text. The children nod and smile in response to the reading, and Judy takes her cues from their faces. These are the teachable moments. Their attention and body language communicate to her how much she should tell them and what she may need to repeat, relate, or extend. In sharing *Digging Up Dinosaurs* (Aliki, 1981), Judy demonstrated a range of literacy behaviors: that reading proceeds from left to right and top to bottom, that pages are turned from right to left, that print and illustrations work together, and that diagrams present factual information. In one reading, Judy's demonstrations allowed all the children to enter into the world of print, the "literacy club" (Smith, 1992), from different places.

Judy provides explicit demonstrations of literacy behavior that express her feelings about literature and its part in her life and in the classroom. There are always books on tables, racks, shelves, and the teacher's desk. Books are constantly being read, listened to on tape, and referred to. Everyone "reads" and uses books. There are few conversations in which books do not play some part. Frank Smith (1981, p. 112) says "Children's brains are not easily fooled. They learn what we demonstrate to them, not what we may hope and think we teach." A teacher who reads a book at the beginning of the day and never refers to it again demonstrates that books and reading are not an integral part of kindergarten learning.

Since learning is a social process, Judy's classroom is arranged to take advantage of peer demonstrations, too. Anyone familiar with classrooms has seen how one child's demonstration—such as a little heart to dot an *i*—will spread throughout the classroom in a matter of minutes. Peer demonstrations are powerful examples. Mary and Layla's book about the Stegosaurus created an interest in starting a special dinosaur library in the classroom. Each book would give information about only one dinosaur instead of many different ones. Nick and Charlie were among those who wrote books about their favorite dinosaurs.

Teacher-Student Dialogue

Mary and Layla have been sitting at the writing table all morning working on their book. Judy can easily keep track of the things they are doing and saying as she works with the other children at the writing table. She decides to join them to talk about their dinosaur book.

01 JUDY: How is your book coming along? Tell me about it.

02 LAYLA: It's a book 'bout a Stegosaurus . . . It's called *Stegosaurus* . . . but we're not finished yet.

03 MARY: Yeah . . . we did it together . . .

04 JUDY: Well, would you read me what you've got so far?

05 LAYLA: I'll read it . . . 'cause I did the writin' . . .

06 MARY: And I'll show my pictures.

07 LAYLA: [Reading] *Stegosaurus* written by Layla, illustrations by Mary. "The Stegosaurus likes . . . leaves" . . . I forgot to put "tender" . . .

08 JUDY: Can you fit it in there? . . . Do you remember that little trick writers use when they want to squeeze in a word?

09 LAYLA: They put this upside down *V.* [She draws in a caret.]

10 JUDY: Yes . . . now write the word real tiny . . . Why don't you start the story from the beginning again?

11 LAYLA: "Stegosaurus likes tender leaves."

12 MARY: Now . . . I made Stegosaurus's armored plates on his back . . . and there he eatin' the tender leaves . . . and . . . His tail is up . . . 'cause dinosaurs didn't drag their tails . . .

13 JUDY: Is that so? How do we know that?

14 MARY: 'Cause scientists haven't found any tail prints.

15 JUDY: Wow! What's going to happen next, ladies?

16 MARY: We don't know . . . We haven't written it yet!

17 JUDY: Well . . . let's think of some ideas . . .

18 LAYLA: Uh . . . Triceratops could come . . . and . . . uh . . . kills Stegosaurus and eats him!

19 MARY: Yeah . . . that's good!

20 JUDY: Wait a minute, wait a minute! Help me, my brain is feeling confused . . . [Mary and Layla shrug their shoulders. Take several deep breaths.]

21 LAYLA AND MARY: [Together] Uh . . . well . . . we could . . . I don't know . . .

22 JUDY: Nick, Nick, could I interrupt you for a minute? Layla and Mary are writing this dinosaur story . . . and . . . my brain's just confused. Could you give us some help? Could you listen to their story? Ladies, read Nick your book . . .

23 LAYLA: [Reading] *Stegosaurus* written by Layla and illustrated by Mary. "Stegosaurus likes tender leaves."

24 JUDY: Tell Nick what you're thinking could happen next . . .

25 LAYLA: Triceratops comes and eats Stegosaurus . . .

26 JUDY: My brain is mixed-up . . .

27 NICK: [Interrupts] Hey! Triceratops wouldn't eat Stegosaurus! He's a plant-eater!

28 LAYLA AND MARY: [Together] Oh! We gotta have a meat-eater . . . like Tyrannosaurus Rex . . . or . . . like that . . .

29 JUDY: Do you want to use Tyrannosaurus Rex?

30 NICK: I'm writin' about Tyrannosaurus Rex . . . you could use my book . . .

31 LAYLA: Naaahhh . . .

32 MARY: Yeah . . . we want a different dinosaur.

33 JUDY: Do you want a meat-eater or a plant-eater? . . . Why don't you get the blue book and look through for your own dinosaur? You might want to use a dinosaur no one else has used . . . [Journal entry, May 1992]

From the very beginning of the conference, Judy's questions convey support and respect for Layla and Mary's ability to choose, and explore a topic of interest. She views their work as a serious effort to write about the Stegosaurus. She enters into conversation with the two girls as an equal, not in knowledge but as a participant in a dialogue. When teachers are supportive and treat a topic in an exploratory fashion, as Judy does here, children are more willing to express their thinking or to ask questions and reveal to the teacher the framework they are using to interpret the information (Wells, 1986).

When viewed alone, Layla and Mary's text provides a limited view of the girls' understanding of dinosaurs and writing. Judy needs to ask questions to determine the girls' purpose in writing their book. During the conference, the girls will reflect on their original idea for the book, tell how they delegated the work, and explain the processes they used to write. The text *and* the talk together enable Judy to discover the skills and intellectual processes the girls are using in this learning situation. Without this information, Judy cannot ask the questions or design the activities that will enable the girls to extend their knowledge of content or strategies.

When Judy stopped Layla (20), she said it was because the story wasn't making sense to her. Judy's confusion compelled the girls to go back and examine their work. She wants Layla and Mary to reflect on what they want to do and how they are attempting to do it. It is not her purpose to look for errors; rather, she wants to use the dinosaur book as a learning opportunity in which the girls can examine and evaluate their knowledge of dinosaurs and writing, all within the context of their book. Judy wants to raise the questions that will lead them to reflect and involve them in a dialogue between teacher and student. Then they will use talk to "think out loud," to inspect and question the information they have in their heads. However, Mary and Layla are not sure about what is wrong or what they should do (21). Judy does not assume control and begin asking for information about meat-eating and plant-eating dinosaurs. Instead, she models a plan of action for the girls. She and Nick (26–33) use talk to examine and analyze thinking. Their conversation serves to demonstrate the internal dialogue that goes on when we are confirming or revising our thinking.

All through the conference, Judy is evaluating the girls' knowledge of dinosaurs and writing, deciding which aspects have the most potential to extend the children's thinking. The teacher's role is not one of judge but of collaborator: "How can I help you write your dinosaur book?" Judy will use the students as her "curricular informants" (Harste and Short with Burke, 1988). She will offer suggestions and extend invitations that are based on the girls' intentions and relevant to their purposes. "How else could you do it?" "What other way might work?" "What would happen if . . ." Capitalizing on children's interest and intent improves the chances that they will incorporate the teacher's input into their own repertoire (Wells, 1986).

In this conversation, the girls were able to talk with Judy about the thinking and decision-making processes they were using to write and illustrate their book. When the meat-eating/plant-eating crisis arose, Judy used talk to model the exploratory thinking process and expressed her thoughts as suggestions, not commands. Together the children discussed and exchanged points of view so the girls could confirm or revise their thinking about dinosaurs.

Student-Student Dialogue

About one week into the study of dinosaurs, the following exchange occurred during Free Choice time, a time set aside for children to explore topics of personal interest. Several children were sitting around the table playing with the dinosaur models when a minor disagreement erupted about the arrangement of the dinosaurs on the table.

01   CLINT: Hey!. . . Why don't we make a museum? [The children move to the block area and start to build a long circular wall. It looks like one large room. Judy walks over to check in with the group.]

02   JUDY: What are you building?

03   CLINT: We're building a dinosaur museum.

04   JUDY: Who's been to a museum?

05   CODY: I went to the science museum with my cousin.

06   JUDY: Oh good, good. What did it look like? Was it one big room, or did it have little rooms . . . or . . . was it like a long tunnel?

07   CODY: When you come in the door . . . You come into a big room . . . and then . . . you kind of . . . kind of follow a maze . . . to see different stuff . . .

08   JUDY: What displays would we put?

09   MOLLY: We could put the dinosaur models on the . . .

10   KATY: [Interrupts] We could put the meat-eaters on this side and the plant-eaters on this side.

11   MOLLY: . . . and we need to make some signs.

12   JUDY: What signs do we need? Do we need a book. . .? [Journal entry, May 1992]

The children collect paper and pencils and begin to make name labels for the dinosaurs. After they have labeled the individual dinosaurs, they make the larger "Meat-eaters" and "Plant-eaters" signs.

At the end of the day, the children place a D NT T (Do Not Touch!) sign on their museum. (Judy will leave the Dinosaur Museum in place for as long as it is of interest to the children.)

The next day Judy walks over to the children's museum. It has been attracting quite a bit of attention from the other children.

01 JUDY: Could I come to your museum? . . . Do I need a ticket? [Molly runs and makes a ticket for Judy.]

02 JUDY: Where do I go? Will someone tell me about this? Is the curator here? The curator is the person who knows all the information about the museum stuff.

03 NICK: I could be the Tyrannosaurus curator . . .

04 CLINT: I could be the Triceratops curator . . .

05 MOLLY: And I could tell about Brontosaurus . . . [Journal entry, May 1992]

The work the children do on their projects involves the building of layers of increasingly sophisticated activity. The initial layer was the children's construction of the dinosaur museum. The next layer was Judy's coming to the museum and issuing invitations to the children to become curators and to tell her about the dinosaur displays. The children extend the invitation by giving tours and "lectures" about dinosaurs. When their classmates wanted to take tours, a problem occurred. The children were touching and knocking over the displays. The next layer, then, involved working to solve this problem. The children decided that they needed a D NT T (Do Not Touch!) sign near the displays. Judy commented that the sign was a good idea, but that people like to touch things, since it helps them learn. The children responded by creating a "hands on" area where classmates could touch the displays. This area included other dinosaur models, puzzles, and dinosaur playing cards. Yet another layer was added to the project when other children wanted to add their own personal dinosaur favorites to the museum. There weren't any models for these dinosaurs, so the children displayed pictures from books or made drawings of these less familiar dinosaurs. Judy asked the children, "Where will you put them? Are they meat-eaters, or plant-eaters?" The children had learned that not all prehistoric animals were dinosaurs, and they researched each prehistoric animal the best they could. However, they still felt they needed a new section labeled NT DNSRS (Not Dinosaurs).

Soon, the dinosaur museum was huge and no one wanted a complete tour. The children added paper slips to each dinosaur so guests could sign up if they wanted to hear the report on that dinosaur. The last layer was added when Judy remarked, "This is such a wonderful museum! It's a shame that no one else is seeing it!" The children made posters to advertise their museum and began giving tours to other classes.

Once again, Judy's role is to raise the questions that lead to reflection and dialogue among the students. She is also the informed guide/collaborator. She helps them reflect on what they know and relate it to what they want to do. She guides them in their exploration of a topic so their good ideas don't fade as a result of inexperience. She is the resource person who provides information or a means of obtaining information. She uses these opportunities to introduce new ideas, concepts, strategies, or skills, all within the context of the museum.

Each layer required the children to extend what they already knew. The children used talk to explore each new phase of their museum and to solve each new problem it presented. They always reflected on what they knew and went on from there. The children needed each other for sharing ideas, clarifying strategies, and giving feedback. They found they needed more than one voice and one idea. Together, they planned, negotiated, and collaborated.

CONCLUSION

As the form of the communication changes, so will the form of what is learnt (Barnes, 1992, p. 15).

As Harste, Short, and Burke (1988, p. 48) explain, "Curriculum is not so much a course of study as it is a transaction between learners in a language setting." The language in such settings serves two primary roles: as a communication system, and as a means of learning (Barnes, 1992). Through their communication systems, their questions, their acceptance of student replies, and their tone, teachers communicate to the students the types of student behaviors—such as language strategies—that are acceptable. This social context, in turn, shapes the way students perceive their role as participants in the construction of knowledge. Teachers who want their students to be active constructors of knowledge must monitor their own language strategies because they may unknowingly place conditions on the ways their students can use language to learn. This relationship—teachers' language to students' participation—is governed by our beliefs about how children learn and it must guide us in developing curriculum.

As I observed Judy's talk and her children's responses, I was amazed at the knowledge and thinking strategies the children used. Such experiences lead us to "question the relationship between teacher's knowledge and pupils' knowledge" (Barnes, 1992, p. 126). Students' knowledge is not an immature version of the teacher's, but the matter is not as simple as replacing an immature viewpoint with a more mature one. Rather, teachers should realize that students have constructed valid viewpoints that they will eventually need to interrelate with adult points of view.

When Judy changed the way she viewed teaching and learning, she began to revise the language she used in the classroom. She moved away from talk that was authoritarian and controlling and gave children choices and asked for their solutions to problems. She began to ask questions that called for reflection and interpretation. The social interaction and the learning atmosphere in the classroom changed. The children displayed a new confidence and a sense of their own value.

On occasion, Judy chose not to talk at all. She conveyed through her silence her expectation that the children would contribute what they knew to the discussion. When teachers stop filling all the silences with their own voices, the children will begin to talk. During their short lifetimes, children have used language to ask questions (Why is the sky blue?), to discuss points of view (I don't need to go to bed because . . .), and to settle disagreements (You can use the shovel after me). If we have not seen these skills used in the classroom, it is because we have not provided opportunities for children to use them (Barnes, 1992).

In our intense effort to make our children better thinkers and learners, we have sometimes tried to bring the elementary curriculum into the early childhood classroom. We thought more skills and more facts would make our students more accomplished thinkers and learners. Instead, children need more opportunities to reflect and relate information and ideas to themselves and their present perspectives. When talk is a valued part of the classroom, we are enriching our curriculum with the children's own thoughts and experiences, raising learning activities to more sophisticated levels, and building strong supportive relationships that, in turn, help our students grow into independent thinkers, life-long learners, and socio-moral individuals.

REFERENCES

Aliki. 1981. *Digging up dinosaurs.* New York: Harper & Row.

Barnes, D. 1992. *From communication to curriculum.* 2nd ed. Portsmouth, NH: Boynton/Cook.

Cambourne, B. 1988. *The whole story: Natural learning and the acquisition of literacy in the classroom.* Auckland, NZ: Ashton Scholastic.

Collier, J. 1990. Personal conversation. Kindergarten teacher. Kirkwood School District, St. Louis, MO.

DeVries, R. with L. Kohlberg. 1987. *Programs of early education.* White Plains, NY: Longman.

Dyson, A. H. 1989. *Multiple worlds of child writers: Friends learning to write.* New York: Teachers College Press.

Edelsky, C. and K. Smith. 1984. "Is that writing—or are those marks just a figment of your curriculum?" *Language Arts* 61(1):24–32.

Forman, G. 1990. "Helping children ask good questions." In *The wonder of it: Exploring how the world works,* edited by B. Neugebauer. Beginnings Books Series.

Glover, M. and L. Sheppard. 1989. *Not on your own: The power of learning together.* Ontario: Scholastic Canada.

Good, T. 1982. "How teachers' expectations affect results." *American-Education* 18(10):25–32.

Harste, J. & K. Short, with C. Burke. 1988. *Creating classrooms for authors: The reading-writing connection.* Portsmouth, NH: Heinemann.

Hays, G. 1992. "Project Construct." *Missouri Schools* 57(3):12–17.

Hendrick, J. 1992. "When does it begin? Teaching the principles of democracy in the early years." *Young Children* March:51–53.

Hitz, R. and A. Driscoll. 1988. "Praise or encouragement? New insights into praise: Implications for early childhood teachers." *Young Children* July:6–13.

Kamii, C. 1984. "Viewpoint: Obedience is not enough." *Young Children* 39(4):11–14.

Missouri Department of Elementary and Secondary Education. 1992. *Project construct: A framework for curriculum and assessment.* Jefferson City, MO.

Nolan, J. and P. Francis. 1992. "Changing perspectives in curriculum and instruction." *Association for Supervision and Curriculum Development* Yearbook:44–60.

O'Neil, J. 1992. "Wanted: Deep understanding. 'Constructivism' posits new conception of learning." *Association for Supervision and Curriculum Development* 34(3):1–8.

Peterson, R. and M. Eeds. 1990. *Grand conversations.* New York: Scholastic.

Power, C. and L. Kohlberg. 1986. "Using a hidden curriculum for moral education." *Curriculum Review* 26(September/October):14–17.

Sheppard, L. 1990. "Our class knows frog and toad: An early childhood literature-based classroom." In Short and Pierce, eds., *Talking about books.* Portsmouth, NH: Heinemann.

Smith, F. 1992. "Learning to read: The never-ending debate." *Phi Delta Kappan* February:432–41.

————. 1981. "Demonstrations, engagement and sensitivity: A revised approach to language learning." *Language Arts* 58:103–112.

Wells, G. 1986. *The meaning makers.* Portsmouth, NH: Heinemann.

Jean Dickinson was teaching fourth grade at Uthoff Valley Elementary School in the Rockwood School District in St. Louis, Missouri, at the time of the inquiry project she writes about in this chapter. She is currently teaching a fifth-/sixth-grade class in a multi-aged, year-round school in Douglas County School District in Parker, Colorado. She enjoys reading and collecting children's literature and uses picture books extensively with intermediate-age students.

Chapter 6
Children's Perspectives on Talk: Building a Learning Community

JEAN DICKINSON

Talk is a daydream in your head. Talk helps us learn, helps us help, lets us tell and ask, and lets us daydream. (Annie)

When we talk we aren't alone. We have more than one answer to think about. We have people to help us. (Adam)

When I talk with my Mom I can get the knots in my head all talked out. (Leslie)

During the 1991–1992 school year, the students in my fourth-grade class joined with me in an inquiry into "talk" in our classroom. Throughout the inquiry process, we identified the kinds of talk we engaged in and shared our perspectives on the role of talk in our learning. The statements quoted above were made by Annie, Adam, and Leslie toward the end of the school year.

As we began our inquiry, I discussed the project with the children. I explained that its purpose was to enlist their ideas about talk and their views of talk as a means of helping them learn. Together, we identified the different kinds of talk in our room: literature discussions, humor and happenings that caused us to laugh, talk in our small group work, social conversations, and the talk that was necessary in conducting our daily routines. It also became clear to the children that talk was an issue important to me as their teacher.

The children and I used talk to assess and evaluate our learning. The children's ideas and insights guided my decisions about my teaching and often gave me reasons to make changes. As we assessed and learned together, each of us became more aware of our own learning.

My beliefs about talk in the classroom have been shaped by seven years of teaching experience, collaboration with other teachers, and continued professional studies. My personal evolution during these seven years has been from traditional teaching toward a more holistic approach. The reading program in my classroom has moved from traditional basal instruction to literature discussion groups using trade books. As I participated in the literature discussion groups with the students, I recognized the dimension that talking about books added to their learning. These discussions clarified story meaning for the children, and as they talked about these stories, they built on their own ideas and the ideas of others, and together we reached new levels of thinking. As a member of these literature groups, I learned much about the children, their understanding of a story, and their personal connections to a story. When given the opportunity to talk in small groups, I saw children go far beyond the expectations that I had set for them. As a result of the literature discussion groups, I first realized the value of talk in our learning.

I supported the inquiry in my classroom in four ways. First, I read *From Communication to Curriculum* (Barnes, 1992). During the 1990–1991 school year I was a member of the study group in St. Louis that met to discuss this book as it related to our teaching. From participating in this group, I realized the impact talk had on my learning and the learning in our classroom. Graduate studies and new opportunities for collaboration with other teachers provided support and gave me a focus for what I was attempting to do in my teaching. Teachers from other schools shared wonderful stories about experiences with students in classrooms rich with spoken language. Carol Gilles and Kathryn Mitchell Pierce challenged my thinking and gave me constructive suggestions for organizing activities that would provide for language-rich learning experiences.

Second, I collaborated with teachers in my own building on the issue of talk, in particular, talk in literature discussion groups. Lori Deubner, a reading specialist, worked in my classroom with remedial readers three afternoons a week. Lori and I brainstormed ideas to improve the literature program, considered modifications, and celebrated the progress students made. We considered new titles to read and tried new ways of setting up the groups and structuring activities. Lori and I continually evaluated what we were doing and how well we felt the children were progressing. A staff study group provided additional opportunities for collaboration with a larger group of teachers. Since all members of the study group were working with literature discussion groups in some form, the group's attention often focused on the talk in literature discussions.

Third, I gave much time to reflective thinking about my teaching. A fifty-minute drive to and from school was perhaps a "blessing in disguise." The drive each day provided time to assess individual needs and time to assess what was working or not working in the classroom. I used this time to listen to tape recordings of the literature discussions, and as I listened I recognized great value in revisiting these discussions. During this driving time I stepped back from the daily events and had a better overview of the larger picture. Day-to-day progress is often difficult to recognize. By looking at longer periods of time, I saw the progress we were indeed making, both individual children and the entire classroom. I used this time to "debrief myself" and was able to keep less important issues in perspective and stay focused on what I believed were the issues most important for the children. By now, there was a frame of reference for my reflective thinking based on professional studies, collaboration with other teachers, and insights shared by the children. I was a more skilled and informed "Kid Watcher" (Y. Goodman, 1985) and I recognized and valued the ideas and thoughts expressed by the children. My reflective thinking was done with a purpose and with input vital for making constructive decisions.

Fourth, I kept a computer log during the school year and wrote entries several times a week. Initially, I had no clear objective for those entries, I just typed! But as time went by, it became clear that I was recording the changes I observed in the class, the progress of individual students, and important curricular decisions such as our use of picture books. My log also allowed me to record the reflective thinking that I was doing on the long drive home. There were evenings I couldn't wait to get to the computer to write—other school work waited. I recorded frustrations and failures, celebrations, and "moments to remember."

We began our inquiry using a framework comprising my initial thoughts about talk. At the end of the year I found that my initial beliefs still held true, but they were now reinforced by our shared experiences. These beliefs had moved to the forefront of my thinking and curriculum planning.

Beliefs About Talk in a Learning Community

1. Talk is the means by which the students and I come to understand one another. It is through talk that we create a safe and secure learning environment conducive to risk taking. *It is through talk that we build our learning community in the classroom.*

2. As the classroom community grows and becomes stronger, students take ownership of their own conflict resolution. As the community becomes strong, humor becomes a part of much that we do. *When the*

community is established, students participate in curriculum planning and assume ownership of their learning.

3. For students whose lack of writing skills stand in the way of their effective written communication, talk is the means by which I am able to convince them that what they have to say is important, not only for them but for the entire class. Talking with the students brings them to the realization that they have important ideas to share and wonderful stories to tell. *By talking with each other, we support the telling and writing of stories in our community.*

4. Together the students and I create strategies that help us look at our talk and reflect on how talk helps us learn. *Given guidance and direction, students develop methods that enable them to identify their own best learning strategies. The students participate in evaluating and planning curriculum.*

5. Talk is the means by which children build on their ideas and the ideas of others. Talk is the avenue to higher-level thinking skills. It is through talk that children make meaning of the world around them. *It is through talk that children learn.*

THROUGH TALK WE BUILD LEARNING COMMUNITIES IN OUR CLASSROOMS

In his book *Life in a Crowded Place: Making a Learning Community*, Peterson (1992) writes that "life in a learning community is helped along by the interests, ideas, and support of others. Social life is not snuffed out; it is nurtured and used to advance learning in the best way possible. Caring and interest of others breathes purpose and life into learning" (p. 3). Peterson continues, "When teachers join with students to make a learning community, they have two broad goals in mind; first, they want to make a place that challenges students intellectually, and second, they want students to value learning and be up to the challenge" (pp. 65–66). As their teacher, I wanted to make a place for my students to learn and a place in which they wanted to learn. I found the shared reading of picture books to be essential in creating that place. Other factors important to building our community were the read-aloud chapter books, poems we learned together, and the phrases and expressions that became a part of our shared language.

Shared Picture Books

The children brought to my attention the important role that picture books had in building our community. Near the end of the year, I asked students how our class had changed since September. There was no response for a few moments. Then Brian remarked that we talked more because we had gotten to know each other better. I asked if there was one particular thing or event that had "pulled us together," anything in particular that had happened last fall. There was a unanimous response: "You read *The Very Quiet Cricket* (Carle, 1990) to us!" To this day, it is still amazing to me how that one picture book did so much to build a foundation for our classroom community. *The Very Quiet Cricket* was voted the class favorite at the end of the year. Along the way, we had revisited the book many times and had shared the story with friends, family, and visitors to our classroom.

A friend, Claudia Prentice, introduced me to picture books about six years ago. Claudia used picture books extensively in her first-grade class. Until that time I had not used picture books in my fifth-grade class, nor was I familiar with authors and titles. As we studied different units, Claudia would bring books to me, place them in my hands, and say, "The children might enjoy these." Little by little, she opened the world of picture books to the students and me. Oh, how those books enriched our literature discussions, our study of American history, and our writing!

Why was there obviously such a strong connection between "talk" and picture books? Perhaps it was because those stories gave us so much to talk about. Perhaps it was because shared reading times became an enjoyable and expected part of our daily schedule. Perhaps it was simply because the children and I loved those books. As I reviewed my log entries, it was obvious that the reading of a picture book triggered exciting discussions or led to an event that became a highlight of our day.

Reading picture books gave students the opportunity to respond to literature with a free sharing of ideas and feelings in nonthreatening situations. Because there was no writing, no worksheet, and no assignment connected with these stories, the children were free to enjoy and become totally involved in them. During these shared reading times the children would sit on the floor as close as possible to me. DeAndre, my only city-transfer student, would hold onto my arm or hand as I read, the only time he would make physical contact with me. I saw DeAndre's response as our way of "talking" with each other.

The year following the inquiry project with my fourth graders, I began teaching a multi-aged class in a year-round school in Denver, Colorado. Yes, I was a bit apprehensive about the reactions of fifth and sixth graders when I read picture books to them, but I continued to share picture books with the students during our first six-week session. On the last day of that first session, our "track-out day," the students asked for time so they could read picture books. I placed piles of books at each group of desks. For one hour, there was silence in the room; *every* student—the best readers, the reluctant readers, and those with reading difficulties—was totally involved in reading. It appeared that picture books would again lay the foundation for our classroom community.

Read-Alouds

Besides the picture books, there was always a read-aloud chapter book being shared. Phrases from these shared literature readings became a part of the mortar that held the community foundation together and gave us a common bond. Kids loved to hate "the dirty old Fat Man" in *Pigs Might Fly* (King-Smith, 1980). As we completed chapters in *There's a Boy in the Girl's Bathroom* (Sachar, 1987), the whole class chorused, "Last row, last seat." *The BFG* (Dahl, 1982) brought tears of laughter each day as we read the story. Because I read the books aloud, reluctant readers and students with reading difficulties were confident about these stories and shared their ideas about them. These children experienced the story just as if they had read the book themselves. When we talked about these read-alouds, all readers brought to the discussions a common literary experience.

The minute the students saw a book in my hands, they were ready for the story. We referred to books we had shared throughout the year, and the students revisited the books continually. Shared literature caused us to laugh, exchange ideas, think, and sometimes cry. It brought us together and opened doors of discussion. Through these doors we not only talked about literature, but we came to know and understand each other. From these times came the richest, most insightful ideas and responses. I remember the wide-eyed look on Danny's face when he correctly predicted, just as I was about to turn the page in *The Gift of the Magi* (Henry, 1991), that Jim had sold his silver watch to pay for the combs for Della's hair. Danny made an accurate prediction and was obviously immersed in the story; this response from a student who was a cause of concern.

Poems We Learned Together

As I reflected on my own log entries, I noticed that poetry had also helped us build the community foundation. In addition to reading poetry to the class, I asked my students to memorize a poem each week. On Monday morning I wrote the poem on the board and students were to copy it and memorize it by Friday. My initial intent was to expose the students to the process of memorizing. This activity also introduced a variety of poets and poems to the class. As the year went by, it became apparent that something else was happening when the children memorized these poems. They found it fun to recite the poems in unison, and our repertoire became larger and larger. Often, reciting in unison occurred spontaneously during the day or as we waited for the dismissal bell in the afternoon.

The first poem we learned was Vachael Lindsay's "The Turtle" (Lindsay, 1983). Because it has a rhythm and a pattern that makes it easy to learn, it has been a favorite with all my classes. We revisited this poem often during the year and asked guests in our classroom to hear this and other poems we had learned.

Phrases Unique to Our Community

Toward the end of the 1991–1992 school year, I asked the students to share words and phrases that had come to have a special meaning to us, words that would probably mean nothing special to those outside our class but that for us would have a common meaning and take us back to something we had shared during the year. In "Once Upon a Time There Were Three," Mem Fox (1992) writes about the shared phrases that "created in our family a literary and emotional togetherness" (p. 167). So, too, did certain words and phrases create a "togetherness" in our classroom.

One day we filled the board with words and phrases from the year. The class listed some of my words that they had come to know so well: "boof" and "oops" (meaning mistakes) and "bingo!" (my way of saying "You got it!"). But one of the children's favorites was "airmail!" "Airmail" referred to the day the class teddy bear went flying through the air. Joey was giving our bear to Adam for the evening and had asked me if "airmail delivery" was O.K. As I signaled my "go ahead," the bear went flying across the room just as our principal, Dr. Cozette, walked in. What fun—what laughter— and "airmail" became a part of our community vocabulary. (Dr. Cozette laughed, shook her head, and left the room.)

In the introduction to his book *Life in a Crowded Place,* Ralph Peterson (1992) writes that "one could use the word 'family' to describe life in a learning community, since the same underlying structures that appear in a healthy family occur in the classroom." He continues, "As teachers, we can choose to provide a healthy place for our students— a place where they belong and are helped to grow in their learning, feeling and thinking" (p. 3). Our "family" in Room 203 had grown in our learning, feeling, and thinking. Along the way we shared words and phrases that held special meaning and we laughed as we recalled the incidents brought to mind by these words and phrases.

At the end of the school year, I read my reflective log entries from the entire year. In this rereading, it became clear how far we had come since September in our building of a community. Several log entries made our progress apparent:

As math papers were corrected and we had a few "answer sheets," the students began walking quietly around the room to offer their papers as guides for other students to correct their papers. Those who understood the assignment began helping those in need of help. (Nov. 12, 1991)

Children have moved from viewing working together as "cheating" and something that a teacher "allows" them to do to seeing a real value in collaboration and helping each other. As they work on assigned written activities, they compare information, compare written responses, point out information in printed materials, and in general help each other. (Feb. 6, 1992)

Watched the Kiddos this afternoon about 3:20. *Every* student totally involved in group project work. Lots of talking, some laughing, and all kinds of ideas flying around the room. Lori (reading specialist) stopped by. We both noted that it was hard to believe it was the same group of children that came in September—the same class that I had doubts would ever function well in group situations. (It's wonderful when I'm wrong!) (May 11, 1992)

Peterson (1992) believes that the process of creating a community is circular: "as the group comes together, the individual is strengthened, and as individuals grow in confidence and expression, they increase their caring contributions to the group" (p. 66). The May 11 log entry illustrated how we had come together, grown as individuals, and were making caring contributions to the group. I believe Peterson would agree that our classroom community was, in Leslie's words, "a warm place to be."

THROUGH TALK STUDENTS BEGIN TO ASSUME OWNERSHIP FOR THEIR OWN LEARNING

As I gained experience in the classroom, I realized that if I would "allow" it and provide the opportunities, children could participate in all decision making and ultimately make decisions about their own learning. Claudia, the friend who had introduced me to picture books, usually stopped by my classroom after school. She would listen to me wrestle with a problem, often long after dismissal time, and then would say, "Talk with the kids. Ask *them* what *they* think." And always, a student or the entire class would share insights or suggestions that I had overlooked—obvious answers to our dilemma.

As I continued to negotiate the curriculum with the students, I began to see the power and potential of talk in solving problems or conflicts among them. When I put the responsibility for conflict resolution on their shoulders, I saw them solve their own problems with far more lasting results.

My fourth graders knew that one way we approached conflict resolution was for the two students involved to "take a walk to talk." The "walk" meant going from our room to the far end of the primary wing—a long walk that usually allowed for a cooling-off time. "Taking a walk" was optional and would happen only when both students agreed to doing so. Even so, the students always chose to try this strategy.

I noticed from my log entries that the children were beginning to take ownership in solving their own conflicts:

> Brian and Joey into it again on the playground. Simply asked them if they thought a walk would help. Both boys agreed, returned a few minutes later and assured me that all was well. (April 7, 1992)

> Today, Katie and Carrie returned to the classroom from a "walk to talk." Both girls said their problem was resolved, but the look on their faces sent a different message. I talked briefly with the girls again. *They* decided another walk might help. The girls left the room again and returned later, smiles on their faces, and assured me that all was well. Katie's comment, "It was just a misunderstanding!" (May 26, 1992)

Having the students "walk to talk" was helping, but I wanted to support this practice by helping the children realize the value of talk in resolving problems. It was about this time that our librarian introduced us to the book, *Albert's Toothache* (Williams, 1974). The story was perfect! Again, a picture book laid the groundwork for thinking and talking about an issue important to all of us.

Albert's Toothache is the story of a turtle and his toothache. But turtles have no teeth! No one in the family would believe Albert when he said he had a toothache. At last, Grandmother *asked* Albert, "Where do you have a toothache?" Albert showed Grandmother his left toe and explained that when he accidently stepped in a gopher hole, the gopher bit him. Albert did indeed have a "toothache"!

After I read this story to the class, we brainstormed ideas and identified the problem, the cause, and possible resolutions. As our responses were recorded on the board, it became clear that everyone in the story was *talking*, but no one was *listening*. It took Grandmother's *asking* to finally bring a solution to the problem. Comments shared by the students included:

"Albert should have *told* his mother!"

"They should have had a family meeting to talk about it."

"Grandmother *asked* Albert what hurt."

"No one talked with each other—they needed to talk with each other."

"They *miscommunicated*!"

As the class looked at the list on the board, it became apparent that there were a number of simple solutions that could have resolved the problem.

Talk—or the lack of it—was what the story was really about. The students noted that along with talk, we need to ask questions and we need to listen to the other person. This is what students were doing as they were taking their walks to talk. As Adam wrote in his log, "Talk does not work if the other person does not understand you." We were recognizing the importance of talk in helping us understand each other.

One of my log entries was about a discussion all the girls had about some minor conflicts involving many of the girls in our class. I asked all the girls to eat lunch with me in the room so we could talk. The girls thought this was a good idea and our discussion was open and honest. During our lunch talk, Nancy shared a story about how her two cousins were always arguing and that one day she simply told them to stop. The girls laughed and understood the message of Nancy's story.

In that situation, I had simply provided the opportunity for the girls to talk during lunch. They set their agenda and had complete ownership of the discussion. The girls came a long way in resolving their conflicts and they felt proud of what they had accomplished.

Another entry demonstrates how ownership had transferred to the student:

> Leslie approached me about an on-going problem with her best friend in the class. We have talked about this before. At this point, I asked Leslie if she would like for me to get involved. She thought for a few moments and then responded by saying she would like to try a few more things and would talk with her friend again. She added, "I'll let you know if I need your help." (May 11, 1992)

Leslie had talked with me and then made her own decision about how to approach her friend in an attempt to resolve the conflict.

The children had progressed in their ability to use talk in resolving conflicts, and I was learning the power of talk in helping children take ownership and responsibility, not only in solving problems but in every aspect of life in our classroom.

As our community became stronger and students assumed more ownership in our classroom, I was increasingly aware of the humor we shared. The students also noted the humor in their logs and in our discussions. Certain events caused us to laugh when they happened and again each time we recalled them. On one occasion, I asked the students if there were any restrictions or guidelines for our laughing. Julie commented that "we never laugh until we make sure the other person is laughing and that they are O.K. We never laugh *at* anyone, we only laugh *with* them."

Years ago, I heard a teacher in a program for gifted students comment that the one trait common to all students in her program was a sense of humor. Are we not looking at high-level thinking skills when children create humor and play with language in the learning environment? It is my guess that as time goes by, the children will forget the details of what made us laugh. But I hope they look back on our year together and remember our laughter and that laughing was very much a part of our community building and learning experiences.

THROUGH TALK, WE SUPPORT THE WRITING OF STORIES

The best stories throughout the year, the stories the students felt good about (by looking at their faces and into their eyes I can tell when they have written a story that really "clicks" for them) were the stories about real people and real events. So many times students approached me, often first thing in the morning, excited about something that had happened in their lives. When I remarked that they had a wonderful story to share, they often responded by saying it really was not that exciting. I assured them that it was wonderful and others would love to hear it. But . . . I was passing judgment on their ideas, and even though they were positive, my comments obviously were not always credible to the students. The solution seemed to be to provide time for sharing these stories. As the children shared these personal stories with each other through talk—when the class applauded Joey's story about his lost dog and Annie's story about her dad allowing her to drive the new car—they came to appreciate their own stories and those of others.

When children struggled to write stories, I talked with them and together, we built and expanded the story. Telling me the story made it possible for a student to put the story on paper. In cases where students seemed to have the pieces of a good story in mind, talking it through made it possible for them to put the story on paper. Students' log entries reflected their understanding of the role of talk in supporting the writing process. These ideas were shared after we published our books for Young Authors' Week in May:

> I wrote three stories that I started over. My 4th story was the charm! The only reason I started over was because when I talked with Mrs. Dickinson she said my words were filling up space but not telling my story. I am glad I started over because "My Angel!" story worked peerrrffffeeeeecccctttttt! (Annie)

> My friend Annie helped me get my idea for my story. Annie said, "What about writing about your puppet." I said "OK" and the idea worked. (Nancy)

> I talked to my mom about what would be a wonderful and exciting story! She said, "Remember when we got a flat tire on the way home from Kathy's?" Oh, Yeh, I remembered! Then that night I wrote down what Mom and I talked about. I know my story is MARVELOUS! (Joan)

Talk enabled children to identify topics for stories, encouraged them to expand on story ideas, and helped them value their own stories and those of others.

Graves (1983) writes: "If children don't speak about their writing, both teachers and children lose. Until the child speaks, nothing significant has happened in the writing conference" (p. 97). I have come to realize that talking with children about their writing need not be confined only to designated conference times. The writing "conference" may occur as we walk down the hall, or when we talk before the school day begins—any time we seize a moment to talk about a story.

THROUGH TALK, WE CREATE STRATEGIES TO ASSESS OUR LEARNING

The students and I used a number of strategies to help us assess how talk affected learning in our classroom. Each student had a talk log, a small booklet made of unlined white paper. The fact that the paper was unlined might be the reason Julie suggested that we do a web as an entry, and Brian proposed that we "draw a picture of talk in our room." Students used the logs for any written response in our current inquiry. Our log entries addressed such topics as "What we think talk is," "Things we talked about during (a certain class time)," "How talk helped us form our community," and "How talk helped us learn."

At times, we shared ideas about talk on the board or on the overhead projector, so the children could visualize the responses and build on what others said. The overhead transparency also made it possible for me to have a written record of our discussion for later reference. However, neither the board nor the overhead was easily accessible when we gathered in a circle on the floor. Butcher paper and chart paper were effective and could be used anywhere in the room. The key was to use a variety of strategies. As time went by, I learned to ask the students how *they* wanted the strategy designed.

Another strategy we used was the "T" chart (Hill and Hill, 1990), an idea shared in our study group by Mary Ann Rankey. We considered what factors were present when our literature discussions went well and what might have caused difficulties when they didn't. An interesting result of one "T-chart" brainstorming session was our realization that literature time often did not go well on Tuesday afternoons. Tuesday literature time was immediately after art class, and the children said they simply had a difficult time settling down. As a result, we added more transition time and included a quiet read-aloud time before we began literature groups.

T CHART
LITERATURE GROUPS

<u>LOOK LIKE</u>

1. Kids in groups
2. People at tables and some on pillows and some on the the floor
3. Kids reading books
4. Writing in journals
5. Doing art work
6. People thinking hard
7. Comfortable
8. Sometimes "goofing off"
9. Cooperating in groups
10. Excited about a story
11. Fun
12. Writing letters

<u>SOUND LIKE</u>

1. Happy
2. Everyone talking; sounds loud
3. Sharing ideas
4. Like we're all friends
5. Serious about what we're talking about
6. Hear ideas about plays and about the books
7. Sometimes SILENCE
8. Laughing

Figure 6.1 *"T" Chart for Literature Groups*

Figure 6.1 shows the students' responses to the questions "What do literature groups look like?" and "What do literature groups sound like?" The responses indicate the children's recognition of the sharing, cooperating, and thinking that were a part of our literature groups. They noted that there were "silent" times and "loud" times. The students demonstrated an awareness of atmosphere in the room when they listed the words "comfortable," "fun," "happy," and "excited." Brian noted that discussion groups "looked like we are all friends," indicating his awareness of our learning community.

In preparation for Spring Parent/Teacher Conferences, I asked each student to complete a reading interest survey. Two questions on the form asked for ideas about "Why they *liked* literature discussion groups" and "What they did *not* like about discussion groups." Their answers gave me insights into their thinking, but most important, the questions required that they think about their literature discussions and their learning.

> The best thing about lit groups is the fact that we use teamwork. Talking about the book makes the story more interesting. (Julie)

> When I don't understand something in the story, there is someone to help me and I don't have to wait for the answer. (Karen)

> We get more ideas to think about when we have someone to talk with. (Matt)

Among the responses to the question asking what they didn't like about literature groups were these comments:

> Having something to say but don't know how to say it. (Carol)
> When people interrupt and when you get out-voted. (Adam)
> Some people talk too much and talk when it's your turn. (Carrie)

John wrote that he didn't like the groups when people argue. His idea was the same one shared by many of his classmates. Because of John's response I realized that the children viewed any difference of opinion as "arguing." I raised this issue with the class and we began to examine the value of sharing different ideas and the importance of considering other people's perspectives.

The children told me they preferred meeting around a table for literature discussions. The groups had the choice of meeting in a circle on the floor, pushing desks together, or meeting around one of the tables in the room. Although they enjoyed reading while stretched out on the floor or curled up on pillows, the children decided that for the actual group sharing, meeting around one of the tables was most satisfactory. We further noted that we preferred a round table as opposed to the oblong table. At a round table, we were all equal members of the group, since there was no place for a "leader" or a person "in charge." Again, these decisions were a result of ideas they brought up during a class brainstorming session, a time when we talked about our learning activities.

At the end of the year, some students chose a staff member to interview as part of our inquiry. Each student generated his or her own questions about talk and presented these questions to the staff member. For example, Scott asked Dr. Cozette, our principal, if talking in our classroom was different from that in other classes she visited. He also asked her how talk in the office was different from talk in the classroom. Several students asked teachers how they thought talking helped children learn better. Little did we appreciate what we had accomplished until the students shared the responses to these questions. Those who had not experienced what we had did not seem to understand what we had come to value. Some did not appreciate the potential of talk in building community and in learning.

In looking at the strategies we used to help us assess the talk in our classroom, it is clear that talking yielded more ideas and better insights than individual written responses. It seemed that asking for a written response burdened the process for many children. When we talked, we heard the ideas of others and could build on them. Talk was the means that served our purpose best in assessing our learning.

THROUGH TALK, CHILDREN LEARN

I continued to look for and call students' attention to those moments when talk enabled us to reach new peaks in our thinking and new heights in our understanding. One such moment occurred during a math lesson on fractions. After a spirited discussion about a number of ideas, Carol drew an illustration on the board to represent her idea. After further discussion, the class decided that her illustration did not correctly represent what she was saying. Nancy walked to the front of the classroom to address her classmates. She said to them, "But you know, Carol tried something new and she made us all think." The children responded to Nancy's offering with a round of applause. Not only had Nancy recognized the value in what Carol had done, but both knew that within our community they could go before their classmates with tentative ideas and the class would respond with support and appreciation. As their teacher, I had moved to the side of the room, relinquishing my "place of control" at the center front. This was truly their classroom. Barnes (1992) uses the term "exploratory talk" for the times "when children rearrange their thoughts during improvised talk" (p. 108). Kathryn Pierce (1992) elaborates on this when she writes that exploratory talk in small groups is "that in which participants use language to move the group along to new understandings" (p. 204).

As I considered talk in the classroom and reviewed the children's talk log entries in preparation for writing about our inquiry, it became apparent to me that what we had accomplished could not and would not have taken place in my classroom a few years ago. I was aware of changes in reading and writing in my classroom. Others went unnoticed as we restructured learning activities and the students began to negotiate the curriculum with me. These transformations were completely changing how our learning looked and sounded. The children were now talking because I wasn't, and I was now listening to what they had to say. These changes helped draw our attention to the role of talk in our learning and made it possible for us to pursue our inquiry collaboratively. We were learning *about* talk while we were learning *through* talk.

Supporting Talk in Our Classroom

A learning community is necessary to support the kinds of talk we use to learn. That community must be continually nurtured and revitalized. Within it, there is respect for each other and an environment in which all members feel safe and secure and free to be risk-takers. I have learned that establishing a community requires time and patience, and that occasionally it suffers setbacks. There were times when I "stepped back" too soon and put too many responsibilities onto students. A classroom community requires support, negotiated guidelines, and clearly stated expectations. No community is without problems; what makes a difference is how we work with children in meeting these challenges.

Children must also have something to talk about. In our study group Kathryn Pierce reminded us, "If we want children to talk, we must give them something worth talking about." This is certainly evident in literature discussions. Given a piece of wonderful literature, children will make connections to the story, discuss character development, and find issues to debate and clarify. I find that in all group work, children are most successful when they enter into the assignment with a clearly stated purpose and ownership in the activity.

I allow and encourage talk during the school day and provide opportunities for talk. My students talk during transition times and speak together quietly while completing written assignments. Talk is central to literature discussions and small group work. Whole-class activities incorporating talk include brainstorming sessions, whole-class discussions about read-alouds, and class meetings, when we talk about the decisions affecting all of us. Daily plans are structured to include activities incorporating talk, and I am increasingly aware of the unplanned moments during the day when an issue arises that is worth taking time to talk about. I expect students to contribute to discussions. It is my responsibility as the teacher to communicate these expectations and negotiate the guidelines with the children. If I expect children to talk, it is necessary for me to help them realize the importance of talk in their learning.

We must come to an understanding of the kinds of talk that are appropriate and constructive to our learning. During our inquiry, the students identified the kinds of remarks that are harmful and hurt others' feelings. We made it clear that certain language was not appropriate in a school setting. We identified changes we could make in discussions that would encourage quieter students to be active participants. We established guidelines for being an attentive audience when a classmate was speaking.

Students must be immersed in all kinds of literature to build a learning community. Literature was the common thread throughout our curriculum. Poetry and picture books supported our learning in social studies and science as well as in language arts. It was the literature we shared that gave us something to talk and think about as we began our year together. Because I love the books we read and the poetry we share, I give a part of myself to the children as I share literature with them.

A Learner in Their Midst

I see myself as a learner in the classroom. As I listen to the children, I learn from them. As I learn from them, I change my lesson plans, my thinking, and my teaching. Barnes (1992) believes that a meaningful curriculum is one enacted by both students and teachers. To enact means to come together in a meaningful communication. Talk was the means by which we came together in the classroom to learn and enact our curriculum.

Barnes notes that children will quickly forget what has been taught them if the they don't make sense of the experiences, try out ideas and skills for themselves, make links to previous experiences, and apply new ideas to new contexts. We used talk to articulate our ideas and questions, and we used talk to make sense of our experiences, try new ideas, and link previous experiences to new contexts. When the children talked, they resolved problems, played with language, and laughed together. When the children talked, learning was rewarding and exciting.

Pierce (1992) writes, "Barnes values the role of talk in the classroom as both a vehicle for learning and as a rich source of data for analyzing and evaluating classroom experiences" (p. 203). The purpose of incorporating talk into the classroom is to give students tools for learning and a desire for knowledge. It is through the children's talk that avenues for obtaining information are opened. When the children in my classroom talked, learning was exciting and rewarding for them. And because I was now learning with them and from them, the children provided me with a "rich source of data for analyzing and evaluating classroom experiences."

June 7: Room 203

Our desks were in a circle for the last day. Joey was late—arrived carrying a single red rose bud for me. His classmates applauded Joey as he entered the classroom . . . the same Joey who stood on top of his desk during literature time the first week of school and the same classmates who united and stood in support of Joey and were his friends throughout the year. At 1:00 we had our last twenty minutes all to ourselves. I asked the class what book they would like to select as a final reading for the year. The choice was *Heckedy Peg* (Wood, 1987). After reading *Heckedy Peg,* I told them I would read *my* favorite and so we revisited *Wilfred Gordon McDonald Partridge* (Fox, 1985). As the excitement was mounting in the building, waiting for the final bell, we in Room 203 sat on the floor and shared these stories. With sixty seconds left on the clock, we recited our last poem of the year, "Keep a poem in your pocket. . . . ." by Beatrice Schenk de Regniers.

In the words of Mem Fox, on our last day together, "we had created in our family a literary and emotional togetherness."

REFERENCES

Barnes, D. 1992. *From communication to curriculum.* Portsmouth, NH: Boynton/Cook.

Carle, E. 1990. *The very quiet cricket.* New York: Putnam and Grosset.

Dahl, R. 1982. *The BFG.* New York: Puffin.

De Regniers, B. S. 1983. "Keep a poem in your pocket." In *Random House book of poetry for children,* selected by Jack Prelutsky. New York: Random House.

Fox, M. 1992. "Once upon a time there were three . . ." *The New Advocate.* 5(3): 165–74.

———. 1985. *Wilfred Gordon McDonald Partridge.* New York: Kane/Miller.

Goodman, Y. 1985. "Kid-watching: Observing children in the classroom." In *Observing the language learner,* edited by A. Jaggar & M. Smith-Burke. Urbana, IL: National Council of Teachers of English; Newark, DE: International Reading Association.

Graves, D. 1983. *Writing: Teachers & children at work.* Portsmouth, NH: Heinemann.

Henry, O. 1991. *The gift of the magi.* Morris Plains, NJ: Unicorn.

Hill, S. and T. Hill. 1980. *Collaborative classrooms: A guide to cooperative learning.* Portsmouth, NH: Heinemann.

King-Smith, D. 1980. *Pigs might fly.* New York: Viking Penguin.

Lindsay, V. 1988. "The turtle." In *Sing a song of popcorn: Every child's book of poems.* New York: Scholastic.

Peterson, R. 1992. *Life in a crowded place—making a learning community.* Portsmouth, NH: Heinemann.

Pierce, K. 1992. "Afterword." In *From communication to curriculum,* by D. Barnes. Portsmouth, NH: Heinemann.

Sachar, L. 1987. *There's a boy in the girls' bathroom.* New York: Knopf.

Williams, B. 1974. *Albert's toothache.* New York: E. P. Dutton.

Wood, A. 1987. *Heckedy Peg.* New York: Harcourt Brace Jovanovich.

Part Three

DISCOVERING THE POTENTIAL OF TALK AS A STRATEGY

Kathy G. Short has focused her inquiry and teaching on children's literature and on reading and writing as authoring processes. She teaches graduate courses in children's literature at the University of Arizona in the department of Language, Reading, and Culture. She has worked extensively with teachers to develop curricula that actively involve students in using reading and writing to learn. Much of her work has centered on integrating children's literature into the curriculum and literature circles. She is co-author of *Creating Classrooms for Authors* (Heinemann, 1988), *Talking About Books: Creating Literate Communities* (Heinemann, 1990), and *Creating Curriculum: Teachers and Students as a Community of Learners* (Heinemann, 1991).

Junardi Armstrong is a classroom teacher in the Tucson Unified School District. She recently served as coordinator for the Center for Insect Science Education Outreach at the University of Arizona. She worked on a National Institute of Health-Science Education Partnership Award creating and piloting a national program that uses insects to teach health concepts and science and math processes in elementary classrooms. The program integrates children's literature and discussion into science processes and is multidisciplinary.

Chapter 7
"More Than Facts": Exploring the Role of Talk in Classroom Inquiry

KATHY G. SHORT AND JUNARDI ARMSTRONG

The role of content and process in learning has long been a source of debate among educators. Traditionally, education has focused primarily on content and final products, emphasizing the learning of a particular body of knowledge or skills. Many educators have argued vigorously against this emphasis on content because they believe that students need to become lifelong learners who understand the process of how learning occurs. The process movement in writing, for example, has focused on learning environments that immerse students in authentic writing experiences and in exploring writing strategies rather than in learning isolated pieces of information about grammar or spelling. Although this focus on process has opened up learning experiences in schools and allowed students to become actively engaged in the construction of meaning, many teachers are returning to their earlier concerns about content and seeking ways to integrate content and process. They realize that they need to be concerned with both the *how* and the *what* of learning, that it does matter *what* students are learning when they are engaged in process activities.

The most common approach to integrating content and process has been through theme units, which cut across various subject areas and periods of the school day. While these units have brought more student interest and involvement to the content areas, they are often characterized by "cute" activities and superficial exploration of content. Rarely do they move into inquiry on topics of scientific or social significance or involve questions that matter to students. While these theme units include the use of children's literature rather than content area textbooks, students are still reading to "get the facts" instead of becoming actively engaged in exploring and constructing concepts for themselves from inquiry experiences.

In Chapter 2, Barnes argues that learning is not simply adding new information but involves the reconsideration of past understandings based on new experiences, ideas, and ways of understanding. He points out that this process occurs over time and that talk plays a critical role in supporting students as they make new connections between past and present understandings. These connections, in turn, change how they think about the world. While the process of connecting what is already known with new ideas is at the heart of learning and inquiry, it is rarely supported by school experiences.

Our concern with the integration of process and content led us to work together in exploring inquiry related to cycles and ecology with second grade students. Junardi has a strong environmental science background and her curriculum revolved around active engagements with scientific processes and concepts. The language arts, however, were taught separately and in a traditional manner. When she heard Kathy talk about literature circles, she was excited about the possibility of integrating literature into science. Kathy was interested in Junardi's invitation to work together because she saw an opportunity to expand her previous work with literature circles to content area inquiry (Short, 1986, 1992). Both of us were concerned about the role of talk and literature and the integration of content and process in scientific inquiry. We wanted to set up an environment that would encourage children to talk about science experiences and to use literature discussions to explore scientific concepts as well as personal and literary connections.

In this chapter, we will describe our experiences in creating an environment that supported children's scientific inquiry and their talk about literary and scientific experiences. While students experienced many difficulties in finding and exploring their own questions and engaging in exploratory talk about science and literature, we were able to work together within the curricular framework of the inquiry cycle to build a strong learning community. This inquiry cycle supported our negotiation of curriculum with students and was based in our beliefs about inquiry and the role of literature and talk in inquiry.

TAKING AN INQUIRY PERSPECTIVE ON CURRICULUM

Instead of a focus on "covering" topics, we believe that curriculum should be based in the search for questions significant to the lives of learners.

Typically, the questions explored in classrooms are determined by the teacher, the textbook, or the school curriculum guide rather than by learners. Children's research in theme units often focuses on finding answers to questions and fails to include the search for significant questions. Inquiry does not necessarily begin with a question but with exploring and searching to find a question that's worth pursuing. Inquirers are both problem-posers and problem-solvers (Freire, 1985). Because teachers have been the primary problem-posers, they have had to "motivate" students to do teacher-based inquiries instead of supporting students in their own inquiries. Our role as teachers in this inquiry process is one of selecting experiences and establishing learning environments that have the most *potential* for raising problems for students rather than predetermining the problems (Dewey, 1938). A critical feature of this environment is that it encourages and supports a wide range of talk so that students can search out and investigate their own questions related to content area concepts and content.

If teachers take an inquiry perspective on content area studies, then the role of talk and literature is to support students in finding and pursuing their own questions. In classrooms where students previously read from textbooks to learn about science or social studies, talk about literature has often been substituted for the textbook but still serves the same purpose—to give students information. Students spend their time reading *about* science rather than actively engaging in doing science through observing, experimenting, and forming and testing hypotheses (Harlen, 1989). Talk about literature should be part of active engagements in the "doing" of science, not a replacement for observation and experimentation.

Literature provides alternative perspectives on how people live and learn and so can support inquiry and exploratory talk in ways that textbooks cannot. Because textbooks are distillations of already known knowledge written to inform, they do not include enough evidence to recreate the author's inquiry process. Well-written nonfiction, in contrast, is more modest and focused, with a more intimate and personal perspective. Instead of informing, the authors' perspective is that of sharing their inquiry with other interested people. Enough data are provided so readers can form their own opinions.

While nonfiction literature is essential to inquiry, other types of literature, such as poetry and fiction, also play an important role. Through fiction, children are able to look at facts through a different perspective, a "more human frame of reference" (Huck, 1989, p. 618). Story plays a critical role in transporting children to countries, cultures, and time periods far different from their own and allowing them to explore moral and social issues. As Rosen (1984) points out, stories are an essential function of the human mind, not an optional extra. Storying is a meaning-making strategy used by humans to bring meaning and moral significance to their life experiences.

Rosenblatt (1978) argues that readers bring a particular stance or purpose to their reading that influences the meaning they construct in the reading event. If readers take a predominantly *efferent* stance, their focus is on getting information to take away from the experience. They narrow their attention to the facts or answers they want to carry away. When readers take a predominantly *aesthetic* stance, they immerse themselves into the world of the book and focus their attention on what they are "living through" during the reading event. They consider a broader range of feelings, thoughts, and personal connections so that they are involved in a "whole" experience. While both stances are always part of a reader's response, the choice of which stance to highlight is primarily determined by readers and their view of the reading task within a particular context. If literature is to support inquiry, then opportunities for readers to engage in the entire continuum of aesthetic and efferent stances must be available so that children's talk about literature can go beyond listing facts.

Another way in which talk and literature can support broader inquiry is through integrating affective and cognitive ways of knowing. Many scientists have an aesthetic appreciation of their work that is eliminated in textbook accounts. Knowing and feeling, the heart and the mind, provide scientists and social scientists with a more holistic view of the world (Eisner, 1982). Children's experiences in reading and talking about literature can support that same integration in their inquiry.

EXPLORING TALK WITHIN A CYCLE OF INQUIRY

We began our focus on ecology with these beliefs about inquiry, but putting our beliefs into action was more difficult than we had imagined. We found that we needed a curriculum framework within which we and the children could negotiate the content and processes of classroom experiences. Eventually we adapted an inquiry cycle developed by Carolyn Burke (1991) to give us a framework for planning inquiry experiences with children. This cycle is based on the authoring cycle (Harste, Short, with Burke, 1988) and Dewey's (1938) description of the scientific method as a learning cycle of forming ideas or hypotheses, acting on those ideas to test them out, observing the conditions that result, and then organizing the facts and ideas for future use. This cycle draws from the same theoretical beliefs that Barnes (1989) uses to characterize active learning: as a process that is purposive, reflective, negotiated, critical, complex, situation-driven, and engaged.

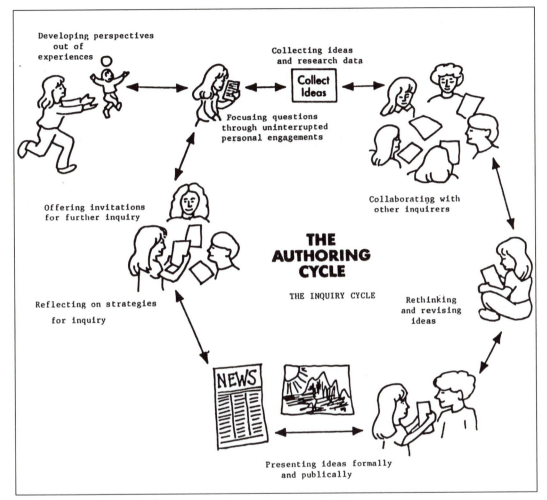

Figure 7.1 *The Inquiry Cycle*

The arrows in Figure 7.1 go both ways, indicating that there is continual movement back and forth between the different aspects of the inquiry process rather than a sequence or a hierarchy. The inquiry cycle became the curriculum framework within which we developed a two-month focus with second-grade students on the theme of ecology and interrelationships. Because this focus occurred in the early spring, students had already developed their conceptions of how the classroom operated, and the shift to active and critical small group engagements with literature and science was difficult for them.

We struggled with how to appropriately support their problem-posing and exploratory talk. Because the children in this urban classroom came from a wide range of cultural and socioeconomic backgrounds, they brought diverse experiences and learning approaches that required flexibility in our support of their inquiry.

We began the inquiry with a broad focus on cycles and interrelationships. We based this focus on our knowledge of science content and processes and of the specific children in this classroom. From this broad theme, the more specific topics and questions the class, small groups, and individuals pursued were open to negotiation. The children explored common cycles of life and nature through literature and their own experiences to develop understandings about interdependence, a broad concept that ran throughout our different explorations of ecology. We then moved into looking at ecosystems, and the children formed small inquiry groups to study the different parts of an ecosystem, such as plants, animals, birds, people, insects, and water. Groups read literature and conducted experiments and research related to their focus. As the groups shared with each other, we realized that they were having difficulty seeing how the parts related to each other, so the class examined a particular ecosystem the children found interesting, the rainforest. Through studying the rainforest, the children were able to relate their inquiries to each other and began to build better understandings of ecological interrelationships. Because of the children's experiences in living in another distinctive ecosystem, the Sonoran desert, the class then began a study of the desert, and children pursued a variety of individual and small group inquiries (see Figure 7.2).

The inquiry cycle provided a framework within which we could plan and evaluate these major experiences with the children. It allowed us to build a "cycle of meaning" in which science concepts, content, and processes could be revisited with new insights and perspectives. In the next section, we will

Cycles	Ecosystems	Rainforest	Desert
• Cycle Text Set	• Text Sets and inquiry	• Whole class and	• Desert browsing
• Nature cycles	groups on people,	individual inquiries	• Brainstorming of
	birds, animals, etc.	• School presentation	connections and
	• Small group logs	on the rainforest	questions
	• Class presentations		• Paired book groups
			• Desert animal groups
			• Cultural centers
			• Field trip

Figure 7.2 *Time Line of Major Experiences in Inquiry on Ecology*

briefly describe each component of the inquiry cycle, the types of talk which occurred within that component, and the ways in which we worked at trying to support children's talk and inquiry.

Developing Perspectives out of Experiences

The inquiry cycle is based in children's own life experiences, from which they draw the perspectives that inform their inquiry. Children need to be able to connect to, and build from, their own life experiences through talk. The open-ended nature of many of the inquiries and literature experiences in our ecology theme gave children *choice* in the problems they pursued, the books they read, and their talk about those books and science experiences. Because of these choices, they were able to select experiences that connected to their own lives. In small group literature discussions, we did not give the children questions to discuss but asked them to share their initial responses to the books and then to reflect on those responses more closely in relation to their inquiries. When we began a new focus, such as the rainforest, children used talk to list what they already knew and what they wanted to know more about to help them connect with their own experiences.

We began talking about cycles to establish a broad theme from which children could make connections to their life experiences and to ecosystems as another cycle in their world. The class explored cycles that were part of children's daily lives, such as getting ready for school, and looked for cycles in literature, such as those portrayed in *The Quarreling Book* (Zolotow, 1963) and *The Very Hungry Caterpillar* (Carle, 1969). Children shared their experiences and talked about the similarities and differences across these cycles. At the same time, Junardi introduced children to cycles in nature—such as producers and consumers, predators and prey, and the water cycle—through charts on the board, predator and prey simulation games, and experiments with condensation and evaporation. The talk that occurred during these initial engagements primarily involved children in sharing observations about what was happening rather than exploring or critiquing their own experiences. From these discussions children then made connections between cycles in nature and in their own lives in order to develop a broad conceptual understanding of "cycle" they could use to support more in-depth talk about various ecosystems.

Focusing Questions Through Uninterrupted Personal Engagements

Learners need time to find and focus their own questions. As they explore broadly and engage in the uninterrupted "doing" of science and social studies, they discover questions that matter to them. They move from their initial questions and beliefs to more focused investigations. We saw this uninterrupted "doing" as time to explore by observing, experimenting, reading, writing, and talking. The talk that occurred during these engagements often began with sharing their personal stories and connections and then moved toward exploratory and hypothetical talk.

When we started the exploration of ecosystems, we had students talk about what they wanted to know and used those questions to form groups. But because their initial questions were too specific and fact-oriented, "How many legs does a spider have?" "Where do bears live?", the children had difficulty focusing their inquiry in these groups.

This experience made us realize that we needed to give students time to explore in order to find questions they could pursue productively. We began the desert focus by filling the room with all types of literature, displays, and observation centers on the desert and allowed students a week to explore them. The children were not expected to write down what they were finding or engage in systematic inquiry, but they were simply to explore and enjoy. We did arrange an informal sharing time during which children could talk about something they had noticed or discovered—a book, an observation, an "I wonder" question, or a connection to their own lives. We also read related pieces of literature aloud. Through this exploration and informal sharing, they were able to make connections to their own desert experiences and to ask questions about those experiences that allowed their talk to become more hypothetical.

After this week of exploration, we brainstormed together as a class on what children knew and wanted to know about the desert. Because they had already been thinking and exploring, their connections and questions showed greater depth and complexity. They asked, "How can the desert have flowers with so little water?" "Why did Native Americans of long ago want to live in the desert when it was so hot?" "How do horned owls live? What do they eat? Why are they called horned owls?" Of course, their questions continued to change as they went along, but because they had the chance to talk and explore informally *before* focusing on their own questions, they were able to make more powerful connections. This process of making connections is essential to meaning making and the creation of more complex understandings about life (Hartman, 1990). The preliminary browsing and exploring also supported their understanding of inquiry as problem posing, not just problem solving.

We made one other change in the class engagements with brainstorming. Because of our previous experience, we were concerned that the children were focusing so much on "facts" in their talk that they were ignoring their feelings. To encourage them to bring affective and cognitive ways of knowing science and literature together, we initiated the brainstorming by reading *The Desert Is Theirs* (Baylor, 1975) while Navajo flute music played in the background. As the music continued, the children individually brainstormed by drawing or writing about what they *knew* and *felt* about the desert and shared these impressions with each other in small groups. Then we brainstormed as a class. Thomas, for example, drew a picture (see Figure 7.3) and talked about it in terms of his knowledge of the birds, scorpions, and ants that live in the desert. He also talked about the feeling of "heatness" in the desert as the sun's rays went everywhere, blocked only by the mountains.

Throughout the desert focus, we encouraged children to share what they were learning and feeling as they participated in literature and "hands on" science experiences. We also continued to often play background music with desert sounds because, as Maria said, "the music makes me feel like I'm in the desert reading, not sitting at my desk." This environment encouraged talk that involved their feelings and reactions, connections to their own experiences, wondering questions, and further exploration of their initial questions and ideas with other learners. By helping children see what they already knew, we believed they would be more likely to connect those

Figure 7.3 *Desert Brainstorming (Thomas, Grade 2)*

experiences to new ideas, find powerful questions for inquiry, and have a common basis for further discussion with classmates.

Collecting Ideas and Research Data

As learners explore and inquire, they need informal ways of collecting and organizing ideas. They need a place to reflect and "discover" ideas as well as to preserve their thinking and support their talk with others. As they focus their questions and inquiries, they need to keep track of their data and organize connections in their data to make sense of what they are finding. These collections of ideas might take the form of a research journal, learning log, web, chart, brainstorm, graph, or time line.

When children were involved in their ecosystem groups, we gave each group a log and asked them to write down whatever they wanted to remember. Because the children did not yet have their own questions to guide them in finding significant ideas to write down in the logs, they used them to record isolated facts from books. The logs and the way we had introduced them to the children convinced them that we wanted them to search for facts, and so their talk in groups consisted of telling each other facts. It was not until the end of their small group discussions that they began to focus their questions in ways that could have led to productive inquiry.

Later, we moved them away from logs to try a wider range of curricular strategies, such as free writes and sketches of their initial responses to their reading. Students particularly liked using webs, charts, diagrams, and graphs to keep track of their thinking and learning during experimenting and reading. We found that they needed these ways to organize the ideas and information they were finding or they got lost in a "sea of facts" and were unable to find a strong sense of focus in their talk with others.

Collaborating with Other Inquirers

As learners develop questions they want to explore in more depth, they seek out opportunities to think and talk with peers. They need collaborative groups of learners whom they trust to help them think through their rough draft ideas and to support them in collecting, analyzing, and interpreting ideas related to their questions. These collaborative groups encourage exploratory, tentative talk and hypothetical thinking (Barnes, 1992). Students come to understand and develop their thinking by trying to explain it to others and to consider new perspectives by listening and building from what others have to say.

Talk about science and literature served several functions in supporting children's inquiry. Sometimes the groups used literature and other experiences to find information related to their questions and to develop and test out their hypotheses. They formed research groups in which they shared the ideas and information they were finding and explored their questions with each other. Literature was not the focus but simply one of the resources they used to support their talk. In the desert unit, students divided into groups to research one of the animals a visiting docent was bringing to the classroom. Their group discussions consisted of comparing what they were learning about their animal from books, filmstrips, pictures, and the animal's visit to the classroom.

Literature can also play a more central role in students' inquiry in literature circles in which students discuss powerful pieces of fiction and nonfiction that relate to their group inquiry. These small group discussions can be focused on a shared book set, text sets, paired books, or class read-aloud books (Short and Klassen, 1993).

Text sets consist of a small set of related titles that have been carefully selected to represent a range of perspectives and genres, including fiction, nonfiction, and poetry (Short, 1992). The ecosystem inquiry groups each had a text set of about fifteen titles related to their group focus. The bird set, for example, included *I am Phoenix* (Fleischman, 1985), *Chickens Aren't the Only Ones* (Heller, 1981), *Inch by Inch* (Lionni, 1960), and *The Chick and the Duckling* (Ginsburg, 1972). The four students in each group all read different titles from the set and then came together to share with each other and compare their books as they searched for similarities and differences. We chose text sets because we wanted students to read more critically and to encounter different perspectives, connections, and information on their topics. Because the sets mixed fiction and nonfiction, we hoped to encourage a wider range of talk.

In planning the text sets on ecosystems, we made several mistakes that made talk about these sets difficult for the students. The sets we developed were too large (ten to fifteen books per set), and the connections too diverse and broad. Because students had not previously participated in literature groups and were not sure how to talk about literature, they needed smaller sets of closely connected books. Because the sets contained books from different ecosystems, students were unable to see the interdependence across any one system. Most of their learning remained fragmented and unconnected, and their talk never really moved from sharing facts and personal responses to the kind of critical dialogue that could help them make sense of larger concepts and issues. Their talk consisted primarily of retellings in which they reported facts to each other rather than explored their understandings and connections with each other. They were much more concerned about behavior than meaning and spent more time reporting to us on who was misbehaving than talking about books or science concepts.

The children's responses indicated their need for support in knowing how to talk about literature and science and how to interact in groups with informal structures. They were used to answering specific questions in basal reader groups or on worksheets. Although they had previously engaged in many science experiences, they had neither talked nor reflected on what they learned from these experiences. Their previous small group experiences had been structured cooperative learning groups in which specific tasks and roles were assigned, and they were unsure of how to talk collaboratively *with* others.

We tried to support children's talk in several ways. Each day before the children broke into their small groups, we read a picture book aloud and had a short whole-class discussion. These discussions introduced children to ways of thinking and talking about ideas with their classmates other than reciting facts or story details. Because children were having difficulty understanding how they could use fiction and nonfiction to explore science, we also talked about connections to science concepts and ecology.

In addition, the class often met after their small groups for a short reflection time. We asked students first to talk about *what* they were discussing in their groups and then *how* the groups were functioning. We did not want the major focus to be on behavior, so we began the reflection with the content and ideas they had discussed in their groups. We then asked about any problems in the groups and brainstormed ways to deal with these problems so that the children could develop new ways of working with each other.

Another strategy Kathy used to shift students' attention from behavior was to ask "What are you talking about in your group?" when students came to "tattle" on each other. Students were frustrated with her unwillingness to discuss behavior, but her question communicated that our concern was not with how well they were behaving but with the ideas they were exploring.

We wanted to move children's talk not only from behavior to exploring meaning but also from overemphasizing isolated facts to immersing them-selves in the world of the book (Rosenblatt, 1978). To encourage them to enter more fully into the world of the book, we gave each group a shared book set of a fiction or nonfiction title related to their text set focus. The bird group, for example, had *Owl Moon* (Yolen, 1987) and the people group had *Tight Times* (Hazen, 1979). Because each person in a particular group had read the same title, we felt there would be less retelling and more sharing of responses to the book. To further encourage dialogue, we asked the children to make sketches of the meaning of the book using a curricular activity called Sketch to Stretch (Harste, Short, with Burke, 1988). They read

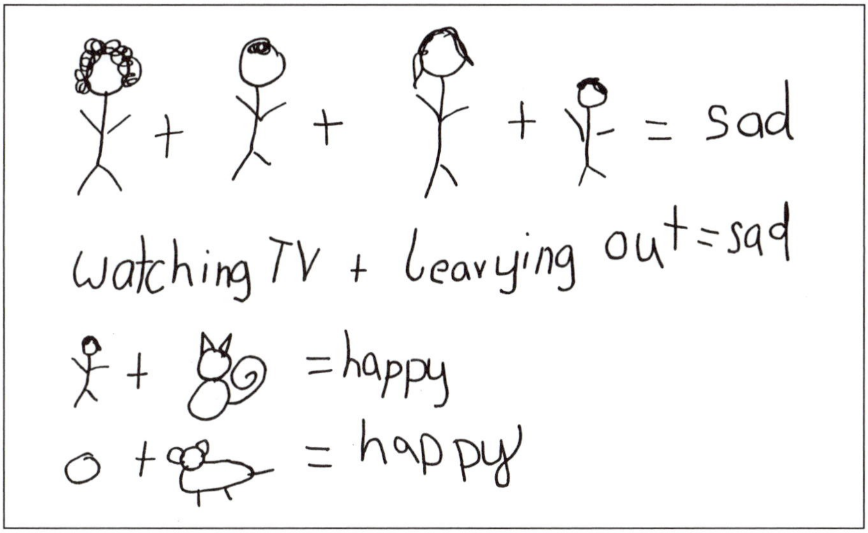

Figure 7.4 *Ben's Sketch to Stretch for* Tight Times

the book, made a sketch, and then brought the sketch to the group to share. This strategy encouraged them to talk about group members' different interpretations and connections to the same story. We introduced Sketch to Stretch with a class read-aloud book before asking students to try the strategy in their groups.

Ben had read *Tight Times* (Hazen, 1979) about a boy who desperately wants a dog but is unable to have one because his family is going through tight financial times. When he finds a starving kitten on the street, he is allowed to keep it and names it "Dog." Ben drew a sketch (see Figure 7.4) and said, "The family plus the babysitter equals sad because everybody is sad. When the babysitter watches TV and leaves out the boy, that's sad too. When the boy gets the cat, he is happy because he has someone. When the cat eats his lima beans, he is even happier."

While we believed that reading was just one way to explore science concepts and needed to be integrated with other experiences, our difficulties in supporting talk in the literature groups led us to emphasize reading *about* ecosystems. We realized that we need to engage children in other experiences, and so we quickly integrated experiment cards into their ecosystem text sets. Students used the suggestions and questions on these cards to talk about and develop their own experiments and surveys related to their group focus. In their groups, they began to move back and forth between reading, observing, experimenting, and discussing to include more ways of knowing and exploring science. Junardi also incorporated more simulation experiences, observation centers, and experiments into the class, such as "Oh, Deer," a game that involved playing out the effect of the environment on population control. She supported these experiences with discussions that encouraged exploratory and reflective talk about what children were seeing. As Paul pointed out, "When I see it, do it, read it, and talk about it, then I can get my own ideas and really learn. I can understand why things happen."

For the ecosystem focus, we began with talk about literature and then developed other science experiences around the text set groups. In contrast, during the desert focus, we began with students' questions and organized small and whole-class inquiries so they could explore those questions. Literature was used when it was appropriate to facilitate that inquiry. This shift in our primary focus from literature to inquiry allowed for a more integrated approach that better supported talk and children's scientific problem-posting.

Instead of one major desert inquiry project, students engaged in a number of smaller inquiries. This change seemed to allow them to focus on particular aspects of the desert and to engage in exploratory talk, unlike their ecosystem group discussions, which stayed at a sharing and retelling level. The inquiries included small groups on animals of the desert, a whole-class inquiry on coyotes and insects, and centers on cultural artifacts of the Anasazai and Hohokam cultures. The children also read poetry about the desert and Navajo coyote tales in their literature discussion groups. These experiences were pulled together by a visit to a desert environmental science center where the children engaged in experiences involving the environment and Native American cultures.

One of our most successful experiences was with paired books. Because students were interested in comparing the desert to other ecosystems, we paired two books that had a similar theme or topic but were set in different ecosystems, for example, *Amigo* (Baylor, 1963) and *Thy Friend, Obadiah* (Turkle, 1969), or *Desert Giant* (Bash, 1989) and *The Park Bench* (Takeshita, 1989). The children chose the book they wanted to read with a partner and talked about their responses to the story and what they would need to tell others so they would understand the story. Then they met with the two children who had the other book in their set, retold their stories to each other, and searched for similarities and differences across their books and ecosystems. Their talk during these groups was much more tentative and exploratory than that we had observed in other groups. As the group compared *Amigo* and *Thy Friend, Obadiah,* for example, Ben commented, "Both animals went after the boys to their friends, but both boys had to train the animals how to act with humans. I wonder if the animals had to train the boys, too."

The exchanges during these paired book experiences fit what Barnes (1992) calls "exploratory" talk. Students used language as a way to work toward their own science and literary understandings, although much of their language was hesitant and tentative, with many qualifying phrases, such as "maybe" and "probably." While initially the children simply accepted what others had to say, they soon began to challenge others' comments and sometimes were able to build from their ideas. They began using talk as a way of building new understandings.

Rethinking and Revising Ideas

As students struggle to explain their tentative ideas and to listen to the ideas being explored by other learners, they encounter new perspectives and make new connections. These interactions often naturally encourage them to re-think and revise their ideas about the topic under consideration. They are able to distance themselves from their own ideas and take a more reflective stance toward their inquiry. The insect group, for example, engaged in exploratory talk about whether spiders and scorpions were insects; that led several children to revise their previous thinking. They discovered that spiders are a separate class of arthropods with different body parts than insects and that insects are just one of four classes of arthropods, not a category that includes all bugs.

Presenting Ideas Formally and Publicly

The inquiry cycle highlights informal exploration and collaboration, but at some point students want to share their discoveries with others. When they go public with what they know, they have to pull together what they have learned from reading, experimenting, and discussing and find a way to present these understandings to others. These presentations or documents are not final but simply a formal presentation of what they currently know.

When the ecosystem groups presented their discoveries to the class, they included *every* piece of information they had gathered, even though we had spent time brainstorming ways they could summarize their learning through diagrams, cycles, webs, pictures, and graphs. Their presentations were long and full of isolated information. Since they had not previously experienced summarizing their learning through presentational talk, they did not have a sense of audience or of how to sort out what was most important.

We looked for opportunities to support their presentational talk. When the class engaged in a short inquiry on rainforests, they were given the opportunity to create a mural and make a presentation on rainforests as part of the school assembly on Earth Day. This presentation gave Junardi the chance to work with students on how to summarize and present ideas to others. In the desert inquiry, students gave many small presentations instead of a major presentation at the end of the inquiry. The paired book groups prepared charts, webs, and diagrams to share their ideas and connections from their book set with the rest of the class. Because the information was not so overwhelming, these smaller presentations were easier for children to pull together. They had less difficulty organizing their ideas.

Reflecting on Strategies for Inquiry

Throughout such active and collaborative engagements in inquiry, learners need time to step back and reflect on what they are learning (content), how they are learning (process) and why they are learning (purpose). When our focus was ecosystems, they reflected as a class on what they were learning about the environment, but they also talked about their discussion strategies in the literature groups, their notetaking strategies for research, and their reading strategies for nonfiction books. This reflective talk occurred primarily as short whole-class discussions right after the inquiry groups met.

Reflection occurs throughout the entire inquiry process, but we found that as learners pull together a particular inquiry to share it with others, they are able to take another step back and reflect more broadly on their learning. Through their reflections on process, content, and purpose they reach a more general level of understanding and integrate this understanding into their frames of reference—the "anticipatory set" within which they continue to learn and interact with the world.

Offering Invitations for Further Inquiry

The inquiry cycle renews itself by offering new invitations to learning that move learners through the cycle again. These invitations encourage learners to ask new questions and to pursue ideas that will lead them to further inquiry. All the members of the community—teachers and students—are responsible for offering these invitations to continue inquiry. Sometimes such invitations come as students share their presentations with each other. Sometimes teachers offer invitations for particular learning experiences based on their own interests or topics in the school curriculum. In our inquiry project, the class presentations of the ecology groups led to further research on the rainforest because children raised a number of questions about how their different ecosystem groups were related to each other. New ideas and questions lead to invitations that keep the inquiry process continually in motion.

CONCLUSION

Our experience with creating a learning environment to support classroom inquiry provided new insights and raised new questions for us as educators. We gained a clearer sense of our roles as teachers in providing demonstrations and of the curriculum structures that would support a wide range of talk in classroom inquiry. Opening up classroom experiences to more exploratory talk by offering choices did not automatically produce that kind of talk from children. Because of their instructional histories, they needed encouragement along with our demonstrations of how they could use talk to explore and present their discoveries to others.

As we examined the talk that occurred throughout the inquiry cycle, we found a tremendous range of types. Children used talk to connect with their past experiences, to share new experiences and their responses to them, to explore and re-consider their own experiences and ideas, to consider new perspectives, to build on the ideas of other students, to hypothesize and explore half-formed thoughts, to ask questions, to develop a focus, to reflect on their inquiry process, and to present their understandings to others. Each of these types of talk played different roles in helping them bring together content and process. As we examined their talk, we also came to understand how we could integrate literature into their inquiry in ways that included both the literary experience itself and science concepts and processes.

Through these experiences we came to value the significance of connections in children's learning. The class's focus on cycles highlighted the importance of connections not only across nature but across all learning. "Learning itself is the search for patterns that connect" (Harste, Short, with Burke, 1988). Without connections, learning and talk remain fragmented and rarely move beyond "getting the facts." Children made connections between various aspects of nature, their life experiences, their school experiences, their own and classmates' ideas, different ways of knowing about science, and literary and scientific concepts. Because their school experiences did not artificially separate cognitive and affective ways of knowing, they were able to engage in more powerful learning. Their search for connections created a cycle of meaning that gave depth to their talk and allowed them to make sense of their world.

REFERENCES

Barnes, D. 1992. *From communication to curriculum*. 2nd ed. Portsmouth, NH:Boynton/ Cook.

———. 1989. *Active learning*. Leeds, England: Leeds University TVEI Support Project.

Bash, B. 1989. *Desert giant*. Boston: Little, Brown.

Baylor, B. 1975. *The desert is theirs*. New York: Macmillan.

———. 1963. *Amigo*. New York: Macmillan.

Burke, C. 1991. Informal communication.

Carle, E. 1969. *The very hungry caterpillar*. New York: Philomel.

Dewey, J. 1938. *Experience and education*. New York: Collier.

Eisner, E. 1982. *Cognition and curriculum*. New York: Longman.

Fleischman, P. 1985. *I am Phoenix*. New York: Harper.

Freire, P. 1985. *The politics of education*. Granby, MA: Bergin and Garvey.

Ginsburg, M. 1972. *The chick and the duckling*. New York: Macmillan.

Harlen, W. 1989. *Developing science in the primary classroom*. Portsmouth, NH: Heine-mann.

Harste, J. and K. Short, with C. Burke. 1988. *Creating classrooms for authors*. Portsmouth, NH: Heinemann.

Hartman, D. 1990. "8 Readers reading." Unpublished doctoral dissertation. Urbana, IL: University of Illinois.

Hazen, B. 1979. *Tight times*. New York: Penguin.

Heller, R. 1981. *Chickens aren't the only ones*. New York: Grosset.

Huck, C. 1989. *Children's literature in the elementary school*. 4th ed. New York: Holt.

Lionni, L. 1960. *Inch by inch*. New York: Astor-Honor.

Rosen, H. 1984. *Stories and meaning*. London: National Association of Teachers of English Papers in Education.

Rosenblatt, L. 1978. *The reader, the text, and the poem*. Carbondale, IL: Southern Illinois University Press.

Short, K. 1993. "Making connections across literature and life." In *Journeying: Children Responding to Literature*, edited by K. Holland, R. Hungerford, and S. Ernst. Portsmouth, NH: Heinemann.

———. 1986. "Literacy as a collaborative experience." Unpublished doctoral dissertation. Bloomington, IN: Indiana University.

Short, K. and C. Burke. 1991. *Creating curriculum: Teachers and students as a community of learners*. Portsmouth, NH: Heinemann.

Short, K. and C. Klassen. (1993). "Literature circles: Hearing children's voices." In *Children's voices: Talk in the classroom*, edited by B. Cullinan. Newark, DE: International Reading Association.

Takeshita, F. 1989. *The park bench.* Brooklyn, NY: Kane/Miller.

Turkle, B. 1969. *Thy friend, Obadiah.* New York: Viking.

Yolen, J. 1987. *Owl moon.* New York: Philomel.

Zolotow, C. 1963. *The quarreling book.* New York: Harper.

Virginia "Gennie" Pfannenstiel grew up on the Great Plains where the sky touches the earth as far as the eye can see. In this environment of vast space she created images that led her to inquire about the surrounding world. As a teacher, Gennie asked questions about language learning that led to her doctoral research while studying at the University of Missouri-Columbia. She now works as an ESL supervisor for the state of Missouri.

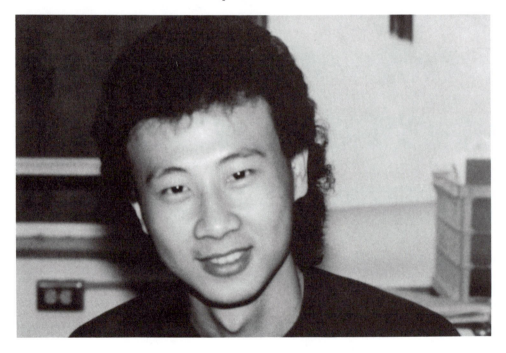

Chapter 8
Liberating Inner Voices and Accessing Inner Visions Through Dialogue

VIRGINIA PFANNENSTIEL

At the end of his English as a Second Language resource study period Sarith announced, "I feel like skipping history next hour." I asked, "What's wrong, Sarith?" "Nothing," he said in a dismissive manner. "What are you talking about in history now?" "I don't know. We watch movie and we have papers to do but I don't know anything." "Well, there must be something you know." "No," he said, "Never mind. Just forget it." When I spoke with his history teacher, she told me that they were studying a film, *The Twenties*. Having known Sarith as a hard worker, we both agreed that he was having difficulty imagining this period in American history because it was so different from Cambodia and his present experience.

I spent the 1990–1991 school year gathering data in an English as a Second Language high school program while working as a full-time aide under a Title VII grant. As I watched the students and listened to their voices as they encountered text in particular content areas, I observed what I will call a *"hindered state,"* when they simply could not contextually process information. Sarith could not access a personal storehouse of information when viewing *The Twenties*. Likewise, when Marcus, who came from Brazil, was asked to complete a worksheet about a familiar object—the microscope—he said, "I have no questions, because I no understand."

Using gestures, Marcus upon further interaction, was able to demonstrate proficiency in using the microscope, yet he adamantly held to the notion that he understood nothing—a state James Moffet (1985) has described as *obsession*. Moffet sees it as a halting of inner speech due to "dominant emo-tions, motives, and fixed frameworks. When the learner can no longer take in new information for 'development'—('. . . the sustaining of a line of thought far enough to allow combinations of inner material to occur that one has not so combined before'), the discovery process is blocked" (p. 306). This is a recurring phenomenon for many students in various schooling situations. With firm convictions, students in hindered states will say they can't do something, they don't understand, or they don't have any questions. Possibly they will sleep, not attend, or disrupt others. These fixed ideas hinder students' ability to take in new information and make discoveries. This state, however, is transitory and students can liberate their inner voices, changing their lines of thought. As teachers listen and students talk, we become learners together, moving to a role of sharing dialogue.

LISTENING TO STUDENTS' VOICES

I saw students in a self-contained study hall and provided help for those who needed to learn the academic language of their mainstreamed classes. The students I worked with were enrolled in ESL classes taught by Carolyn Collins or Betty Belcher. It was my role to be accessible in the study hall and to offer invitations for interactions that would guide students in formulating knowledge while embedding content-area language. In terms of the subject matter, they were the experts and I was the learner. My primary responsibil-ity, as defined by the grant guidelines, was to concentrate on providing supplemental assistance in acquiring language concepts related to science and social studies.

It was in a listening role that I was able to gain the trust of twenty-seven teenagers representing eleven countries. They expressed evidence of this trust in the letters, illustrations, and photographs they included in the fare-well notebook they presented to me on my departure. To preface this collec-tion from their students, whom I aided, Carolyn Collins included a poem written by Betty Belcher. The following excerpts portray the theoretical view-points toward learning that molded the relationships within the ESL commu-nity.

Requirements for the ESL Aide
Someone kind,
someone good,
who makes us feel
the way we should

About ourselves,
about our classes,
which include
square roots and masses.

She must read
with us each day
and show us books
for which we may

Take knowledge,
pleasure and laughs
while keeping us
from taking naps.

. . .

She must ask questions
which turn on lights.

She must respect us
and then give choices
to us while straining
to hear our voices. . . .

The collection offers a window into the lives of the students whose paths I crossed again and again. They shared their experiences and became discoverers of "white sands" and "blue water," as Dais, a student from Japan, wrote (see Figure 8.1).

In Betty Belcher's words, I was "straining to hear [their] voices." As an ESL aide, I was able to get to know the students during the first semester before I taped their voices in the latter half of the second. Gina, a student from Taiwan, offered reassurance in her farewell letter: "You really don't make me feel like you are a 'teacher' at all. I can talk about anything with you . . . you've been really helpful to my homework and tests." The majority of the students expressed comments about the importannce of talk either verbally or in writing, changing my pattern of teacher-dominated interactions.

MOVING FROM THE HINDERED STATE THROUGH DIALOGUE

When we encountered problematic text together, I noted that learners often experience the hindered state I have referred to, in which they are unable to use their inner voices to gain access to their personal storehouses of knowledge. In his discussion of Vygotsky's work, Alex Kozulin (1990) addresses the theoretical premise underlying this common occurrence—when

Figure 8.1 *Dias' Poem*

language minority students struggle to develop a schema that conceptualizes history from an unfamiliar culture. He quotes Vygotsky: "Man makes use not just of physically inherited experience: throughout his life, his work and his behavior draw broadly on the experience of former generations, which is not transmitted at birth from father to son. We may call this historical experience" (p. 81).

Sarith's own historical experience was not helping him bring American history to his consciousness. Vygotsky presents another social component of human experience, which allows the individual to live in the experiences of others through the use of interpersonal communication. As Kozulin (1990) describes it, "We literally live in the experiences of others. Speech plays the decisive role in this transformation of the experiential field. Speech is a special kind of stimulus that can be reproduced by individuals and thus through it they can identify themselves with others. "In a broad sense," wrote Vygotsky, "speech is the source of social behavior and consciousness" (p. 81).

In other words, Sarith's problem stemmed from his feeling of exclusion, which deactivated his inner voice. Like many other students, he did not talk to those who were there to help him because he felt he had nothing relevant to say.

The hopelessness Sarith experienced is prevalent among the oppressed and excluded. Individuals lacking a shared cultural fulfillment with the community at-large feel forced to become a part of what Paulo Freire (1972) called "a culture of silence." Sarith, who was overwhelmed by a "whole stack of work" he had not completed, told me that his history teacher had said, "You didn't watch the movie; you slept." To which Sarith admitted to himself, as he relayed the situation to me, "Yeah, I put my head down because the movie wasn't talking to me." These "sleeping" students are our society's concern. They need to learn how to make meaning in their lives within the social system. As Charity James (1974) says of learners, "They need to be able to make works of art or inventions or communications according to their *inner vision*, to make good guesses about human behavior and, for that matter, about the behaviors of newts or molecules or spacecraft. They also need to see that they can make a difference to their social environment" (p. 10). Students like Sarith are hindered by an enculturated silence. According to Freire and Faundez (1989), they are not engaging their inner visions or inner voices to create a dialectical relationship between reflection and action, so the activity becomes meaningless and they appear vacuous to the teacher who in turn sees them as "refusing to try." These individuals should not be viewed as lacking knowledge or the ability to learn, but as lacking praxis—the ability to put knowledge into practice (Freire, 1972). It was Sarith's belief that "the movie was not saying anything to him" that kept him from applying new textual information to old experiences.

MAKING INQUIRIES TOGETHER

The aim of my classroom research was captured by Andrea, who, in her Portuguese dialect, explained the nature of my role to a new student: "It's like this. You say, 'Ms. Gennie I need help.' She says, 'Tell me what you know.' You say, 'I know this, and this, and this . . .' She says, 'What is your question?' You say, 'It is this . . .' Ms. Gennie says, 'What do you think?' You say, 'I think this . . .' Then you say 'AHHHH!' because you know the answer. You are so surprised! You see, that's what you do and that's what Ms. Gennie does." What an insightful informant! That's exactly what happened when students approached me in their study hall.

"Meeting the students where they are at" involves having them tell you what they know. Initiating an interaction with a question can hinder students in accessing their personal knowledge if they do not know the answer. Saying "Tell me what you know" allows students to bring forth bits and pieces of their inner voices and visions about a particular topic. As they weave their thoughts with language, they produce their personal knowledge. When Chamreun was taking her English test under my jurisdiction, she said: "Ms. Gennie, I can't write the answer to this question until I talk about it, so I know what it is that I know." Likewise, the special education teacher teaming in a "class within a class" arrangement spoke of the learners in Marcus's basic American history class: "When the students are asked specific questions by the district-wide curricular exam, they do poorly; when they are asked to write about what they know, they shine." As these informants, who represent the teacher/student dichotomy, illustrate, once the students identify what they know, they can ask about the unknown or be asked about the known.

In my research, I refrained from asking students specific content-related questions to spur an interaction. During the first semester, I had discovered that asking direct questions led to dead ends—it did not "turn on lights." Yet it was my role to do just that by approaching the unapproachable. Some students are convinced that their situation is hopeless, so that help is unnecessary. Why engage in a conversation that leads to questions they cannot answer? "Do you need help with your history class?" quickly received a flat "No!" from a napping student who was about to flunk. These noninteractive sleeping students are the concern of all teachers.

In looking at the work of Belenky and her colleagues (1986) I found evidence of the power of oppression: "The silent women had limited experience and confidence in their ability to find meaning. . . . For them school was an unlikely place to 'gain a voice.' For them the experience of school only confirmed their fears of being 'deaf and dumb' " (p. 23). The isolation these women felt is the same as that experienced by many of the second language learners in this study.

Gina, "the artist" in the ESL community, was described by her art teacher as having no interest in art: "I showed a filmstrip on pottery to expose the students to various images and possibilities to explore, and she wouldn't even keep her head up to look at it." During study hall I offered Gina an invitation: "Tell me about your art class." She replied, "Well you see, uh, we are not doing much in there right now, uh, it's pretty boring, you know, uh, we just watch this film, and it's boring." "Tell me about the film," I coaxed. "Well, you see, I really don't know much about it because it started saying all these things I didn't understand, so I put my head down on my desk." Gina's response is compelling! Although she is a competent artist, the overwhelmingly incomprehensible language used in the narration created a hindered state, one in which she became uninterested because she felt disenfranchised. When I showed this to Gina almost a year later, she said, "Yeah, I remember that, I felt really out of it!"

For Gina, the way to no longer "feel out of it" was simple and the outcome was remarkable. I asked to borrow the filmstrip from the art teacher and during study hall Gina and I looked at it together, without the soundtrack. As we viewed the frames, I asked her to tell me about what she thought of each photographed clay creation. Sometimes we spoke using free association: something looked like "a fish," or "madness." We laughed at the humorous objects (a fully clothed man drinking tea in a bathtub), and when the curious ones piqued our interest to the point of asking questions ("I wonder why they made that look like something Chinese," Gina asked from her Chinese viewpoint), we read that section of the script to learn about the background of the sculptures. We discovered that some of them were intended as metaphors.

Our discoveries were made possible by experiencing the objects themselves through our own inner vision, which engaged our inner voices, and then relating them to the contextual information. Gina and I glowed with discovery. We had gained a new level of meaning in our interactions about the filmstrip, and she felt a part of its curricular purpose. She was no longer "hindered" but felt the value of accomplishment. Later, while sharing my notes with Carolyn Collins, she asked Gina, "What did you think of how Ms. Gennie wrote about you? Was it O.K.?" Gina replied, "No, it wasn't O.K., it was GREAT!" Gina's contribution to my "farewell notebook" was a drawing that captured my "presence" trying to redirect the paths of "hindered" students. I assumed a stance of persistent, friendly invitation (see Figure 8.2). With one hand extended and one hand contained, I tried to balance the role of "doing" and "being," just as I encouraged Gina to take the lead as a discoverer.

Discovery is a hero's venture. The moment it happens, it is made known. Much to my surprise, Beth made one of her earliest Americanized verbalizations by raising her arms, clenching her fists, and simultaneously exclaiming *"yesssssss!"* while forcefully pulling her hands downward. Her outburst happened at the moment that she made a "cellular" discovery, while telling me, with limited English, about her biology notes written in Chinese. In this encounter, and others, students registered their discovery in such vocalizations as "ahhh," "ah ha," or "oh yeah!"

Figure 8.2 *Gina's Drawing*

As we sat at our desks pulled together in a spiraled circle one day during fourth-hour study hall, I found myself listening to four students taking turns telling me what they knew. Sadie told me about a story for her English class while posing a question about an event. She then redirected her attention to the text, while Chamreun told me about "weathering" for her geoscience class. Andrea got my attention to ask a question about the historical period during which Marian Anderson lived. As Marcus took his turn to talk about water purification, Chamreun (rereading her text at my elbow) exclaimed *"aahhh, I get it!"* when she answered her question about the differences between physical and chemical weathering. Meanwhile, on the other side Sadie softly lipped "ohhhhh" as she looked up from reading about the critical event in her story.

As I wrote about the students and interpreted the transactions that were documented through our interactions, I discovered that we shared the same approaches to problematic text. Granted, they were teenagers faced with unique problems and second language speakers learning a new culture, but we are all learners. As we approached unfamiliar topics together, I discovered that learners who share common ground withhold personal judgment, which builds trust. Again and again, students commented that I didn't seem like a teacher because I listened to them. Again and again in my research role,

I learned that to be a good teacher I must be a co-learner: I am not "the expert" but "a facilitator" of dialogue.

LEARNER BEHAVIORS

From their writings and my taped encounters with the twenty-one high school students in the English as a Second Language Program resource classroom a number of learner behaviors emerged as they moved from a hindered learning state to talking through textual transaction: *taking risks:* acting upon one's perceptions; *experiencing knowing:* assimilating knowledge for making changes in adopting new information; *perceiving symbols:* using language for labeling; *making connections:* matching symbols to culture; *using the imagination:* renaming, reinventing, and recreating symbols for a new community; *invoking culture:* drawing communal knowledge from one's world; and, as students begin *self-initiating inquiry:* asking questions about the known to get answers to the unknown.

At the end of the school year, I asked students to respond in writing to the statement: "Before I had my resource hour with Ms. Gennie, I used to . . . but now I . . . ." The students offered insights about our time together, and their eclectic voices focused my observations.

Taking Risks

Stephane: Before I had my resource hour with Ms. Gennie, I used to . . . when I do my homework, I try to do the best that I can. When I am in my classes, I listen very carefully to the directions and when I do my homework it will be easy for me because I finish myself. I always say "yes I can do it" and I make it, but when I am not true in myself, I ask Ms. Gennie to help me. Before to ask her, I try to understand but if I really don't understand, I ask her. When Ms. Gennie finishes to explain to me I can understand because she does it carefully and after she gives to me some examples. So, it's easy for me to understand and after I do it by myself.

Stephane is a risk-taker. That is his strength, but when he is not "true" in himself he needs an "example" or an experience that aesthetically moves him to understand the meaning. For him, often a song, a story, or a photograph exemplifies inner meaning.

According to the theories of John Dewey (1934), for Sarith to take a risk he needed an aesthetic experience that would free him from the forces that impeded and confused the development of meaning. As Maxine Greene (1978) says of Dewey:

> He was, of course, fundamentally interested in the ways in which works of art concentrated and enlarged immediate experiences, in the ways in which they moved people to an imaginative ordering and reordering of meanings, to the effecting of connections, to the achieving of continuities. He spoke in various ways of the "gap between the here and now of direct interactions whose funded result constitutes the meanings with which we grasp and understand what is now occurring" and he went on: "Because of this gap, all conscious perception involves a risk; it is a venture into the unknown, for as it assimilates the present to the past it also brings about some reconstruction of that past." (p. 171)

Unfortunately for students like Sarith, the gap may seem to be too wide for risk taking. Dewey views experience in totality; for Sarith, the forces that hinder him are more prevalent in his experience than his knowledge of *The Twenties.* Thomas Alexander (1987) explains: "experience for Dewey emerges from the complex interplay between the biological organism and a physical environment mediated by participating in a culture of symbols" (p. 9). According to Clifford Geertz (1983), it could be said that Sarith has a storehouse of visions and voices, but as an individual with unique local knowledge (Cambodian culture transplanted to mid-America), he did not perceive them as connected to the cultural symbols of the historical period being introduced to him.

According to J. Berryman (1983), "immigrant children must have survival needs met before they can move to the higher levels of development of social interaction and self-esteem . . . the learning climate must be conducive to security" (p. 6). Carolyn Collins, the ESL classroom teacher who was the respondent for my research, commented on Berryman's statement:

> Do you think Sarith's survival needs are unmet in this culture? I think that they are met, but I think his low self-image in academia may be rooted in his childhood experiences of which we know little or nothing. We can only surmise from *Killing Fields:* Sarith was a child who lost both parents, who watched a brother drown because he was too little to help and no one else came to his rescue.

Collins was concerned about Berryman's claim because she felt it did not apply to Sarith, who had survival skills: even in this culture he has maintained a job and a home. Perhaps he is referring to the root of survival needs. Sarith's early life was traumatized by war and the death of loved ones. Unmet childhood needs are carried over into his later adolescence, and to be successful, Sarith definitely needs a secure learning environment where his stories can be told.

When Leslie Marmon Silko, a contemporary Native American writer who was a minority learner in a dominant culture, was asked by Laura Coltelli (1990) to tell her story, she replied,

One of the things that I was taught to do from the time I was a little child was to listen to the story about you personally right now. To take all of that in for what it means right now, and for what it means for the future. But at the same time to appreciate how it fits in with what you did yesterday, last week, maybe ironically, you know, drastically different. And then ultimately I think we make a judgment almost as soon as we store knowledge. A judgment that somehow says, "I've heard stories like that" or "I would tend to judge her harshly except I remember now . . ." All of this happens simultaneously. (p. 141)

In talking about her success as a beginning writer in a college creative writing class, Silko explained that it was possible for her to take the risk of writing a story because she had experienced a lifetime of personal stories. "The best thing, I learned, the best thing you can have in life is to have someone tell you a story" (p. 145). "I just grew up with people who followed, or whose world vision was based on a different way of organizing human experience, natural cycles" (p. 138). For this writer, it was simply a task of putting her knowledge of human experience into a symbolic art form using standard English. So too, Sarith has a profound knowledge of human experience that needs to be connected with story.

Experiencing Knowing

Emmanuel: I used to have a poor grade, like a 'D' in most of my classes and I also had a hard time studying for a test or a quiz. Since Ms. Gennie come to my resource hall, she have been doing great, by helping us, when we need her help. Since she has been helping me especialy in biology, I've been doing a lot better, and my grade moved from a 'D' to 'B' now. And I am a kind of thankful to her for being in my resource hall.

In reviewing the tapes, I discovered that there was only one interaction with Emmanuel related to biology, during which I had shown him pictures of *biomes* in a calendar filled with breathtaking photographs of landscapes. I remember his enthusiastic reply: "I know what biomes are!" This one word had hindered him from experiencing knowing as he struggled through the unit on biomes.

Carolyn Collins told me that during the next school year Sarith continued to struggle with risk taking in her ESL class. When I gave a conference presentation with Betty Belcher, Sarith's ESL reading teacher, she told me a powerful story about Sarith. In her class they were reading about the Santa Fe Trail. She said that the book *Trees in the Trail* (Holling, 1942) contained many proverbs, which she discussed with the students in order to gain an understanding of that historical time. Then she asked the students to write down proverbs from their own cultures. As she described it, the students "immediately flew around the room grabbing markers and enthusiastically writing their proverbs." When she asked Sarith why he wasn't attempting to participate, he said that he had nothing to say. While the other students began telling stories and were very animated in their presentations, Sarith sat silently.

Belcher asked him about the Khmer words on his jacket: "What about that writing you have on your jean jacket?" "What does that mean?" Sarith couldn't translate it into English, so he asked Bun Quan to help him. After their discussion, he wrote: "One fist can kill a whole family." For Sarith, this was a monumental moment. It was a transaction that embodied particular truths through the reorganization of experience, making necessary modifications to present them in the symbols of the English language (Britton, 1970).

Bun Quan was able to help Sarith because he too had had similar experiences and had written about them in Carolyn Collins' ESL class during the previous school year in a piece he called "Remembrances and Pains of Bun Q. Tang." He was able to hear the voices of his parents, who stayed in Cambodia as he faced the realities of life in a new land away from family and friends.

> Bun Q. Tang is a Chinese person. I was born in Cambodia's capital city, Phnom Penh. My family had eight persons, no including me. After 1975 my family left from the city to go to the countryside because in 1975 the Khmer Rouge attacked Phnom Penh City. The government of the Khmer Rouge had announced to all Cambodians that they had to leave from the city as soon as possible . . . [He went on to describe the loss of his siblings]
>   . . . my parents said, "Khmer Rouge is the murderer and very cruel to people." Because in 1975 to 1979 there are two million people were killed by Khmer Rouge's fist . . .
>   . . . I have a good luck because I discover the information from my uncle in United States, he has been in Missouri for eight years. So now a day I live with him, but I am still unhappy because I am often homesick.

Bun Quan's writing includes the same symbolic fist depicted in Sarith's proverb. Perhaps it was this experience, which Bun Quan had symbolically represented through his writing, that made it possible for him to help Sarith. Because of the collaborative classroom atmosphere, Sarith was able to accomplish with the help of a peer what he was not able to risk on his own. According to Vygotsky (1962), Sarith was operating in a "zone of proximal development," which allowed him to perform at a higher level while working with a more capable peer.

Perceiving Symbols

> *Wing-Kin:* Before I had my resource hour with Ms. Gennie, I used to have too much vocabulary word I don't understand or sentences I don't know. So this was difficult for me to do my homework or test, but now I can do it easily and I can understand the questions.

When Wing-Kin first arrived, he was dependent on his hand-held computerized dictionary, which he used as a translation device. Often he had difficulties because the cultural symbolism of the words did not carry over in translation. Wing-Kin and I compared the meaning of our perceptions by drawing miniature icons next to the printed word.

A section of Bun Quan's writing demonstrates his ability to perceive cultural symbols while gaining insights about facelessness, the negative identity of the oppressed:

> After 1979 Vietnam's soldier came to save the lives of Cambodian until today, Cambodian is fortunate get alone well, but it is the Communist country because the government are weak and other government control . . . they look down on Chinese people, they have number to serial the Chinese people were called (351) these number is mean he dog. Therefore, if I still stay there forever might be my life is lifeless. So my parents left me escaped from them to find my future.

Bun Quan expresses the realization that he was viewed as a dog. When a people have become targets in war, it is because they have become nonpeople. When Josef Skvorecky, a writer against revolutions, spoke at the 1981 Amnesty International congress called "The Writer and Human Rights," he said:

> James Joyce once wrote: "It's so easy to kill real people in the name of some damned ideology or other; once the killer can abstract them in his own mind into being symbols, then he needn't feel guilty for killing them since they're no longer human beings." The Jews in Auschwitz, the zeks in the Gulag, the bourgeoisie in a communist Iran. Symbols, not people. Revolutionsfutter. (Toronto Arts Group, p. 119)

Bun Quan, literate in Chinese, Khmer, and English drew from the voices of his people—their stories—to know his inner self, holding onto his valued image reflected in that mirror.

Joseph Campbell (1988) reassures us about what happens when we live according to the mythology of our culture:

> One thing that comes out in myths is that at the bottom of the abyss comes the voice of salvation. The black moment is the moment when the real message of transformation is going to come. At the darkest moment comes the light. (p. 37)

For some of our students the light has not yet come. In her talk to teachers at a conference in St. Louis Maya Angelou (1992), poet and writer, beseeched them to give their students hope. She gave personal testimony of a teacher from her past who had used poetry to help her regain her voice after a period of silence in her childhood. "A teacher becomes that rainbow to young men and women who otherwise might see no light" (*St. Louis Post-Dispatch*, p. 8A). As the reader of poetry and story or the participant in other art forms perceives symbols related to a personal world, the contextual experience becomes a part of that reader, or that participant.

Robert Bly's translation of a poem by Juan Ramon Jiménez offers me as a reader an experience of knowing the mirrored image of the inner self, the one who is willing to take risks in order to perceive symbols:

> I am not I.
>
>   I am this one.
> Walking beside me, whom I do not see,
> Whom at times I manage to visit,
> And at other times I forget.
> The one who forgives, sweet, when I hate,
> The one who remains silent when I talk,
> The one who takes a walk when I am indoors,
> The one who will remain standing when I die.
>   (*Iron John*, 1992, p. 51)

Our perceptions of the inner self are enhanced after reading a poem like this. We can go back to this poem again and again, and each time we will read it in a new way, according to our personal experiences and reflections. Dewey saw the viewer (reader) as transacting with art by adjusting, adapting, and assimilating perceptions.

Making Connections

Marcus: In my first semester (very begin of the school year), I feel lost and my homework was crazy for me. I just was crazy with those lots of things to translate. Ms. Gennie helped me to understand what the words means, and now I fell more secure when I give my works because she can said what is wrong, right, etc. Even in slangs that I almost went to hit one guy because of that, she helped me to understand the meaning. Ms. Gennie is not only a teacher, she is more, she is a friend wait to help in all the ways. I feel better and on the way now.

Marcus had difficulty linking language to the culture of his new environment. It was through the dramatization of his personal experiences, our dialogue of gestures and facial expressions to probe his story, that he was able to see the connection between thoughts, language, and actions.

David Johnson (1990), an English professor and poet whose teaching encourages students to create stories from their personal histories, wrote in response to a poem: "Each of us has the capacity to re-create these images for ourselves and slowly weave a web of relationships with other humans" (p. 177). Johnson metaphorically equated poetry to word weaving, a phrase he chose for the title of his book:

> Although *Word Weaving* is about poetry, the larger issues are self-expression and creating a human world for ourselves and others. When we choose language as a medium for this adventure, then we write. Some of that writing might end up as poems; some might be reflective or analytical. In the integrated curriculum, in the best of all possible classrooms, different kinds of writing would complement every phase of learning, since there is always an inside view and an outside view, a personal perspective and an objective perspective. A biology unit on the physiology of birth could also integrate writing about one's own beginnings and use poems by women about the birthing experience. (p. 6)

In a similar way, Marilyn Zurmuehlen (1990) described an artist as repeating a "cycle of intending, acting, realizing, and re-intending" (p. 2). She presents this involvement as a universal act—the "originator instinct," moving from unreflective to reflective thought. Zurmuehlen also posited that the culture influences the naming of the art.

Alland (1983) researched the naming of artwork with children from six different cultures. He found that the children from Ponape, Taiwan, and Bali were not concerned with naming their drawings and did not respond to his prompting or questioning, whereas, the children from Japan, the United States, and France were more interested in representational art. His conclusion was that "representation and symbolism are things children are consciously or unconsciously taught to do by adults and other children" (p. 214). Since naming is a culturally influenced language activity, the testing of naming can produce hindrances in making connections.

While individuals begin to see connections between their inner selves and their outer worlds, they develop a sense of relevancy that can be seen by the mind's eye as patterns channeled through their cultural viewpoints (Samuels and Samuels, 1990; Bateson, 1979). In *Seeing with the Mind's Eye*, (1990), Mike Samuels, an immunogeneticist, and Nancy Samuels, an educator, have written:

> What people "see" when they look at an external object is dependent upon who they are and what they are interested in at that moment. For example, a butcher might look at a bull and see beef steaks, a county judge might see the bull's good or bad lines, and a city dweller might see the bull as an object of sheer terror . . . . There is no single valid external reality—reality is multifaceted. (pp. 7–8)

Having grown up on a farm, I know that the "bull" should read "steer," because bulls are not used for beef steaks, naming information I know because of my background.

"Seeing" is an experience that perhaps could be associated with connecting realities or responding to the patterns of a multi-faceted reality. In *Mind and Nature*, Gregory Bateson (1979) bridged aesthetics with patterns: "By *aesthetic*, I mean responsive to the pattern which connects" (p. 9). He further challenged my thinking by adding: "I offer you the notion of *context*, of *pattern through time*" (p. 15). As the reader perceives the symbols of the text and takes risks to see connections, the reader transcends time within the context.

Using the Imagination

> *Bun Quan:* I always reading my history book at four hours before I have a test or quiz from Mr. Nevins and I used to study the terms and sometimes to study over my notes. When I don't understand the questions, I ask Ms. Gennie for help. If it still don't impress about the question she draw a picture to help me out. Now I felt better than before but sometime I still have problem with the new words.

When Bun Quan was unable to express himself orally, we exchanged dialogue by drawing. He drew from his imagination to learn new words and concepts.

As Sarith struggled to reconstruct the order of his experiences, he needed to use his imagination to weave a contextual pattern through time from the people in the film *The Twenties* to the people in his present and past worlds. Alexander (1987) exemplified this aesthetic experience as he discussed Dewey:

> To understand the experience embodied in the Parthenon, Dewey comments, at some point we must take into account "the bustling, arguing, acutely sensitive Athenian citizens" and attempt to connect them "with people in our own homes and in our own streets." (AE, 4; LW10:10). The ability of the Greeks to give expressive shape to their art arises from the same human ability to take sensual delight in the world. Whatever the difference in the culture of fifth century Athens and twentieth century America . . . works of art are developments of general habits of perception connected with a world of cultural meanings. Cultures teach us to see and respond to the world in a variety of ways. Art is simply an intensification of this process. (pp. 188–189)

In her discussion of making and then naming art, Zurmuehlen (1990) says that the third dimension is seeing. "Seeing is forgetting the name of the thing one sees" (p. 6). To see the Parthenon, one does not necessarily need to know the name, one needs to see the people, their lives, and their aspirations. Zurmuehlen admits that "for many adults, seeing is forgetting the name of the thing one sees may be a startling notion . . . young children, however, do not have to forget a name in order to 'see' " (p. 6). For Sarith, viewing the film meant taking notes of names of people, places, and events. It did not mean "seeing." We often hear the prophecy: To see is to understand. We compliment scholars by calling them "visionary thinkers." Yet, we often concern ourselves with a curriculum that asks for naming instead of seeing.

At exam time, Sarith attested, "Ms. Gennie, I fell through the trees; I flunked my history test." When I asked him why, he said, "All I saw was words." Chamreun expressed a similar experience, which was evident in her comments as we reviewed for her American History test: "Oh, I remember, I read that last night" and "Yes, I remember, he [her teacher] talked about that in class, but when I go to take the test I have troubles; my mind goes blank." Sarith and Chamreun have read words, but they have not imagined the words; the meaning of the words has not become a part of their experiences.

My fieldnotes record three students from Cambodia entering the world of the unknown by using their imagination when studying the Incas. During their resource hour, I decided to show them a filmstrip of Machu Pichu to help them "see" the people and their culture. Each student found personal connections with those people of long ago. Rorith, who noticed people's facial features and gestures, commented that the Incas' faces looked like Cambodians. Chamreun, who told me at Penh's wedding that when she gets married she will have "lots and lots of real flowers all around," expressed an interest in the garden terraces snaked around the mountain tops. Kheun, a fashionable young man adorned with gold necklaces and rings, was fascinated with the Incas' jewelry and their metaphors: "gold is the sweat of the sun" and "silver is the tears of the moon." The students made comments about their Cambodian culture and drew parallels between the Inca people and their environment and their own personal worlds. They were able to enter an unknown world and rename and recreate its symbols "through the system of knowledge of language attained and internally represented in the mind/brain" (Chomsky, 1986, p. 24).

If Sarith can look at his world of work, billiards, music, and art, and then imagine *The Twenties,* he will see similarities and differences. This knowledge will move him from a blank state of "I know nothing" to an active imaginative state of reacting and doing. Ann Berthoff (1984) builds a case for reclaiming imagination "as a name of the active mind, the mind in action making meaning" (p. 22). I too believe that using the imagination is a cognitive act necessary for creating meaning, and thus I see the importance of integrating the fine arts with the language arts.

Invoking Culture

Jin Kyung: I used to do my homework myself. In the school, I was too busy. It make me so tired. Most of the people like to figure themselves. I don't like it. So I started to question to the teachers. I needed to talk with somebody in the school. I have no American friends. I often wished how can they talk really well. I loved English when I was in S. Korea. We started to talk and my English respond better than before. Now, I have some friends and I can understand what the teacher say, but still I have some language problems. Usually the people talk naturally, but it's bother me. It's hard. I try to talk naturally with Ms. Gennie. Some vocabulary words are hard to understand, but I think I can do it.

Jin Kyung's writing portrays an invoking of both of his cultural realities in order to be a second language user.

In order to embody the truths necessary for survival, individuals must learn to evaluate their personal experiences while comparing their cultural perceptions of symbols with those of the dominant culture (Mills, 1959). Teachers must actively engage their students' imaginations in activities (Berthoff, 1984) that require problem-solving which is related to their worlds. In guiding students through the creative process while they interact with the arts and literature, or, as Dewey (1934) said, as they broaden their consciousness, learners become risk-takers. As teachers, it is our role to introduce strategies that allow us to become aesthetic learners with our students and to sharpen our vision in order to recognize new and unseen truths (Bersson, 1982). To invoke our personal culture in tandem with *experiencing knowing* within the mainstream curriculum is an art. In *The Educational Imagination*, Elliot Eisner (1985) defined teaching as an art. In one sense, Eisner felt that teaching "can be performed with such skill and grace that, for the student as well as for the teacher, the experience can be justifiably characterized as aesthetic" (pp. 175–176). The aesthetics of learning allow students to invoke their culture from home and at school.

Eisner makes us look at ourselves, not only as teachers, but also as individuals "who work and live within a culture. This culture functions as an organic entity that seeks stability yet reacts to changes in one part from changes made in others" (p. 22). Eisner advises teachers to understand these interactions in order to make significant changes in schools. "The study of curriculum in isolation from the rest of schooling is not likely to reveal the ecology of the school" (p. 22). If we perceive the school as having an ecology shaped by the individuals within that community, then we realize that as members come and go, they have an impact on the system through their individual cultures, as they in turn are molded by the school and its guiding force—the curriculum. According to Eisner, those students whose personal cultures do not match the mainstream curriculum adhere to the *hidden curriculum*. These are the students who create their own agenda for getting through school because they feel unable or uninvited to invoke the culture of the mainstream.

Self-initiating Inquiry

Olga: Before I had my resource hour with Ms. Gennie, I used to read the book skipping the words I didn't know, sometimes I don't get the whole meaning, but, now I read to try to make a *picture* of what I'm reading; it helps. When something happens I ask myself questions like: why? how? who? when? If someone reads to you it helps because perhaps you have heard a word before but when you read it you don't recognize but if someone read it to you, you understand it.

Olga asked questions about the known in her story to create a picture in her mind, offering answers for the unknown.

To help Sarith infuse his culture into the mainstream as he talks about life in Cambodia, we can guide him in making connections to life in America by offering dialogue that allows him to make inquiries about the pictures in his mind. As teachers become listeners, as students use dialogue to illustrate their inner visions, we can identify cultural similarities and differences. When we overcome our hindrances we develop a new consciousness that allows us to share the experiences of others. As students and teachers collectively come to know, we are able to focus our inquiries to tap the unknown. It is a transactional process, one that spirals into cumulative discoveries, an act of self-initiating inquiry.

As learners perceiving symbols, we are sensing the world and channeling those sensations into perceptions. While using our imaginations to create images that produce feelings necessary for risk taking, we experience knowing in our thinking. Whatever route we take, we are guided by a personal force that comes from invoking our culture. Wells and Chang-Wells (1992) explain the interdependence of individual and society. Not only is culture the product of social interaction but

> individual activity is always specific to a particular culture at a particular point in the historical development of that culture and dependent on the tools that the culture makes available. Thus, like the culture itself, the individual's knowledge, and the repertoire of actions and operations by means of which he or she carries out the activities that fulfill his or her perceived needs, are both constructed in the course of solving the problems that arise in goal-directed social activity and learned through interpersonal interaction. Human development and learning are thus intrinsically social and interactive. (p. 29)

Interaction is critical in developing both the individual and the culture.

My research captured the interactions between student and adult (or more capable peer). It investigated the course of the dialogue leading to self-initiating inquiry. The outcome is a composite of stories illustrating problems that learners face within a goal-directed social activity called schooling. The interpersonal interactions that took place revealed the need learners had to tell their stories—the telling of stories is a social need. As stories are told, metaphors are born and inquiries are posed, because life is dynamic when there is dialogue.

REFERENCES

Alexander, T. 1987. *John Dewey's theory of art, experience & nature: The horizons of feeling.* Albany: State University of New York Press.

Alland, A. 1983. *Playing with form: Children draw in six cultures.* New York: Columbia University Press.

Bateson, G. 1979. *Mind and nature: A necessary unity.* New York: Bantam.

Belenky, M. F., B. M. Clinchy, N. R. Goldberger, and J. M. Tarule. 1986. *Women's ways of knowing.* New York: Basic Books.

Berryman, J. 1983. "The importance of self-esteem in second language acquisition." *TESL Talk* 14(4):3-14.

Bersson, R. 1982. "Against feeling aesthetic experience in a technocratic society." *Art Education* July: 34-39.

Berthoff, A. 1984. *Reclaiming the imagination: Philosophical perspectives for writers and teachers of writing.* Portsmouth, NH: Boynton/Cook.

Bly, R. 1992. *Iron John.* New York: Vintage Books.

Britton, J. 1993. Language and learning. 2nd ed. Portsmouth, NH: Boynton/Cook.

Chomsky, N. 1986. *Knowledge of language: Its nature, origin, and use.* New York: Praeger.

Coltelli, L. 1990. *Winged words: American Indian writers speak.* Lincoln: University of Nebraska Press.

Dewey, J. 1934. *Art as experience.* New York: Minton, Balch & Co.

Eisner, E. 1985. *The educational imagination: On the design and evaluation of school programs.* 2nd. ed. New York: Macmillan.

Flowers, B. S., ed. 1988. *The power of myth: Joseph Campbell with Bill Moyers.* New York: Doubleday.

Freire, P. 1972. *Cultural action for freedom.* Baltimore: Penguin Books.

———. 1972. *Pedagogy of the oppressed.* London: Penguin Books.

Freire, P. and A. Faundez. 1989. *Learning to question.* New York: Continuum Publishing.

Geertz, C. 1983. *Local knowledge.* New York: Basic Books.

Greene, M. 1978. *Landscapes of learning.* New York: Teachers College Press.

Halliday, M.A.K. 1973. "The Functional basis of language." In *Class, codes and control. Volume 2: Applied studies toward a sociology of language,* edited by B. Bernstein. London: Routledge & Kegan Paul.

Hick, V. 1992. "Angelou: Students need hope." *St. Louis Post-Dispatch* April:8A.

Holling, H. C. 1942. *Trees in the trail.* Boston: Houghton Mifflin.

James, C. 1974. *Beyond customs: An educator's journey forward.* New York: Agathon.

Johnson, D. 1990. *Word weaving.* Urbana, IL: National Council of Teachers of English.

Kozulin, A. 1990. *Vygotsky's psychology: A biography of ideas.* Cambridge, MA: Harvard University Press.

Mills, C. W. 1959. *The sociological imagination.* New York: Oxford Press.

Moffett, J. 1985. "Liberating inner speech." *College Composition and Communication* 36:304–308.

Samuels, M. and N. Samuels. 1990. *Seeing with the mind's eye: The history, techniques and uses of visualization.* New York: Random House.

Toronto Arts Group for Human Rights, Ed. 1983. *The writer and human rights.* New York: Anchor Press/Doubleday.

Vygotsky, L.S. 1962. *Thought and language.* Cambridge, MA: M.I.T. Press.

Wells, G. and G.L. Chang-Wells. 1992. *Constructing knowledge together.* Portsmouth, NH: Heinemann.

Zurmuehlen, M. 1990. "Praxis, symbol, presence." *Point of view series: Studio art.* Reston: National Art Education Association.

Nancy Y. Knipping is Associate Professor of Early Childhood Education in the Department of Curriculum and Instruction at the University of Missouri-Columbia. She enjoys collaborating with teachers to develop curricula that support young children's active construction of knowledge. Her most recent work has explored the influence of drama on language and literacy learning.

Chapter 9
Using Dramatic Talk to Explore Writing

NANCY Y. KNIPPING

Seven-year-old Nick giggled as he prepared to read his story to the class. Based on the television show, "The Simpsons," his emerging text had received comments of approval from the boys with whom he had shared it, and Nick was eager to learn the responses of the rest of his classmates. There was frequent laughter as he read his completed draft:

Bart vs. Maggie

"Bart!"
"What, Dad?"
"Go play with Maggie."
"No!"
"Yes!"
"No!"
"Yes!"
"O.K., I'll go play with Maggie."
"Gosh, Maggie is in trouble. I better go help her. Oh, no! She's going to drop the lamp. Mom and Dad will be mad at me. I will get in big trouble."
"Wait, Maggie! I'm coming to save you. I'm running as fast as I can. I got you! That was close!"
The end.

THEORETICAL CONTEXT

For two years Sheryl McGruder and I had examined the use of drama as a means of helping her second-grade authors reconsider their original written stories. Now in October, as I recorded the events on videotape, Sheryl was familiarizing a new class with a strategy we were developing. It involves dramatizing and discussing children's stories as a way to help young authors "re-see" (Graves, 1983) their work and possibly revise it. Our research (Knipping, 1989; 1991) with her former students had convinced us of drama's potential for helping writers distance themselves from a piece in order to critique it. As actors and author collaborate to plan an informal drama, enact it, and reflect on their work with audience members, they engage in what Barnes (1990) terms "working on understanding" (p. 49). Knowledge is collectively constructed as children consider tentative ideas and hypotheses, reinterpret old conceptions, and shape new ones.

During the first month of school, the children in Sheryl's class have many opportunities to dramatize adult-authored stories, and in so doing, to improvise action and conversation for the characters they portray. In October, Sheryl invites her student writers to volunteer to have their stories dramatized. She explains that the strategy provides a way for the class to think together about what is good about a piece and to consider possibilities for making it even better. Throughout the year, the number of volunteers varies depending on what kinds of writing the children are doing, but Sheryl's students dramatize and discuss an average of one or two stories a week. The process requires an average of thirty to forty-five minutes per story.

The drama/discussion procedure begins with the author reading his or her working draft to the class and asking for volunteers to play the various characters. The children who do not have parts in the story then return to ongoing work as the author and actors collaborate on how to present the piece. The author usually retells the story to make sure that each actor knows when to come in, and the children discuss what the actors might do or say. Since the actors' main purpose is to help the author consider possible revisions in the story, they try to stay loosely within the story line while improvising conversation or action that might make the story better. Time is not taken for an actual rehearsal before the drama, but the cast considers possibilities: "Maybe you could say . . ." or "Then I might. . . ." Sheryl is available if her help is requested, but the children usually work alone in negotiating the group's agenda. As they think aloud, they address each other directly to raise questions, and shape answers collectively by extending and modifying one another's contributions.

After the actors and author have talked through the story, the audience gathers on the floor along one side of an open area of the room that serves as the stage. The author, as narrator and director, begins the drama by reading the title and as much of the story as necessary before the actors take over. Sheryl helps the actors and author share the story by reminding the author to pause so the actors can play out a scene and by prompting the actors when necessary: "What might you say and do to show that you were really happy?" or "Mother, how might you react to what your daughter just did?" During this improvisation, the story is tentatively extended, and often modified, to offer the author another perspective on his or her work.

After the drama, the children gather in a circle on the floor to talk about what they liked about the story, to raise questions about it, and to make suggestions for improvement. This is another time for exploring possibilities: "I hope you keep the part about . . ." or "Maybe you could have the kid say . . ." or "I thought the mother should. . . ." Sometimes, in response to a suggestion, two or three actors move to the center of the circle to play out a possible new scene. Sheryl works hard to offer her opinions without judging or assessing the offerings of other class members. She explains her ideas and the reasons for them and lets the author decide which, if any, suggestions to act upon. Her intent is to encourage her students to "bring out existing knowledge to be reshaped by new points of view being presented to them" (Barnes, 1992, p. 111).

At the end of each discussion, Sheryl moves from her place in the circle to the overhead projector. She writes the title of the story at the top of a transparency and asks the children what notes she should make for the author. As the children repeat the main ideas, she talks with them about the process of taking notes rather than writing full sentences. When the last notation is completed, a photocopy of the transparency is made and given to the author so that the ideas discussed can be remembered. The author then considers classmates' suggestions and decides whether, and how, the story will be revised.

As the children work through the strategy, they engage in both the tentative, hypothetical thinking aloud that Barnes (1992) labels "exploratory" talk, and the polished, well-formed, final draft language he categorizes as "presentational." Drama is by nature presentational. Even when improvising, actors take the stage to *present* their views of the story in a form as well-shaped and polished as possible. However, for Sheryl's students, drama also generates a context for the exploratory talk they use to refine and revise their understanding of writing.

This chapter will examine the ways second-graders have used talk throughout the drama-discussion strategy: to collaborate on possibilities for dramatizing a story; to try out characters' personalities and possible twists in plot; and to share notions about what makes a story good and possibilities for making it even better. Two examples of the strategy in action, one from early in the school year and one from late May, provide a small sampling of the kinds of revisions authors have made, the ways in which stories have built on one another, and, more generally, the manner in which Sheryl's students have used dramatic talk to explore writing.

NICK'S CONSIDERATIONS: THE INFLUENCE OF DRAMATIC IMPROVISATION ON A REVISION

Nick's story, dramatized in mid-October, provided the first demonstration of the potential for a dramatization to modify the plot and thus to add humor to a piece. During the previous weeks, actors had easily pantomimed action as authors read their stories, but they relied on Sheryl's prompting to expand dialogue and inject action that was not originally scripted into the dramatization. However, when an unexpected turn of events during the dramatization of Nick's story provided an obvious opportunity for improvisation, Ryan, Cristy, and Lewis were ready. Without missing a beat, they were able to cooperate to extend Nick's original idea in two directions, and in so doing, to provide the group an occasion to consider the appeal of various versions of the piece.

During the brief planning session, Nick reviewed the actors' roles. Although in a form much more abbreviated than would be common later in the year, both Ryan and Cristy proposed ways to embellish the script:

01   LEWIS (HOMER): What should I do?

02   NICK: First you go like this [shakes finger] and tell Bart to go play with Maggie. Then you say "yes" when Bart says "no."

03   LEWIS: O.K., that's easy.

04   NICK: Maggie, you don't say anything; you just knock over the lamp.

05   CRISTY (MAGGIE): I'll go get something for the lamp, so I can really knock it over.

06   RYAN (BART): I say "no" when Lewis says "yes," and then I say "O.K." and I could call, "Maggie, where are you?" Then, "Oh, I can't find Maggie. I must go and find her." Then I walk into the living room and see her holding the lamp and yell at her not to drop it. Then I dive and catch it.

07   CRISTY: Then after you put it down, I'll crawl over and knock it off the table on purpose.

08   RYAN: O.K.! Should we really do that?

09   CRISTY: I'll think about it.

10   NICK: Well, after you catch the lamp, Ryan, you say, "Oh, I got you. That was close." [To Sheryl, who was nearby but not in the group] O.K., now we're done.

11   SHERYL (WALKING OVER TO GROUP): Do you all have ideas about what to say and when?

12   CRISTY: I don't say anything!

13   RYAN AND LEWIS: Yes.

When the audience had assembled, Nick introduced the story by narrating Homer's first line. Lewis repeated the line, and then the actors took over. Ryan and Lewis said their lines as scripted, until Ryan gave in to Lewis's demands, "O.K., I'll go play with Maggie" and then improvised, "Maggie, where are you?" Cristy crawled across the stage and picked up the shoebox that had been designated as the lamp. As she held the lamp over her head, Ryan yelled, "Oh, no, Maggie. Don't drop the lamp!" Cristy released the lamp and Ryan dived to catch it but missed. He immediately improvised, "Oh, I missed it! Dad's gonna kill me." As she backed away from him, Ryan held the box out to Cristy and begged, "You've gotta glue it together." In role as a child too young to speak, Cristy shook her head and pointed to him. He replied, "Why me?," but when she kept shaking her head, he resigned himself to the task, "O.K., where's the glue?" When she shrugged, he pointed at her and accused, "Maggie, did you eat the glue again?" This time she smiled and nodded. Ryan replied, "Oh, yuck!"

As laughter from the audience quieted, the action stopped at this point, and Sheryl asked if they were finished. When Nick said he could not go on because Ryan missed the lamp, Sheryl asked if he wanted the actors do that part again. Nick did. Several audience members protested that the story was funnier the way it was first dramatized, and Sheryl promised that the class would talk about both versions later. She cautioned Cristy to drop the box so Ryan could catch it, and the scene began again. This time Ryan caught the lamp and improvised, "Dad, Maggie dropped the lamp." Lewis entered and scolded Cristy, "Bah, humbug! Now go to your room." Ryan then bragged to Lewis, "But I catched it, Dad. I catched it. How much money is it worth?" Lewis turned the lamp over in his hands, put it on the table, and answered, "Nine hundred dollars." "Oooo!" sighed Ryan. As Ryan and Lewis talked, Cristy sneaked out of her room, crawled over to the lamp, and knocked it off the table. While laughter rang from the audience, Sheryl nodded to Nick, "They changed it on you again, didn't they? Well, let's talk about the story."

The children formed a circle on the floor and began to tell Nick what they liked about his piece. Although they did not build as directly on each other's ideas as they later would learn to do, their comments and suggestions illustrate their evolving notions of effective plot development, humor, and character development.

01 LYLE: I liked when Maggie knocked over the lamp after Bart catched it.

02 ANDREW: I thought it was great when Maggie knocked over the lamp, but Bart didn't catch it.

03   CARRIE: I liked it when Bart said, "I catched it, Dad. I catched it!" That was funny.

04   KAREN: I liked that part and then where Bart asked how much money the lamp cost and Homer said, "Nine hundred dollars."

05   ANTHONY: I liked the first time when Ryan missed it and he said, "Oh, no! I missed the lamp!" That was funny.

06   ANGELA: I liked that part too, and I liked the second story. That was a good one. I liked when Homer said, "Bah, humbug! Go to your room!"

07   CRISTY: I thought it was funny when Ryan asked if I ate the glue.

08   SHERYL: I thought that was funny, too. O.K., suggestions?

09   KYLE: I think Maggie should burp when Bart asks her if she ate the glue.

10   ANDREW: Nick should keep the part about where Homer and Bart are talking about the lamp after Bart catches it and Maggie crawls up and knocks it off the table.

11   CARRIE: He should keep the part where Bart asks Maggie if she ate the glue.

12   CRISTY: I just thought of something. After he asks me if I ate the glue, I should nod my head and he should say, "Open up; let's see," and my mouth should be stuck shut.

When there were no more suggestions, Sheryl moved from her place in the circle to the overhead projector. She titled a blank transparency "Bart vs. Maggie" and asked what notes she should make about the discussion for Nick. As children repeated the main ideas, she reminded them that she was not writing in full sentences but just taking notes. She wrote:

Bart & Homer talking about lamp. Maggie crawls up and taps lamp off table.
Bart asks Maggie if she ate glue.
Maggie nods head about glue then burps.
Mouth stuck shut.
Maggie knocks lamp off. Bart misses.
Maggie knocks lamp off. Bart catches.

As she made the last notations, Sheryl said to Nick, "You'll have to decide which way you want the story to go. Did you like it when Bart missed the lamp or when he caught it better?" Nick responded, "I like when he missed it. That was funny."

After careful consideration, Nick decided to incorporate only a few of his classmates' suggestions into his revision. Although he was selective about the changes he made, the influence of the dramatization of his story on his revision is immediately apparent. He omitted the last line of dialogue so that the plot could change. (Children's stories have been reproduced with conventional spelling and punctuation as a courtesy to the reader; any revisions in their usage were not considered attributable to the drama strategy. Text added to or substituted for the original is underlined; omitted text is included in brackets.) Here is his revision:

Bart vs. Maggie

"Bart!"
"What, Dad?"
"Go play with Maggie."
"No!"
"Yes!"
"No!"
"Yes!"
"O.K., I'll go play with Maggie."
"Gosh, Maggie is in trouble. I better go help her. Oh, no! She's going to drop the lamp. Mom and Dad will be mad at me. I will get in big trouble."
"Wait, Maggie! I'm coming to save you. I'm running as fast as I can. [I got you! That was close!] I missed the lamp!"
"Bart, what was that?"
"The lamp."
"Go to your room now! If you don't do it, you will get in horrible trouble."
"O.K."
The end.

Sheryl's usual practice after hearing a revision was to ask the author what changes he or she made and what factors influenced his or her decisions. Among the factors mentioned were thinking about the drama, remembering suggestions or questions that arose during the discussion, referring to the summary notes written at the end of the discussion, talking to a friend or family member, and just thinking of an idea oneself. Nick said he added parts he liked from the dramatization of his story, and he explained that he decided not to include the part about the glue that his classmates thought was funny, "because," as he said, "this way is more real."

Nick's revision decisions were well reasoned. Although authors were asked to explain their choices, decisions of whether and how to revise were unquestionably their own. The purpose of the dramatization-discussion strategy, to help children collaborate in examining a story's potential, had been fulfilled.

KAREN'S CONSIDERATIONS: THE INFLUENCE OF PREVIOUSLY DRAMATIZED STORIES ON AN AUTHOR'S WORK

Karen's story, dramatized in late May, illustrates the powerful influence of previously dramatized stories on subsequent pieces. Karen's work is based on an idea originally developed by Cristy and later modified by Gina and Joan (Knipping, 1993). Cristy's piece, "The Magic Kite," dramatized in late November, was the first of several stories Karen's classmates wrote about troublesome magical objects. Gina's story, "The Runaway Shoes," added a foreshadowing of trouble that appeared in many subsequent stories: the sales clerk asked the protagonist if she were sure she wanted the item she was about to buy, and the child was resolute. Karen also drew from a story written by Stephen about a fight between a cat and a dog. The story ends as the dog ruminates about the cat, "My best enemy. Or is it my worst enemy?" Here is Karen's story:

The Alive Doll

Once there was a girl named Cristy and she loved dolls. Well, one day she was watching TV and she saw a commercial for a doll that talked.
"Oh, Mom, I have to have that doll."
"Well," said the mother, it costs a lot of money."
"Please!" said Cristy.
"O.K.," said the mom, but you have to do some chores, so go rake the leaves. Tomorrow we'll go buy the doll."
So the next day they bought the doll. The salesperson said, "Are you sure you want this?"
"Yes," said Cristy.
O.K.," said the clerk and then he told the mom it was twenty-four dollars.
"What?!" said her mother.
"Prices are prices," said the clerk.
So when they got home she opened the doll and tried it, but it would not work. "Let's go back to the store." So they did.
"The doll's not working," said her mom.
"Well, use some batteries!"
So they did, but it did not work. "Bummer," she said.
So her mom said, "We'll have to buy a regular doll." So they did.
When she got home, she called her friends Gina and Kristen.
So when they got there they said, "Why did you invite us over?"
"Because I got a new doll."
"Oh," they said.
"So, I'll go get it," Cristy said.
"Wow," they said. "What is her name?"
"I'll answer that," said the doll. All the girls screamed.
"I thought it was a regular doll," said Kristen. "I mean, really. I think you played a joke."
"No, I did not!" said Cristy.
"Will you listen to me?" said the doll.
"No!" they said. So they took the doll, wrapped it up, and gave it to their best enemy.

Th e
n
d

Immediately after Karen read the last line, she thought aloud, "Maybe I'll make it their worst enemy." Stephen smiled as hands went up to volunteer for roles. Karen had asked her friends' permission to use their names in her story, and she chose Cristy, Kristen, and Gina to play their namesakes. As usual, Sheryl asked who had not had a turn in the most recently dramatized story, Karen chose the remaining actors from those volunteers, and the cast gathered to plan their action. By this time in the year, the children built more readily on each others' ideas than they had in October. Ryan focused initial consideration on how past groups had efficiently organized the planning procedure, and then he quickly raised another organizational question. With that settled, Karen moved to the plot, and Carrie called her attention to a logical gap in the story resulting from omitted information.

01   RYAN: Do the little parts first, O.K.?

02   KAREN: O.K., Carrie [doll], you have a little part. You're a really mouthy doll. You say [speaking in a haughty voice], "I'll answer that!"

03   RYAN: But what about the first doll? Who will be that doll?

04   KAREN: Oh, yeah! Well, Carrie can be that too.

05   CRISTY: Yeah, Carrie can be both dolls, since she has a little part.

06   KAREN (TO CARRIE): When you're the first doll, you just don't work and then you fall apart.

07   CARRIE: Oh, you didn't say that in the story. I fall all apart?

08   KAREN: Yeah.

The children then drew on their life experiences as they considered the humor and believability of proposed dialogue and voice inflection.

09   GINA: What do me [friend] and Kristen [friend] do?

10   KAREN: O.K., when you ring the doorbell, you say [with her arms crossed, and in an accusing tone], "Why did you invite us over?"

11   KRISTEN: But she's her best friend. She wouldn't be mean to her.

12   GINA: I'll say it nicer, "Why did you invite me over? I was right in the middle of my favorite T.V. show."

13   KAREN: Yeah! Do that!

14   CRISTY: Or, "Why did you invite us over—to watch our favorite T.V. show?

15   GINA: Or Kristen could say [in a neutral voice], "Why did you invite us over?" And I'll say [in a hopeful voice], "To watch our favorite T.V. show?"

16   KRISTEN: I'll say, "Why did you invite us over?" And you say,

"Probably to watch my favorite T.V. show, because I was right in the middle of it."

17 GINA: Yeah.

. . .

22 KAREN: Ryan (clerk), do you know what to do?

23 RYAN: Let's make sure. When they say they want to buy the doll, I ask the girl, "Are you sure you want this?" She says yes; then I say (in a slow, silly voice) "Well, the price is twenty-four dollars."

24 KAREN: O.K., but don't talk like that, O.K.?

25 CRISTY: Talk like you did when you were the doctor in Gina's story.

26 RYAN: O.K., I'll be more serious. Then I'll tell them they need batteries.

As the children finished reviewing Ryan's part and took up Cristy's, they considered stage directions and continued to carefully match improvised dialogue to the action scripted or implied.

31 KAREN: But they go home before that, so you leave real quick.

32 RYAN: O.K., exit stage right!

33 KAREN: O.K., Jessica (mother), when Cristy asks for the doll, you say it's a lot of money.

34 JESSICA: I'll say "probably," because I wasn't watching the commercial.

35 KAREN: Then you finally say "O.K., but you have to do some chores first."

36 JESSICA: O.K., I'll think of what else to say.

37 KAREN: And Cristy (girl), you have to ask Jessica if you can have some friends over.

38 JESSICA: And I'll say, "I guess so." And then I'll go take a nap.

39 CRISTY: Or a shower.

40 KAREN (TO CRISTY): Do you know the rest?

41 CRISTY: Yeah!

As Karen read her story during the dramatization, the cast improvised in several ways, some of which were discussed in the planning session. The first one occurred after Cristy asked her mother for the doll. Jessica said, "Well, it probably costs a lot of money." Cristy replied, "I know, but Mom, I really want that doll!" Jessica then asked, "What are you going to do with it?" Cristy mused, "I don't know; I'll take real good care of it and add it to my collection."

The next improvisation came when Ryan asked if Cristy was sure she wanted the doll. "Yes, of course I do!" answered Cristy, "She's cool." Ryan quoted the price and answered the mother's surprise with a firm, "Prices are prices," as scripted. Cristy then added, "Yeah, Mom, prices are prices!"

When she could not get the doll to talk, Cristy threw up her hands and said to Jessica, "Mom, this dumb doll won't work!" Both Jessica and Cristy tried several imaginary knobs on Carrie's back before Jessica announced, "Well, we'll have to take it back to the store." As the three girls walked across the stage, Ryan came out to meet them. "You have to use batteries," he said. Sheryl reminded him to let the girls tell him what was wrong first. Cristy said softly, "Sir, this doll doesn't work." Ryan asked, "Have you put in batteries?" Cristy shook her head, and Ryan added, "You need two batteries, size A." Cristy repeated, "O.K., size A."

The trio went home and put batteries in Carrie's back, but when she still would not work, Jessica began to shake Carrie by the shoulders. Cristy improvised, "Oh, no! Everything's falling apart. This doll is ruined. I think we better throw it in the trash." Jessica replied, "I'm sorry, Dear. I guess we'll just have to buy a regular doll." Cristy protested, "But, Mom," and Jessica became cross, "Well, the other dolls like this probably work the same way!"

When they went back to the store, Cristy said to the clerk, "I'd like this doll now." Ryan quoted the price, "It's ten dollars," and Jessica said brightly, "Oh, that's cheaper than last time." At home, Cristy asked Jessica, "Can I call Gina and Kristen to come over and see my new doll?" Jessica replied, "I guess so. I'm going to take a nap." Cristy called each friend in turn and asked if she could come over and play. Gina said, "Sure," and Kristen answered, "I'll be right over." When the doorbell rang, Cristy greeted both girls with, "Hi!" Gina immediately asked, "Why did you invite us over now? I was right in the middle of my favorite T.V. show." Cristy said, "Sorry. I want you to see my new doll. I'll go get it." As she left, Kristen said to Gina, "It's probably really neat." Cristy came back holding Carrie by the shoulders as they walked. "Here she is," Cristy smiled. Kristen cooed, "Wow! That's cool," and Gina asked, "What does she do?" Cristy answered curtly, "She's just a regular doll." "Well, I didn't know," pouted Gina, "What's her name?"

At Carrie's, "I'll answer that!" all the girls screamed. Jessica called from off stage, "Stop screaming. You're too noisy!" Cristy apologized, "Sorry, Mom." Gina asked, "Is this some kind of a joke?" and Kristen added, "Yeah, I thought it was a regular doll." Cristy defended herself, "I didn't know she could talk." Carrie then cried, "Why won't you listen to me?" Kristen urged, "Put her back in the box!" As the girls spun Carrie around, pretending to wrap her up, Carrie protested loudly, "Don't do that! Hey, stop it!" Karen then read, "They wrapped her up and put her in the mail to their best, or is it their worst, enemy," over Carrie's shouts, "Let me go! Let me go!"

During the discussion, Karen's classmates proposed a new twist for the ending and commented about character development. At Sheryl's initiation, the group also considered the authenticity of the plot. In fulfilling her role as a group member, Sheryl was careful to explain the criteria on which she was basing her opinions, and she posed her ideas as tentative possibilities. By this time in the year, the children were much more comfortable in talking directly to one another rather than to Sheryl and in collaborating to develop ideas than they were in October.

01 ANDREW: Did you get the idea from Chuckie [character in the movie *Child's Play*]?

02 CARRIE: She probably hasn't even watched that movie.

03 KAREN: I know that's a horror movie, and I didn't get my idea from there! I got it from all the stories about alive things: Gina's "Runaway Shoes," Cristy's "Magic Kite," Joan's "Magic P.J.'s." I just thought, though, that I should change the title so I don't tell the surprise at the end.

04 SHERYL: Do you have an idea for a new title?

05 KAREN: I think just "Cristy's Doll."

06 CRISTY: I think you could add that the enemies bring her back to my house and she says, "I'm back!"

07 SHERYL: That would be like a horror story. Do you want to make it scary? [Karen shook her head.] Personally, I liked the way you ended. It finished what had been happening in an interesting way.

08 RYAN: At the end, the mailman could deliver the doll back to Cristy from the enemies. It could just be annoying, not scary.

09 KAREN: I think I might do something like that or maybe do a new story about that.

. . .

14 JANIE: I liked when Carrie screamed and kicked and didn't want to be wrapped up.

15 JOAN: I liked the part when Ryan said, "A price is a price."

16 CARRIE: I liked that part and then when Cristy added, "Yeah, Mom, prices are prices."

17 NICK: When they throw away the doll that didn't work, Cristy could say, "There goes twenty-four dollars!"

18 SHERYL: In real life, what else might they do with a doll that didn't work?

19 NICK: Take it back.

20 SCOTT: Yeah, my mom would make them take it back or give her money back.

21 CRISTY: They might recycle the good parts and throw the rest away.

22 MARY: Like what?

23 KAREN: I've been thinking about that part. I meant to put in the story that when they tried to put the batteries in, the whole doll falls apart.

24 RYAN: Ooh, yeah, the arms and legs.

25 KAREN: Yeah, the arms and legs and hair and everything. Then they take it back, and the sales clerk says, "I don't want that broken doll!"

26 CRISTY: If it's all torn up, and all the parts and wires are on the floor, how will they take it back to exchange it for another doll?

27 SHERYL: In some stores, the clerk might say, "Surely you can't expect me to exchange a doll you tore up."

28 BOB: You could take it back to [local store].

29 SHERYL: Yes, if you have a receipt, [local store] will take back anything.

30 KAREN: I'm going to add that the store won't take it back.

31 CRISTY: I don't think the friends would wrap up a friend's doll.

32 KAREN: They thought it was a joke or maybe they were a little spooked.

33 MARY: You said the girl did a lot of chores, didn't you? What did she do?

34 KAREN: It was fall and they have a big yard, so she had to rake a lot of leaves.

35 SHERYL: Anything else? Karen, did the drama give you any ideas?

36 KAREN: I liked when the doll was real mouthy. I might add more for her, and I'm going to put in the part about the doll falling apart. I think I'll write a new story about what happens next, but I'm not going to tell that now.

Karen's revision incorporated improvisations added during the drama and ideas suggested during the discussion, including her own realization that the title should be changed. She decided not to add more dialogue for the doll in the revision but to include more lines for her in the sequel, "Chapter 2," which she had begun writing. Karen said she was more excited about working on this new chapter, which opened with the delivery of a doll-sized package for Cristy, than she was in revising the first chapter. We found this practice of incorporating ideas from the drama and discussion into new stories, rather than working them into existing drafts, common among Sheryl's students. Here is Karen's revision:

[The Alive] Cristy's Doll

Once there was a girl named Cristy and she loved dolls. Well, one day she was watching T.V. and she saw a commercial for a doll that talked.

"Oh, Mom, I have to have that doll."

"Well, I don't know," said the mother, it probably costs a lot of money."

"Please!" said Cristy. "I promise I'll keep it with my collection."

"O.K.," said the mom, but you have to do some chores, so go rake the leaves." [Tomorrow we'll go buy the doll.] <u>So she did. Since it was fall, raking the leaves was a very big job.</u>

So the next day they <u>went to buy</u> the doll. <u>And when they did,</u> the salesperson said, "Are you sure you want this?"

"Yes, <u>of course I do,</u>" said Cristy.

"O.K.," said the clerk. "That will be twenty-four dollars."

"What?!" said Cristy's mother.

"Prices are prices," said the clerk.

<u>Cristy smiled at her mom and said, "Yeah, Mom, prices are prices."</u>

So when they got home she [opened the doll and] tried <u>and tried to make the doll talk</u>, but it would not work.

<u>"Mom," said Cristy, "this stupid doll does not work."</u>

["Let's go back to the store." So they did.] <u>So they went back to the store.</u>

"The doll's not working," said her mom.

"Well, [use] <u>you need two</u> batteries!" <u>said the clerk. "Size A."</u>

So they <u>got batteries</u>, but [it did not work] <u>the whole doll fell apart when they put in the batteries. So when they went back to the store, they asked the clerk if he would take it back and he said, "No way! You broke it!"</u>

"Bummer," [she] said <u>Cristy.</u>

So her mom said, "We'll have to buy a regular doll." So they did.

When she got home, she called her friends Gina and Kristen.

So when [they got there they] <u>Gina came, she</u> said, "Why did you invite us over? <u>I was right in the middle of my favorite T.V. show.</u>"

"<u>Oh sorry,</u>" said Cristy, "I got a new doll <u>I want you to see.</u>"

["Oh," they said. "So,]

I'll go get it," Cristy said.

"Wow," they said. <u>Gina asked,</u> "What's her name?"

"I'll answer that," said the doll. All the girls screamed.

"I thought it was a regular doll," said Kristen. ["I mean, really. I think you played] "<u>What</u> a joke!"

["No, I did not!" said Cristy.]

"Will you listen to me?" said the doll.

"No!" they said. So they took the doll, wrapped it up, and <u>sent</u> it to their best, <u>no, their worst</u> enemy.

Th e
n
d

OPPORTUNITIES FOR EXPLORATION

The dramatization and discussion of Nick's and Karen's stories provide examples of the various ways in which Sheryl's students use dramatic talk to explore writing. The strategy provides young thinkers opportunities to "work on understanding" as they use language to interpret and reshape developing notions. Improvisational drama, closely related to the familiar dramatic play of early childhood (Wagner, 1990), encourages Sheryl's students to "play out" their ideas quite literally. When interviewed at the end of the year about the strategy, the children commented that this process helps them think about the stories (Knipping, 1993). As Vygotsky (1978) reminds us, what children first do most easily through action and speech, they later do internally as thought.

Through the processes of planning the drama, dramatizing the story, and then discussing the dramatization, Sheryl's students have many opportunities to consider a story carefully. As they work, they use language to extend thinking in three ways: "by providing a new idea, question, or observation; by providing cognitive conflict; and by providing collaborative assistance . . . or support" (Lindfors, 1987, p. 274).

Planning sessions give rise to new ideas, such as Cristy's suggestion that Maggie intentionally knock the lamp off the table after Bart saved it. Actors' questions and comments about their roles, such as Carrie's observation that Karen had omitted necessary information about what happened to the first doll, provide opportunities to clarify confusing plot lines and unclear descriptions.

Both Nick's and Karen's stories demonstrate how the actual dramatizations provide a context for collaboration as actors inject humor, elucidate character, and clarify or redirect plot. Audience members pay rapt attention, and their responses are duly noted by author and actors alike.

Group discussions following the drama give the children an opportunity to reflect on their work and to bring their responses to a conscious level. As the children comment on what they like about a story and give suggestions for improvement, they develop an evolving, collective, concept of story. The discussion of Nick's story illustrates the children's early considerations of humor, character definition, and plot development. By May, their discussion of Karen's story demonstrates additional considerations: sources of ideas for the story, the amount of information to include in the title, the mood of the piece, and the believability of characters' actions.

CYCLES OF MEANING

The children's consideration and reconsideration of ideas as they planned, dramatized, and discussed Nick's and Karen's stories demonstrate the cycles of meaning that developed among Sheryl's students. Whether or not they choose to include those ideas in revisions of their work, authors have the benefit of their classmates' and teacher's collaborative thinking about their stories. The time taken to work through the strategy does not benefit the author alone, however. Figure 9.1 illustrates opportunities the strategy provides for all of Sheryl's students to construct new meanings about good writing and to return to those ideas to reconstruct and extend them. The outer oval depicts the steps in the drama-discussion strategy, and the inner arrows denote opportunities each step offers for considering revision of the current piece and for conceptualizing a new story.

The cycles of meaning that develop over time as the children use interpretations from previously dramatized stories to write, dramatize, and discuss new pieces illustrate the concept of "intertextuality" (Short, 1986), or "the process of interpreting one text by means of a previously composed text" (Cairney, 1992, p. 502). The children's work with Karen's story abounds with examples of such intertextual ties. As Karen explained, the idea for her story came from three previously dramatized stories about "alive things" written by classmates, and her original working draft contained ideas from their pieces (the trouble caused by a magical object and the foreshadowing of that trouble by a sales clerk). Other ties became evident as the children worked through the strategy. In the planning session, Cristy encouraged Ryan to talk as he had when he played the doctor in Gina's story. During the dramatization, when Ryan asked Cristy if she was sure she wanted the doll, Cristy responded with the reply common in other stories, "Of course I do," in addition to the scripted, "Yes." Finally, all of the ideas considered in the discussion of Karen's story had roots in previous discussions. As described earlier, the children's collective concept of story had been evolving throughout the year.

Karen's use of intertextual ties is not unique. Often, the ties from a new piece to a previous story are clear, as in the language Karen borrowed from

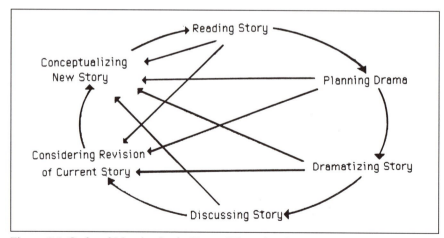

Figure 9.1 *Cycles of Meaning in the Drama-Discussion Strategy*

Stephen, "their best, no their worst enemy." Other times, a more general concept is reflected, such as Karen's notion that "mouthy" characters are appealing. As Sheryl saw how her students included ideas from the dramatization and discussion of previous works in their new stories, she became convinced of the value of the strategy even for those children who do not choose to revise their drafts. Dramatizing and discussing peers' stories provide a rich context for all of Sheryl's students to reconsider and reorganize their ideas about writing, which is what learning to become a better writer entails.

REFERENCES

Barnes, D. 1992. *From communication to curriculum.* 2nd ed. Portsmouth, NH: Boynton/ Cook.

———. 1990. "Oral language and learning." In *Perspectives on talk and learning,* edited by S. Hynds & D. Rubin. Urbana, IL: National Council of Teachers of English.

Cairney, T. H. 1992. "Fostering and building students' intertextual histories." *Language Arts* 69:502–507.

Graves, D. 1983. *Writing: Teachers and children at work.* Portsmouth, N.H.: Heinemann.

Knipping, N. Y. 1993. "Let drama help young authors "re-see" their stories." *Language Arts* 70:41–46.

———. 1991. "Developing civic discourse: A 2nd-grade example." *Childhood Education* 68:14–17.

———. 1989. "The value of drama in the composing processes of young children." In *National Reading and Language Arts Educators' Yearbook,* edited by S. Hoffman. Kansas City, MO: National Reading and Language Arts Educators. 135–57.

Lindfors, J. 1987. *Children's language and learning.* 2nd ed. Englewood Cliffs, NJ: Prentice-Hall.

Short, K. G. 1986. "Literacy as a collaborative experience: The role of intertextuality." In *Solving problems in literacy: Learners, teachers, and researchers,* edited by J. Niles & R. Lalik. Thirty-fifth Yearbook of the National Reading Conference. Rochester, N.Y.: National Reading Conference.

Vygotsky, L. S. 1978. *Mind in society.* Cambridge, MA: Harvard University Press.

Wagner, B. J. 1990. "Dramatic improvisation in the classroom." In *Perspectives on talk and learning,* edited by S. Hynds & L. Rubin. Urbana, IL: National Council of Teachers of English.

M. Ruth Davenport has just completed her doctorate in reading education with Dr. Dorothy Watson at the University of Missouri-Columbia. In addition to teaching undergraduate classes on integrated curriculum and content-area reading, she supervises student teachers and instructs the reading clinicians at the UMC Child Study Clinic in miscue analysis. When she's not on campus, you'll find her at her piano studio learning a new Mozart Sonata or teaching "whole music" to over twenty young children.

Chapter 10
Reflecting Through Talk on Content-Area Reading

M. RUTH DAVENPORT

Twenty five sixth-graders sit in a circle on the floor of their classroom. Their teacher, Susan McClintic, passes out a short article on Saturn for them to read, and what follows is an exciting journey into the minds and thought processes of these reflective readers. Engaging in *metacognitive inquiry*, the group proceeds to discuss the article, explore their reading and thinking strategies, and discover connections to their background knowledge. They share stories, have conversations about their personal experiences, and become immersed in dialogue through which they gain a deeper understanding of related scientific information.

When faced with unfamiliar words, students offer each other possible options, such as: ask someone else; call my Aunt; throw the paper away; look it up in a thesaurus, dictionary, or encyclopedia; read on and try to use context clues; or try to see little words in a big word. They agree that they don't need to know the meaning or pronunciation of every word, especially when faced with difficult words. One student encountering the word "phenakistoscope" decides, "I didn't want to be stuck on that word forever and I knew it was some kind of scope, I thought of "telescope," so it has to do with sight, it's not important to know how to say it right, I'll read on . . . Oh! It tells what it does!"

Another student decides that even though she doesn't know the word "Hubble" she does know "Bubble," and since the two words look alike, she'll just replace the "B" with an "H." She reads further and finds out that the passage describes a telescope in space and that it is "high above Earth's murky blanket of air." An in-depth discussion follows about the advantages of space-based telescopes, the flaws in the mirrors, the scientific implications, as well as the students' speculations on the effects of the loss of the ozone layer and what it's like above the clouds. These students sustain a lively, hour-long discussion on this brief text, making connections to what others have said, reflecting on their background knowledge, and actively constructing meaning through metacognitive inquiry.

At the beginning of the school year, Susan introduced metacognitive inquiry to the whole class by demonstrating her own thinking while reading aloud. Over the next two weeks, she invited students to participate in the strategy several times as a group. The class then collaborated on making a list of the reading and studying strategies they had noticed they use. Throughout the year, Susan and her students referred frequently to this list, added to it, and continued to discuss their reading and learning processes in all the content areas on an informal, in-context basis. For example, when students engaged in partner reading, they suggested strategies to each other when they were having difficulty with a word or concept. Susan also asked students what strategies they had already tried before making suggestions for a different approach to a learning task, math problem, or unfamiliar word.

At the end of the year, each student in Susan's class selected a country to study and used a variety of encyclopedias and tradebooks as resources for the report. Students selected one of these texts to read, and Susan and I recorded conversations with six of her students while we engaged in metacognitive inquiry. What we learned from these sessions is that talk during metacognitive inquiry provides a valuable means of helping learners understand difficult content-area text.

WHAT IS METACOGNITIVE INQUIRY?

Metacognitive inquiry is a conversation between a teacher and student, or among several students, during which the reader is assisted in actively constructing meaning by talking about the process of thinking and understanding a text. After reading a brief passage, readers stop and talk with the teacher or a peer about their thinking. They discuss their comprehension of concepts and vocabulary, make connections with their own lives, or ask questions. The inquiry procedure for both individuals and small groups involves asking frequent, open-ended questions that invite students to explore their thinking processes, their understanding of the content, and their knowledge and use of reading or studying strategies.

During metacognitive inquiry, the teacher and students talk about their thought processes and their ways of making sense of the text. As Barnes and Todd (1977) stated, this type of collaborative talk "must lead to [the] construction of new ways of understanding" (p. 50). In content-area reading metacognitive inquiry is particularly helpful, since it offers students a way to monitor their comprehension, regulate their use of strategies, attend to and use text features to aid understanding, pose questions, make personal connections, and identify and resolve misconceptions. By engaging in talk during metacognitive inquiry, students take control of their own reading process. They begin to see reading as an active transaction with the text.

HOW IS METACOGNITIVE INQUIRY CONDUCTED?

When students are first introduced to metacognitive inquiry, it is helpful for the teacher to demonstrate what goes on in the mind of a proficient reader by thinking aloud as she reads (Davey, 1983). As adults, we take for granted or are unaware of how actively we construct meaning when we read. By thinking aloud as they read, teachers show students how to sample text features such as headings, pictures or graphs; make predictions; deal with unfamiliar words and concepts; reread to clarify meaning; notice and correct miscues or deviations from the text; and think through misunderstandings. Teachers can show how they form hypotheses about what the text might mean, organize information through mental images, call on prior knowledge and experiences, monitor their comprehension, and attend to comprehension problems.

The introductory think-aloud is best accomplished by selecting a passage that "contains points of difficulty, contradictions, ambiguities, or unknown words" (Davey, 1983, p. 45). The passage is shown on an overhead transparency, and as the teacher reads the passage aloud, students follow along silently.

In one think-aloud, for example, I demonstrated my thinking for Susan's students as I read an article from *Science News* (Hoppe, 1992) about a space shuttle mission. I stopped after reading the title and then after brief sections of each sentence in order to tell the students what I was thinking:

"Shuttle Mission Yields Surprising Results": Well, this makes me think of the last shuttle mission when they were in space for the longest time ever. I wonder if that's this one. I'm also wondering, what were the results, and why were they surprising?

"Biologists may have to rethink traditional theories about how the human body functions . . .": Well, I'm thinking about all the human biology classes I had in high school and college. What do we have to rethink?

". . . in light of new results from experiments conducted on shuttle astronauts . . .": I love that expression "in light of." It makes me think of shining a light on something in a dark room. It really makes it stand out. So these results are really standing out, are important somehow. I wonder about conducting the experiments on the astronauts themselves. I always think of planting tomato seeds in space or trying to make perfect ball bearings, not experiments on the people themselves.

". . . during last June's Spacelab Life Sciences-1 Mission, scientists announced last week."

Oh, it *was* the mission I was thinking about, the really long one. I wonder what "Spacelab Life Sciences-1" means. Maybe it's the name of a special set of missions to see what happens to people in space.

Following a think-aloud, the teacher then engages a student, a small group, or the entire class in metacognitive inquiry by asking them to read a short passage from a textbook or tradebook either orally or silently. According to Palincsar and Ransom (1988), students need ample practice with daily school tasks using a variety of reading material following think-aloud demonstrations "if the strategies are to come under the ownership of the learner" (p. 788).

Having the students read two or three sentences before they stop is optimal, particularly during their first few experiences with metacognitive inquiry. The most common opening question after students have read a short passage is, "Tell me what you're thinking right now." Further questions follow the students' "train of thought" as they talk about their understanding of the text, and are intended to elicit clarification ("What do you mean by that?") or further discussion ("Tell me more about that"). The teacher also helps readers discuss sources of knowledge ("How did you know that?"), understand why certain strategies are appropriate ("Why do you think you did that?"), identify reading strategies ("What did you try there?"), attend to miscues ("Did you notice what you said here?"), or clarify misconceptions ("Do you know what that means?").

These actions help readers use talk to bring their reading and learning processes to the conscious level and thereby gain a better understanding of the passage. The intent of the questions is to help readers follow their hunches and intuitions as they approach understanding. Barnes (1991) identified this type of talking as "exploratory talk" and stated, "How can we expect children to arrive [at understanding] if we don't allow them the journey [through talk]?"

During metacognitive inquiry, the teacher also helps students identify the points they consider important in the passage and assess their own comprehension. The teacher frequently asks students to clarify their meaning ("I'm not sure I follow your thinking there") or restates what a reader has said ("So you think it's confusing that the names of the countries are so similar?"). At times, direct teaching takes place, particularly if a student has tried a variety of strategies and still does not understand the passage. The teacher can suggest strategies for students to try if they've run out of possibilities or explain difficult words or concepts.

WHAT ARE THE PURPOSES OF METACOGNITIVE INQUIRY?

Most important, metacognitive inquiry helps students use talk as a way of making sense of what they are reading. The strategy helps students take the language of tradebooks and content-area textbooks and make it their own, thereby assisting them in gaining meaning. By talking about the content, students become more comfortable with vocabulary and concepts and incorporate the texts' language into their discussion. As Lemke (1989) stated, in order to comprehend text, "we need to be able to paraphrase it, restate it in our own words, and translate its meaning into the more comfortable patterns of spoken language" (p. 136).

Content-area texts are often difficult to understand because they are dense with new words and unfamiliar concepts. To aid in their comprehension, students can use metacognitive inquiry to relate stories about their own experiences, carry on conversations about related topics of interest, and collaboratively engage in stimulating dialogue to arrive at a deeper understanding. When students think through and talk about content-area reading strategies, they improve their reading and comprehension of expository text. Students also learn about themselves as readers and learners and about the active nature of the reading and learning processes. By recognizing the characteristics of their thinking processes, they become empowered to regulate their use of various strategies. Students become more adept at using the most appropriate strategy in a given situation. The following list summarizes other purposes of the metacognitive inquiry procedure that can assist students in becoming more proficient readers.

Purposes of the Metacognitive Inquiry Procedure

- Use talk to make sense of what you're reading.
- Take textbook language and make it your own.
- Become aware of the active nature of the reading process.
- Observe yourself as a reader.
- Notice how well you're understanding what you read.
- Attend to and correct miscues.
- Become aware of yourself as a learner and your learning process.

- Clarify misconceptions.
- Call on relevant background knowledge and experiences.
- Set purposes for reading.
- Use text structure and text features to aid comprehension.
- Help teachers assess students' understanding.

The following examples of students' talk demonstrate some of these purposes of metacognitive inquiry. They are taken from conversations conducted with six of Susan's students while they were reading content-area tradebooks. The first example illustrates one purpose of metacognitive inquiry, to help students gain a better understanding of what they are reading through talk.

Kevin had selected a text on ancient Egypt and was having difficulty with a long sentence about a funeral procession. The sentence had several concepts that were hard for him to understand. By discussing brief segments of the sentence, he was able to clarify his understanding of unfamiliar words and concepts. According to Lemke (1989), we need to help students become active in thinking through what they read and thereby construct meaning by making "the text talk in [the students'] own voices, not by reading it, but by elaborating on it themselves, building on it in their own words, and making its words their own" (p. 138), as Kevin did here:

01   TEACHER: What do you think about that, did that make sense to you?

02   KEVIN: No.

03   TEACHER: What could we do to figure that out?

04   KEVIN: Keep rereading it.

05   TEACHER: O.K., let's take a section of it at a time and reread it—let's take this first part.

06   KEVIN: "Upon arrival at the tombsite . . ."

07   TEACHER: O.K., what does that mean?

08   KEVIN: That means they arrived.

09   TEACHER: When they got there, O.K., and when they got to where?

10   KEVIN: Tombsite.

11   TEACHER: Do you know what that is?

12   KEVIN: Yeah.

13   TEACHER: O.K., all right.

14   KEVIN: ". . . the footsore procession was more than ready to rest . . ."

15   TEACHER: O.K., is this giving you a problem right there?

16   KEVIN: Kinda.

17   TEACHER: What do you think this means?

18   KEVIN: Footsore, I don't know.

19   TEACHER: What two words make up that word?

20   KEVIN: "Foot" and "sore."

21   TEACHER: So what do you think?

22   KEVIN: Your foot's sore.

The discussion continued until Kevin understood the meaning of "procession" and "funerary banquet." By using information from earlier in the text, applying the rereading strategy, calling on his background knowledge, and analyzing word structure, Kevin was able to talk his way to understanding. His voice rose in intonation and his expression became bright and excited when he realized he knew the meaning of the entire passage.

Another purpose of the metacognitive inquiry procedure is to help students become aware of the active nature of the reading process. By observing their own thinking and how they use a variety of strategies, they begin to develop the notion that the reader engages in an active transaction with text to construct meaning. In the following example, Kevin realized several things about his reading process: that reading should make sense, that he reads at different rates, that sometimes he doesn't comprehend, and that he actively questions the text:

> I was kinda slow because some of it didn't make sense and [when] I would get to one part that made sense, then I'd keep reading and I would forget it and I would have to go back over it. I was confused. I was like, "What did that say? Why did it say that?"

Kevin later shared with me that the metacognitive inquiry procedure helped him to discover:

> . . . a lot of things about my reading, rereading, using context clues, using parentheses, knowing what the paragraph's about, asking questions at the end. That helped me a lot, me asking myself questions. When you did that at the end of each one, I think that it's a habit now since you've been asking me. I usually do it now.

Kevin is taking on the responsibility of engaging with the text actively and independently, one of the important goals of the metacognitive inquiry procedure.

Still another purpose of metacognitive inquiry is to help students observe themselves as readers and assess how well they are understanding what they read. This strategy also helps students become aware of other strategies and when to use them. When reading about the German government, Alicia was aware that there were times when she was confused and that the text had helped her clear up her confusion in one instance by immediately providing a definition in parentheses. She also knew that the text had not helped her when she came to another unfamiliar word, "chancellor." In this case, she used a strategy she knew, continuing to read and attending to context clues, to figure out the meaning:

> "Chancellor," that kinda confused me until it explained what it was, 'cause up here it says, after "the commander," which means "leader of the army" and it has that in parentheses, and this didn't have it. So I was kinda confused. So I read on, and it says he "runs the Republic."

Another purpose of metacognitive inquiry is to help students attend to and correct their own miscues. In this example, Alicia knew she hadn't pronounced "crooked" correctly, but by questioning herself as she read and continuing to read for context clues, she was able to combine this information with her background knowledge, catch her miscue, and realize that she understood the meaning of the word:

23   TEACHER: O.K., what are you thinking?
24   ALICIA: When I got to "crooked" (pronounced as "crookt") or whatever, I was thinking, "Well, I've heard that before but, do I remember what it means?" and I'm like, "O.K.," and I was just thinking about some of the old streets that we have here and how the road had "crooks" in it and just a bunch of things, and then I got down to "cobblestones" and I'm like, "Oh, now I know what it is!"

Metacognitive inquiry can also help students become aware of themselves as learners and their learning process as they encounter new information. Through dialogue with their teacher or peers, students realize the active nature of the learning process as they call on prior knowledge to make sense of what they are reading. They often express surprise or interest when they discover something unexpected about their topic, as Cindi did in the following example. After reading about the religious civil war in Chad, Cindi compared what she knew about religious freedom in the United States with the information in the passage:

> Um, it's interesting to find out that in one country, between the north and the south they were fighting. They were fighting over religion, and mostly here religion is whatever *you* want.

Metacognitive inquiry can also help students clarify misconceptions. Through their discussions, students recognize when the text contradicts their current understanding of the information presented. In this example, Thom clarified his misunderstanding about India's global ranking relative to its economic status:

> Well, I was thinking, 'cause I read earlier it was big income. Ecomics [*sic*], that's what it is, and it was poor, and I was thinking like, "Oh, it's the 24th

richest in the world," but it's the 24th poorest country! . . . I thought it was kind of, it was kind of strange that I read like three or four encyclopedias and two other books and they didn't have it and finally I found it. It's kind of interesting that this book would have it.

Through metacognitive inquiry, students call on relevant background knowledge and experience to help them understand what they are reading. Barnes and Todd (1977) described "cognitive strategies" that readers or groups of readers use to pose their own questions, hypothesize about meaning, and find evidence to support these predictions as they come to understand a text (p. 50). In this way, learners use "what they already know in order to give meaning to new insights or information which they are given. New understanding is likely to be a reorganization of old knowledge rather than an addition to it." Frequently, through dialogue with the teacher during the metacognitive inquiry procedure, students use previous knowledge to "throw light on the matter in hand" (p. 56) and thereby gain new insights and reorganize old knowledge.

In addition, students often relate personal experiences and family stories that help them connect to the text. A description of a German building reminded Alicia of a family vacation to Louisiana and a tour of old mansions, and a passage about African tribes and religions reminded Cindi of a conversation with a man from Kenya about Muslims. Such recollections help students gain a richer understanding of what they read. Barnes and Todd (1977) state that it is

> important not to restrict the construction of knowledge so that it applies only to knowledge distant from the knower's own concerns, since our most important knowledge is not of that kind. The knowledge which bears directly on children's daily lives, and on which they base their actions, has its own part to play in school learning, and it is well not to forget this. (p. 50)

Metacognitive inquiry also helps students to set purposes for reading and to use text structure and features such as maps, charts, and headings.

Through metacognitive inquiry teachers can assess students' comprehension of what they are reading as they talk through their understanding of difficult vocabulary and concepts. As Lemke (1989) states, we need to help students develop their ability to "restate a sentence or passage in their own words as [this is] the surest sign of comprehension" (p. 139). In the following example, Sylvia was reading about Zaire, and demonstrated her understanding of "Pygmies" by making inferences based on the context clues "inhabitants" and "prehistoric":

30 TEACHER: What are you thinking?

31 SYLVIA: I'm thinking about pie-ga-mees.

32 TEACHER: O.K., what do you think that is?

33 SYLVIA: I know it's a group of people . . . 'cause it says "first inhabit-
    ants." I'm also thinking they lived there way back. They've been
    there for a long time, thousands of years, because it says "they have
    been there since prehistoric times."

Sylvia used the language of the text to help explain how she came to understand both who the Pygmies were and how long they had lived in what is
now Zaire.

In the next example, Cindi talked her way to understanding a passage
on men's clothing in Chad. She used what she knew about the word "skull"
to speculate on the meaning of "skullcaps":

34 TEACHER: What are you thinking about?
35 CINDI: I was thinking, "Skullcaps, that sounds kind of crazy."
36 TEACHER: Why does it sound crazy?
37 CINDI: 'Cause skullcaps . . . your skull . . .
38 TEACHER: Yeah, what do you think that is?
39 CINDI: I guess maybe it's a headdress or headband or something
    that's really tight around your head or something.
40 TEACHER: Why do you think so?
41 CINDI: 'Cause your skull is part of your head but it's inside your
    skin and everything and I guess if it's a skullcap it's just really close.

The metacognitive inquiry procedure offers teachers a view of the reader/
learner unavailable through other means of assessment. It provides teachers
with a window into the thought processes of students as they actively engage
in the interpretation of content-area texts. This in-process information is
valuable in grouping students with similar needs. For example, the teacher
may identify students who are able to articulate the use of certain strategies
but have difficulty applying this knowledge when reading. Four or five
students could be involved in metacognitive inquiry in order to encourage
them to become more proficient in using the reading and studying strategies
they can talk about.

WHAT IS METACOGNITION?

To understand the basis of the metacognitive inquiry procedure, it is helpful
to examine the nature of metacognition and the implications of using talk
to aid in content-area learning. Simply stated, metacognition is thinking
about your own thinking. Metacognition includes an awareness of cognitive
activity when reading or studying and the regulation of one's own thinking

processes and use of strategies. It is knowing whether you understand what you are reading and doing something about it when you don't (Zabrucky and Ratner, 1990).

Different areas of metacognitive awareness, which are interactive and not mutually exclusive, are available when reading and studying. They include: *procedural knowledge* ("What are the steps in this strategy?"), *conditional knowledge* ("When and why do I use this strategy?"), and *declarative knowledge* ("What do I know about myself, this reading task, and the strategies I can use?") (Billingsley and Wildman, 1990; Wade and Reynolds, 1989; Paris, Lipson, and Wixson, 1983) (see Figure 10.1). Barnes and Todd (1977) referred to metacognition as "reflexivity" (p. 61), and described students' self-awareness and their ability to monitor strategy use, both of which, they noted, are dependent on the capacity for thinking about one's own thinking.

Procedural knowledge is the learner's awareness of how to perform a particular strategy or task. It is understanding "how particular reading skills operate and how to use the various steps or procedures that are part of a skill or strategy" (Billingsley and Wildman, 1990, p. 19). For example, readers with the procedural knowledge needed for understanding the gist of a chapter may skim the title, read the summary, review chapter headings, and develop an overall impression of the passage. Next, the reader may skim the passage, then read it in detail. Procedural knowledge involves specifying the task, confronting the reader, selecting a method or strategy, and knowing the steps needed to perform the appropriate strategy.

In the following example, Thom shows clear intentionality as a reader and learner when he recognizes the need to select a new section of text to read. He goes about this task by defining his purpose, consulting the table of contents, monitoring his process, then giving a reason for his selection:

> I'm looking to see what I want to read. I'm just looking at the different sections. I'll look up facts about it. I'll look at "Looking in the Future." I haven't read that.

Conditional knowledge is the awareness of the reasons certain strategies are helpful and the contexts in which they should be used (Billingsley and Wildman, 1990; Paris, Lipson, and Wixson, 1983). If learners know when and why certain strategies are most appropriate to aid comprehension, they will be better able to use different methods flexibly in a variety of reading and learning situations.

Conditional knowledge provides the reader with the rationale for using certain strategies in different contexts. As Paris, Lipson, and Wixson (1983) suggest, conditional knowledge is the "glue that holds skill and will together in our analysis of reading strategies. Usually children are told when to perform the 'strategy.' Seldom are they told why" (p. 312). When students

M. RUTH DAVENPORT

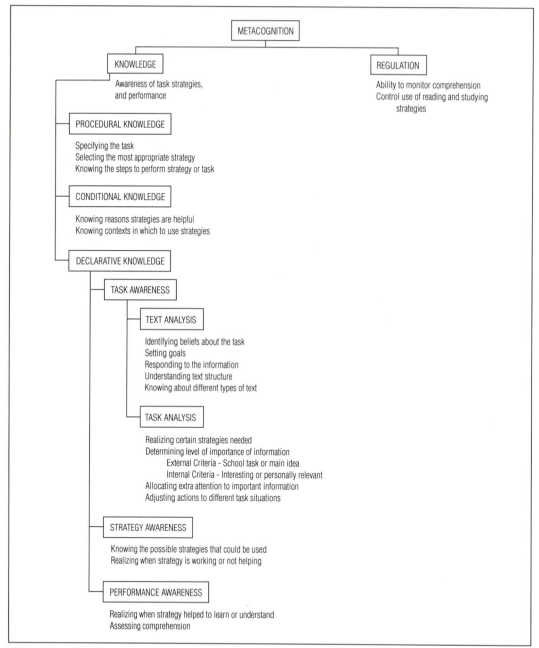

Figure 10.1 *An Overview of Metacognition*

know when and why a particular strategy is useful, they are able to connect their ability to engage in an active transaction with a text and their motivation to do so. In this way, conditional knowledge orchestrates the use of declarative and procedural knowledge by helping readers apply this information to particular reading and studying tasks.

In the following example, Sylvia was aware of several options when faced with "diplomatic," an unfamiliar word. She tried one strategy, realized it didn't work for her in that context, and then relied on context clues to guess the meaning:

43 TEACHER: What are you thinking?

44 SYLVIA: What in the heck is "dimomatic?"

45 TEACHER: What could you do to find out?

46 SYLVIA: I might look it up sometime, or ask somebody, if I hear it again I probably will.

47 TEACHER: What else could you try?

48 SYLVIA: I can read the paragraph again.

49 TEACHER: O.K., why don't you do that?

50 SYLVIA: (Rereads silently) I guess it's um, that didn't really help me.

51 TEACHER: What were you going to guess?

52 SYLVIA: What I was guessing didn't make sense. It has something to do with "established relationships." That's what I'm thinking.

This dialogue continued about the ways countries establish relationships and what "diplomat" meant, thereby helping Sylvia come to understand how "diplomatic" was used in the sentence and that she had made a reasonable guess at its meaning. Her conditional knowledge of various strategies allowed her to apply an appropriate strategy, rereading and using context clues.

Declarative knowledge is defined by Billingsley and Wildman (1990) as "incoming knowledge [that] is represented in memory as facts, concepts, rules, strategies, and beliefs" (p. 19). Declarative knowledge includes three domains: *task awareness* ("What type of book is this? What kind of reading will I be doing?"), *strategy awareness* ("Should I slow down here to reread to better understand this? Did this strategy help me?"), and *performance awareness* ("Am I understanding this?").

The first domain, *task awareness*, includes: identifying beliefs about the task ("I think this is going to be easy"), setting goals for reading ("I need to find the reasons for the decrease in production"), responding to the information ("This is interesting"), and understanding text structure ("Bold headings give me important clues"). This domain also includes the reader's knowledge of the characteristics of different types of texts and the appropriate strategies for each type. Our rates of reading and purposes change as we move from a mystery novel to an instruction manual or a science textbook, and therefore we need a variety of reading and studying strategies (Wade and Reynolds, 1989).

Readers must also determine the level of importance of the information in each type of text, and they use two types of criteria to do so (Shirey and Reynolds, 1988). The first is external: readers attend to information because it is relevant to school tasks or represents the main ideas of the text. The second is internal: readers identify information as interesting or personally relevant.

In the following example, Thom had been reading about the different sports played in India. He determined that the information was important using both internal and external criteria. He was interested in the various sports and connected the text to his personal experiences in gym class. He also decided he could use this information in his research:

53   TEACHER: What are you thinking?
54   THOM: I was thinking about what kind of games, like if I played them, like what I'm playing in gym, like what games. Actually, I was trying to remember it so I could write it down in my report.

Another factor in *task awareness* is the ability to allocate extra attention to information that has been deemed important. The learner must know "what information in a text is relevant to success in a particular learning situation and thus deserving of greater attention" (Wade and Reynolds, 1989, p. 7). Information considered personally relevant will be remembered more easily, and information that is important based on external criteria will require extra attention in order to be learned (Shirey and Reynolds, 1988). Thus, task awareness involves both *text analysis* ("What do I need to do to learn and remember this type of information?") and *task analysis* ("This seems important, I should pay more attention to this part").

Task awareness also includes information that helps readers adjust their actions to different task conditions (Paris, Lipson, and Wixson, 1983). In the following example, Alicia is aware of how she adjusted the pace of her reading and why:

> I think I kinda slowed down on this paragraph because of all the new words that I'm trying to figure out, and also because if I've never really read something before, I always slow down, if it's something new, because I always remember about it. It helps my mind to clarify it, like, and keep it in my mind for a longer period of time.

The second domain of declarative knowledge is *strategy awareness* (Wade and Reynolds, 1989). Learners and readers must be aware of a variety of reading and studying strategies and be able to make decisions about what methods are the most appropriate for each text and each task. For example, studying tasks make greater cognitive demands on the reader when analysis, synthesis, and evaluation are required. Learning and reading about topics in which students have a greater interest and about which they have more background knowledge will require fewer cognitive resources. Readers must not only be able to select the most appropriate strategy for a given reading or learning experience, they must also realize when a strategy is working for them and when they need a new one.

In the following example, Cindi used a categorization strategy to figure out the meaning of "sorghum," an unfamiliar word. In this case, it was the most appropriate strategy to help her understand the meaning:

49 TEACHER: What do you think that is?

50 CINDI: Sorghum.

51 TEACHER: Yeah, what do you think "sorghum" is?

52 CINDI: Um, I think it's maybe kinda like a grain or something, because it says "millet, sorghum, and rice," and millet, it's kinda like a grain, and rice is a grain. So I think maybe it's a grain.

The third domain of declarative knowledge is *performance awareness*. According to Wade and Reynolds (1989), students must be able to evaluate the effectiveness of a strategy, which they determine by the effect it has had on their learning. A strategy cannot be conceptualized as "either existing or not existing" (p. 11). That is, students can use a strategy without increasing their understanding or their efficiency as readers. Metacognitively aware students realize when a strategy helped them to understand what they read or learn new information and when it did not prove useful. By assessing their comprehension, students learn to take corrective action when strategies fail, and thereby become flexible strategy users.

WHAT DO STUDENTS THINK OF METACOGNITIVE INQUIRY?

Although there are numerous benefits to the use of the metacognitive inquiry procedure, it is not a panacea for all students' learning and reading difficulties. The procedure provides teachers with a window on students' thinking and reading processes, but not without cost. Students were asked what they liked and didn't like about engaging in metacognitive inquiry, and their responses were very informative.

Alicia thought the procedure helped her learn to think about her reading, recognize when she needs help, and identify what she needs to learn. She was surprised that she could read and understand such a wide variety of content-area texts.

Thom showed an awareness of his audience as he compared reading orally and silently. He miscued frequently in addition to having articulation difficulties, although his comprehension was excellent. Through metacognitive inquiry, he became more aware of what he sounds like to others when reading orally:

> Now I hear myself, like I'm actually reading and in my mind I'm not doing that (making miscues) and it's coming out like that. *I* understand it and the people next to me are like, "What is he saying?"

Cindi noticed that metacognitive inquiry

> helped me look a little bit closer and stop skipping sentences. I do that a lot. I'm noticing what I read. It helps everything make sense more, and it helps me figure out the words and not skip over them.

Kevin thought teachers should show students the use of the metacognitive inquiry procedure to help them pay attention to their reading strategies and "to show that reading is important and there's a lot of ways to think about what you're reading."

Encouraged to be honest and assured they would not hurt my feelings, students gave candid responses to the question, "What *didn't* you like about doing the interviews?" Cindi and Alicia gave similar responses about repeated questions such as, "What else would you like to tell me about what you're thinking right now?" Alicia said, "When you keep on asking me what I'm thinking, and I feel like I've told you all I know, I just don't have any more to give." This type of response prompted a great deal of reflection and discussion, causing Susan and me to re-examine our sensitivity to the students' ability to continue to report their thoughts on a passage.

Several students said they disliked having to stop so frequently. We discussed this with them and explained that this was the only way "to pick their brains" and help them learn more about themselves as readers, thinkers, and learners. Thom expressed his involvement with the text and his frustration at having to stop:

> I couldn't see what was going on next. I wanna know about that and I wanna know about that, and I can't know because I'm stopping. I just like to read straight on through without stop, stop, stop, because then it doesn't sound interesting when you stop every paragraph.

However, he later conceded:

> I liked more than I didn't like. I liked when we stopped and we talked about what I read, after I got used to stopping. I like to know how I sound and what I did. It makes me a better reader but it takes more time.

Greg was not as talkative as the others during the interviews, often responding with "I don't know." Although his willingness to share his thoughts improved with each session, it usually appeared that he would rather be doing something else. When asked what he didn't like about the sessions, he replied, "Now that I think it's all done, I feel that it was great, but during the interviews, I thought, 'When is this session going to be over?' and 'I really hate this.' "

Greg also commented that he liked the sessions best when he was able to select his own texts to read because "I wanted to read about it, and it was something I was interested in." He also realized that he "never really thought about which strategy I was doing" and that this procedure helps students "understand what they're doing when they're reading."

Students also made suggestions about how the procedure could be conducted differently, and their responses often reflected their prior classroom experiences with exploring their thinking as a group. Most of their suggestions involved conducting metacognitive inquiry with several students at once. They all recognized the benefits of additional input from others, which reflected an intuitive awareness of the social nature of the learning process (Vygotsky, 1986).

Alicia commented that at times she felt a little "on the spot" and uncomfortable working one-on-one with me, since she didn't know me well. She suggested an alternative that would alleviate this concern and also allow students the chance to learn from each other's ideas:

> I think it would be nice to see if we did this in groups of two or something. It would make everybody feel less tense and get a little bit more information out of it. If somebody brought up an idea, we could all learn from it, and plus it would make us think of other things that we'd already read.

Thom's comment was similar but also shows a sensitivity to individual learning styles:

> You could have done it with everybody else, and then we all compare and we see what different kids know and how they learn. Each kid learns different.

Kevin was asked whether he would use the metacognitive inquiry procedure if he were a teacher, and responded:

> I would do it with my whole class so I know altogether what people are really thinking. Actually I would do it one-on-one and then get everybody together so everybody could combine their thoughts. I think there would be a lot more talking and a lot more thinking about what the paragraph is about.

These students offered many helpful insights about participating in this type of inquiry as they were "metacognating" on their metacognition. Certainly the metacognitive inquiry procedure has many benefits for both teachers and students and is worthy of closer examination. Although the procedure slows down the reading process, if our goal is more enthusiastic and proficient readers of content-area text, as Thom suggested, it's worth taking the time.

REFERENCES

Barnes, D. 1991. Presentation at University of Missouri-Columbia, Columbia, MO.

Barnes, D. and F. Todd. 1977. *Communication and learning in small groups.* London: Routledge and Kegan Paul.

Billingsley, B.S. and T.M. Wildman. 1990. "Facilitating reading comprehension in learning disabled students: Metacognitive goals and instructional strategies." *Remedial and Special Education* 11(2):18–31.

Davey, B. 1983. "Think aloud—Modeling the cognitive processes of reading comprehension." *Journal of Reading* 27(1) 44-47.

Hoppe, K. 1992. "Shuttle mission yields surprising results." *Science News* 142(5):70.

Lemke, J.L. 1989. "Making text talk." *Theory into Practice* 28(2):136–41.

Palincsar, A.S. and K. Ransom. 1988. "From the mystery spot to the thoughtful spot: The instruction of metacognitive strategies." *The Reading Teacher* 41(8):784–88.

Paris, S.G., M.Y. Lipson, and K.K. Wixson. 1983. "Becoming a strategic reader." *Contemporary Educational Psychology* 8(3):293–316.

Shirey, L.L. and R.E. Reynolds. 1988. "The role of attention in learning and recalling interesting and less interesting sentences." *Journal of Educational Psychology* 80:159–66.

Vygotsky, L. 1986. *Thought and language.* Cambridge, MA: MIT Press.

Wade, S.E. and R.E. Reynolds. 1989. Developing metacognitive awareness. *Journal of Reading* 33(1):6–14.

Zabrucky, K. and H.H. Ratner. 1990. "Children's comprehension monitoring: Implications of research findings for the classroom." *Reading Improvement* 27(1):46–54.

Part Four

EXPANDING THE POTENTIAL OF LITERATURE DISCUSSION GROUPS

Carol Gilles is interested in talking and learning in small groups, influenced significantly by her experience with students labeled learning disabled. She has co-written *Whole Language Strategies for Secondary Learners* and was a contributor to *Talking about Books.* Currently she is a Visiting Assistant Professor at the University of Missouri-Columbia in Continuing Professional Education where she works with practicing teachers in reading, language, and literature.

Chapter 11
We Make an Idea: Cycles of Meaning in Literature Discussion Groups

CAROL GILLES

Seated in the "special ed trailer" in the parking lot behind the junior high, I interviewed Chris, a tall, quiet seventh-grader, who wore his black trench coat in and out of school. I asked Chris to tell me how he and his classmates engaged in literature discussion groups.

01 GILLES: Can you describe what makes a group go well?

02 CHRIS: What's discussed, the connections that are made. When people share the ideas they have and then come up with one. *All the ideas are shared and then matched together and we come up with one* [my emphasis].

03 GILLES: One new idea?

04 CHRIS: Yeah, a big new idea.

05 GILLES: Does this happen very often?

06 CHRIS: Yeah, it happens in almost every group. Not on as big a scale sometimes, but it happens pretty regularly. (Gilles, 1991)

I often ask teachers to talk about their experiences with literature discussion groups (LDG). Their comments are very different from Chris':

MARIE: Sometimes I'm just not sure if my kids are getting enough out of the discussion. It seems like we talk about so many different things!

BARBARA: The literature study is exciting to me. I feel like what we're doing is right, but should I try to get the kids to spend a longer time on certain topics?

CHARLIE: The talk goes by so quickly. I don't know what we have covered and what we haven't. I wonder if we're getting to the important stuff.

As participants talk about literature study groups, they are exploring the implied question "How is meaning made?" Chris, who hadn't finished reading an entire book before seventh grade, felt sure that meanings were made slowly, tentatively, by all the members of the group. He felt that the members of the group made an idea together by sharing their reactions to the book. The teachers, on the other hand, seemed to be questioning how meanings are made and more specifically, their own role in the meaning making. Since literature group discussion is vastly different from the question-response-evaluation mode traditionally used, teachers have legitimate concerns about how the discussions should proceed.

As a junior high learning disabilities teacher, I had some of the same concerns. I found that my questions were not fully answered by reading journal articles about literature discussion, nor were they completely answered by listening to presentations of teachers who implemented literature discussion groups. In order to answer the difficult questions, I had to slow down the talk of the participants and examine it. Thus, I became an observer in my colleagues' classrooms, tape-recording the discussions of their students and analyzing that talk.

MY INQUIRY

In order to explore how meanings are made, I recorded, described, categorized, and analyzed the talk of thirteen junior high school students labeled learning disabled. I audiotaped the discussions in Marc Vandover and Shirley Johnsen's class called "Reading Trade Books." Students in this class selected, read, wrote about, and discussed trade books through literature discussion groups. (Watson and Davis, 1988; Gilles, 1989; Peterson and Eeds, 1990.) I hoped that by carefully recording, transcribing, and then counting and analyzing the utterances, I could document how meanings were created. However, I soon found that by using my procedure I was missing important information. Barnes and Todd (1977) explained that "It often seems that the features which are most visible, most readily isolated, are those which are least important: whilst those features which the observer focuses on as being most significant are precisely those which are hardest to categorize in a reliable way" (p. 7). So it was with my study. Important questions such as "How are meanings made?" "Do some meanings occur over time?" "Are important topics reinitiated over time?" were not being answered by counting and categorizing. In order to answer these questions, I found that I had to examine discussions over a number of sessions and track particular topics and events. In this chapter I explore the meaning-making process by examining in depth how students engaged in literature discussion.

HOW DO STUDENTS ENGAGE IN LITERATURE DISCUSSION?

Barnes (1991) suggested that exploratory talk is a vehicle to "journey into a book," an appropriate metaphor. These junior high students labeled learning disabled each chose a book from three possible choices, read a portion of their book silently, and then recorded an *agenda* item in their journals. These agendas were issues they valued and wanted to discuss. Agenda topics were often the connections students made between one book and another book or event, a retelling of a part of the book they liked, questions about an event or word that confused them, or their reactions to an episode in the book. Each group had a volunteer leader whose job it was to make sure everyone had a turn to talk, to keep the discussion moving, and to stay on the topic. The journal agendas served as reminders of the topics they wanted to discuss.

The discussion often began with students retelling an interesting or helpful part of the book. Sometimes the retelling took the form of *collaborative storying*, which Hurst (1988) defined as "collaboratively picking up the thread of the narrative from one to the other in a series of short, often unfinished exchanges" (p. 182). One student might begin the retelling and then, nearly midsentence, another would take over. Together a number of students retold the story. This was an important process, for as students retold the story, they verified that the meaning one person had constructed from the story was similar to the meaning constructed by another. Sometimes the retelling was followed by some of the questions students had recorded in their journal agendas about the story, the plot, the characters, or words that had confused them. Discussing these questions provided immediate information that made it easier for the students to reenter the book for the next reading. The first part of their "journey into a book," then, included talk that constructed and verified broad meanings.

As they continued their journey, the students often moved into making connections between the book and their lives, other people, or other books; discussing the author's style or purpose; reflecting on their own thinking as they used reading strategies; visualizing what was happening in the book;

or responding to other group members' comments. These comments often helped students to explore deeper meanings. When the students were reading *Where the Red Fern Grows* (Rawls, 1961), they found it helpful to discuss the author.

46 ANDY: Oh, he's a good . . . he or she are good describers.

47 MIKE: Two people, a "he" and a "she."

48 ABE: No, it's just he.

49 ANDY: It's just a he.

50 MIKE: Just a he? Well, that explains a lot of things.

51 ANDY: Did this really happen to him?

52 JOHNSEN: No.

53 MIKE: Well, I thought it really actually did . . . I guess he didn't actually have those adventures.

54 ANDY: Read about the author. [He shows Mike the back cover where there is a short biography.] (Gilles, 1991)

Speculating on the life of the author helped these students understand the basis of the story. Mike believed that Rawls and his wife had written the book and that it described Rawls' adventures as a boy. Discussing the author and reading the short biography provided background information that helped these students construct meaning. Johnsen further extended students' background information by sharing details from a presentation by Rawls that she had attended.

Another way students considered deeper meanings was by hypothesizing about the plot, characters, setting, or symbolism and asking one another "hard" questions. The meanings created by this process were more sophisticated than the general awareness students used to verify that they were "on the right track." On these occasions, students collaborated by "working on understanding" (Barnes, 1992).

An example of "working on understanding" in LDGs occurred when students were reading *The White Mountains* (Christopher, 1967). The book is an adventure story set in the future. Tripods, huge three-legged metalic creatures, have invaded the earth. Society has been destroyed and humanity has gone back to the premachine era of the Middle Ages, although there are still vestiges of some of the old "machines" around. When teens reach their fourteenth birthdays, the Tripods find them and make them board Tripod ships. When the teens return, they each have a small, metal cap in their skull and have lost their ability to question and be curious. Will does not want to be "capped" and begins a journey to the "White Mountains," a place where a resistance movement is forming.

One issue that was especially puzzling to group members Mike, Matthew, Billy, and TJ, was the issue of "capping," the implanting of thin metal strips in the heads of young people to curtail curiosity:

99   MATTHEW: Someone needs to figure out how to destroy those Tripods!

100   TJ: The Tripods are people who know everything. They can't be stopped.

101   MATTHEW: Some people have escaped.

102   BILLY: How?

103   MATTHEW AND MIKE: From the inside . . .

104   VANDOVER: When Jack was capped, did he try to escape?

105   MATTHEW: We still have 3,000 questions! [General agreement]

106   MATTHEW: It's curious to me. If the kids question the capping, then why don't they fight it!

107   TJ: One part of them wants the cap, to be a man, and one part doesn't.

108   MATTHEW: But it is incredible. If you knew that would happen to you at, say at age sixteen, wouldn't you fight?

109   MIKE: Well, I saw this on TV. They had these huge elephants and they had just small elastic strings to restrain them. And the elephants didn't try to get away. But when the elephants were babies they used big ropes, so, so they could't get away. I think that's how these kids feel. They are used to the idea of capping from the very beginning. (Gilles, 1991)

In this exchange students asked themselves and one another some of the puzzling questions this book evoked. Matthew demonstrated some frustration when he commented that they still had 3,000 questions to ask (105). Then Matthew raised an issue central to the book: Why did the people in the book not fight against their captors? TJ reminded Matthew that the act of capping was culturally correct or expected in that society. That didn't satisfy Matthew. He repeated the question by making it more personal. Mike then made a connection to elephants that clearly illustrated the idea that when something was expected from childhood, there was less resistance. He then drew a parallel that moved the readers back to the book.

In this example, the issue of resisting the capping was considered collaboratively, and all group members were engaged. They expanded, reiterated, and connected the topic to their life experiences and then moved back to the book. Mike probably would not have remembered the elephant story had it not been for Matthew's insistent questions.

DIALOGUE

The talk in this episode could be considered *dialogue*. Dialogue has been defined by Moffett (1967), Freire (1970), Thelen (1981), Peterson (1988), and Berthoff (1990), among others, but Thelen's and Peterson's definitions are most relevant to this discussion. Thelen, who was concerned with education and curriculum, used the notion of dialogue to convey the mutual support that members of a group give one another. He described it metaphorically as a quartet of four string players in a room tuning up for a concert and later performing the concert. In both situations the players are in the same room, may play similar notes, and get some personal satisfaction out of playing. Yet there is a great difference between four individuals practicing in the same room and a quartet performing. Thelen suggested that the quartet is disciplined by a sense of context and of form. The context includes the awareness of the other players' contributions, the intention of the group as a whole, and the particular contribution of each player. The group's success then depends partially on the extent to which its members are genuinely working together for a common end and trying to understand one another and communicate (Barnes 1992, p. 38). Dialogue, from Thelen's point of view, is that balance or harmony between an individual's contributions and the common understandings of the whole group.

Peterson (1988) sees the potential for dialogue in literature study groups as a resource for students in constructing meaning:

> Reaching beyond a mere exchange of information and sharing of ideas, participants in dialogue seek to disclose "original meanings." They collaborate one-with-the-other to comprehend ideas, problems, events and feelings in the light of their own background, experience and intent. Through heartfelt responding, partners in dialogue work to expand what they know of the world's meaning. (p. 1)

Seventh-grader Chris' account of making ideas is reminiscent of those of Thelen and Peterson. He believed that participants shared ideas about the book and that a new idea was formed from that sharing. Charlie, a ninth-grade student labeled learning disabled, who was enrolled in a building trades course, described the process a bit differently:

> Everybody put together what they knew [about the last book] and made a base for the time being, 'till they could find out what is really goin' on. So the base . . . wasn't permanent. . . . Whenever we find a new part in the book that we don't understand and it doesn't go with what we've made, then we just change something and make it fit, to where we understand everything. Each time we find a new clue, we just replace part of it, until finally we get the foundation, the permanent foundation. (Gilles in Short & Pierce, 1990)

Both boys understood how important it was for the group to work collaboratively together. Stanley Fish (1980) reminds us that "meanings are not extracted but made and made not by encoded forms but by interpretive strategies that call forms into being" (p. 183). One of the interpretive strategies that creates meanings is dialogue. Dialogue is, at its heart, a kind of problem solving. As the group struggles to share and build on understandings, they impose a "collaborative explicitness" (Barnes, 1992) on one another. The questions that group members ask one another force them to be more explicit in their thinking than they are on their own. Through this spoken collaboration, new thinking occurs, an idea emerges, a permanent foundation is formed.

SOCIAL TALK

The social talk that regulated the group activity also helped propel students on their journeys through books. At the beginning of the session, the students talked about who might be the leader and how much of the book the group should discuss. During their meeting they might discuss specific problems, such as inviting the quieter members to share their thinking or how to help a member who was behind in the reading. At the end of the meeting they might ask if everyone who had something to say had a turn and decide how far to read for the next meeting. This kind of talk helped students negotiate some of the social parameters of their discussions. Teachers were not the undisputed authority figures, and students had to negotiate and collaborate with them on how routines would be carried out and how differences would be settled. Such talk was usually brief, but it occurred in every group.

When conversations broke down, the teachers encouraged students to consider why their discussions were not working, so that students would have experience in evaluating each member's participation. The students learned how to be productive group members by actually participating in groups and by talking about their participation. Talk that established organizational routines was essential for the group's success.

Within social talk, students searched for areas where their lives intersected. The connections they made with the literature they were reading often provided an opportunity for them to share personal stories. Through these stories they built ties with one another and with their teachers that formed the fabric of the group community. As Thelen reminds us, productive group talk is based on the balance or harmony between an individual's purpose and the group's purpose. Social talk helped students develop the trust and the cohesiveness needed to function as a productive group.

The kinds of talk used in the LDGs had few boundaries. Students never moved in a linear fashion from retelling the story to discussing deeper meanings and then to considering the group's routine. Instead, meanings interwove in a tapestry of social talk. They emerged through talk that moved from conversation to dialogue to story and back again. Few topics emerged neatly. Students often moved quickly from one topic to another and returned to those they considered important. This dynamic, circular movement I've labeled "cycles of meaning." Barnes and Todd (1977) helped me consider the notion of cycles:

> On one hand, a very great deal may go on in just one utterance: the observer may feel that several equally important things are happening at the same time. He cannot put utterances into categories on a one-to-one basis, because some utterances seem to belong in several categories. On the other hand, it also seems that meanings for what is going on in the conversation are constructed not from any one utterance on its own, but from cycles of utterances, perhaps over quite lengthy sections of the interaction. (p. 17)

I began to wonder how long those sections of interactions might last and if the cycles might extend beyond one conversation. It became evident that "the cycle" was not so much the verbal turn or utterance, but the meaning that was created from the transactions of the speakers. Cycles of meanings are more than utterances; they are the meanings and understandings that individuals and groups create over time as they transact with one another by discussing rich texts.

MIKE REVISITS A TOPIC

In order to discuss one way learners cycle into meaning over time, I return to the discussion of *The White Mountains*. Mike, Matthew, Billy, TJ, and their teacher, Marc Vandover, read and discussed the book in late April. At the beginning of one LDG session, Vandover asked students to prepare their agendas to bring up anything they wanted to talk about. Mike began the discussion by asking:

35   MIKE: In the book . . . it told about parallel lines. Is it a road or something like that?

36   BILLY: There were these horses and wagons.

37   MIKE: And two men, yeah. But what would these two parallel lines be?

38   BILLY: And they were pulling stuff.

39   MIKE: But what were the parallel lines?

40   VANDOVER: Well, let's see. [Begins to look through the book.]

41   MIKE: Mr. Vandover will read it out loud to us, O.K.?

42   TJ: Yeah.

43   VANDOVER: Will you show me where it is? [They all look in the book except Mike.]

44   TJ: [To Mike] You brought it up, you should be looking for it. [Mike takes the book and begins reading.]

45   MIKE: (Reading) "Looking down he could see a track made of two parallel straight lines, gleaming in the sunshine, which ran from town and disappeared in the far distance." I want to say it's a road, but if it gleams . . . What would gleam? Oh, a river. It's probably a river of some sort.

46   BILLY: Well, if you read page 80, you'll know. [Mike finds page 80 and reads to himself.]

47   MIKE: Oh, it's a train track, an old train track.

48   VANDOVER: How do you figure that?

49   MIKE: Well, it says, "You follow the now empty lines away from the town. They were of iron, their tops polished to a brightness, and were fastened on massive planks." I think it's the massive planks. It's like the second paragraph down.

50   VANDOVER: Then what were the horses used for?

51   BILLY: To pull it. They had 20 horses.

52   MIKE: Yeah, they had something like a boiler thing to get the things started to go. It's like a train, but they're not using . . . It's sad, it's really sad. Like why can't they just invent it [machines] all over again? Invent the trains and stuff. This is terrible.

53   TJ: The Tripods don't know all about this stuff.

54   MIKE: That's why Beanpole [a character], he has all these inventions! That's why Beanpole doesn't want to be capped because of how he got in trouble with the hot air balloon. It's an old idea. (Gilles, 1991)

Mike began by asking about the concept "parallel lines." Billy tried to help by directing him to the context of that section, but Mike still didn't understand. When the teacher entered (40), Mike sat back and let the other students look for the part of the text that had confused him. TJ considered this to be unacceptable behavior and he reminded Mike, "You brought it up, you should be looking for it." This was primarily a social interaction; it did not begin an argument but served to move Mike into the book. Once Mike found the section, we can see his mind working as he predicted possible explanations for the parallel lines. Billy gave Mike hints but left the work to Mike.

Once Mike had decided that "parallel lines" referred to a train track, Vandover asked him to be more explicit in his thinking (48). This caused Mike to enter into the text and explain what key phrases had led to his conclusion. Vandover continued to probe by asking Mike to explain the role of the horses Billy had introduced earlier. At this point we see why Mike initiated this topic: his real concern was not a vocabulary word that gave him trouble but the fact that so much technology available to him was withheld from the characters in the story (52). Mike wondered aloud why the characters could not just reinvent machines to help them escape. In the last line he connected the lack of technology to Beanpole's insistence on joining Will to escape the capping and continue inventing. Perhaps Mike was beginning to infer that Beanpole's role in the story was to invent machinery that would help the characters escape.

Later in the discussion, after the group had speculated on the setting, Mike returned to the technology issue: "That makes me mad. I mean, we have already invented all those things and here they think it's something really good that they have invented. It's already been invented in the olden days." Mike was probably referring to the part of the book in which twenty horses were pulling a train that at one time was steam powered.

Three days later the group met again. Because the students had been asked to put up posters in the main building for the upcoming student council election, they chose to discuss *White Mountains* as they put up their posters. Mike again brought up the issue of technology: "In a way it's too bad that we couldn't enter the book as characters because we appreciate machines and we could help others appreciate machines." Mike had continued to think about the issue of technology over the three-day interval since the last discussion.

If students come upon a troublesome issue in their literature study or in other study groups, we can't expect that a single group conversation will settle the questions in their minds. Readers may continue to mull over the problem at home and at school, trying out options and looking in the book or asking others for various solutions. Like Mike, readers may need to reintroduce topics they are trying to understand. Because the group's approach to the task was open, Mike felt comfortable mentioning his uncertainty and his tentative hypotheses about machines. As Barnes (1992) states,

> This open approach implies a collaborative social relationship in which pupils make frequent use of one another's contributions by extending or modifying them. They address one another directly, sometimes by name, and occasionally ask one another to explain or extend what they have already said. They deal with disagreement in open discussion in order to reach verbal clarification of the difference. (p. 67)

We can see from their discussion that the group was collaborative in nature. The boys were patient as Mike discovered the meaning of the parallel lines for himself. This is only one example of a phenomenon that happens regularly in such groups: students bring up topics, work out understandings for themselves with the help of the other members of the group, and reflect over time on issues within the group and outside of it.

A GROUP REINITIATES A TOPIC

Often important topics are not identified quickly during one discussion but established over time as members of the group reiterate them. The setting of *The White Mountains* is important to the story but difficult for many readers to establish. The story begins in England, but the characters escape by sea to France and then continue on their journey to the white mountains near the French/Swiss border. Although hints about the characters' travels are given, placenames are never revealed. The issue of "white mountains" was introduced by Billy the first time the group met:

21　BILLY: Jack [a character in the story] said, "I want to meet you again, in the white mountains."

22　MATTHEW: Why not go to the white mountains before they are capped?

23　BILLY: I don't know.

Mike reestablished the topic early in the next session when the group was talking about Ozymandias, a vagrant who acted crazy but who passed information to the characters about escaping from the Tripods to the white mountains.

15　MIKE: He's a really weird dude. Not a regular guy. He comes from the white mountains. [Mike looked up at the topographical map on the wall, which showed white-capped mountain peaks.] You know, whenever I look up, I just see those white mountains.

16　VANDOVER: How do you picture it?

In the interchange that followed, the group again considered the setting. TJ believed that the story was taking place in England, because "the speech is real refined, and they live in little villages, but it seems near a big city. They go by the ruins of a big city." Although Mike expanded further on the notion of *ruins* and Vandover on *city*, the topic of setting was dropped for that day. TJ's hypothesis was correct, but *no one reacted to or extended his contribution.* Yet it had sparked an idea about where the quest could have begun.

In the next session the group met without Vandover, and setting was not discussed. However, at a later session Vandover brought up the topic of setting and explained how he established setting as he read:

> When I read something, especially a story like this, I try to picture what's happening as I read. I've got to know the place and usually I start in Columbia . . . until I read something that tells me it's not Columbia. Like if they are talking about ocean spray I know immediately it's not Columbia. So I have to use my head and go other places.

This explanation began another discussion of where the quest began. Students considered the possibility that it had begun in various parts of the United States until TJ said:

76 TJ: Well, I never believed [it was set in the United States] because they had the rusty old ship at the ruins.

77 VANDOVER: How did that help you decide?

78 TJ: Well, it's huge so it couldn't have been a little ship and we don't have huge ships here.

79 VANDOVER: Where are you picturing this thing?

80 TJ: Along the coast of some country in Europe or something.

Although TJ was incorrect in assuming there were no large ships in the United States, he was correct in identifying where the story began. His suggestion initiated speculation about the location of the white mountains, where the quest would culminate. Using the clues from the book, Mike considered the Great Lakes, and thought about the high mountains of China. TJ replied:

86 TJ: [Almost to himself] [It] could be the Alps.

87 BILLY: Could be Hong Kong.

88 BILLY: Could be going to the South Pole.

89 TJ: Not enough mountains [at the South Pole].

Again, TJ was hypothesizing correctly, but no one else expanded on his ideas. During the last week of school the group met again. This time Mike began the discussion of where the characters were heading:

18 MIKE: He's in the castle.

19 VANDOVER: I know, but do you know where [the castle] is?

20 MIKE: France, I think.

21 VANDOVER: Uh huh, that's what I think.

Mike went over to the map, and the group began to talk about where the characters were traveling:

28   MIKE: Now are they traveling north? They could have it they traveled
     for one day, got to about here. [He points on the map.] Then they
     took that long train cart and got on somewhere.

The group took turns hypothesizing about where the characters traveled
and used the map to trace the paths their guesses led to, until TJ said:

34   TJ: So maybe they were heading for the Alps.

35   MIKE: These mountains? [pointing to the Alps]

36   TJ: Yep. The Alps is where they are headed.

Mike found an encyclopedia and the group read about the Alps, discovering
that the highest mountain in the range was Mount Blanc (French for "white
mountain.") The group was positive that the characters were in France,
headed for the white mountains in the Alps.

The setting changed as the characters made their journey, and was never
mentioned directly. Instead, clues were scattered throughout the story, and
readers had to consider each clue to establish the changing setting. Over
four literature discussions, from May 15 to June 7, the group discussed the
setting seven times. TJ had figured out where the book began the second
time it was introduced; he speculated that it was England. However, other
group members were not ready to accept that interpretation, and the topic
kept recurring.

Smith and Edelsky (1990) call topics that use literary elements to elicit
deeper understandings *literary balloons*. TJ sent up one such balloon with
his speculation that the journey began in England. Although students often
catch these balloons and expand on the topic, the group at first ignored TJ's
insights. Because the topic of setting was important to the story, the students
continued to return to it. In a mini-lesson Vandover explained how he identified setting. Mini-lessons offered students strategies to use as they tried to
identify or describe the conventions of a story, such as setting, plot, or
character. Vandover followed up on his mini-lesson by asking students to
explain their thinking ("How do you figure that?"). Thus students were
given still more practice in searching for clues that might suggest a particular
setting.

Why didn't the group accept TJ's pronouncement about setting the first
time? It was not that the other students were inattentive to his contributions
but that his contributions were first accepted, like all contributions, as speculation. Although TJ leaped to a correct interpretation of setting, other group
members needed to talk through this issue. Over time they were successful
in creating and negotiating meanings recursively. Had the teacher stopped
the speculation and clue searching by evaluating the response ("Good work,
TJ, England is where the book begins"), all the strategies these students used

to develop the setting would have been lost. The practice they have had in reintroducing the topic, speculating and looking for clues, matching their clues against the book and a map will be helpful as they encounter other books in which the setting or other information is important but not easily determined.

RETURNING TO SIMILAR TOPICS IN SUCCESSIVE BOOKS

Not only did students return to topics that were puzzling or confusing within one book, they also returned to topics in preceding books that had yielded important discussions. This was well illustrated when Vandover's group was reading Fred Gipson's *Old Yeller* (1956). In the book, Travis is left with his mother, sister, and dog when his father is called away from home. Vandover first asked students why Gipson removed the father so early in the story:

39   VANDOVER: What about the beginning of the book the father leaves. What about that?

40   DAN: I thought that he would never come back . . .

41   TJ: . . . I mean the guy has got to make a living . . .

42   DAN: . . . I mean I thought that they would have to make a sequel.

43   VANDOVER: If you were the father, would you have left your family?

44   ALL: No!

45   DAN: He had to get out there and get some money. Until winter came.

46   JOSHUA: Stock up on food.

47   ALL: Yeah.

48   JOSHUA: I think they needed to mention more about the father, I mean . . .

49   DAN: As soon as you start the book, he's already leaving.

50   JOSHUA: There needs to be more about the family as a whole [The group continues talking about why the father should have been included for a longer time.]

 . . .

76   JEFF: Well, part of the book is how they live without the dad, or something like that.

77   TJ: Well, it was nice that they didn't have Dad in there, because some of the things that happened, wouldn't have happened if the father

was there. But they need to explain a little more about the father, especially at the end.

As the group talked, they continued to come back to the fact that the father had been removed too early in the story. This inquiry resulted in a group letter, which they wrote and mailed to the author:

> *Dear Fred Gipson,*
>
> We are students in Columbia, MO. and we are all in a reading class here. We have finished your book *Old Yeller* and we have the following comments about the book.
> Out of six of us, five think that the father should be included in two or three more chapters. On a scale of one to five, (five being the best), we of this reading class rate it a four. Also we all think you should write a sequel. We all want to know if this story relates to you in any way. Please reply. This letter was written by students with no teacher involvement.
> *Sincerely,*
> [The Students]

The class members prided themselves on the fact that they had independently constructed the letter. One member of the group then visited the library to find Fred Gipson's address only to discover that he was deceased. The boys were mortified. They had spent all that energy writing to a dead man! Vandover persuaded them to send the letter anyway, and the publisher replied to it with a great deal of information about the author.

The students were concerned enough about the author's decisions and purposes to write a group letter to him. Vandover had raised the literary balloon of the author's purpose, and students had pursued the idea. In so doing, they had deepened their understanding of the story.

In the next literature discussion group each student chose a book for independent reading and then used the group meetings to talk about the books and their similarities and differences. Students continued to be critical of the authors' purposes and decisions. Tom reported, "This book has too much detail," and compared his book to *Old Yeller*. Joshua stated:

35   JOSHUA: This book and that book [points to Tom's] are too detailed. [But] it doesn't even give the father's name, just Dad!

36   TOM: You don't know the father's name in *Old Yeller*.

37   JOSHUA: But Dad is gone early in the story!

The boys consistently returned to the issue of Dad's absence in *Old Yeller* and seemed to use it as a gauge to evaluate the authors' decisions in their current reading.

For the next book, *Snowbound* (Mazer, 1973), the same group stayed together. This time Vandover brought up the author's purposes: "Do you think the author—when he was writing about the stray dog, what was his purpose?" Students discussed what effect the author might have wanted to achieve. Then Tom suggested, "Let's write him—if he's alive—and ask him!"

The next choice was *Ace Hits the Big Time* (Murphy, 1981). Once again the group stayed nearly intact, with five members choosing *Ace.* As in previous books, the group members were critical of the author and his purposes. Andy mentioned, "The book isn't as good as I thought it'd be. The author spends too much time in like one part, it's too dragged out." Bringing up questions about an author's purposes and then being critical of the author had become a part of the way students analyzed the books they read.

Some topics, such as the author's purpose, provided productive discussions for one book and were initiated again for succeeding books. When students raised a topic that initiated a productive discussion, they seemed to internalize the topic. It became a part of their *inner repository of responses,* which they used to consider books. We know that young children learn from hearing stories that many fairy tales begin "once upon a time" and end with "happily ever after." Similarly, through their discussions these adolescents learned how to question the author's motives and purposes, how to figure out strategies to identify the setting of a book, and how to decide if characters were strong or weak. When a topic led to a critical perspective and a productive discussion, the same topic tended to be raised with ensuing books.

Returning to topics that have proven productive in preceding books is important in creating richer discussions, but it is also important in enabling students to read more proficiently. To be a proficient reader, one must be active in constructing meaning within, between, and among books. If students have questions in their heads as they read, they will be more active, critical readers (Goodman and Burke, 1980). Likewise, after a productive discussion they will approach each new experience in a more complex way (Dewey, 1938).

THE TEACHERS' ROLES IN MEANING MAKING

These seventh-grade learning-disabled students did not create meanings alone; their teachers played an important role. The teachers selected books worth reading and discussing. Vandover and Johnsen were confident that their students were up to the task of responding to literature, and their confidence helped to create a sense of trust in the groups. These teachers realized that in all groups some social talk is necessary to build trust. When students briefly strayed from the topic, the teachers waited for a student or an incident to bring them back, and they were rarely disappointed for having waited.

Both teachers were members of the discussion groups—more knowledgeable and more sophisticated members, perhaps, but still members. That doesn't mean that productive groups can't meet without a teacher; they often do. However, when teachers are present, following the lead of students can support productive talk. The teachers often urged students to be more explicit in their thinking and to talk about how they came to certain conclusions. Through his contributions to the discussions, Vandover explained his own reading and writing strategies (for example, how to figure out setting) and demonstrated how he created meaning. Reminding students of important issues was another important role for the teachers. When the students considered the authors' purposes in three books, for example, but ignored the topic in the fourth, Vandover brought it up. He realized that this kind of talk would help students create important insights.

The talk in the discussion groups I observed wasn't always as exemplary as the excerpts I have cited. Some days the book did not seem compelling enough to inspire the discussion of important topics, the students were silly, the teachers were tired, or there just didn't seem to be enough to talk about. But we were confident that the process was valuable. Students were learning how to work collaboratively in a group to make sense of their reading. In the fall the students were reading Beverly Cleary books and pointing out their favorite parts. By winter they were devouring *Old Yeller* and *The White Mountains* and critiquing the author's purposes. Their reading, writing, talking, and thinking had become more complex and sophisticated.

COMING FULL CIRCLE

In writing this chapter, I have begun to see similarities between cycles of meaning in oral language and cycles of meaning in writing. As we write, we revisit topics we have raised earlier and reconsider them through new lenses.

As we reconsider Chris's and Matthew's assessments of literature discussion groups, their insights take on even more power. They believed that meanings in literature study groups were made by all the members, in their own ways at their own speed, that by collaborating together members came to new understandings.

Now let us reconsider the teachers' questions mentioned previously: Marie wondered about the value of talk that covered so many topics, and her concern was quite valid. The talk of these students ranged over a myriad of topics, but that is the nature of collaborative discussion. Students not only constructed for themselves a sense of what the books were about, they negotiated the routines and purposes of their literature study groups. A discussion is a highly complex event, and teachers might be surprised at the number of topics that must be raised to make it rich.

Barbara was worried about getting students to spend a longer time on topics. Barbara may need to take a cue from Vandover and help students to stop and focus on an especially interesting observation that will carry the discussion to a more sophisticated level. When I observed students, some topics were touched on but never developed while others were reinitiated by students and teachers in later discussions. Knowing that important or puzzling topics do reemerge should help Barbara to understand her students' discussion. She may see that in her own study groups, the discussions continue for more than one session and students *are* thinking outside of school about the connections they are making.

Charlie was concerned that his group might not be getting to the "important stuff," a question I asked myself. Observing in my colleagues' classrooms, I was able to see for myself how important the process was. Students used conversation, dialogue, and story to journey into books. They explored meaning collaboratively with the help of their teachers and helped one another become more explicit in their thinking. They pondered issues at home and raised the topics in later groups. Some meanings were made "on the spot," like the connection Mike made between the elephants being held by ropes and the boys being capped in *The White Mountains*, but others evolved over time. Some of the topics that proved successful to students surfaced later as they encountered similar problems in new books. Meanings were made, returned to, and reconsidered; they surfaced, submerged, and resurfaced. As Mike reported about an especially good group, "I could almost visualize it all happening again. It was a little bit better than actually reading the book, you know?" Talking about books together, collaborating and exchanging ideas, considering the meanings that emerge from the social talk in classrooms is indeed "important stuff."

REFERENCES

Barnes, D. 1992. *From communication to curriculum.* 2nd ed. Portsmouth, NH: Boynton/ Cook.

———. 1991. Conversation with Douglas Barnes. Speech at Columbia, Missouri TAWL, March.

Barnes, D. and F. Todd. 1977. *Communication and learning in small groups.* London: Routledge & Kegan Paul.

Berthoff, A. 1990. *The sense of learning.* Portsmouth, NH: Boynton/Cook.

Christopher, J. 1967. *The white mountains.* New York: Scholastic.

Dewey, J. 1938. *Experience and education.* New York: Macmillan.

Fish, S. 1980. Interpreting the *Variorum.* In *Reader-Response Criticism.* Ed. Jane P. Tompkins. Baltimore, MD: Johns Hopkins University Press. 164–85.

Freire, P. 1970. *The pedagogy of the oppressed.* New York: Continuum.

Gilles, C. 1991. *Negotiating the meanings: The uses of talk in literature study groups by adolescents labeled learning disabled.* Unpublished dissertation. University of Missouri: Columbia, MO.

———. 1990. "Collaborative literacy strategies: 'We don't need a circle to have a group.' In *Talking about books: Creating literate communities,* edited by K. Short & K. Pierce. Portsmouth, NH: Heinemann.

——— 1989. "Reading, writing and talking: Using literature study groups." *English Journal.* January:38–41.

Gipson, F. 1956. *Old Yeller.* New York: Scholastic.

Goodman, Y. and C. Burke. 1980. *Reading strategies: Focus on comprehension.* New York: Holt, Rinehart and Winston.

Hurst, K. 1988. "Group discussion of poetry." In *Young readers responding to poems,* edited by M. Benton, J. Teasy, R. Bell, & K. Hurst. New York: Routledge.

Mazer, H. 1973. *Snowbound.* New York: Dell.

Moffett, J. 1967. *Drama: What is happening: The use of dramatic activities in the teaching of English.* Urbana, IL: National Council of Teachers of English.

Murphy, B. 1981. *Ace hits the big time.* New York: Laurel Leaf.

Peterson, R. 1988. "Story elements: Teaching about literature." Presentation at the CEL Conference, Feb.18–19. Winnipeg, Manitoba.

Peterson, R. and M. Eeds. 1990. *Grand conversations: Literature groups in action.* New York: Scholastic.

Rawls, W. 1961. *Where the red fern grows.* New York: Bantam.

Short, K. and K. Pierce (eds.) 1990. *Talking about books: Creating Literate Communities.* Portsmouth, NH: Heinemann.

Smith, K. and C. Edelsky. 1990. *Literature study: Karen Smith's classroom.* Video. Tempe, AZ: Center for Establishing Dialogue in Teaching and Learning.

Thelen, H. A. 1981. *The classroom society: The construction of educational experience.* New York: Halsted.

Watson, D. and S. Davis. 1988. "Readers and texts in a fifth-grade classroom." In *Literature in the classroom: Readers, texts and contexts,* edited by B. Nelms. Urbana, IL: National Council of Teachers of English.

Lauren Freedman has taught seventh- and eight-grade language arts for the past thirteen years at Townsend Middle School in Tucson, Arizona. Since 1990, she has been part of an interdisciplinary team of teachers who work collaboratively to integrate language arts, social studies, and science at the seventh-grade level. Her current areas of interest are teacher research, the use of literature across the curriculum, literature discussion and classroom talk, multicultural education, and integrating whole language philosophy with middle school philosophy. She serves on the board of Tucson Teachers Applying Whole Language and is currently working toward a Ph.D. in Language, Reading, and Culture at the University of Arizona.

Chapter 12
Teacher Talk: The Role of the Teacher in Literature Discussion Groups

LAUREN FREEDMAN

> While it [open-mindedness] is hospitality to new themes, facts, ideas, questions, it is not the kind of hospitality that would be indicated by hanging out a sign: "come right in; there is nobody at home." It includes an active desire to listen to more sides than one; to give heed to facts from whatever source they come; to give full attention to alternative possibilities; to recognize the error even in the beliefs that are dearest to us.
>
> J. Dewey

In thinking about teacher talk, I am struck by the relevance of Dewey's statement. It describes the foundation of the classroom as a community of learners and the talk that sustains that community. If teachers and students are to engage in conversation, story, and dialogue as a means of learning, they must be willing to do so with open minds.

Although the research on teacher talk is narrow in scope, it seems to confirm that teachers believe in class discussion as an important way to learn. The problem, however, is that in many cases discussion is not a particularly useful learning tool because the teacher tends to control it, almost with a set of vise grips. In a study done by Alvermann, O'Brien, and Dillon (1990), a discrepancy was observed between the teachers' thinking and their practice:

> In the intellectualized definitions, the teachers said that discussions should provide opportunities for open exchanges of students' ideas and opinions.

> They also said that questions should stimulate thought and that questions should come from students as well as teachers. In the interviews, however, teachers stated that they used discussions to evaluate students' recall of facts and that they expected students to raise their hands or write answers to questions prior to discussion. (p. 319)

The reasons teachers gave for limiting discussions were "the demands for content coverage, effective use of time, and classroom order" (p. 319). For many teachers, their need to control content, time, and management—and the fear of losing that control—contributes to their inability to allow for what they seem to agree are the most productive kinds of talk. Dewey's notion of open-mindedness is important: teachers need to realize that being "open" is not the same as being empty. No one would suggest that teachers relinquish responsibility for the learning that takes place in their classrooms. In fact, as Barnes (1992) suggests, "If teachers understand the patterns of communication in their lessons they can take *more* responsibility for what their pupils learn" (emphasis mine) (p. 20).

Teacher talk plays a central role in creating the atmosphere in the classroom. If students are to work collaboratively as a community, then trust is a real factor. Students must feel that all ideas will be listened to and, if not accepted, that they will be challenged in a noncombative, noncompetitive way. They must feel assured that their ideas will generate a reply rather than an evaluation. The following discussion I had with a small group of students about our seventh-grade language arts curriculum offered several perspectives, all of which had validity, and the students were willing to see the merit of each other's ideas as well as mine. (I use numbers rather than names to distinguish between students, since the focus is on the teacher's talk.)

01   TEACHER: Would it have been better to have read folklore in the beginning of the year when you were studying about the First Americans in Social Studies?

02   STUDENT 1: Not really, because folklore was different.

03   STUDENT 2: Wait, I've got another idea of what we should have done for folklore. Instead of reading all that stuff and everything, I think we should have done plays and musicals and . . .

04   STUDENT 3: Yeah, see I like acting out stuff a lot.

05   STUDENT 1: I don't. I like to read. But not . . . well I like to read when I don't have to. I don't like to have to read a certain book by this certain date.

06   STUDENT 3: Yeah, I like reading when I want to.

07   TEACHER: Well, how can we get around that in school? Just say choose

from these ten books, for example, and read it approximately in the next two weeks?

08   STUDENT 2: Yeah, that'd be good.

09   STUDENT 3: Yeah.

10   TEACHER: Sort of like what we did at the beginning of the year with *Light in the Forest* [Richter, 1969], *Sing Down the Moon* [O'Dell, 1970], and *Sign of the Beaver* [Speare, 1983].

11   STUDENT 1: Yeah, but it would be better if you could choose your own groups 'cause a lot of times, if you're with people you like, you want to do more and your group presentation will be better.

12   STUDENT 4: Yeah, but what about, like, when certain friends are together and they just mess around and they don't do anything like [they mention a specific example] . . .

13   STUDENT 2: Oh, yeah I know what you mean.

14   TEACHER: O.K. Let me ask you another question. I understand what you're saying and I see a lot of value in it, but I have a real concern when kids come from such diverse areas as come to this school in seventh grade. I worry that if we just said form your own groups, no one would venture beyond their own small group of friends.

15   STUDENT 4: Yeah, I know. That's what I'm saying.

The conversation went on until the bell rang. We reached very few conclusions but generated a lot to think about. My role in this discussion was to aid the negotiation going on among the students. The issues being discussed were very real ones. The students ignored my initial question and took the conversation into areas of more concern to them. It was up to me to follow their lead and to add another perspective to the issues being addressed. As Barnes argues, "The quality of the discussion—and therefore the quality of the learning—is not determined solely by the ability of the pupils" (p. 71). Rather, the teacher has a great deal of influence on the factors—such as the topic, the purpose, and the knowledge and confidence the students possess—that contribute to a discussion.

Much of the research on teacher talk (Mehan, 1979; Cazden, 1986; Goodlad, 1984; McNeil, 1988; Stubbs, 1983) has shown that the following pattern exists in conventional class discussions: the teacher initiates the talk usually with a question, and a student offers a reply; the teacher evaluates the reply and initiates the next sequence (see Figure 12.1).

The teacher assigns the floor, and then takes it back after the student replies (Mehan, 1979). In such a model of student-teacher interaction, the teacher has a fixed agenda, which allows little room for deviation. It elicits a factory image, a conveyer belt on which empty containers are filled or raw

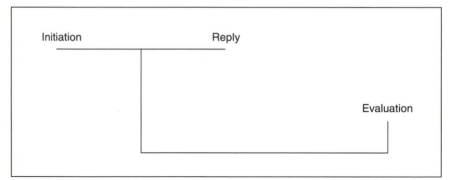

Figure 12.1 *IRE Pattern of Classroom Talk*

metals molded that is reminiscent of Dickens' "little vessels . . . ready to have imperial gallons of facts poured into them until they were full to the brim" (Barnes, 1992, p. 22). Barnes terms this the *Transmission View:*

> The Transmission teacher 1) believes knowledge to exist in the form of public disciplines which include content and criteria of performance, 2) values the learners' performances insofar as they conform to the criteria of the discipline, 3) perceives the teacher's task to be the evaluation and correction of the learner's performance, according to criteria of which he is the guardian, 4) perceives the learner as an uninformed acolyte for whom access to knowledge will be difficult since he must qualify himself through tests of appropriate performance. (p. 144)

The transmission view does not allow for cycles of meaning, since the teacher keeps things moving in a linear direction, feeding the students "school knowledge" and testing their digestion. The fact that students come to school already equipped with a great deal of knowledge is largely ignored. Who the students and the teacher are as human beings and learners is left out of the curriculum, making school a hollow experience to be endured rather than embraced. This view of school and the teacher-student relationship not only discourages open-mindedness, it quite simply does not allow it to exist, and thus prevents the development of learning communities.

The teacher's talk is an essential element in fostering learning in the classroom community. Children do indeed take their learning cues from the adults around them. As Margaret Mead (1975) found in her work as an anthropologist studying another culture, children very quickly learn to do what the adults around them are doing even when these are activities parents would rather their children not learn. In addition, when adults do things regularly but without enjoyment, children learn that these activities are not worth much and that adults can be rather hypocritical.

In order to grow and develop, we need people around us who can guide us, who will listen to us and point us in the right direction. John Dewey (1963) makes the need for adults in the classroom very clear. He suggests that basing education on personal experience requires an increased number of close and varied contacts between teacher and student, and more guidance rather than less. "The problem then is: how these contacts can be established without violating the principle of learning through personal experience" (p. 21).

To facilitate a solution to this problem, Barnes offers the *Interpretation View* of teaching. In contrast to the Transmission View, this view fosters the development of learning communities and nurtures "the pupil's ability to reinterpret knowledge for himself" through collaboration with others (Barnes, 1992):

> The Interpretation teacher 1) believes knowledge to exist in the knower's ability to organize thought and action, 2) values the learner's commitment to interpreting reality, so that criteria arise as much from the learner as from the teacher, 3) perceives the teacher's task to be the setting up of a dialogue in which the learner can reshape his knowledge through interaction with others, 4) perceives the learner as already possessing systematic and relevant knowledge and the means of reshaping that knowledge. (p. 144)

The following six assumptions about learning provide guidelines for Interpretation teachers in structuring and evaluating their talk (Short, 1990):

1. Learning is an active process.
2. Learning is a social process of collaborating with others.
3. Learning occurs when we make connections to our own experiences.
4. Learners need choices to make connections and feel ownership.
5. Learning is reflective as well as active.
6. Learning occurs within a multicultural world with many ways of knowing.

Teacher talk must do many things. It must foster collaboration, challenge thinking, demonstrate thinking, offer ideas, share information, foster social behaviors congruent with a community of learners, offer direction, add to the choices, and offer adult ways of viewing the world. Further, it must be personal as well as social and show that the teacher is also a learner. Thus, the teacher becomes both a guide and a participant.

In thinking about the teacher talk in my seventh-grade language arts classroom, I realized that Barnes' ideas about presentational talk and exploratory talk seem to fit with my notion of the teacher as guide and participant. Barnes (1992) defines presentational talk as polished, complete thoughts, logical conclusions with appropriate supporting details. Exploratory talk is marked by incomplete ideas and interruptions.

As I was considering these ideas, I found it easier to think of them diagrammatically, as in Figure 12.2. This figure contrasts dramatically with the linear Transmission View in Figure 12.1. It depicts the Interpretation View, which allows for the integration of various kinds and uses of teacher talk. The diagram shows two circles that overlap so that only a small part of teacher talk is ever solely presentational (guide) or solely exploratory (participant). The circles illustrate the cyclical nature of talk (the cycles of meaning) and the ease with which teacher talk can move from one mode to another. The area in the center represents the contexts in which teacher talk can include both modes almost simultaneously. It is important to note that although teachers do engage in exploratory talk, it may appear presentational on the surface because adults tend to use more sophisticated language patterns. But the experience of exploring a new idea is certainly as valid for teachers as it is for students. More important, it provides an opportunity for teachers to demonstrate exploratory talk as participants in an open discussion in which students may play off the teacher's ideas as well as each other's in developing their own.

In bringing language into the community of the classroom, the teacher's role is that of a participant in the development of the social community not by engaging in chitchat or making patronizing remarks about a child's hair style or clothes or pretty penmanship but by engaging in the kind of conversa-

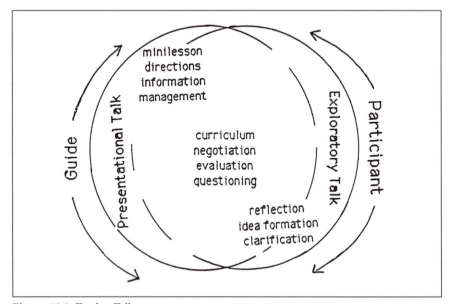

Figure 12.2 *Teacher Talk*

tion that takes place when people know and care about each other. Social conversation shouldn't be relegated to a particular time during the day or a particular class period. People must get to know one another if they are to work well together and enhance each other's learning. Often, talk that appears irrelevant to literature study or some other project may in fact involve issues that need resolution or clarification. And, just as important, conversation is a means of bringing the group closer together.

As Figure 12.2 shows, presentational teacher talk (teacher as guide) most often occurs when the teacher is giving directions, offering information, providing mini-lessons, and managing classroom logistics. Exploratory teacher talk (teacher as participant) occurs when the group reflects, shares opinions and ideas, and asks and answers questions for clarification. In the space between, the two kinds of talk overlap when the teacher and the students engage in talk focused on relating personal anecdotes, negotiating the curriculum, evaluating, pulling examples from the text, returning to the text, connecting the text to other books, and mediating disputes or disagreements.

Last spring during our study of *The Adventures of Huckleberry Finn* (Twain, 1962), I audiotaped several conversations with my seventh-grade students, in small groups of four or five and with the whole class. The students in my classroom come from a variety of economic and ethnic backgrounds and are academically heterogenous. In the following discussion of the kinds of talk teachers engage in as both guide and participant, I have included excerpts from these audiotapes.

PRESENTATIONAL TALK: TEACHER AS GUIDE

The following excerpt offers an illustration of presentational talk. The teacher gives specific information about the social context of the novel. The discussion focuses on the paragraph in which Jim confides in Huck that once he is free, he intends to buy his wife and two children or steal them if necessary. This discussion followed a mini-lesson on satire.

00 TEACHER: [rereads passage.]

01 STUDENT 1: It doesn't sound right.

02 TEACHER: No, it doesn't sound right; there is something ironic about stealing your own children.

03 STUDENT 2: It's not right.

04 STUDENT 3: But he would have to get them back because they were bought into slavery.

05   TEACHER: Now, remember, Twain is writing this after the Civil War.
There is no more slavery when the book was published but only by
about twenty years. So there's still a lot of people in the South feeling
as though getting rid of slavery wasn't such a good thing.

06   STUDENT 4: I thought you said it happened before the Civil War.

07   TEACHER: The story itself is happening before the Civil War. But, it
was published twenty years after. The audience that first read it was
made up of people just twenty years away from the Civil War. There
was no more slavery. So people reading that even in Twain's time
would have been struck by the irony of it. The satire here is very
heavy. How ridiculous—How can you steal your own children? Isn't
slavery pretty stupid? That's the underlying idea.

In this sequence, I offer background information in terms of a time frame
and a historical mind set. The students can then add this information to
what they already know to assess the irony and satire more easily and
accurately.

There are many ways teachers can offer information to help students
to stretch their thinking in a literature discussion that also reflect a true
involvement with the students and an understanding of where they are as
learners. These include mini-lessons, answering students questions as they
arise, or redirecting the question to the whole class or to a student the teacher
knows has an answer. The following two excerpts show two such ways of
offering heuristic information: (1) giving students facts to help them reason
for themselves (in this case, giving them information to help them understand
the importance of the river), and (2) offering an argument to assess the
"truth" of an idea (that all drugs are or are not lethal).

The following discussion focused on the students' ability to visualize the
setting of the novel.

01   STUDENT 1: How big is the river? How wide?

02   TEACHER: It's about a mile wide. That's from Craycroft to Swan [the
school is between these two parallel main streets].

03   STUDENT 2: How long is it?

04   TEACHER: I don't know in miles, but it begins about here [pointing
to map] and goes down to the Gulf of Mexico.

05   STUDENT 3: It's the biggest river in North America.

The discussion ended with a comparison of the Mississippi to the Nile and
the Amazon. Because of the information I supplied, students now had a
more concrete way of reasoning about the role the river might play in the
novel.

The second discussion revolved around a "What if . . ." strategy (what if . . . Huck Finn lived now, what kind of car would he drive, what would he do for a living, what would he do if someone tried to sell him drugs?). One of the students kept coming back to the idea that all illegal drugs are lethal.

01   STUDENT 1: But, if he grew up today, he'd know what it could do, and he wouldn't take the drug.

02   TEACHER: O.K., what do the rest of you think?

03   STUDENT 2: But, he would know about drugs even back then.

04   STUDENT 3: No, they didn't have drugs back then.

05   STUDENT 2: Didn't Coke used to have cocaine in it?

06   TEACHER: I have heard that. Drugs weren't illegal then. There weren't laws one way or the other.

07   STUDENT 1: But, it wasn't lethal then.

08   TEACHER: It's not all lethal now.

09   STUDENT 1: Well . . .

10   TEACHER: No, if all drugs were lethal, then people would drop like flies. I mean, if people were dying right and left, no one else would do them. But, a few people die here and there and lots of people's lives are ruined and . . .

11   STUDENT 2: People die from drug-related accidents, like they can't see well and they drive a car.

We all agreed that drugs cause a lot of pain and agony, but we moved away from blanket statements about "all" and "every." We worked our way from a simplistic view to a more complex view by analyzing the "truth" of the idea that *all* drugs are lethal.

The teacher as guide may also serve as a clearinghouse. The teacher knows who is working on what and which groups are reading which books, and thus can refer students to each other as well as to other resources. As Carol Gilles (1988) states, "A collaborative environment is nurtured by a teacher who considers everyone to be a resource, who allows risks to be taken and mistakes to be made, and who doesn't always have the right answer" (p. 31).

SHARING TALK: TEACHER AS GUIDE/PARTICIPANT

If, as Barnes (1992) suggests, "the central problem of teaching is how to put adult knowledge at children's disposal so that it does not become a strait-jacket" (p. 80), we must be able to move freely back and forth from teacher as guide to teacher as participant and engage in both presentational and exploratory talk. We must share our talk with our students because:

> people whom we collaborate with in an unthreatening relationship are likely to influence us more deeply since we shall have to achieve sympathetic insight into their view of reality in order to collaborate successfully with them. (p. 110)

The following discussion demonstrates this movement within the two circles of talk. This discussion centered on Jim's and Huck's realization that they have gone beyond Cairo.

01 TEACHER: Do you have any respect for the fact that Huck is willing to go against the laws of his society and do what he thinks is right even though . . .

02 STUDENT 1: Can't he buy Jim? Doesn't he have enough money to buy Jim? How much is Jim?

03 STUDENT 2: $800.

04 STUDENT 3: Is he old enough?

05 TEACHER: There weren't the age limits back then like there are now.

06 STUDENT 1: I think he should just buy Jim and they can just still be friends and he couldn't get in trouble if they found them.

07 TEACHER: He can't because he can't get his money unless he goes back to Judge Thatcher and owns up to being alive.

08 STUDENT 2: Oh yeah, they only have the $40. I thought they had $400.

09 STUDENT 1: Yeah, they have no chance, do they, of getting to the North.

10 STUDENT 3: Not on a little raft.

11 STUDENT 2: They'll get a canoe.

12 STUDENT 1: Well as soon as they get to the North can't Huck buy him for 40 bucks?

13 TEACHER: He has to buy him from his owner. Who would he buy him from?

14 STUDENT 3: He could sell him and buy him back couldn't he?

15 STUDENT 1: I don't get that. I think it should be like, you know, Capture the Flag.

16 TEACHER: The game?

17 STUDENT 1: Yeah. When you—let's say this is your side. O.K. Now you can't get tagged over here. Say this is the South.

18 TEACHER AND OTHER STUDENTS: O.K. [Throughout this sequence, we periodically said O.K. to indicate that we understood.]

19 STUDENT 1: You're someone's property right here [in the South]. But if you go over here [to the North] you can do anything you want,

but you can get caught. But, as soon as you get this—as soon as you get the flag, and that's like Huck getting, like Huck buying Jim, then you just go over here and the game's over.

20 TEACHER: So when you're over here you can't do anything but you can't get in trouble, is that right? Let's say this is the North and this is the South.

21 STUDENT 1: O.K. Now, if you're over here, you can do whatever you want but you can get into trouble for it. Now let's say the flag is Huck, who wants to buy you. But Huck can't get you, you have to get him. So here's Jim and he's gotta run away here, but as soon as he gets over here there are more white people here trying to catch him, but if he gets around them, he gets Huck—the flag—and Huck buys him. But for Huck to buy him, he has to get over here. As soon as that happens the game's over and Jim is free. Isn't that how it goes? So, if you go to the North and you get bought, you don't have to buy from the owner, do you?

22 TEACHER: You don't have to buy at all. Once Jim gets to the North he is free.

23 STUDENT 2: But people can still get him.

24 TEACHER: He has to be very careful that he finds support among people who believe in abolishing slavery because you're right, he could get captured and taken back.

25 STUDENT 1: But couldn't Jim sell himself to Huck because he's a free man right now?

26 TEACHER: But why would you sell yourself?

27 STUDENT 1: If Jim sold himself to Huck, he and Huck could stay in the North and be safe.

28 STUDENT 3: If he's in a free state, he's just free, right?

29 TEACHER: Yes. He just needs to be careful to contact people who believe in the abolition of slavery.

30 STUDENT 2: And if someone in the North, a white man say, kidnaps him and takes him south then he is a slave again.

31 TEACHER: A lot of bad stuff went on. So Jim had to be careful because in Missouri, he was someone's property.

The discussion included the laws of reciprocity among the states. It was beginning to occur to these four students that things could get rather complicated. As the teacher, I had a golden opportunity, as long as I was patient and listened, to help the students see that in the adult world there are few simple answers, even though our beliefs and values tell us there ought to be. The student who made the analogy between escaping from slavery and a Capture the Flag game was working through his confusion about what it meant to be "free" in the North if you were a runaway slave. In listening to the tapes, I realized that my talk moved fairly easily from presentational to exploratory: students responded to my role as guide with questions and concerns and to my role as participant with their own comments. As a participant, I followed the students' reasoning to the point where I could enter the discussion as a guide and help to clarify where the knot of confusion was and suggest how to untie it.

In the next excerpt, we were discussing the issue of slavery. Again, my talks falls more inside the circles of the diagram between presentational and exploratory talk, showing that we are sharing talk effectively. This is especially true as the students changed the direction of the conversation by making a connection that I, as an adult, would probably not have made. It reinforces the idea that if teachers set the agenda and limit the content with our talk, we often lose the students and hinder rather then help them make meaningful connections.

01   TEACHER: Even in the best of circumstances even if you were well fed, clothed, housed, and treated kindly, you were still a slave. What does that mean to you?

02   STUDENT 1: Yeah, like being a kid. No freedom.

03   STUDENT 2: Someone bosses you around, tells you what to do.

04   TEACHER: Who you can be with.

05   STUDENT 3: I wouldn't like that. It's really not fair.

06   TEACHER: How many of you want to spend your adult lives with your parents the same way you are now?

07   STUDENTS: (Many voices at once): No way, not me, it would be awful.

08   STUDENT 2: Yeah, I want to make my own decisions.

09   STUDENT 4: And money. I want my own money, too.

10   STUDENT 1: I would have hated it. I'd have run away too, like Jim.

And there we are back in the novel. The students were able to make a very personal connection with Jim and his plight. As guide, I began the discussion with a description of slavery under the "best" of circumstances. The students made an analogy between being a slave and being a minor which, as a member of the group, I picked up on and added to (04). Thus, my movement from presentational talk to exploratory talk influenced the students' efforts to work toward an understanding of what it might have been like to be a slave.

In the next sequence, the teacher talk can be said to fall in the center of the diagram, where the teacher is almost simultaneously acting as guide and participant. This transcript is from the discussion about Jim "stealing" his children. It led to what I consider a rather startling connection the students made between Jim's stealing his children and noncustodial parents' doing the same thing.

01 STUDENT 1: But, you *can* steal your own children.

02 STUDENT 2: Yeah, when people get divorced if they want their children and they don't get to see them or something.

03 TEACHER: Interesting connection—we are running into this same problem in a very different way today, that's true.

04 STUDENT 2: Because of divorce.

05 STUDENT 3: Why would they do that?

06 STUDENT 4: Because they love their children.

07 STUDENT 5: You'd think the child would want to call for help, not the parent.

08 STUDENT 4: They're afraid they'll never see them.

09 STUDENT 3: I don't think that's right.

10 STUDENT 6: Like if a parent abused them, I can understand them. But then they could visit with people around.

11 TEACHER: Unfortunately, and I'm sure there are folks sitting in this room whose parents have been through fairly nasty divorces.

12 STUDENT 1: They want to get back at each other.

13 STUDENT 2: Yeah, revenge.

This is a good example of how teacher talk follows the students' lead. Divorce and "kidnapping" are important issues in the lives of many students. Were I directing the discussion according to the traditional format of question-reply-evaluation and my agenda were set, I would see this kind of digression as an unnecessary disruption to "learning." Not only would I have turned the kids off at that point had I squelched their discussion, I would have made them associate their feelings of frustration and neglect with *The Adventures of Huckleberry Finn* (Twain, 1962), and they probably would have left the classroom muttering about how much they hated the novel. As it was, they made a powerful connection with the novel and spent the remainder of the period delving into all the ramifications this connection had in their own lives.

The tapes reinforced the fact that "children can be responsible and independent learners if they are involved in a curriculum that supports them in making choices, setting goals, and being self-motivated learners. We have not turned the classroom over to children. Instead, we have learned how to collaborate with the children in sharing the classroom" (Kauffman and Short, 1990, p. 131). This approach to sharing expresses the movement taking place inside the circles.

EXPLORATORY TALK: TEACHER AS PARTICIPANT

Exploratory talk occurs when ideas are not fully formed. Instead, they are suggested tentatively, and the talk is marked by interruptions during which new or additional information is offered by the same speaker or by someone else (Barnes, 1992). While it is often true that even in open discussions teachers have preformulated ideas they want to share with students, it is equally true that during the same discussion a teacher may be struck with a new idea to be explored. There are times in my teaching when I am very much in an exploratory stance, sharing a new idea that is just then forming itself. I want to toss it out to the students, who may accept it as something to explore further or reject it as irrelevant.

An example of exploratory teacher talk occurred during a discussion of the section in which Huck decides it's easier to do "wrong" and help Jim than to do "right" and turn him in. Here my talk demonstrates thinking aloud and offers an idea for consideration. The teacher talk in this excerpt adds to the students' discussion instead of directing it. As we were talking, it occurred to me that perhaps one way to see the problem facing Huck was the idea of two consciences (04). The students accepted my perspective as worthy of consideration, and we explored what might be involved in Huck's struggle with what his "society" conscience calls right and what his "personal" conscience calls right.

01 STUDENT 1: They're saying wrong and right are the same thing.

02 STUDENT 2: Well, it sort of is.

03 STUDENT 3: Well, if you don't get in trouble, or get caught lying.

04 TEACHER: What *is* the struggle here that Huck's having? Is it fair to say that Huck has two consciences?

05 STUDENT 2: Yeah—one from how he was raised.

06 TEACHER: What society has taught him.

07 STUDENT 4: The other side has being fair.

08 TEACHER: Loyalty.

09 STUDENT 5: Friendship.

10 STUDENT 3: But, Huck believes in the rules.

11 TEACHER: He just doesn't follow them all the time or even most of the time.

12 STUDENT 2: Could Huck get in big trouble, I mean hanged if he got caught helping Jim?

13 STUDENT 1: It's sort of like Nazis killing Christians when they helped the Jews.

In this sequence, I felt very much a participant, anxious to share additional thoughts as they occurred to me. In line 08, I offer an addition to Student 4's notion that fairness played a part in Huck's dilemma. In line 11, I followed up on Student 3's statement that Huck did indeed believe in the rules. This was an exciting sequence for me to listen to as I transcribed the tape. Although students often engage in this sort of exploratory talk, teachers don't always see that it is a tremendous opportunity to demonstrate that adults also explore ideas, that we are not automatically equipped with them at every turn just because we are adults.

As teachers we tend to talk too much (I found that almost embarrassing while listening to the tapes). Probably the single most important thing a teacher can do is listen. We must listen to our students and observe them, so that we know what they already know and what they want or need to explore next. We need to let the students tell us where they want to go. That's why in much of the discussion (in large and small groups) that goes on in the classroom, students do not have to raise their hands (although many of them do out of habit). The ritual of raising hands tends to keep the talk directed toward the teacher, inhibiting students from talking to each other. This seems chaotic, but it isn't. Students engage in conversations all day long with a variety of people. They know that if they don't talk one at a time, much of what they say gets lost. Students who are involved in a class discussion listen closely enough to each other to know who wants to talk next. That's not to say there isn't rivalry and competition and several voices going at once, but it usually sorts itself out. When it doesn't, or if I notice that a student has been trying to speak for quite a while, I will intervene and direct the conversation, but again, more in a participant style. I want to demonstrate for the students that as a member of the group I have noticed that someone has something they want to say and that I want to hear it. Often when the students are working in small groups and I am not a member, I will overhear them using this strategy for including everyone. The same thing holds true if a group member is monopolizing the conversation. I demonstrate not "as the teacher" but from a participant stance how to redirect the floor. I'll ask a question directly of another student—not a question presuming a certain answer but one to elicit that student's ideas.

I believe that it is important to offer students structure in a discussion and that teachers should not place narrow limits on the content. This is particularly important when students are engaging in discussion without the teacher. Much of what I have said about the teacher's role in literature discussion can be accomplished by the students themselves. As I move from group to group listening to students, I hear them moving freely from guide to participant as their knowledge base and experience allow. To facilitate this movement and to offer a structural framework, I sometimes suggest that the students begin with a "grand tour" question (Spradley, 1979) and see where it leads them. A grand tour question is one that opens the discussion in very general terms, such as "What are your thoughts and feelings about Huck's and Jim's relationship?" Students record the questions they begin to ask each other as a result of their exploration of the grand tour question. Sometimes I have the students brainstorm questions to begin a discussion. I see questions as the spark, the impetus, and the result of a discussion. What did you want to know? What did you have to say about it? What new questions do you have as a result?

CONCLUSION

At the Victoria Symposium in 1982, there were three points about literacy all the participants agreed upon:

(1) all children learn constantly, without the need for special incentives or reinforcement; (2) children learn what is done by the people around them; and (3) children learn what makes sense to them. (Smith, 1988, p. 32)

Yet students come into our classes—particularly in middle school and high school—all too ready to engage in the kind of linear discussion patterns revealed by much of the research to date. How do we change this? Certainly, the most significant change must be in the kinds of talk we engage in with our students.

As I have tried to show, students do indeed pick up on what is being discussed. When provided with an open, supportive atmosphere, they will freely involve themselves in the exploration of ideas, building on one another's talk and that of the teacher. Students want information so that they can more readily make sense of the world around them—their world. But the information will only be useful to them if it is given for an authentic purpose, one which makes sense to them.

Teachers are changing. We are becoming more open-minded in Dewey's sense and more knowledgeable about how learning occurs. To more successfully align our classrooms with how people learn, we must participate in and provide demonstrations of the ways *we* use both exploratory and presentational talk. We must think of ourselves as both guide and participant, taking on each role as dictated by the needs of our students, learning and practicing ways to move freely between these two roles. We must understand that communication and learning to communicate are inextricably linked and that "learning to communicate is at the heart of education" (Barnes, 1992, p. 20).

REFERENCES

Alvermann, D., D. G. O'Brien, & D. R. Dillon. 1990. "What teachers do when they say they're having discussions of content area reading assignments: A qualitative analysis." *Reading Research Quarterly* 24(4):296–322.

Archambault, R.D. Ed. 1974. *John Dewey on education.* Chicago: University of Chicago Press.

Barnes, D. 1992. *From communication to curriculum.* 2nd ed. Portsmouth, NH: Boynton/ Cook.

Barnes, D., J. Britton, & M. Torbe. 1990. *Language, the learner and the school.* Portsmouth, NH: Boynton/Cook.

Barnes, D. & F. Todd. 1977. *Communication and learning in small groups.* London: Routledge & Kegan Paul.

Cazden, C. B. 1986. "Classroom discourse." In *Handbook of research on teaching.* 3rd ed., edited by M.C. Wittrock. New York: Macmillan.

Dewey, J. 1963. *Experience & education.* New York: Collier.

Gilles, C. 1988. "The power of collaboration." In *Focus on collaborative learning,* edited by J. Golub. Urbana, Il: National Council of Teachers of English.

Goodlad, J. L. 1984. *A place called school: Prospects for the future.* New York: McGraw-Hill.

Kauffman, G. & K. G. Short 1990. "Teachers and students as decision makers: Creating a classroom for authors." In *Portraits of whole language classrooms,* edited by H. Mills & J. Clyde. Portsmouth, NH: Heinemann.

Lindfors, J. W. 1980. *Children's language and learning.* Englewood Cliffs, NJ: Prentice-Hall.

McNeil, L. 1988. *Contradictions of control: School structure and school knowledge.* New York: Routledge & Kegan Paul.

Mead, M. 1975. *Growing up in New Guinea.* New York: Morrow Quill Paperbacks.

Mehan, H. 1979. *Learning lessons.* Cambridge, MA: Harvard University Press.

O'Dell, S. 1970. *Sing down the moon.* Boston MA: Houghton Mifflin.

Richter, C. 1969. *The light in the forest.* New York: Knopf.

Short, K. 1990. Six assumptions about learning. Syllabus for LRC 582 Children's Literature in the Curriculum, University of Arizona, Tucson.

Smith, F. 1988. *Insult to intelligence: The bureaucratic invasion of our classrooms.* Portsmouth, NH: Heinemann.

Speare, E. 1983. *The sign of the beaver.* Boston, MA: Houghton Mifflin.

Spradley, J. P. 1979. *The ethnographic interview.* Fort Worth: Holt, Rinehart and Winston.

Stubbs, M. 1983. *Language, schools and classrooms.* 2nd ed. London: Methuen.

Twain, M. 1962. *The adventures of Huckleberry Finn.* New York: Scholastic.

Charlene Klassen taught elementary students for ten years in central California. Working with predominantly migrant and immigrant students, she focused on creating collaborative learning experiences throughout the curriculum. Currently Charlene is completing her doctoral studies in Language, Reading, and Culture at the University of Arizona. Her dissertation explores the use of multicultural children's literature with preservice teachers.

Chapter 13
Exploring "The Color of Peace": Content-Area Literature Discussions

CHARLENE R. KLASSEN

Educators whose classroom practices evolve from their beliefs about the social nature of learning are exploring the various roles literature can play in inquiry. Intensive and extensive opportunities for reading literature are being examined for their usefulness in providing students with multiple ways of learning about themselves and their world (Harste, Short, and Burke, 1988; Peterson and Eeds, 1990). By considering the various purposes for inquiry with literature, teachers can ensure that books are not used in only one way in classrooms but rather in multiple ways for generating knowledge. Teachers are currently exploring four different ways to use literature for learning: as a way to learn language; as a way to know about literature itself; as a way to learn other content, such as math or social studies; and as a way of exploring social, political, and cultural issues (Short and Klassen, 1993). While a specific inquiry might highlight one way of knowing through literature, a study usually encompasses more than one focus.

In order to consider how I enact my beliefs about learning as a social process, I asked my fourth-grade students in Fresno, California, to reflect on our literature experiences. Halfway through the school year I posed the following question to them: How would you explain our literature experiences (specifically our literature discussion groups) to a new student, the principal, or your parent? My purpose for asking this question grew out of a need to reflect on what we already knew by bringing our current understandings to a conscious level and to use our present knowledge to direct the upcoming literature discussions centered on our inquiry study of peace and conflict. Chanthalansy wrote:

> It is about reading, feeling, laughing, true, false, historical fiction, being smart, writing, learning, caring, helping, talking at conferences, war, peace, the past, the future, the present, crying and work.

USING LITERATURE, TALK, AND DIVERSITY FOR LEARNING

Chanthalansy's words depict how he is making sense of his current understandings about the usefulness of literature for learning. His description includes all four of the ways I focused our literary experiences. *Reading* and *writing* experiences with books provide Chanthalansy and other students with opportunities to learn more about their first and second languages. This first role of literature focuses on learning language through literacy events.

Living in the author's world evokes aesthetic responses (such as *feeling, laughing,* and *crying*) for Chanthalansy and others. This second role focuses on the transactive reading event, in which literature experiences become a way of learning about the author's craft and also about the readers' own lives and the world (Rosenblatt, 1978; Peterson and Eeds, 1990). *True, false, historical fiction, the past, the future,* and *the present*—these words describe some of our previous studies with literature centered around history. In this third role, literature offers a way to explore content-area subjects (such as science, math, and history). Themes, topics, and issues of interest create a focus for classroom literature experiences (Edelsky, Altwerger, and Flores, 1991; Harste, Short, and Burke 1988). Personal and global issues like *war* and *peace* are also relevant concerns that can be explored through literary events. Through this fourth role, literature is a way to explore social, political, and cultural concerns that help to form a critical consciousness about reading the word and understanding the world (Freire and Macedo, 1987). This focus emphasizes the notion that reading and learning result in action. In his second language, Chanthalansy describes the power of literature for exploring multiple ways of knowing about language, literature, content areas, and social, political, and cultural issues (Short and Klassen, 1993).

One striking feature of Chanthalansy's description is its interconnectedness. He has made no effort to separate the uses of literature. Instead, he has portrayed the consolidated whole of our learning experiences with literature across the curriculum. His words illustrate how interwoven explorations with literature can be in actual classroom practice.

Chanthalansy's description also points out the social nature of our learning with literature (Vygotsky, 1978). Words such as *laughing, caring, helping, talking at conferences,* and *crying* highlight the active experience of learning and talking in our class. Creating knowledge is a reciprocal process in which learners collaboratively explore topics and issues of concern. Chanthalansy's focus on various forms of talking with other students underscores the generative power of language (Berthoff, 1987). Language as a means for learning in one's first or second language plays an essential mediating role for learners as they construct meaning from their world (Harste, Woodward, and Burke, 1984; Smith, 1983).

Because of my pedagogical belief that knowledge "is both out there in the world and in here in ourselves" (Barnes, 1992, p. 79), from the first day of school I worked to engage students in using their own experiences for learning. Individually and collectively, we gathered knowledge from the world. Topics for inquiry grew out of students' interests and questions. One of my central purposes was to educate critical citizens/students who would actively participate in our nation's democratic system (Giroux and Freire, 1989). Learners needed opportunities to critically reflect on their world and their place within it. I hoped these reflections would lead us to take purposeful action within our social, political, and cultural communities.

It was through talk that I provided demonstrations of my willingness to listen and "take students' views seriously" (Barnes, 1992, p. 110). Three days before our school's winter break, a shooting occurred at a local high school. In the aftermath of this killing, students needed an opportunity to express their disbelief and fear. During whole-class meetings each morning after the shooting, they asked questions about their sense of right and wrong and the need for justice. The intensity of their responses seemed to present a compelling occasion for constructing new understandings of their world.

The diversity of perspectives in our classroom and the political nature of a study about peace and conflict forced me to consider the usefulness of exploring this controversial topic carefully. Some students expressed deep concern about the possibility of another shooting at neighboring schools, while the goal of other students was membership in ethnic gangs. I believed that the multiple voices in our classroom deserved an opportunity to express their views. Talk provided a way to explore our differences and similarities and initiate reflection.

Cultural diversity was the cornerstone of our classroom. We represented six diverse ethnic groups: Mexican Americans (46%), Hmongs (16%), Laotians (13%), European Americans (13%), Cambodians (5%), and African Americans (5%). Half of the students' first language was not English. Because of grade-level misplacement due to language barriers, the ages of our class members ranged from nine to thirteen. Religious and spiritual beliefs ranged from animism to Buddhism to Christianity. The class was also "severely labeled" (Limited English Proficient: 40%, Non-English Proficient: 7%, Special Education: 10%, Gifted: 5%, Below grade level in reading and language: 91%, Below grade level in math: 77%). Students' prior schooling experiences ranged from several months to five years in an American public education system. The one unifying cultural aspect was social class: a majority of the students' families received some form of federal financial assistance each month. The attrition rate for our class was 40%. This level of diversity is not uncommon throughout many other local schools in central California.

This cultural pluralism could have overwhelmed our learning community. Ethnic and familial clashes led to the shooting that precipitated our study, and divergent world views could potentially silence some of these voices. I wondered how our diversity could be used as a generative tool for learning about peace and conflict. Finding ways to embrace the plurality of voices and histories within our classroom was one of my primary goals.

Chanthalansy's use of terms like *feeling, laughing, being smart, caring,* and *helping* to describe our class offered a stark contrast to our "disadvantaged" educational, linguistic, and economic status. The reality of learning in our classroom every day combined the best we had to offer as depicted by Chanthalansy and the struggles we faced in overcoming a severely labeled past both inside and outside school. Throughout our curriculum, cultural similarities and differences became catalysts for learning.

Literature, talk, and diversity were critical elements for learning in our classroom. Literature provided new insights students could explore as they constructed knowledge for their own purposes. Talk with other learners enabled first and second language learners to reflect on their current thinking and consider other points of view. Diversity of perspectives offered multiple viewpoints to examine for potential growth. These three elements each played a central role in this inquiry on peace and conflict.

INITIATING OUR INQUIRY ON PEACE AND CONFLICT

This inquiry offered our fourth-grade class an opportunity to examine and build on personal, community, and world experiences. The thematic approach to this study of content differed from traditional units in several ways. The students and I posed problems and questions for exploration throughout the study, and all participants reflected upon and shared new knowledge (Altwerger, 1990). The three main components of our eight-week inquiry study included (1) literature discussions that evolved from our readings of historical and biographical books, (2) expert groups centering around our major social concerns, and (3) courtroom skits we wrote and performed using the information we gathered through literature and expert groups (see Figure 13.1).

Whole-class discussions about local conflict initiated our study. Students and their parents were greatly concerned about the violence in the neighborhood. Discussing fears publicly in school was not the norm, but five months

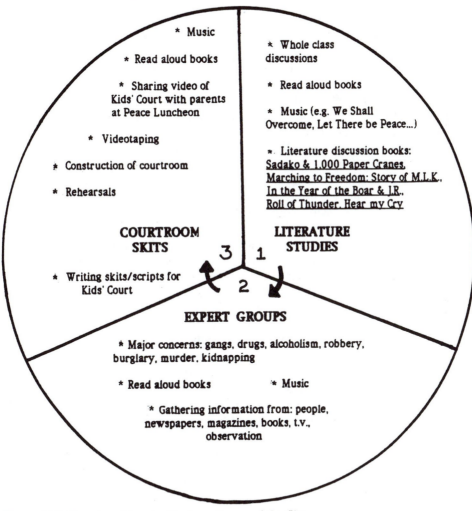

Figure 13.1 *Overview of Inquiry Study on Peace and Conflict*

of interacting in our fourth-grade community led students to realize that it was possible to risk talking about controversial issues. To further our understanding of the shooting, students began bringing in newspaper clippings, which they shared with the class. The day before winter break, I asked the class if our next inquiry study should center on these concerns. A majority vote led me to begin gathering materials for a study, including four historical and biographical books. When we returned to school in January, we continued our discussions about the shooting within a broader inquiry on peace and conflict.

Several times a day from the beginning of school, I had read a wide variety of books aloud and initiated literature discussion groups about various topics and issues. In order to continue and broaden our discussions about the shooting I shared books (such as *The Land I Lost,* Nhoung, 1982; *People,* Spier, 1980; *Faithful Elephants,* Tsuchiya, 1988; *Nettie's Trip South,* Turner, 1987; *A Chair for My Mother,* Williams, 1982; and *We Came to America,* Wolters Elementary students, 1984) that provided various cultural perspectives on peace and conflict. The class discussions following the sharing of a book enabled us to talk our way to a better understanding collaboratively than we had individually (Barnes, 1992).

Because half of the class was reading in their second or third language, I provided many whole-class and small group opportunities to engage in talk. For some second language learners, whole-class discussions seemed less risky, since there was more think-time available for considering their thoughts privately in their first language before sharing them in their second language. These discussions generated a variety of perspectives beyond those shared in a small group. However, for some first and second language learners, whole-class discussions were occasions when they chose simply to listen because of intimidation or the fear that they might not appear as "smart" as others. For other learners, whole-class discussions caused frustration because they could not get enough "air time," since we worked to provide all learners with equal time for sharing. Public and private occasions for talking with others became complex interchanges because of multiple first and second language issues.

The four historical and biographical books I selected for our literature discussion groups were *Sadako and the Thousand Paper Cranes* (Coerr, 1977), *In the Year of the Boar and Jackie Robinson* (Lord, 1984), *Marching to Freedom: The Story of Martin Luther King, Jr.* (Milton, 1987), and *Roll of Thunder, Hear My Cry* (Taylor, 1976). But these Asian American and African American texts did not adequately represent the cultural diversity in our classroom. Therefore, I continued to read aloud a cross section of multicultural books. I introduced the four literature texts through book talks, which consisted of a brief overview of each book and a description of key characters and their surroundings. These "hooks" into the author's story world focused on the dilemmas characters faced in their historical settings.

Students used ballots to record their first and second choices for a literature discussion group, which met on a rotating basis twice a week. My decisions about the size of the groups, whether or not I would remain in groups as a participant, and how often to meet with groups affected our discussions in various ways (Hanssen, 1990). For management reasons, I chose to form only four discussion groups, so that the number of students in each group ranged from five to seven. Less "air-time" was available for each student, yet the larger groups allowed second-language learners more think-time during group discussions.

I decided to remain a member of each discussion group for several reasons. Since half of the students were reading and writing in their second language, I wanted to continue to demonstrate how one person could take up another person's half-formed idea and extend that reader's thoughts. Some class members were recent immigrants. I wanted to support these readers as they risked talking in their second and third languages. In addition, I wanted to be available to pose questions and provide historical information when appropriate.

In order to provide continuous support for learners negotiating their reading experiences in a second or third language, I also chose to meet with each literature discussion group as they read their book. Since an earlier set of discussion groups had become problematic for some students attempting to read an entire book without enough discussion, we rotated between reading one day and meeting to talk the next day. Second language learners found it helpful to talk with other group members while they read the texts. Discussion time throughout the reading of the book gave them opportunities to raise questions and clarify any misconceptions about confusing terms or issues. To provide additional support, students chose a partner within their discussion group so that during their independent reading time between each group meeting they had another person with whom to explore their current understandings.

THE GENERATIVE NATURE OF TALK AND DIALOGUE

Literature discussion groups gave our class the opportunity to engage in the active construction of knowledge together. Although a good deal of our talk occurred at a conversational level, it was my goal to create an environment that promoted dialogue. The difference between talk and dialogue is one of intensity and focus. Talk implies a conversation that can take many directions, dialogue connotes a focused exchange of ideas in which all learners are changed through the collaborative production of meaning. Learners who come together in order to make sense of anomalies are receptive to hearing divergent voices (Peterson, 1992). In these four literature discussion groups, I wanted to bring to life the power of dialogue (Short and Pierce, 1990).

The talk and dialogue supported our learning in numerous ways (see Figure 13.2). Talking about literature was a way for us to learn about language (first role): (1) learners posed questions about difficult words and terms in their second language. Our talk about literature was a way for us to learn about literature itself (second role): (2) students had an occasion to live in the author's world and (3) consider the author's intent in writing the literature we were examining. Talk about literature was also a way for us to learn about content (third role): (4) learners gained a personal perspective on history. In addition, our talk about literature was a way to learn about social, political, and cultural concerns (fourth role): (5) students dealt with social conflict, (6) made sense of life experiences, (7) considered tensions in their lives, and (8) reshaped their perspectives on peace and conflict.

Learning a Second Language

First and second language learners used our discussion time to pose questions about new or confusing words and phrases. One morning during our discussion of *Sadako and the Thousand Paper Cranes* (Coerr, 1977), Sanhya, who was Laotian, started our group meeting by making a comment about

	FOCUS OF INQUIRY STUDY			
	Lit. as way to learn language	*Lit. as way of knowing about literature*	*Lit. as way to learn content*	*Lit. as way to explore social political and cultural issues*
TYPES OF TALK	1) Learn a second language	2) Live in author's world 3) Consider author's intent	4) Gain personal perspective on history	5) Deal with social conflict 6) Make sense of life experiences 7) Consider tensions in lives 8) Reshape perspectives on peace and conflict

Figure 13.2. *Ways of Using Literature for Inquiry.*

the term "lazybones." After reading aloud Coerr's use of this word from page ten, he remarked that it was a weird and funny word. Others agreed that it "was a great word." In the midst of reading this story about a young Japanese girl stricken with leukemia as a result of atomic bomb radiation, Sanhya was noticing new words in his second language. The following week he asked his group to help him understand what it meant for Sadako's "legs to get energy." When no one offered an example, I joked that, at recess, Sanhya's legs appeared to have "lots of energy" for running around the school yard chasing his friends. We went on to talk about other times during the day when we had lots of energy.

Second language learners like Sanhya often used their second language to pose clarification questions. Demonstrations by bilingual learners over the previous seven years had helped me begin to understand that optimal learning occurs in the students' first language. (Cummins, 1981; Freeman and Freeman, 1992). Since I was fluent in English, one of the five languages spoken in our classroom, I worked to create a collaborative environment in which students supported each other in their first language while other class members and I supported learners in their second. Whether students communicated in Spanish, Hmong, Lao, Khmer, or English, we focused on gathering knowledge collaboratively and generating new meaning. Our classroom community worked to value an exchange of ideas, where students used their first and second languages as a central means for organizing and reflecting on their current understandings.

Although most of our discussions about Coerr's book were quite emotional, Sanhya knew that our small group discussions were also occasions to ask questions about his second language. A list of tips we wrote to help students prepare for literature discussions included one that suggested they record confusing words or phrases while reading and then ask the group for clarification at the next meeting. Sanhya had demonstrated a willingness to risk posing questions to six other learners. Our talk in literature discussions reminded me of the vital role a community of readers plays in supporting students as they learn (Lindfors, 1987; Freeman and Freeman, 1992).

Living in the Author's World

The members of the literature discussion group on *Sadako and the Thousand Paper Cranes* openly expressed their feelings about the "lived-through experience" of reading this poignant book (Rosenblatt, 1978). During our second discussion, Mo commented that Sadako was "too young to die." He had read the epilogue, which noted that she died on October 25, and thought it was strange to think of death so near Halloween, a newly discovered celebration for this recent Hmong immigrant. Later, Sompat shared that she "felt scared last night" as a result of reading the book. Angel stated, "I don't know how it feels to die," and Sompat said how lucky she felt to be so healthy. The group went on to consider how the author might have collected information about Japanese children who got leukemia after the atomic bomb was dropped on their city during World War II. Angel then referred back to his earlier thoughts by calling attention to the death of one of Sadako's friends in the hospital on page forty-two of the book. He felt "sad, mad, and angry" that children would die. Mai expressed how scared she felt when people talked about death.

In looking over my field notes after this discussion, I wondered why students spent so much time sharing their emotional responses. I noted the numerous lapses into silence between statements. There seemed to be an uneasiness in talking about this subject. I wondered if the four Southeast Asian refugee students in the group faced death as they fled their homeland. When I described this literature discussion to another teacher, he told me that Southeast Asian parents advised their children not to talk at school about what they experienced before arriving in America.

While the talk in our second discussion encompassed the historical context, the author's perspective, and the genre of historical fiction, I realized how legitimate it was for students to explore their aesthetic responses (Rosenblatt, 1978) to peace and conflict concerns. The world created by Eleanor Coerr's words evoked a variety of feelings, many of them left unsaid at our group discussions. As I considered the life experiences behind the students' words, I was reminded that literature could help us learn more about our own lives and the world (Peterson and Eeds, 1990). These discussions provided time for us to respond as people with deeply felt emotions.

Considering the Author's Intent

Another literature group reading *Roll of Thunder, Hear My Cry* (Taylor, 1976) used their discussion time to explore why the author wrote the book. The story about the Logan family provides an insider's perspective on African American life in the South during the 1930s. At our first conference, Samuel wondered if Taylor wrote the book because she did not like the idea of slavery. He relayed a discussion he'd had with his mother one evening. She had indicated her agreement with the author's purpose by stating, "Peace is the right way." Jee asked if Mildred Taylor was black. He wondered if she wrote it because she did not want people "to be prejudice."

The following week, Pa continued to explore the author's intent, along with other issues, in her literature log. She wrote:

I felt sad reading the book. I had felt like crying but I know that no one won't cry with me. Cassie is such a wonderful kid and her mind works out good but she's got a miserable life. I wish that I was Miss Crocker so I can be nice to Cassie forever and be nice to the other different kids like Black and White in the story book. I think I know why the book is call *Roll of Thunder, Hear My Cry* because Cassie cries and she wants the thunder, the Lord, and the sky to hear her cry. I guess that's why it's call *Roll of Thunder, Hear My Cry.*

Pa's empathetic response to Cassie, the main character, prompted her to want to take action by entering into the story world in order to promote positive change. She was disturbed by the injustices she encountered through her reading. The recognition of prejudice was not enough; it demanded action. In her log she took time to consider various responses, and although she never chose to share this entry with our group, it was a generative experience for her. She used writing as a time to wonder and explore her current thinking. Her response to Taylor's symbolic "cry" to recognize and address prejudice was to take personal action by wishing to change Cassie's world.

Samuel's, Jee's, and Pa's thoughts about Taylor's purpose in writing this book emphasized their awareness of the writer's social and cultural concerns. Writers are people who have questions about peace and conflict just as we do. These three students knew personally what it meant to experience prejudice. Samuel, an African American student, had recently moved from the South to Fresno; Pa and Jee were Hmong immigrants from Laos. Through discussions of this work of historical fiction, we were able to reexamine historical events in order to see what we could learn from them. Our consideration of Taylor's intentions moved us toward a greater understanding and awareness of our world. The insights about peace and conflict we gained from the story of Taylor's life helped us reconsider personal issues of peace and conflict. We explored the fact that authors are sometimes prompted to write in response to some of the same social and cultural dilemmas we face (Meltzer, 1989).

At the close of our last discussion we created our own "I [We] have a dream" speeches, expressing our desire for schools free of prejudice, knives, fighting, hatred, and killing. Clarifying our goals was one step toward taking some sort of action against prejudice. Taylor's words pushed us to respond to prejudice within our own community.

Gaining a Personal Perspective on History

Students used our literature discussions as a time to consider historical events in light of their own experiences and thus gain a personal perspective on history. During our first discussion about *Marching to Freedom: The Story of Martin Luther King, Jr.* (Milton, 1987), Jenifer began reflecting on the experiences of her people. As this African American ten-year-old read Milton's account of the struggles Martin Luther King, Jr., faced throughout his life, she noted how much people "talked about peace" during his life and wondered how we could get people "talking about peace again." Later in this same discussion, she brought up the subject of the Jim Crow laws, which were still in effect during King's life. Her comments led the group to talk about the unfair treatment of African Americans throughout our nation's history, starting with their arrival as slaves. Jenifer wondered, "Why was there slavery?" Seated around a map of the United States we examined the need for cheap farm labor in the 1600s. Using a world map, we traced the journey from Africa to the plantations in the southeastern United States. Then we moved over to the historical timeline (posted across the front of our classroom) and traced the hardships African Americans faced from the days of slavery through the Civil War when they got their "freedom" to the Jim Crow laws still in effect when Martin Luther King, Jr., was born.

Following this discussion, Jenifer continued to reflect on power relations between ethnic groups through her writing in her literature log. She was working to make sense of the injustices in her life experiences, which paralleled the injustices King encountered as a child.

> I wonder why the Blacks can't have peace and freedom in the world. Now there's freedom in America. Martin Luther King treated the White people good and the White people treated him bad.
>
> I had a friend like that and she was prejudice of me. I never noticed until one day, I called her and her mom answered the phone and said that she's gone and so I went over to her house and she answered the door and I said, "Your mom said that you wasn't here," and my friend said, "Oh, my mom said you and me can't play together," and I just walked away and I cried. It just isn't fair to have Blacks not to play with Whites and I went back home and so I cried and cried.

Historical events took on new meaning when Jenifer perceived them through the lens of her own life experiences. Her critical consciousness of the world increased as she compared her own struggles with those of King. I was still concerned about helping students gain a clearer understanding of American history as it related to the struggles of African Americans. Our sweeping discussion only highlighted general concerns across hundreds of years. I also felt the need to examine slavery and Jim Crow laws, not in terms of one ethnic group versus another, but in terms of a human struggle across many ethnic groups. Somehow we needed to examine the multiple perspectives affecting issues of slavery and prejudice. I suggested that students use their literature logs to pose historical and critical questions for clarification.

Andrea wrote the following entry one week later as she worked to explore half-formed thoughts and organize questions in preparation for our next discussion.

> I think it was a sad life he [King] led. I am glad I was not in it. I could not imagine what it would be like if I was Black. I think it was sad for the Black people. I think the reason why Joy wrote is for people to live a better life. Why did they shoot Martin Luther King? I think it was sad when he shot him. Why did they call him the peacemaker? How old was Abraham Lincoln when he got shot? Where did Abraham get shot? I did not like wetting [spraying with water hoses during marches] the Black people. I did not like when they said that they would blow up his house.

In her writing, Andrea was laying out what she knew and what she needed to know in order to gain a larger perspective on the historical struggles facing African Americans. Andrea's people had also faced similar struggles. I wondered if she would consider her own history as a Mexican American in conjunction with our look at the difficulties faced by African Americans.

At our next discussion, Andrea asked a number of questions. She wanted to know, "How did the law start [about the buses]?" which led our discussion back to the Jim Crow laws and the Civil Rights Movement. I referred to our earlier discussion about the prejudice African Americans have faced throughout our history. We talked about the days of slavery and the Civil War, which brought up the topic of the Emancipation Proclamation. I used pictures to refer to Abraham Lincoln and his efforts to free the slaves. After looking at Lincoln's picture, Andrea wondered, "Was Abraham Lincoln Mexican?"

Near the end of this discussion, Andrea returned to her questions by wondering why "no Mexican names were mentioned in this book." I explained that I had not been able to find any books about Mexican American people quickly enough for our literature discussion groups. I agreed that we needed to read some of these books, since many students in our class were Mexican American.

The need for a personal perspective on historical events was clear in Andrea's statement. Her poignant comment focused on my inability to represent all ethnic groups in the books for literature discussions. Finding culturally diverse historical fiction books for the elementary classroom was not simple, and yet I needed to find ways through the texts I shared to support the Mexican American students who formed half of our class. Literature books were one powerful avenue to help us develop "a sense of history, a personal perspective, and a wisdom that [would allow us] to examine the present and project the future in light of historical processes" (Baldwin, 1981, p. 242). Andrea wanted this opportunity. One of my solutions was to share more literature about Mexican American culture during our read-aloud time each day.

The talk about issues that evolved from our own transactions with literature helped readers to begin exploring their own histories and voices while adding to their knowledge of the world. I was beginning to understand that a historical inquiry needed to connect with the students' own history. Historical lessons about peace and conflict were most useful when examined through both a personal and a historical lens.

Dealing with Social Conflict

Students' lives outside of our classrooms are full of conflict. My fourth-graders readily recognized and discussed conflicts they saw in the literature books we read. Two different literature groups addressed the problem of the interpersonal struggles that result from larger social conflicts through discussions about the characters in their books.

Lor considered the plight of the main character in *In the Year of the Boar and Jackie Robinson* (Lord, 1984) as she talked about her efforts to endure the taunts of classmates. The central character, Shirley, a recent arrival from China, was a fluent Chinese reader and writer but understood little English. Her first months in a Brooklyn school were filled with turmoil as she struggled to find her place among the other class members. Lor, a Hmong immigrant, readily empathized with Shirley's struggles. During one discussion she shared that she would "cry a lot if the students called me names." Lor went on to ask why they thought Shirley's classmates yelled, "Are you stupid?" when she did not respond with the correct answer in class one day. Noutchary responded by stating how sad and scared she would feel if someone talked to her that way. Kosal added that it was hard when you "don't understand what they say." These first language speakers of Hmong, Lao, and Khmer implicitly understood the need for friends and the turmoil of struggling to comprehend another language in a strange, new country. The characters in Lord's book worked to cope with social conflicts similar to those facing immigrants like Lor, Noutchary, and Kosal.

During the last discussion of the group reading *Marching to Freedom: The Story of Martin Luther King, Jr.* (Milton, 1987), Teresa summed up what she had learned from reading the book by explaining that if "there was no more segregation," there would be "no more prejudice," which would "take a lot of courage." She went on to ask why people used "cuss" words to describe African Americans and why the author referred to those words in the book. I commented that even though we normally never discussed swearwords in school, sometimes we needed to in order to examine an issue. I asked the group to think of other words people might use against their ethnic group. Teresa mentioned a derogatory word for her Mexican American people. We talked about where the term came from by using a map to locate the Rio

Grande River and went on to discuss some of the struggles Mexican American people had faced throughout American history.

Teresa's question highlighted the fact that we live in a world of people with conflicting views. Once Teresa had initiated the topic, my goal was to move this literature group toward reflection through the use of their personal perspectives. Over the course of five months of learning together, I had frequently heard them use disparaging phrases against each other. Milton's reference to people's use of these detracting terms during the civil rights era helped us begin to "make the familiar strange." Stepping outside of our own use of similar terms and examining their use historically provided personal, cultural, and historical insights. The disjunction Milton created by referring to disparaging words helped us come to a greater awareness of historical events and construct new understandings of our own experiences.

Lor's and Teresa's comments provoked our thinking about the kinds of cultural prejudice that can pervade people's responses to many "minority" groups. Interpersonal conflicts often grow out of people's stereotypic beliefs. Our talk about literature offered us a way to examine relevant cultural and social issues at personal and public levels. I wondered how these insights would affect their daily interactions with each other and if they would extend into their families and communities. During the last literature discussion in Teresa's group, I asked the students to think about why we read and talked about prejudice so intensely. Sonephet shared, "It's important to remember so we don't do it anymore," thus touching on our ability to use new knowledge in order to understand and change our interpersonal interactions in the world (Barnes, 1986.)

Making Sense of Life Experiences

Students used their literature discussions to examine and cope with difficult life experiences. They needed time to talk about struggles they had faced with a community of trusted co-learners. The last discussion with the students reading *Sadako and the Thousand Paper Cranes* (Coerr, 1977) proved to be such an occasion. Angel started by stating, "I hate it!" He explained how it made him mad that Sadako missed her graduation because she was too sick to leave the hospital. Sompat shared, "I hate the dying part." Sanhya told us he hated page thirteen, where the author explained how the atomic bomb, dropped on Hiroshima ten years before, was still killing many Japanese people. Later in the discussion, Milagritos continued to delve into the topic of death by sharing, "I don't like the dying part because my sister died." The other group members and I did not know how to respond except with respectful silence. Finally I asked Milagritos if she would tell us more. Five years ago, at the age of two, her little sister Crystal had died. After more silence, Mai quietly stated that she felt scared of death; the book "reminds me of my dad dying" in Laos. Angel went on to share that his uncle died. He said he hated the "feeling like you're going to cry." I explained that I too felt fearful when thinking about death but that someday each of us would die, that it was difficult for me to talk about this topic but I felt the need to think more about my fear of death in order to make peace with it.

I was not sure how to close a discussion in which students had shared their feelings so honestly. I asked the group what we should do. One student suggested that we read the book to the class and ask them what they thought of it. Another recommended that we have a peace celebration with the whole class. Still another proposed that we create mini-skits about the book to show our favorite parts. The group decided to share Sadako's story with the class and consider experiences they could include in a peace celebration.

The next day I began reading *Sadako and the Thousand Paper Cranes* to the entire class during our read-aloud time after lunch. One student suggested that we try to fold one thousand paper cranes and hang them from the ceiling of our room as a sign of peace. The following afternoon several students demonstrated origami techniques to the whole class, and we hung our first twenty-six paper cranes from the ceiling in symbolic response to Sadako's story and our desire for peace in the world.

I sensed that these small group discussions about the text offered a fleeting glimpse of the students' thinking. Their lives were filled with conflict. As a result of the Vietnam War, one third of our class became refugees, and now their neighborhood showed signs of unrest (through the shooting at the high school and increased gang activity).

A few weeks later, I discovered one immigrant student's efforts to deal with his own history and life experiences through his writing. During our literature discussions, I became aware of Mo's struggle to share his thoughts verbally because of his uncertainty about speaking in his second language. I read *The Land I Lost* (Nhoung, 1982) aloud to the class during this investigation of peace and conflict issues. Mo chose a similar title for a piece about his homeland and the conflicts he encountered.

How I Lost My Land

All I really know is he take us to a nice new house. We have a backyard. There was three trees. It was a apple tree, also a orange tree and a pear tree. We live there for five months. We was live in peace.

Through extensive discussions with classmates and me, Mo's final draft of his experiences in his homeland expressed the struggles of a refugee family. Three weeks after writing his first draft, he had completed the following piece describing his experiences in Laos and Thailand:

How I Lost My Land

When we were living in Laos, the mean Vietnamese soldiers came to take us
for their slaves and even kill us if we do not do what they said. So one day
my father said, "We have to leave this land and go find freedom." When we
came to the Mekong River, it was so big that we could not swim across so
everybody had to get in the boat to get across the river. We crossed safely to
the other side. After that we still had to go a long way. We had to go up hill
and down hill, and we crossed many rivers on the way. After many days we
came to Thailand. On the way my grandmother was not the lucky ones. She
was sick and die. My family was very sad. I remember we were so tired and
hungry. After living in Thailand for many years, my father said, "There is
nothing here for us. We had to go on to find freedoms in the United States of
America." When I got on the airplane, I was so scared. I did not eat or drink
because I lost my appetite. When we got to America I always think about my
grandmother and how I lost my land.

Years after traumatic struggles, Mo, Milagritos, Mai, and Angel were still
working to gain a greater understanding of their life experiences. Dialogue
in small groups and writing offered these learners a chance to reflect upon
these experiences within a community of trusted co-learners. The words of
Mai and Mo, in part, initiated whole-class discussions about the complex
political events in their homeland of Laos. We struggled to gain a larger
perspective on the hostile interactions involving the Laotian, Hmong, French,
Vietnamese, and American people. My awareness of the range of human
experiences these nine-, ten-, and eleven-year-olds brought to our community
of learners was profoundly deepened. Mo's focus on freedom and hope
reminded me of all I had to learn from my students. My understanding of
the usefulness of literature increased as I recognized the need for students
like Mo to make sense of their life experiences within the larger framework
of historical and political events.

Considering Cultural Tensions in Our Lives

Our literature discussions gave us an opportunity to learn more about the
cultural tensions that affected our daily lives. We began to recognize some
of these disjunctions by talking about the shooting at the high school and
the conflicts different story characters encountered. We were able to see
anomalies in others' lives and examine how they chose to deal with them.
I wondered how to address the conflicts in their lives more directly.

Lor, who was reading *In the Year of the Boar and Jackie Robinson* (Lord,
1984), provided a bridge into our own lives by using her written response
time as an occasion to reflect on her own struggles as a Hmong refugee.
Since the beginning of the year, students had been using the literature log
as a place to wonder and pose questions about their reading. Up to that

point, I had not seen Lor reflect on her immigrant experience through her writing. But near the end of our literature discussions, she indicated her desire to write about the struggles of her people, which paralleled the conflicts the characters in her literature book encountered. I readily agreed that reflecting upon her life experiences was an essential part of our study about peace and conflict. That morning Lor spent thirty minutes intently focused on writing.

> I lost my land because American they try to get our land. When they try they have to use their hands with weapons. America, when they first started, they lie and [were traitors] to us. That killed our own tradition . . . The Americans trick us . . . Later they [Americans] lose and we was scared . . . we are against you Americans . . . I don't like America land because in our land we don't have no robberies or murders. In America . . . they don't care . . .

Reading her literature log that evening, I was stunned by Lor's anger. Her powerful reflection demanded action. Before school the next morning, I asked Lor if she would share her thoughts with the class at the whole-class discussions we held prior to our literature groups. When she declined, I asked if I could read her literature log entry to our class that day without disclosing her identity as a way to promote a whole-class conversation about the social and cultural tensions in our lives. I felt the need to bring these issues out into the open for consideration by the class. I wanted to collectively recognize tensions throughout our class and world community. Recognition of conflicts precedes being able to deal with them effectively (Freire and Macedo, 1987).

The class discussion that evolved after I had read this entry was quite discomforting. Other immigrant students voiced their frustrations about being labeled newcomers by unfriendly Americans. By posing questions, I asked them to share their understandings of the turmoil that initiated the Vietnam War in order to gain a greater understanding of the tensions they felt in their homeland and in our country. I did not feel prepared to deal with the fear, anger, and hostility I heard from students. Their feelings of being isolated as outsiders, their unsettled state of mind about living in the United States, and their intense desire to return to their homeland shocked me. I felt like a learner working to gain a more critical consciousness of my world. This opportunity, for me and our classroom community to hear multiple perspectives concerning the cultural and social conflicts facing immigrants, generated knowledge which could help us more effectively understand and change our world. I decided to present the divergent views surrounding the issue of the Vietnam War. Immigrants, soldiers, and governments all had strong, often opposing viewpoints. "Hearing" all of these voices in our learning community proved to be a complex process.

The tense discussions that resulted from reading Lor's entry to the class did not magically solve these students' dilemmas. Naming the problems publicly did not eradicate international tensions. Instead they appeared more overwhelming the longer we examined them. In one of these whole-class discussions, we listed the social concerns we felt in our neighborhood and recorded some of the conflicts students dealt with everyday. As students shared stories of family and community struggles, we generated a long list of concerns, including gangs, drugs, alcoholism, robbery, burglary, murder, and kidnapping. In order to examine these social dilemmas further, I proposed that we explore these issues through expert groups after we completed our literature discussion groups. Three to four students focused on one topic and gathered information from people, newspapers, magazines, books, and television. Two weeks of collecting information produced a wealth of notes and facts. Through an extensive class discussion, we decided to write court-room skits for a Kid's Court in which we would examine conflicts through the court system. After we wrote the scripts, rehearsed our parts, and constructed a courtroom, we videotaped our Kids' Court and showed it to parents at a Peace Luncheon and Celebration.

Our literature discussions and class discussions about cultural and social tensions in our lives did not lead us to any definitive answers. Our questions about the war, immigrant struggles, and social issues like drug abuse or alcoholism led us to more questions about the nature of peace and conflict. Throughout these discussions, I was forced to reconsider the role of education and my role as a teacher. Actualizing my democratic beliefs by encouraging a critical consciousness helped to bring out into the open the disequilibrium students felt. Disjunctions presented opportunities to grow individually and collectively.

Literature provided a way for us to know more about social and cultural tensions. The purpose of our inquiry into peace and conflict was not to magically discover the "right" answer. Instead it was an opportunity to productively discuss matters with others who think differently (Britton, 1986). The complexities we examined in our discussions created greater awareness. Our talk persuaded me to explore immigrant issues. I was working toward a greater understanding of what it means to negotiate the curriculum with students, thereby acknowledging my role as co-learner (Wells, 1986).

RESHAPING OUR PERSPECTIVE ON PEACE AND CONFLICT

Near the end of our literature discussion groups, Jee considered his newly acquired knowledge of historical events in light of his hopes for the future.

> I think in this book people hate Black and judge them by their color. I hope some day all the people doesn't care about color. They only care about peace.

> Peace is [more] important than prejudice. Prejudice is not good. But people sometime can break the law. After when the American want freedom they treat people bad. But I'm glad it don't happen in Room 19.

In his second language, Jee reflected on his current perceptions of peace and prejudice, an outgrowth of discussions with other students reading *Roll of Thunder, Hear My Cry* (Taylor, 1976) and whole-class discussions. Indirectly he acknowledged the power of our learning community in providing an example of people who "[do not] care about color" but focus on "caring about peace." Jee recognized and began to work through the disequilibrium created by learning about prejudice in the South during the 1930s, prejudice he felt directed toward the Hmong people, and demonstrations of peace he experienced in our classroom.

When examined over time, learning often provides a clearer view of the ways in which students are making connections. Three weeks after we finished our inquiry study, Samuel was still reshaping his current knowledge through his writing. During our Writer's Workshop time, he wrote the following piece in an effort to integrate his thoughts about his people, his perspective on slavery, and his notions of peace. He read it to the class and asked for their response.

> Once, a long time ago, Black people were slaves. It wasn't a very peaceful time for Blacks. The only thing you could hear was Blacks crying and whips cracking in nearby fields. Suddenly a man came along who must have took a smoke from a peace pipe and began to straighten out the world. His name was Martin Luther King, Jr., yes the peacemaker, who died for his rights and yours.
>
> Martin fought and went to jail a lot but he didn't care because he was a man of peace. To me Martin Luther King, Jr., saw only one color, the color of peace. He believed that no one man, woman, or child should be judged by the color of his skin but by what was in his heart.

Having lived in the South all his life before moving to central California, Samuel did not appear to have questioned the limited position in which society placed African Americans. The Logan family in *Roll of Thunder, Hear My Cry* provided divergent role models, ones he had not previously considered. Our whole-class discussions about Martin Luther King, Jr., shed new light on his prior perceptions. Dialogue within our community pushed him to create new understandings as he worked to embrace diverse perspectives about himself and his world, therein reshaping his beliefs about *the color of peace.*

Our literature discussions provided the impetus for reflective thinking long after we completed our inquiry. Talking and writing were a constructive force for future learning. Through an exploration of literature, students like Samuel were coming to view themselves in a new light, as viable, contributing members of our classroom and society. The learning community's ability to value learners' knowledge affected students' perceptions of themselves.

EXPLORING THE COLOR OF PEACE

Literature discussions encouraged students to work toward the simultaneous reading of the word (historical fiction books) and the world (social, political, and cultural issues throughout history). The concurrent act of reading both text and context promoted a more critical consciousness of their personal and global place in the world (Freire and Macedo, 1987). The disequilibrium created through reflection provided a generative opportunity to clarify personal perceptions and hear the multiple perspectives present in the classroom, thereby generating new knowledge to be explored in future inquiries.

This focus on using literature to learn about a content area (history) and to examine social, political, and cultural concerns enlarged my understanding of the usefulness of literature discussion groups. Although our literary experiences were a way to learn language and know more about literature (the first and second roles for literature), this inquiry centered on issues of peace and conflict. Literature provided a way to explore historical, social, political, and cultural problems (the third and fourth roles for literature).

The nucleus of Samuel's essay, *the color of peace*, focused on the central purpose of this inquiry, that of working toward a greater understanding of the complexities inherent in peace and conflict issues. Although we grew as individuals and as a learning community, engaging in this exploration did not make the problems we examined disappear. After our study, the multiple perspectives present in our class seemed even more apparent. Our celebration to "conclude" this study, the Peace Luncheon with parents, appeared to "initiate" the actual work of using our new insights.

We discovered no simple solutions to our questions. Instead we were faced with some of the same complexities that initiated our study; only now we were able to recognize and consider new strategies for facing these conflicts. Our collective study of problem-posing and problem-solving appeared to highlight the multiple contexts for future exploration inside and outside of the classroom (Short and Burke, 1991). One student provided a powerful demonstration of working to face the complexities in her life by inviting her father, who had recently gotten out of jail, to our Parent Luncheon. I discovered another student's efforts to use her knowledge through her mother. At our next student/parent/teacher conference, her mother commented that she noticed a more thoughtful attitude in her daughter, who was attempting to respond in a different way to her siblings. I was also pushed to apply my insights by one administrator, who felt my decision to have students write courtroom skits and enact what we had learned about peace and conflict was not a wise use of instructional time.

Our conversations and dialogue about relevant personal and community issues at literature groups and whole-class discussions urged us to reconsider our prior beliefs and utilize the multiple perspectives present in our lives to work toward new understandings of peace and conflict. Our very diversity became a productive tool for learning. In essence, it was our goal to use our current insights into *the color of peace* to generate new cycles of understanding and meaning for our personal, community, and global purposes as learners.

REFERENCES

Altwerger, B. 1990. "The theme cycle—an overview." *Connections* 6:7–8.

Baldwin, R. 1981. "When was the last time you bought a textbook just for kicks?" In *Reading the content areas: Improving classroom instruction,* edited by E. Dishner, T. Bean, & J. Readance. Dubuque, IA: Kendall/Hunt.

Barnes, D. 1992. *From communication to curriculum.* 2nd ed. Portsmouth, NH: Boynton/Cook.

———. 1986. "Language in the secondary classroom." In *Language, the learner and the school.* 3rd ed., edited by D. Barnes, J. Britton, & M. Torbe. Portsmouth, NH: Boynton/Cook.

Berthoff, A. 1987. Foreword. In *Literacy: Reading the word and the world,* edited by P. Freire & D. Macedo. South Hadley, MA: Bergin & Garvey.

Britton, J. 1986. "Talking to learn." In *Language, the learner and the school.* 3rd ed., edited by D. Barnes, J. Britton, & M. Torbe. Portsmouth, NH: Boynton/Cook.

Coerr, E. 1977. *Sadako and the thousand paper cranes.* New York: Dell.

Cummins, J. 1981. "The role of primary language development in promoting educational success for language minority students." In *Schooling and language minority students: A theoretical framework,* edited by the California State Department of Education. Los Angeles, CA: California State University Dissemination and Assessment Center.

Dewey, J. 1938. *Education and experience.* New York: Macmillan.

Edelsky, C., B. Altwerger, and B. Flores. 1991. *Whole language: What's the difference?* Portsmouth, NH: Heinemann.

Freeman, Y. and D. Freeman. 1992. *Whole language for second language learners.* Portsmouth, NH: Heinemann.

Freire, P. and D. Macedo. 1987. *Literacy: Reading the word and the world.* South Hadley, MA: Bergin & Garvey.

Giroux, H. and P. Freire. 1989. "Editor's introduction." In *Education and the American dream,* edited by H. Holtz. Granby, MA: Bergin & Garvey.

Hanssen, E. 1990. "Planning for literature circles: Variations in focus and structure." In *Talking about books: Creating literate communities,* edited by K. Short & K. Pierce. Portsmouth, NH: Heinemann.

Harste, J., K. Short, and C. Burke. 1988. *Creating classrooms for authors: The reading-writing connection.* Portsmouth, NH: Heinemann.

Harste, J., V. Woodward and C. Burke. 1984. *Language stories and literacy lessons.* Portsmouth, NH: Heinemann.

Lindfors, J. 1987. *Children's language and learning.* 2nd ed. Englewood Cliffs, NJ: Prentice-Hall.

Lord, B. 1984. *In the year of the boar and Jackie Robinson.* New York: Trumpet.

Meltzer, M. 1989. "The social responsibility of a writer." *The New Advocate* 2:155–57.

Milton, J. 1987. *Marching to freedom: The story of Martin Luther King, Jr.* New York: Dell.

Nhoung, H. 1982. *The land I lost.* New York: Harper & Row.

Peterson, R. 1992. *Life in a crowded place: Making a learning community.* Portsmouth, NH: Heinemann.

Peterson, R. and M. Eeds. 1990. *Grand conversations: Literature groups in action.* New York: Scholastic.

Rosenblatt, L. 1978. *The reader, the text, the poem.* Carbondale, IL: Southern Illinois University Press.

Short, K. and C. Burke. 1991. *Creating curriculum: Teachers and students as a community of learners.* Portsmouth, NH: Heinemann.

Short, K. and C. Klassen. 1993. "Literature circles: Hearing children's voices." In *Children's voices: Talk in the classroom,* edited by B. Cullinan. Newark, DE: International Reading Association.

Short, K. and K. Pierce. Eds. 1990. *Talking about books: Creating literate communities.* Portsmouth, NH: Heinemann.

Smith, F. 1983. *Psycholinguistics and reading.* New York: Holt, Rinehart & Winston.

Spier, P. 1980. *People.* New York: Doubleday.

Taylor, M. 1976. *Roll of thunder, hear my cry.* New York: Bantam.

Tsuchiya, Y. 1988. *Faithful elephants.* Boston: Houghton Mifflin.

Turner, A. 1987. *Nettie's trip south.* New York: Macmillan.

Vygotsky, L. 1978. *Mind in society.* Cambridge, MA: Harvard University Press.

Wells, G. 1986. *The meaning makers: Children learning language and using literature to learn.* Portsmouth, NH: Heinemann.

Williams, V. 1982. *A chair for my mother.* New York: Scholastic.

Wolters Elementary Students. 1984. *We came to America.* Fresno, CA: Migrant Publishing.

Kathleen Crawford is a teacher at Maldonado School in Tucson, Arizona. She has taught first, second, and fourth grade. Kathleen is also working on a doctorate in Language, Reading, and Culture at the University of Arizona. She is a member of the Editorial Advisory Board for the "Children's Books" column in *The Reading Teacher*, published by the International Reading Association. With Dr. Kathy Short, she has published articles on teacher study groups and the inquiry cycle. She has also presented at national and local conferences. Kathleen is interested in teacher research in her classroom and is involved with teacher study group research.

Theresa Hoopingarner is a Chapter I Program Facilitator at Los Amigos Elementary School in Tucson, Arizona. Previously, she had thirteen years of experience teaching first graders. She is the Coordinator and Trainer for the district's Chapter I summer school program. She has given presentations and workshops on her work with Language Arts curriculum and literacy strategies.

Chapter 14
A Kaleidoscope of Conversation: A Case Study of a First-Grade Literature Group

KATHLEEN CRAWFORD AND THERESA HOOPINGARNER

Although we have both been interested in literature groups for some time, we had many questions about how first graders would interact in these groups. However, we found only limited information in professional articles and decided to work collaboratively on a project with first graders who were just beginning literature group discussions. We were interested in seeing how these discussions would develop over time and what kinds of talk the first graders would use to explore their understandings of literature.

Because we work in different schools and in different districts in Tucson, Arizona, we knew our roles in this project would be different. We decided to look at the talk of first graders in Kathleen's classroom. Kathleen had a personalized, daily view of the community, while Theresa brought the view of an outsider looking into the classroom to try to understand small group interactions. We met often to talk about the classroom and our perceptions of what we were experiencing.

The children in Kathleen's classroom had previous experience in using literature in discussions at home, in total group classroom settings, and through independent reading. Yet they had not formally participated in small group literature discussions with the teacher as a collaborator. We wondered whether first graders participating in literature discussions immediately engage in conversations at the level of complexity we so often read about in books such as *Talking About Books* (Short and Pierce, 1990) and *Grand Conversations* (Peterson and Eeds, 1990). We felt that published examples make it seem much more successful than it might be in real life in an everyday classroom. We did not doubt that conversation would occur in our literature groups but wanted to know when and how.

Before we began the project, we talked about our beliefs and our philosophy of learning. We agreed that children need to work in an environment that supports and demonstrates a collaborative atmosphere throughout the day. We knew that the small groups would become mini-communities within the large classroom structure because of the experiences they would share in daily group meetings. We also felt that children need to be able to choose what they want to read and that the teacher needs to become a member of the group rather than the leader or director. Yet we also knew that the teacher's comments and questions would play an important role in demonstrating ways of talking about literature and stretching the discussion.

INQUIRY PROCESS

In our study of a beginning literature group, we taped and transcribed the discussions of a small group of first graders over time. To set up the first round of literature groups, we chose six books that dealt with a theme currently being considered in the class. Kathleen read each of the six books aloud to the children, and they wrote down their titles in order of preference for reading and discussion. Once rankings were made, Kathleen divided the children into groups according to their first or second choice. We followed this process each time a new round of literature groups began. On the first day of the group, children took a copy of the book home to read to or with a family member. They were asked to express their reactions, comments, and questions in a variety of ways, such as sketching, writing, or retelling (Harste, Short, and Burke, 1988). The following day the children met and discussed the book with the other group members. It was at this point that we taped and transcribed the discussions for later analysis.

We decided to analyze the transcripts from the second meeting of the discussion groups because we felt that the first meeting was primarily spent in building community in the group and sharing initial responses to the book. We found that the children often used the first day to warm up to the subject and become accustomed to the use of audio and video recordings (Barnes, Churley, and Thompson, 1971). The second meeting was generally a time for questions and comments about the book and so seemed the more productive day to tape their discussions. The literature groups met every day for twenty to forty minutes. At the end of every meeting, the children reflected on where they were and where they wanted to go with the discussion for the next meeting. The groups discussed and negotiated their plans for what they wanted to do next; each group continued for about two weeks. Kathleen began as a facilitator, helping the children refocus when their conversation started drifting away from the topic. As the group's discussion progressed, she became an equal participant within the group.

Our research group of children remained together for three different book studies. We were pleased to see these children repeatedly pick the same book as a first or second choice, so the group was not a forced grouping. For the third literature book, another student joined the group because of her preference in book selection.

As we read through the transcripts of the children's discussions, we looked for specific types of conversations and created labels for the categories of talk that emerged from our analysis. We then developed a list of categories to use in analyzing the kinds of talk occurring in literature groups (see Figure 14.1). We saw the list as a guide for future literature groups. We knew that actually transcribing each literature discussion of all the groups in the classroom would be an impossible task and assumed that developing the list would allow us to analyze a literature group discussion quickly without a transcript. We knew that the categories would change as the children and literature changed, but that the list would provide a beginning point for evaluating children's talk about literature.

FIRST LITERATURE BOOK: *HAWK, I'M YOUR BROTHER*

We began by video and audio taping a literature discussion with Kathleen and four boys: J.R., Jamey, Michael, and Carlos. The literature groups were each reading books related to the classroom's focus on the desert. This group chose *Hawk, I'm Your Brother* (Baylor, 1986), a story about a Native American boy who captures a hawk. He wants to keep the hawk to satisfy his feelings of loneliness but realizes that he must release the bird back to nature. As we examined the boys' talk, we noted several areas where the discussion did not seem to move into those highly developed "conversations" we had read about in published articles. Our analysis of the boys' discussion showed that they kept returning to ideas for a response activity rather than talking about the meaning of the book.

01 J.R.: We were talking about at first we were going to do the *mural*. Then the second thing we're going to make a *book*.

02 JAMEY: We're going to do the *book* first if we can't do the *mural*.

03 KATHLEEN: Do you remember what we talked about yesterday?

04 ALL: Yeah.

1.	Discussion: details	The question/answer is explicitly stated in text.
	inferences	The question/answer is implied in text, sometimes the readers are required to synthesize content from more than one sentence or paragraph.
	opinion	The question/answer comes from a reader's use of background knowledge/prior experience, the reader is required to elaborate, embellish what was read and make inferences about the topic.
2.	Revisiting the Text	Returning to the book to find support for points under discussion.
3.	Predictions	Predictions about the plot or characters in the story.
4.	Personal Reaction	Making a judgment, giving a reaction about the book based on a personal response.
5.	Clarifying Concerns	Discussing parts of the story that the readers do not understand.
6.	Retelling	Discussion/comments are a retelling of the story.
7.	Literary Element	Comments can be classified as an understanding/concern dealing with one of the literary elements.
8.	New Insight	Discussion leads child/children to a new or different understanding than previously held.
9.	Connections: Literature	Making connections to other books previously read.
	Personal	Making connections to own life experiences.
	Class Theme	Making connections to class theme presently being studied.
	Content Areas	Making connections to other content areas or past theme studies.
	Conversation	Making a connection to a statement made by a group member that does not relate directly to the book.
	Broader Society	Making a connection to how this text connects to a child's view of the world.
10.	Future Inquiry	Question/comment provides opportunity for a further study.
11.	Conversational Maintenance	Comments which are used to begin conversations or keep them going. Comments that might direct the discussion in a different way.
12.	Conversational Stretch	A group member makes a statement that would encourage opinions or responses.
13.	Summary	Group member summarizes thoughts presented in the discussion.

Figure 14.1 *Categories of Talk in Literature Discussion*

05   KATHLEEN: About how you guys were going to talk about the book.
06   ALL: Yeah.
07   KATHLEEN: Is there anything you want to talk about in the book?
08   J.R.: Hmm, I think so.

We realized that the boys' focus on "what to do" in the group was an outgrowth of their prior experiences with whole-class literature studies. In those instances, after a book was read aloud the class talked together in one big group and decided whether to perform an extension of the book, such as rewriting the story, making it into a play or song, or drawing a mural. Because of their previous experiences, it is not surprising that the boys focused on end products and celebrations instead of on discussion. Exploratory talk about meaning needed to become the focal point of the group if meaningful literature discussions were to take place.

Initially, we noticed little exploration and discussion of the content of the story, but as we examined the transcript, we saw that even the "most insignificant" conversation revealed useful information (Barnes, 1992). The boys' discussion was not just about the details of the story. They were also making inferences and giving their opinions about the story through their questions. We were pleased to see the connections they made between the book, their own lives, and the classroom study of deserts. One connection was with the illustrations of cacti.

105   CARLOS: There are cactuses in this book.
106   JAMEY: But not like jumping chollas. Not even one jumping cholla. They're all ocotillos.
107   CARLOS: I know why you got this book. Because it's about the desert.
108   JAMEY: Here's one saguaro.
109   MICHAEL: Look, look it. Back here. They're not all ocotillos.
110   J.R.: Most of the ocotillos are big, but when she put the other cactuses they're kind of small. You can hardly see them. You need to take a magnifying glass to make them bigger.

They were able to identify and correctly name the cacti pictured in the book that grew in their familiar southern Arizona environment.

As we reviewed the transcript, we also found that the children had asked thought-provoking questions:

13   MICHAEL: Does it have a father? The baby chick.
26   J.R.: Why did he steal the hawk?
41   MICHAEL: Does the hawk have a brother?

75 JAMEY: Hey, I've got a good idea. I've got a good idea. We can study about the Santos Mountains.

76 MICHAEL: Yeah, what are the Santos Mountains?

82 JAMEY: I wondered why he said, "Hawk, I'm your brother."

Hearing their voices on the tape reinforced for us the importance of listening to everyone in the group. All the members came to the group with questions and seemed so excited about sharing them that they had a difficult time sticking to a specific topic and really listening to the comments of other group members. We saw this as an indication of their excitement about the book and the opportunity to meet as a group, not as a management problem, but we still felt that it was important for everyone's question to be heard. One child, Carlos, talked only at the beginning of the discussion. Unlike Peterson and Eeds (1990), who found that some children participate in groups by listening because they do not feel secure about sharing their ideas or experiences, we attributed his quietness to the fact that the group did not respond to the question he asked. On the tape, Carlos could be heard asking his question over and over, but no one responded and he became quiet throughout the remainder of the discussion.

We decided to share the transcript with the children to see if they could identify the strengths and weaknesses in the process of the discussion. Kathleen invited the students to listen as she read the transcript aloud several times. The children enjoyed listening to their actual talk and looking at the transcript. The second and third readings prompted an analysis of their own talk. They began to notice that they had not discussed the book but had "talked about their own stuff."

The children's analysis of their group's conversation was helpful for them because they were able to get a better sense of the process of group dynamics. After hearing the transcript read aloud, the boys realized that they had addressed very few questions. They thought it was because they were not listening to each other. To find out, they counted the number of questions asked and looked to see if anyone answered or responded to them. They realized that they were right: they were not listening to each other. After much debate and voting on different ways of solving their problem, they decided to come to the next group meeting with their questions written down in their literature logs. They would begin the group by having each person read a question aloud, one at a time. The logs would then be put in the middle of the table and one chosen at random to begin the discussion.

Looking at this literature discussion in more depth caused our perceptions of the group's discussion to change. Drawing on our impressions and the children's decision making altered our methods for the next literature book discussion. We were eager to see if the solution they had agreed upon would be implemented with the second literature book and what impact it might have on the discussion.

SECOND LITERATURE BOOK: *A LIVING DESERT*

After spending a couple of weeks on the first book, the boys decided they wanted to know more about the desert. We looked in our school library and found a multiple copy set of a nonfiction book, *A Living Desert*, by Guy Spencer (1988), which gives information on plants and animals of the Sonoran Desert. The boys were thrilled to find the book and began reading it right away.

The group came to the next discussion with their literature logs containing their questions, concerns, and comments about the desert book. As we had previously decided, they began the discussion by having everyone read their questions, which included: How does the saguaro grow so tall? How did the prairie dogs get their food? How does the mountain lion climb? Why can't you see the mountain lion's claws? When do the prickly pear cacti bloom? We felt that these questions would lend themselves to open-ended comments and future inquiries. The group then randomly selected Carlos' question to begin the discussion.

05   CARLOS: How did the mountain lion climb?

06   JAMEY: They are probably born and know how to climb already.

07   J.R.: Or maybe, they don't know how to climb and their mother has to teach them.

08   CARLOS: Kind of like people.

09   MICHAEL: They jump.

10   J.R.: Or maybe they have to jump to get a start and then they have to climb the mountain. They have to find a place where it is real easy to jump onto, and then they jump onto it and then they climb from there.

13   MICHAEL: Maybe they have to jump to somewhere where it is flat, and they grab onto or jump down, and then they climb to the other spot.

14   J.R.: Maybe the mountain lion can jump and climb because it has sharp claws . . . or maybe they dig.

One of the first things we noticed in analyzing the second discussion was the level of the conversation. It had moved from talk in which children focused on response activities and their individual questions to a discussion full of inferences and the sharing of opinions. This time the children never even mentioned such end products. They followed the guidelines they had set forth; they listened to one question to get them started, and they continued with the conversation until they felt that it was finished. J.R. continued to bring up his question about the mountain lion's claws because the issue was still not resolved for him.

Carlos talked more during this discussion, probably because his questions and comments were heard and discussed by the group. Our analysis indicated that all the children were better listeners. Because of this, we added a new category of talk, which we labeled "Connection: Conversational," to our analysis sheet. This category included those comments that relate to a statement another group member had made. Often these comments, which seemed out of place, made a connection back to a previous comment. Jamey's comment, "maybe mountain lions have houses like Carlos and when they get real hungry they just climb up cupboards," seems irrelevant but is directly tied to what Kathleen said earlier in the discussion. This kind of connection was absent in the first discussion, and it was exciting to see children returning to earlier comments when the connections were powerful or useful to them (see Gilles in this volume).

We saw several other types of talk that led to additional categories. The need for the category Conversational Stretch arose from a clearer understanding on our part of the teacher's role in a discussion group. At appropriate times during the discussion, Kathleen would ask a question that would "stretch" the children's thinking.

41   CARLOS: I think the mountain lion could get the roadrunner.

42   J.R.: I doubt it.

43   MICHAEL: I think the roadrunner could over run the mountain lion.

44   J.R.: That's what I think.

45   JAMEY: I think the roadrunner's a better climber than the mountain lion, probably.

46   CARLOS: Maybe the mountain lion could get the roadrunner. Maybe he could see the roadrunner. Maybe he's a better jumper and he could see it and jump to it.

47   KATHLEEN: Do roadrunners fly?

48   ALL: No.

49   CARLOS: They run fast.

50   JAMEY: They can fly but they can only fly about that high from the ground.

51   KATHLEEN: Uh huh. Do you think the roadrunner is faster than the mountain lion?

Kathleen's question (51) led the students to compare the two animals, which could have led to a new research topic. Since the teacher will not always be the one who asks these thought-provoking questions, we defined our category to include a "stretching" statement by any group member.

Having finished the first round of Literature Circles, we then decided to add a new component to the literature discussion group for the next book. We had read an article by Patricia Kelly (1990) and liked the three discussion questions she adapted from Bleich (1978) to ask her children: "What did you notice in the story? How did the story make you feel? What does this story remind you of in your own life?" (p. 466). We decided to ask Kathleen's students to respond to these three questions in their literature logs next to their own questions, comments, and concerns. The purpose of this strategy was to provide the children with a wider variety of questions for beginning their discussion the first day.

THIRD LITERATURE BOOK: *RAIN FOREST SECRETS*

Most of the students were becoming more aware of environmental issues in the desert. We had gone on several "desert walks" and discovered that the desert needed to be cleaned and preserved. Because the class was also interested in worldwide environmental issues, the books we chose for the next round of literature groups dealt with the environment. The discussion group we were following chose to read *Rain Forest Secrets* by Arthur Dorros (1988), which describes a South American rain forest and its effect on the environment. Jannean joined the group because she, along with all four boys, ranked this book as her number one choice. As we analyzed the group's final transcript, it was evident that the quality and content of their conversation had improved.

23   JR: How does the rain forest get so much rain?

24   MICHAEL: Maybe they got more rivers than we do.

25   JAMEY: . . . and the rivers get soaked up and then it rains.

26   JANNEAN: Maybe the sun doesn't shine on them as much as it rains.

27   MICHAEL: Maybe they have more water than they do on the ground. Then the water evaporates and then it rains again and then it goes up and down. [Michael makes movement with hand to represent rain then evaporation.]

28   J.R.: Hey! That's kind of weird.

29   JANNEAN: That is kind of weird.

30   MICHAEL: Uh-huh!

31   KATHLEEN: Why?

32   JANNEAN: Because I've never seen that happen.

33   MICHAEL: Because you can't see evaporate . . . water evaporating, because they turn into gas and they go up, and then they turn into water.

This time the students focused on the content of the book. They were able to talk about broader issues and their own concerns. We also saw the process of discussion improving as students became more aware of what the others were saying and actually listened to their comments. Questions asked were being addressed (23), and the conversation continued and moved on to new ideas.

This transcript helped us see the advantages of following the same group over several books. The depth of the children's conversation increased because of the group's previous experience in discussing books. Gilles (in this volume) looks at the notion that meanings cycle in a spiral fashion across books. The conversations never really ended when students completed a book. They continued to connect conversations about books they had already read to the book they were currently reading. Not only were their "cycles of meaning" building over time, they were building over books. The students knew they were becoming a community with shared experiences. Knowing stories in common was an important part of building a group history.

Because of this group continuity, other group members were more comfortable this time in letting J.R. know when he was off track and did not let him dominate the conversation as much. As a side note, we were also pleased to note that J.R. himself became more aware of his "off task" behaviors. He commented, "I know it doesn't have anything to do with what we're talking about . . . ," realizing that to be a member of a discussion he needed to discuss the topic currently being addressed by the group.

Even though we support members of a literature group remaining together for several books, we do not think that literature groups need to remain the same for an extended period of time. All the participants gained from this learning experience, but because we believe children need a choice in their selections of books and groups, we would not force a group to remain together.

One problem surfaced in the third group. Kathleen found that giving all three discussion questions at the same time was overwhelming to first-grade students. We would suggest that the group respond to one question. Having children try to write out responses to all three questions turned into a laborious assignment instead of a tool to facilitate discussion.

Being prepared and having time to reflect on the book played a crucial role in the level of participation and the depth of discussion in the group. One day, two of the students admitted they hadn't read the book. They were given class time to finish it and went right from the book to the discussion, where they remained relatively quiet, acting more like observers than participants. We wondered if reading the book is only a small part in the quality of a discussion. Just as adults need time to think and reflect prior to a literature group, so do children.

IMPLICATIONS FOR FUTURE DISCUSSION GROUPS

Because we reviewed transcripts throughout the study, we were able to make changes in the literature group process and see the impact of those changes. We also connected the group's discussion to broader issues, such as the environment, which we will continue to explore in future literature groups in our classrooms.

We found it powerful to share the data attained from literature group transcripts with children. We would recommend allowing children to analyze their transcripts, noting the behaviors demonstrated during literature discussion groups (conversational support, amount or lack of listening, and amounts of talking being done by group members). This sharing should be informative, not embarrassing to children.

The discussion seemed to function more effectively when a fifth person was added to the group. One more person's ideas opened up the discussion. We agree with Barnes, Churley, and Thompson (1971) that in a literature group five is the optimum number.

We agree with Peterson and Eeds (1990) that "children need teachers to demonstrate how to enter into and explore the world of literature" and see the teacher as a significant part of the discussion when beginning literature groups. Because Kathleen was there to demonstrate conversational stretch, conversational maintenance, and quality group membership, group members were able to be more responsible for their own discussion.

We had lengthy discussions about the categories for the types of talk occurring in the literature groups. We constantly redefined and added to our list and our own understandings about children's talk. We realized that different genres of literature lead to different categories of talk and that we could never develop one category sheet that could be used in all situations. After an enormous amount of reading, thinking, and talking, we agreed that children's talk could be divided into three main categories: Literature Discussion, Conversation Discussion, and Connections. All the other categories fell under one of these three. By Literature Discussion we mean specific discussion about the book—its details and students' inferences or opinions.

On our category list, categories 1, 2, 3, 4, 6, 7, and 13 all fell under this broader topic (see Figure 14.1). By Conversation Discussion we mean a conversation that starts with the group book and spirals to other topics or previous comments. From our category list we placed numbers 5, 8, 10, 11, and 12 under this general topic. We found that we were constantly adding more descriptors to our Connections label. Most of the group discussions are built around the ideas in category 9.

Because of our experience with the literature groups, we began to view the discussions as a kaleidoscope. All of the children's comments fit together to make a beautiful design: as conversations turn in a new direction, the same pieces fit differently into the framework of the total picture. As in a kaleidoscope, no two conversations are the same, yet the same bits of conversation cycle back into the discussion to make a new picture.

An important conclusion of our study is that meaningful books lead to meaningful discussions. Kathleen noticed that if a book was powerful and thought provoking, the children's discussions were also. It was also rewarding to observe the children's love of learning. Within the available selection, they were able to choose a book and engage in worthwhile discussions. Their learning expanded more than we would have imagined. We saw children wanting to do more extended research on a discussion topic. They went to the library, searched for materials at home, and read more. They took an active role in their own learning.

During a discussion of *Rain Forest Secrets,* one of the children suggested raising money to buy land in a rain forest so they could play a part in the preservation of wildlife and the rain forest. They wanted to sell pencils as a fund raiser. In a group meeting they decided they would buy land in South America. When they measured the distance they would need to travel to go visit, they found that it was nineteen pencil lengths from Tucson to "their" property. They decided that Michael's grandfather could take them because he had a recreational vehicle. The group was able to move from "how are we going to draw the mural" to thinking about purchasing land to help save an important part of the environment.

We were excited and impressed by the change these first graders were able to make as they participated in their discussions. If others could read about these particular discussions, we thought, they would come away feeling as we did when we read about powerful literature discussions in articles and books. We were amazed by the levels of discussion that occurred in such a short amount of time. Our transcripts of the three literature discussions show that talk does become more productive. We discovered that we could develop categories to examine children's talk even though they might change from genre to genre. And we are convinced that, given time and rich literary experiences, children will exceed the hopeful expectations of teachers as classrooms begin the journey into literature discussions.

REFERENCES

Baylor, B. 1986. *Hawk, I'm your brother.* New York: Scribner.

Barnes, D. 1992. *From communication to curriculum.* 2nd ed. Portsmouth, NH: Boynton/ Cook.

Barnes, D., P. Churley, & C. Thompson. 1971. "Group talk and literary response." *English in Education* 5:3.

Bleich, D. 1978. *Subjective criticism.* Baltimore, MD: Johns Hopkins University Press.

Dorros, A. 1990. *Rain forest secrets.* New York: Scholastic.

Eeds, M. and D. Wells. 1989. "Grand Conversations: An exploration of meaning construction in literature study groups." *Research in the teaching of English* 23:4–29.

Harste, J. C., K. G. Short, and C. Burke. 1988. *Creating classrooms for authors: The reading-writing connection.* Portsmouth, NH: Heinemann.

Kelly, P. 1990. "Guiding young students' response to literature." *The Reading Teacher* 43:464–70.

Peterson, R. and M. Eeds. 1990. *Grand conversations: Literature groups in action.* New York: Scholastic.

Short, K.G. & K.M. Pierce. 1990. *Talking about books: Creating literate communities.* Portsmouth, NH: Heinemann.

Spencer, G. 1988. *A living desert.* Mahwah, NJ: Troll Associates.

Margaret Newbold has been a librarian for grades K–12. She is currently a librarian at South Middle School and South High School in the Fort Zumwalt School District in St. Peters, Missouri. Prior to her work as a librarian, Margaret taught reading and English in grades six through eight. Margaret completed a dissertation through the University of Missouri-St. Louis on students' use of CD-ROM technology as compared to print sources in April 1993. She is forever exploring ways of bringing books and people of all ages together to share in the magic of talking about great stories.

Chapter 15
Literature Discussion Groups Aren't Just for School

MARGARET NEWBOLD

To fulfill part of the requirements for a graduate class, I was instructed to learn all I could about literature discussion groups. I knew I could find a number of books and articles that would address the mechanics of how to organize and evaluate literature discussion groups. I also knew I would be able to read about how other teachers incorporated literature discussion groups into their classrooms and their evaluations of the program based on their personal experiences. But just reading about other's experiences would never really "show me" literature discussion groups. I wanted to see a group in action. I wanted to learn about literature discussion groups by hearing children's talk, seeing their interactions, and sensing their feelings for this type of reading experience. Only then would I feel I had learned about literature discussion groups.

At first, I wasn't sure where I could possibly find a group of children willing to help me "learn" all I could about literature discussion groups during the summer, but eventually I found them in the same place graduate students usually find "willing" subjects—within my own family and neighborhood.

I set out to form literature discussion groups with my two children and their friends. I originally wanted to find out if children's talk about books outside the classroom environment differed from talk in the classroom. I also wanted to find out whether or not literary elements such as plot, characterization, and theme would be discussed if a teacher was not present and in charge. Basically, I wanted to experience a literature discussion group as part of my own "learning." But what actually evolved out of this assignment was something far more remarkable.

One of the groups consisted of my son and another ten-year-old boy, neither of whom had ever participated in literature discussion groups, since both were taught reading in basal text programs. I knew before I began that groups consisting of at least three (Morrow and Smith, 1990) and as many as five members (Barnes, Churley, and Thompson, 1971) were best, but the third member who originally accepted would be away for two of the four weeks of the project. Therefore, I decided to work with the two boys rather than cancel the group. As it turned out, the two-member group was not ideal, but it did allow me to gain some experience and learn a little more about the topic.

After reading Hanssen's (1990) "Planning for Literature Circles" and Peterson and Eeds's (1990) *Grand Conversations: Literature Groups in Action*, I felt I had a sense of how best to organize a literature discussion group and what my role should be as a participant-observer in the group. I believed I was prepared to begin working with a group of my own. The boys first met and decided on a book to read. They wanted to read *Robin Hood* because the movie was being released, and they knew if they read the book, I would take them to see the movie. I had a difficult time deciding among the three versions of *Robin Hood* I was familiar with: Pyle's (1883), McGovern's (1968), and Miles' (1979). I thought the boys would have a difficult time reading the version by Pyle, but I knew that both McGovern's and Miles' versions were appropriate for intermediate students. I took the advice given in *Choosing Books for Kids* (Oppenheim, Brenner, and Boegehold, 1986), which recommended the version by Miles because of its historical detail and wonderful illustrations. This proved to be a good choice for the boys. I then suggested they do two things: keep a journal or a response log (Hanssen, 1990, p. 203) and use yellow stick-on notes to mark places in the book they wanted to talk about or had questions about (Peterson and Eeds, 1990, p. 63). Both strategies were to help the boys prepare for their discussions.

Once the boys had read their assigned chapters, written in their response journals, and stuck notes in their books, I naively assumed they would be prepared to engage in wonderful, even "grand conversations" (Peterson and Eeds, 1990) about Robin Hood and his many adventures. I knew this group would have no difficulty establishing rapport, which seemed to be a common problem that others encountered when forming groups (Peterson and Eeds, 1990; Short, 1990; Watson, Burke, and Harste, 1989). These two boys had been close friends since they were old enough to walk, and talk was something they spent a lot of time doing. So I was sure that talking about a book and sharing their thoughts and feelings about the story and characters would be easy for them.

What I found was that the boys engaged in more "report talking" as defined by Tannen (1990). They would simply take a turn "reporting" information. Their exchanges did not build on, nor did they reflect on, one another's comments:

NATHAN: I like it (the story) because it told fighting and action and they think of real neat ways to do stuff without anybody finding out, like the cave, and then some. I like it because they do neat stuff like build their own huts and stuff, and they have contests for themselves. That's the main reason I like this book.

TIM: I like it because he's [Robin Hood] always nice with animals and that—this part I always (unintelligible) that he'd become an outlaw just to save his dog's paw and wouldn't just say, "Oh it's just a little paw," and that he knows how to make all the animal sounds and that he can shoot straight with the bow and arrow.

The boy's talk did not contain the wonderful "dialogue" (a collaborative, dynamic exchange whereby meaning evolves as the participants strive to comprehend ideas, problems, events, and feelings) that Peterson and Eeds (1990, p. 14) had witnessed in many of the conversations they had heard. There were no "connections" to other books, other movies, or other experiences, which Gilles (1990) and Watson (1990) had heard in successful literature discussions. The boys' conversations had not demonstrated that they were personally connecting with the book. And yet, I knew from the way they were writing in their journals and actually reading the book that they liked this experience and were enjoying the story. I wondered why I wasn't hearing talk that demonstrated that they were reading and discussing what they had read in order to bring meaning to, as well as to take meaning from, the text (Weaver, 1990, p. 178).

Even though I had completed my assignment and had turned my project in, these questions continued to haunt me. I knew I had been successful in "learning" about literature discussion groups, but I did not feel I had answered my original questions about how children's talk about books outside the classroom environment differed from talk in the classroom. And now, even more than how talk differed in these situations, I wanted to learn how to get children engaged in "dialogue" about books. So, I reread the various chapters in *Talking About Books* (Short and Pierce, 1990) and *Grand Conversations* (Peterson and Eeds, 1990) in hopes of finding the key to what had gone wrong. I looked specifically at the sections that discussed how to organize a literature discussion group and how to engage children in conversations about books. And in addition, I read *From Communication to Curriculum* (Barnes, 1992), which explores how children use language to learn. Then I began to see what had gone wrong. I had forgotten a very important component of successful literature discussions, "practice accompanied by feedback" (Peterson and Eeds, 1990, p. 18). The boys did not have a background for sharing books in this manner. They lacked practice in conversing in a way that was both reflective and perceptive. They had never taken part in or observed a group discussing a book. We had "talked" about the purpose of the group as being an opportunity to share their thoughts and feelings about a book. We had "talked" about possible phrases that could be used to encourage the speaker to elaborate and make further connections. We had even "talked" about what made a discussion group successful. The boys had listened to their taped conversations and "talked" about the good parts and about which parts could be improved. But talking was not enough. The boys needed to practice using language and hearing language that invited them to respond to literature before they could be expected to engage in literary discussions on their own.

My son agreed to take part in another "project." I knew the discussion group should consist of more than two people so I contacted a neighborhood friend of my son's. Andrew agreed to be a member of the group, but then Tim decided he didn't want to read another book. Once again I had a group of just two boys, one with little literature discussion experience and one with no literature discussion experience. Nathan mentioned the possibility of including his father in the discussion group, even though his father considers himself to be aliterate, "a person who knows how to read but who doesn't choose to read books for pleasure, nor extensively for information" (Cullinan, 1987). Then I wondered what would happen if Nathan's dad *and* Andrew's dad would both agree to read and discuss a book with their sons. This seemed to be an exciting possibility, yet I knew little about such father-son discussions and wondered if a group such as this would really work.

A precedent had already been set, since both fathers had read to their sons as infants. And as Holdaway (1979) discovered and reported, parents who read to their children experience much satisfaction and pleasure when engaged in reading that is not looked upon as a duty or as an experience to "achieve specific educational advantages for the child" (p. 39). Holdaway also believes that when a parent reads to a young child, a special relationship between the parent and the child will result. The child will get a feeling of security and "special worth" due to the quality of the attention being given and develop strong positive associations with books (Holdaway, 1979, p. 40). Reading and sharing books with the children as infants had been pleasurable experiences for the dads, but I was not sure this would still hold true now that the boys were school-aged.

It is frequently reported that compared to girls, boys in the United States demonstrate a more negative attitude toward reading (Holbrook, 1988). Some researchers believe that our culture plays a significant role in shaping these negative attitudes (Downing and Thomson, 1977; Lehr, 1982). This is largely due to a perception by some that reading is a more feminine activity (Downing and Thomson, 1977; Edwards, 1989). I believed that these fathers would not view reading in this manner, that they would find the opportunity to share a book with their sons to be an acceptable father-son activity.

In a recent study conducted by Gray (1992), it was found that father-to-son reading had a positive effect on intermediate grade boys' reading achievement and attitudes. "Intermediate grade level boys who were read to by their fathers scored significantly higher in CTBS reading achievement than boys who experienced no father-to-son reading" (p. 18). In addition, the boys who believed that their fathers enjoyed reading as well as those whose fathers modeled "pleasure-reading" indicated that they also enjoyed reading for pleasure. Gray also found that boys who made the assumption that their fathers did not enjoy reading demonstrated less desire to read independently. In a literature discussion group, the fathers would not be reading aloud to their sons but would play an important role by engaging their sons in talk about a book. In addition, the boys would be given an opportunity to view their fathers as readers. This opportunity for sharing had great possibilities and, in my opinion, was worth attempting.

Thus, "Dads and Lads" was born. Once again, I did not question the group's ability to establish rapport or create a sense of community, as everyone knew each other quite well. The fathers were neighbors and had developed a friendship over the years. The sons had been friends since they were old enough to walk and frequently did things together. They were all comfortable talking with one another. But I wondered if their talk would go beyond "report talk," talk in which one person states what he has to say while not really inviting others to respond (Tannen, 1990). Several questions came to mind: (1) Would this group be capable of engaging one another in meaningful dialogue? (2) What kind of talk would emerge? (3) Would the talk more closely resemble the "literature lesson talk" common to classroom discussions or the "private, unguided" talk students used when left alone to talk about books (Barnes, Churley, and Thompson, 1971)? These were questions I was eager to answer.

The group first decided which book to read and how much time to allow for reading. They chose to read *Sign of the Beaver* (Speare, 1983), a story set in Maine in the late 1700s about a young white boy, Matt, who is left alone to care for the homestead while his father goes back to Massachusetts to get his mother and sister. Matt must rely on help from an Indian boy and his grandfather if he is to survive. The group then decided to read the entire book before they had any discussions. Two meetings were agreed to: the first to share the book and to determine topics they were most interested in studying or learning more about, and the second to focus more on what they had learned when they reread the book or sections of the book they were most interested in.

When I met with the Dads and Lads, all were told that the purpose of the group was to provide an opportunity to share their thoughts, feelings, and questions about the book they had read. The dads were also reminded that they were not to "teach" the book; they were to engage the boys and each other in conversation that invited sharing. I specifically asked the dads to refrain from using questions that required the boys to answer "yes" or "no," or to direct a question to one boy as if they were a teacher calling on a student. I encouraged all to use questions that were reflective and would invite responses. I suggested phrases such as, "When I read this, it reminded me of . . . ." and "I was wondering about this part when . . . ." The dads then began to reminisce about books they had read or were "made" to read when they had been in school. The boys mainly listened to this exchange but would respond when a familiar title was mentioned. This first unguided, unplanned discussion set the tone for future meetings. The boys saw their fathers engaged in conversation about books they had read and characters they had remembered. The conversation had not been guided by a need to "teach" the boys something. As the fathers shared their own experiences with books, the boys began to see how language was being used to invite one another into the "literacy club" (Smith, 1988), a club the sons were now being invited to join with their fathers.

Certain conditions would have to exist if the boys were to accept the invitation. The boys would have to see themselves as being like their fathers; they would have to believe that by joining, the experience would be meaning-ful, useful, and enjoyable; and, they would have to feel that membership was risk-free, that they would not be punished or embarrassed if they made mistakes (Smith, 1988). The conditions were right and the boys accepted.

The talk the Dads and Lads engaged in was different from those I had read about (e.g., Barnes, 1992; Barnes, Churley, and Thompson, 1971; Peterson and Eeds, 1990). Much of the conversation resembled that of students who were left on their own to discuss books. Just as Barnes had observed in the taped conversations of students' unguided book talking, there was a great deal of "sorting-out" and "re-experiencing" as the members spent time sorting out the plot, confirming their own understanding of events and incidents, as well as sharing special sections they enjoyed. This kind of talk made their discussions different from traditional classroom lesson talk (Barnes, Churley, and Thompson, 1971). Yet, unlike the students' free talk, there were also elements of literature lessons reflected in the discussions. There were moments when a dad would recall a scene in such a way that literary elements, setting, characters, mood, point of view, and even irony and symbols, would be discussed. The dads were not intentionally introducing these elements to their sons, they were simply responding to what they had read as experienced readers respond. The literary elements had been the vehicle the dads had used to reflect on a deeper understanding of the story. The dads' talk also pulled together ideas, provided insight, and shared connections from an adult perspective.

The following excerpt, which draws a parallel between the relationship of Matt and Attean and that of Robinson Crusoe and Friday, can best demonstrate how the dads were able to do this without "teaching," thus turning the discussion into a traditional lesson:

01   DAD 1: The part that made me chuckle when I got to it was when Attean pulled out his only book, er no, he had two books. One was the *Bible* . . .

02   NATHAN: No, that was Matt, not Attean.

03   DAD 1: Er, Matt I mean. When Matt . . .

04   DAD 2: The two books.

05   DAD 1: The two books, the *Bible* and his other book . . .

06   ANDREW: *Robinson Crusoe.*

07   DAD 1: *Robinson Crusoe.* I kind of laughed at that when that . . .

08   DAD 2: For those of you who . . .

09   DAD 1: Why he'd have *Robinson Crusoe* of all books!

10   NATHAN: (Laughs.)

11   DAD 1: Do most of you know about *Robinson Crusoe?*

12   NATHAN: He crashed on a desert island.

13   ANDREW: Yeah. And he had a slave.

14   DAD 1: Yeah. And he was pretty much by himself, right? And had to survive. So what's Matt doing?

15   N & A: Surviving.

16   NATHAN: Except with the Indian, he wouldn't have lived without the Indian.

17   DAD 1: Yeah, but that's why I chuckled when he had, when that was his favorite book. Do you see the connection?

18   N & A: Yeah.

As Dad 1 was "re-experiencing" a favorite part, he was also sharing his insight and understanding of situational irony and metaphor without naming it as such. And although Dad 1 is leading the conversation at this point, he does not take on a teaching role by "telling" or "questioning" in the way teachers often do. Nathan appeared to make the connection when he laughed

(10). It was apparent that both boys knew something about *Robinson Crusoe* (12 and 13), which drew them further into the conversation. It is also interesting to note that Dad 2 was prepared to contribute information if it seemed necessary when he said, "For those of you who . . ." (8) but let Dad 1 continue his "exploring" once he realized the boys were making the connection. As Dad 1 continues (14), he invites the boys to draw a direct comparison between Matt and Robinson Crusoe, a comparison that once made allows the reader to understand one of the story's unspoken meanings.

This exchange demonstrates the friendly and informal tone of the Dads and Lads' discussions as shown by the frequent interruptions (e.g., 2, 4, 6, and 8). And, there appears to be no tension among speakers whenever a mistake is made, as when Nathan adds, "No, that was Matt, not Attean" (02). Mistakes can be made in this "literacy club": the speakers do not have to fear being ridiculed or embarrassed by the other members. Such a climate encourages learners to engage in what Barnes calls "exploratory talk," which he defines as occurring when members of the group collaborate and wish to "talk it over in a tentative manner, considering and rearranging their ideas. The talk is often but not always hesitant, containing uncompleted or inexplicit utterances as the students try to formulate new understanding" (Barnes, 1990, p. 50). Such talk is essential for learners to create new meanings together.

The Dads and Lads group discussion provided ample opportunities for the boys to raise the type of questions Barnes believes are almost entirely excluded from the lesson talk found in classrooms (Barnes, 1992, p. 55), questions generated by the students rather than the teacher. The following excerpt demonstrates how such a question, even if not directly answered, keeps the discussion moving while allowing personal experiences to be introduced:

01   NATHAN: How do you bank a fire?

02   DAD 2: Bank a fire?

03   DAD 1: Well, you take it to the teller and . . . no . . .

04   A & N: (Laugh.)

05   DAD 2: What was that kind of fire the scouts used sometimes?

06   NATHAN: A tee-pee?

07   DAD 2: No. no.

08   ANDREW: A friendship fire?

09   DAD 2: No, no.

10   ANDREW: The lean-to?

11   DAD 2: Yeah. The one that works with the lean-to called the Adirondak.

12 DAD 1: Oh man, that sounds technical.

13 DAD 2: Well, basically you put a stick . . . . We saw them doing it once.

14 ANDREW: You put . . . like . . . well . . . let me show you.

15 DAD 2: If you have a lean-to, say this is the wall . . . [Proceeds to demonstrate the type of fire he and Andrew were trying to describe.]

16 DAD 1: Well, they were talking about banking the fire, apparently to keep it alive.

17 NATHAN: Yeah.

18 DAD 2: Oh, Is that? . . . Maybe that's . . .

19 DAD 1: Yeah, so it wouldn't go out and I'm not exactly sure.

Nathan's original question prompted the others to explore several possible definitions before Dad 1 finally conceded (19) "I'm not exactly sure." However, this exchange did prompt a lively demonstration as Dad 2 and Andrew tried to recall how to make a specific fire, a fire that could be called a "banking" fire. Even though Nathan was never given a definitive answer, an opportunity to draw from personal experience and share information resulted that is usually not present in classroom lesson talk (Barnes, Churley, and Thompson, 1971).

Posing hypothetical questions often allows the readers to reach new levels of understanding. In the following excerpt, the boys are asked to identify with Matt as he faces the dilemma of leaving with the Indians and having companionship or waiting for his father to return and remaining alone:

01 DAD 1: Would you have gone with the Indians or stayed like he did?

02 ANDREW: I'd have gone.

03 NATHAN: I'd have gone.

04 DAD 1: You would have gone with the sure thing?

05 DAD 2: No question, huh?

06 NATHAN: No, not . . .

07 DAD 2: No question about it?

08 ANDREW: It's just the people's tough luck if they can't find me.

09 DAD 1: If I had told you that I was coming back, that I would be back, would you still leave?

10 NATHAN: No.

11 DAD 1: Well . . .

12 NATHAN: You just said would you go with the Indians. You didn't say that you were going too!

13   DAD 1: No, I'm putting you in this position that Matt was in. His father told him he would be back.

14   ANDREW: Well, if you left him that long I might.

15   DAD 1: He told him when to expect [him] to be back, but he told him that, you know, it may not be so easy.

16   DAD 2: He was . . .

17   DAD 1: It's a hard journey and that's, you know, if you had the choice . . .

18   NATHAN: I might go and I might not.

The dads were trying to help the boys realize how difficult Matt's decision was. That this was not easy for the boys is shown in their first, quick responses (02 and 03), "I'd have gone." Unless the boys could empathize with Matt, they would miss the magnitude of this conflict. That the boys could never really identify with Matt is shown in Andrew's comment (14) and Nathan's final word on the subject (18), "I might go and I might not." This may not have been the answers the dads wanted to hear from their sons, but they allowed the conversation to move on: the dads did not tell the boys what they should have done or what they would like for them to have done had they been in Matt's situation.

In another situation where a hypothetical question was raised, the boys seemed better able to identify with Matt because of their ability to draw from personal experiences.

01   DAD 2: What if his [Matt's] folks hadn't come back though? That's a good question.

02   DAD 1: Yeah. What if they hadn't . . .

03   NATHAN: He'd grow old not so gracefully!

04   DAD 2: He might not have made it.

05   ANDREW: [Sighs.]

06   NATHAN: Well, his neighbor . . . [unintelligible]

07   DAD 2: . . . he might have . . .

08   DAD 1: . . . Hey, he was . . . How old was he? He was about your age.

09   NATHAN: Thirteen.

10   ANDREW: Thirteen!

11   DAD 2: Thirteen . . .

12   DAD 1: He was a little older than you . . . 'cause I mean . . .

13   ANDREW: I could survive!

14   DAD 1: Oh . . . Hey . . . Just think about that . . .

15 DAD 2: Me too [inaudible over the other talk].

16 ANDREW: I doubt that . . .

17 DAD 1: Hey, we were just at camp. Now how *dark* is it at night? Out in the woods?

18 NATHAN: Dark!

19 ANDREW: He had . . . fire . . .

20 DAD 1: How do you *feel* out at night in the woods?

21 ANDREW: I hate it!

22 NATHAN: Dark, dark, dark, dark, scared . . .

23 DAD 1: Yeah, this is . . . this is . . . this kid lived, lived this every day.

24 DAD 2: *Every* day.

25 DAD 1: Every day . . .

26 ANDREW: Well, he would get used to it.

27 DAD 1: Well, he *did* get used to it because he had to get used to it.

28 ANDREW: Usually a week long camp, I'm used to the dark by the last night, and . . .

29 NATHAN: [Laughs.]

30 ANDREW: So I'm not scared the last night . . .

31 NATHAN: [Laughing.]

32 DAD 1: Well, Nathan was too . . .

33 ANDREW: But then . . . but I . . . but then I go home for a long time and I get so used to . . . the light. When I go back to camp I get scared again until the last night.

34 NATHAN: [Laughing.] Until the last night . . . what if that last night is two years later?

35 ANDREW: I would [inaudible].

The boys appeared to be better able to identify with Matt in this situation because of their scout camp experiences. Dad 1 urged the boys to remember how dark the woods were at night (16), which seemed to be something both boys found uncomfortable. At this point, there was a noticeable shift in the responses the boys made. Andrew went from making grandiose claims (12) to admitting feelings of being scared (32), which is probably something he never would have revealed in a classroom discussion. And this time, in contrast to the other hypothetical situation, the boys appeared to be able to empathize with some of Matt's feelings—at least what it might have been like to sleep alone at night in the dark.

The boys tended to initiate more "sorting-out" talk (Barnes, Churley, and

Thompson, 1971) than the dads. This may have been because the boys found details to be more important; they may have needed to first clarify the inconsistency they were faced with before they could deal with any new ideas. The dads, on the other hand, appeared less troubled with details and were able to focus on the overall meaning of what was being said. This is most obvious in the following excerpt, where Nathan questions the direction the Indians were headed in when leaving Matt, while the dads were discussing a hypothetical ending to the story in which Matt leaves with the Indians.

01   DAD 1: I think that could have been a happy ending in itself. That he [Matt] could have gone and to be taken care of by the tribe.

02   DAD 2: I think he would have found that first winter kind of a shock.

03   NATHAN: Why?

04   DAD 2: Well . . .

05   DAD 1: And they were going North . . .

06   DAD 2: They were going North for the winter.

07   ANDREW: So it would have been harder.

08   DAD 1: It's colder North.

09   NATHAN: I wonder why they did that.

10   DAD 2: The Indians?

11   NATHAN: I thought they were going West.

12   DAD 1: No, they were going North, uh . . . to hunt . . .

13   ANDREW: Yeah, they said they were going West.

14   DAD 1: Where the . . .

15   NATHAN: They said they were going to go West because . . .

16   DAD 1: Well, they were going to go West, I think, instead of coming back to this place, because didn't Matt ask the question . . .

17   ANDREW: Yeah, they were going to go West after the winter.

18   DAD 1: Yeah, didn't Matt ask the question: Did this land belong to your grandfather?

19   NATHAN: Yeah.

20   DAD 2: And what was the response?

21   DAD 1: I don't think there was a response, was there?

22   DAD 2: Well, kind of . . . and . . .

23   NATHAN: He said, "How can one man own . . ."

24   DAD 2: That's . . .

25   ANDREW: Yeah, how can one man own a land?

26   DAD 1: Oh, that's it . . .

27   DAD 2: Yeah, the idea of owning land was so . . . the idea that you could own land was so alien to the Indian's mind . . .

Nathan appeared confused as soon as Dad 2 brought up the idea that the first winter would have been difficult for Matt: "I think he would have found that first winter kind of a shock" (02). Part of why Nathan may have been confused by the ideas being presented is finally revealed when he remarks, "I thought they were going West" (11). At this point there is a blockage (Barnes, Churley, and Thompson, 1971), and the dads soon discover that the discussion will not proceed until this issue has been fully resolved in Nathan's mind as well as Andrew's, since he too begins to question (13 and 17). The direction the Indians were headed was not the main point of the dads' discussion, but until it was addressed, there would be difficulty moving the discussion forward.

The importance of such "sorting-out" may be seen in line 23 as Nathan once again is able to contribute and help move the discussion forward. "He said, 'How can one man own. . . .' " Nathan may not have been able to recall Attean's response or even attend to this part of the discussion if he had not been allowed the time to sort out the question of direction. But now, because the boys had been allowed to work through this issue, the group was able to discuss and explore one of the book's deeper meanings, the issue of Indian thinking versus white man thinking.

As the dads "explored" the book, they demonstrated talk that showed high levels of commitment to the story and to the discussion by sharing predictions they had made while reading (Smith, 1981). They recalled for their sons points in the story where they had had a feeling that something would happen.

01   DAD 2: I thought someplace in there they would have something about the cabin catching on fire. Right at the beginning they talked about his house . . .

02   ANDREW: The wooden chimney?

03   DAD 2: Yeah, they said be careful of the wooden chimney and I thought for sure that that was going to catch on fire one time, but it never did.

04   DAD 1: No, it never did.

05   NATHAN: He had to watch it though.

At this point, they went on to explore how chimneys had been made and what materials would have been used to prevent a fire. The following excerpt provides an additional example of their discussion of predictions.

01   DAD 1: I felt bad about the traveler taking his [Matt's] gun.

02   DAD 2: Oh yeah. I felt a little bit . . .

03   NATHAN: I felt sorry for him.

04   DAD 1: Yeah, he was betrayed by this traveler who was . . .

05   NATHAN: How do you know that?

06   DAD 1: . . . who befriended him . . .

07   DAD 2: Ben.

08   DAD 1: And then, in fact, I thought after I had read that part where he took off, I expected through the rest of the book that he was going to see him again.

09   DAD 2: That he would come back?

10   DAD 1: That he would come back.

11   DAD 2: That the Indians would see him or . . .

12   DAD 1: I figured they would make it up . . . that he'd make it up to him somehow. But it didn't happen.

Both dads had shared predictions they recalled making while reading. This is something reading teachers try to get their students to achieve because predicting is an essential part of the reading process. In a reading lesson, students are frequently asked to make predictions. However, no one was asked to make a prediction during this discussion. In the course of exploring the text, the dads simply related what they had been thinking as they read. This provided an opportunity for the boys to see how more experienced readers draw meaning from the text and bring meaning to the text. The Dads' demonstrations will influence the Lads as they read future novels.

I had begun the summer wanting to learn more about literature discussion groups and how children use language to talk about books. I learned a little about that and a whole lot about what can happen when fathers invite their sons to join the "literacy club" (Smith, 1988). I was a witness to a wonderful exchange of ideas and thoughts about a story between experienced and novice readers. Fathers and sons, mothers and daughters, or any combination of caring and consenting novice and experienced readers can charter their own club and do what these Dads and Lads did. They can come together and share their thoughts, feelings, and questions about a book they read, inviting all members to engage in dialogue and make meaning out of the text. Our society encourages children to engage in sporting activities with family and friends. Reading is one of our children's keys to success. It makes even more sense, then, to encourage our children to engage in reading with family and friends.

In the "real" world, the true test of a new product's success is if consumers are willing to try it or buy it again. The best indication of the Dads and Lads success was the expressed desire of the group to meet during the following summer vacation. The Dads were especially pleased with this activity and did not mind telling me so. Sharing a book was an opportunity to spend some special moments together.

The Dads and Lads was a successful literature discussion group because the fathers and sons had come together ready to collaborate and experience a story. They were able to establish rapport and create a sense of community that was crucial to its success. Since the members knew and liked one another, no one had to worry about being embarrassed or ridiculed for a mistake. The dads showed through their actions and words that they genuinely cared about what the boys had to say and how they felt. The adults did not pretend to be omnipotent; they shared their thoughts and questions and demonstrated how experienced readers reflect on the words in the text to make meaning. And because the dads were more experienced readers, they were able to share their understanding of literary elements used by the author to add depth to the story's meaning without turning the discussion into a mini-lesson.

This same success is possible whenever and wherever readers gather to discuss and share their thoughts and feelings about literature, providing a similar environment has been created. The members of the group must feel accepted. They must know that it is "safe" to share their thoughts and feelings. And perhaps more important, the members must be given the opportunity to see experienced readers sharing and discussing books. For it is through modeling and being given time to practice the art of communicating in a discussion group that inexperienced readers can learn to be successful, thus enjoying the experience. And if one has enjoyed sharing and discussing books once, it probably will not be the last time.

REFERENCES

Barnes, D. 1992. *From communication to curriculum.* 2nd ed. Portsmouth, NH: Boynton/ Cook.

———. 1990. "Oral language and learning." In *Perspectives on talk and learning,* edited by S. Hynds & D. Rubin. Urbana, IL: National Council of Teachers of English.

Barnes, D., P. Churley, and C. Thompson. 1971. "Group talk and literary response." *English in Education* 5(3):63–76.

Cullinan, B. 1987. *Children's literature in the reading program.* Newark, DE: International Reading Association.

Downing, J. and D. Thomson. 1977. "Sex-role stereotypes in learning to read." *Research in the teaching of English* 11:149–55.

Edwards, I. 1989. "Sex differences and reading gender." Unpublished Master's thesis, Keen College.

Gilles, C. 1990. "Collaborative literacy strategies: 'We don't need a circle to have a group.'" In *Talking about books*, edited by K. Short & K. Pierce. Portsmouth, NH: Heinemann.

Gray, J. M. 1992. "Summary of master's thesis: Reading achievement and autonomy as a function of father-to-son reading." *The California Reader* 25:17–19.

Hanssen, E. 1990. "Planning for literature circles: Variations in focus and structure." In *Talking about books*, edited by K. Short & K. Pierce. Portsmouth, NH: Heinemann.

Holbrook, H. T. 1988. "Sex differences in reading: Nature or nurture?" *Journal of Reading* 31(6):574–76.

Holdaway, D. 1979. *The foundations of literacy.* New York: Ashton Scholastic.

Lehr, F. 1982. "Cultural influences and sex differences in reading." *Reading Teacher* 35(6):744–46.

McGovern, A. 1968. *Robin Hood of Sherwood Forest.* New York: Scholastic.

Miles, B. 1979. *Robin Hood: His life and legend.* New York: Checkerboard Press.

Morrow, L. M. and J. Smith. 1990. "The effects of group size on interactive storybook reading." *Reading Research Quarterly* 25(3):213–31.

Oppenheim, J., B. Brenner, and B. D. Boegehold. 1986. *Choosing books for kids.* New York: Ballantine.

Peterson, R. and M. Eeds. 1990. *Grand conversations: Literature groups in action.* New York: Scholastic.

Pyle, H. 1883. *The merry adventures of Robin Hood.* New York: Scribner.

Short, K. G. 1990. "Creating a community of learners." In *Talking about books*, edited by K. Short & K. Pierce. Portsmouth, NH: Heinemann.

Short, K. and K. Pierce. 1990. *Talking about books: Creating literate communities.* Portsmouth, NH: Heinemann.

Smith, F. 1988. *Joining the literacy club.* Portsmouth, NH: Heinemann.

———. 1981. "Demonstrations, engagement and sensitivity: A revised approach to language learning." *Language Arts* 58(1):103–112.

Speare, E. G. 1983. *Sign of the beaver.* Boston: Houghton Mifflin.

Tannen, D. 1990. *You just don't understand: Women and men in conversation.* New York: Ballantine.

Watson, D. J. 1990. "Show me: Whole language evaluation of literature groups." In *Talking about books*, edited by K. Short & K. Pierce. Portsmouth, NH: Heinemann.

Watson, D., C. Burke and J. Harste. 1989. *Whole language: Inquiring voices.* New York: Scholastic.

Weaver, C. 1990. *Understanding whole language: From principles to practice.* Portsmouth, NH: Heinemann.

Part Five
REFLECTING ON EVALUATION

Kathryn Mitchell Pierce has been involved with several teacher study groups in an ongoing exploration of the potential of literature discussion groups. This inquiry has since broadened to include student and teacher self-evaluation, talking and learning in small groups, and teacher study groups. She is currently teaching graduate and undergraduate courses in children's literature, language arts, and reading at the University of Missouri-St. Louis and working with two area school districts in long-term professional development projects. She is co-editor with Kathy Short of *Talking About Books: Creating Literate Communities* (Heinemann, 1990) and the "Children's Books" column in *The Reading Teacher,* a journal of the International Reading Association.

Chapter 16
Collaborative Curriculum Inquiry: Learning Through Evaluation

KATHRYN MITCHELL PIERCE

As a lifelong student of reading and language, I have always attempted to make sense of the complex processes through which children learn to read and of the actual reading event itself. Initially, as a first-year teacher, I was convinced that a good reader was one who scored four out of five on the comprehension skill tests at the end of the unit. These important tests generally included such skills as identifying the main idea or author's purpose, inferring cause and effect relationships, and predicting outcomes. In short, I defined a good reader by the same skills-driven agenda that most textbooks use to define a successful student.

As my studies continued, I found myself listening in on children and adults discussing books with one another. During these informal conversations readers often engaged in selected retellings of key points in the story in order to make a point or seek clarification; they shared personal connections with the story, to other books, movies, and experiences. Through these conversations, the group members seemed to be building up a shared sense of what the story was "about" and how each of them had connected with that story. In the process, they learned things about one another, changed their experiences with the books, and changed themselves.

In my classroom, my own reading curriculum began to change to reflect these insights into what readers unencumbered by the constraints of schooling do when they have read a particularly moving book. It seems natural that readers turn to one another to share books, and I wanted to create opportunities in my classroom for my readers to engage in the same kinds of discussions. For the past eight years, I have been working with teachers and children exploring "literature discussion groups" as a powerful strategy for helping learners grow as readers. During the early part of this work I defined good readers as those who could construct complex connections as well as explore their responses to books. Still, there was something about the nature of these discussions that eluded me, something that said to me, "You haven't fully understood the reading process."

Then I became a parent, and my outlook on teaching really changed. As someone who also teaches children's literature, I have access to a great variety of books for young children. Watching my two children (ages two and five) interact with these books has been instructive. I guess it is the researcher in me, but for whatever reason I am a student of my children's reading experiences. I take note of the conversations we have about books at bedtime and references to these conversations at other times during the day. I also notice the ways my husband and I use books in our everyday lives—the examples we provide to our children of the ways adults use books and reading.

I know that we as adult readers don't read merely to locate the main idea, although that often plays a part in what we do. I still believe that being able to retell and build connections with books is important, but we pick up our books for larger purposes than that. My family reads many books and magazines that promote a particular "earth ethic." We read about wolves and dinosaurs, and why animals become extinct. We read about tyrants and heroines, and why people don't always do what's best for others. We read about rivers and famous places, and why natural and cultural resources must be protected.

Watching the evolution of our "family" reading has been fascinating. This past summer we read a nonfiction book about butterflies that led Jennifer, age five, into a butterfly research project. She read other books about butterflies, observed butterflies in our garden and in various fields, created and collected pictures of butterflies, and enjoyed poetry that captured the beauty and movement of butterflies. By the end of summer Jennifer had become a butterfly expert. She was convinced she was going to study butterflies when she grew up so they would never become extinct. Later, we read a collection of stories written by children in a homeless shelter and, again, the book moved Jennifer to action. She wanted to know why some children didn't have many toys, and why Santa didn't bring them more toys than he brought to other kids, since homeless children needed them more. I had a hard time answering that question without revealing a still well-kept secret about Santa

Claus, so I diverted her attention by asking what she thought she could do about it. We gathered two bags of treasured but neglected toys and donated them to "Toys for Tots."

Then a friend lent me a copy of *Lakota Woman* by Mary Crow Dog (1990). In this autobiography, a Native American activist writes about discrimination against Indians, women, and individual tribes, about marriage, family relations, parenting and rites-of-passage. After I read it, I was sure I'd never be the same. Through observing my child's and my own reading experiences, I realize what I had suspected for some time: we read in order to change ourselves and thereby to expand our potential to change the world.

So when I look at the books my children and I share at home, I realize that these are books that will help my children develop a sense of who they are and what they can become, respect for others and for nature, and responsibility to unborn generations and a threatened planet. I am no longer content knowing that my children can identify the main idea or create a connection between themselves and a story, although we often talk about these things. When Jennifer begins school next year, I will not be interested in letter grades or developmental milestones. I will want to know in what ways her reading experiences have changed her as a person. I will want to know the new questions she is asking, the new ideas she has about her role in the world, and the new causes she wants to explore.

That's the power of literature: to help us understand ourselves and our world, both present and future, real and imagined (Huck, 1990). The goal of education must be to change us, must leave us able to handle new experiences in more complex ways (Dewey, 1963) and passionate about using our education and our vision to change the world (Freire, 1970). Reading education in our schools should be aimed at nothing less.

REFLECTING ON EXPERIENCES AND BELIEFS

This brief account of my changing concept of readers and learners captures the transactional nature of the learning process. The more I worked to understand the reading and learning processes, and to find ways of evaluating what readers and learners were experiencing, the more I reflected on my basic beliefs about learning, reading, and evaluation. Through this constant interplay of reflection and experience I have changed my values and beliefs, my teaching practices, and my means for evaluating learners.

My learning experiences have been significantly shaped and supported by the various groups of which I am a member, particularly a study group of educators who have been exploring literature discussion groups for almost eight years (Pierce, 1990; 1992). Much of what I claim as my own understanding of evaluation is a reflection of the experiences and perspectives others have shared with me. Each of the contributors to this volume has influenced my thinking about literature discussion groups, evaluation, the role of talk in the learning process, and curriculum. My most intense involvement, however, has been with three elementary teachers, Tonya Dix, Mary Ann Rankey, and Joan Von Dras. Over the years we have worked collaboratively to answer evaluation questions that emerged from our various teaching experiences. Our consideration of these questions has resulted in a cycle of examining our beliefs and changing the ways we define the purposes of reading, facilitate reading experiences, and gather information about and evaluate learning.

Our inquiries, summarized in the questions included in Figure 16.1, have led to several transformations in our beliefs. We have shifted our concerns from answering the evaluation questions asked by those outside our classrooms to seeking ways of involving partners inside and outside the classroom in collaborative evaluation (row 1). We have moved from defining comprehension as a hierarchical set of skills to valuing those experiences with text that changed readers in significant ways, particularly in their relationship to other people and their worlds (row 2). We have moved from using literature extension projects and presentations as opportunities for students to demonstrate specific reading skills to appreciating the role of these presentations in helping readers reflect on their transactions with text (row 3). And we have moved from consulting the "experts" in our teachers' manuals in order to make curricular decisions to valuing our own insights and those of other professionals, our students, and their parents (row 4).

Although, I have presented it in a linear fashion, Figure 16.1 represents a continuous cycle of professional transformations through which we repeatedly examine our beliefs and values in light of our experiences. The means through which we worked at creating answers to these questions include collaboration with other professionals, classroom observations and reflections, collaboration with students and parents, and professional publications and presentations. Posing each new question opened up for us a new inquiry cycle of exploring, focusing, refining, and then reflecting on our classroom experiences. Creating a satisfactory answer for one question raised yet another question, as our inquiry cycle began anew. Dewey (1963) defines transaction as an educational experience that changes the potential of both the learner and the environment. The act of evaluation, therefore, is itself a transactional experience that results in professional growth.

	→	→	→	→
INQUIRY QUESTIONS	How *should* literature discussion groups be done? How can we justify to others that our learners are covering the required skills?	What evidence do *we* accept that our readers are growing? What *is* evaluation?	How do we involve the readers in evaluation, and self-evaluation? How do we communicate to parents what their readers are doing and how we are evaluating it?	How do we communicate *with* parents so that teacher, parent and student perspectives on evaluation are explored and valued?
DEFINING COMPREHENSION	A collection of basal skills: inferring cause and effect relationships, identifying author's purpose, identifying main idea, etc.	Retelling and connecting. Readers who are comprehending are able to retell portions of the text to illustrate a point, and to create connections with the text and life experience.	Increasing ability to build up personal meaning in response to text, within a social context.	Reading experiences leave the reader changed in significant ways, particularly in a developing sense of responsibility toward others and our world.
ROLE OF LITERATURE PRESENTATIONS	Additional contexts within which readers demonstrate application of reading skills.	Options for demonstration of comprehension: art, music, movement, drama, writing, displays, etc.	Opportunities to learn about the personal connections individual small groups of readers make with specific texts.	Evidence that readers have changed as a result of their transaction with text.
SOURCES OF KNOWLEDGE	The "experts" represented in the basal teacher's manual.	The "experts" represented in the professional literature, fellow teachers, the students, and our own professional experiences.	The "experts" represented in the professional literature, fellow teachers, the students, and our own professional experiences.	The "experts" represented in the professional literature, fellow teachers, the students, and their parents, and our own professional experiences.

Figure 16.1 *Time Line of Professional Transformations*

DEFINING EVALUATION AS TRANSACTION

When teachers attempt to evaluate student learning in literature discussion groups, they inevitably learn more about how these curricular engagements function and how to use them more effectively—how to expand the potential of the curricular engagement so that it can better serve the learning needs of the students. At the same time, as teachers reflect on both the curricular engagements they offer students and student learning, they have opportunities and data available to promote their own professional growth (Goodman, 1989).

As teachers think about literature discussion groups and struggle with ways of evaluating students, they find themselves understanding more about the reading process, the social nature of learning, and the role of talk in small groups. Such awareness leaves the teacher better able to guide students in literature discussion groups and other small group experiences. One of our responsibilities as teachers is to work at creating evaluation experiences that have an impact on the learning of both the learner and the teacher, along with the potential for both to use the particular learning engagement.

My own beliefs about evaluation have developed over time through such a transactional process, and I have learned to reject evaluation experiences that fail to meet the criteria implied by my beliefs. I currently believe evaluation is best when it

- Is collaborative.
- Involves systematic and intentional collection of and reflection on data.
- Is multifaceted and includes several different ways of looking at a learner's growth.
- Captures changes over time, presenting a video-view of learning rather than a snapshot view.
- Respects the learner as an individual with responsibility for his or her own learning.
- Offers a sense of perspective or direction for continued learning.
- Communicates useful information to the learner and others interested in the learner's work.

Teachers' actions in the classroom are guided by theoretical belief systems, whether intuitively or explicitly chosen (Harste and Burke, 1977; Watson, in press). When teachers articulate their beliefs, they have control over their own learning (Short and Burke, 1991). The actions teachers take in literature discussion groups (Should I assign book titles to the group? Should I meet with each group each time? Should I interrupt and offer a question or comment?) are based on their values and beliefs (Hanssen, 1990). Reflecting on these decisions helps us clarify our beliefs and bring our actions and beliefs into alignment with one another (Short and Burke, 1991; Watson, in press).

The model that follows depicts the relationships among our beliefs, our actions, and our observations of learners (Figure 16.2). The model is designed to be similar to Neisser's model of perception (1976), which guided its development. Neisser proposes that our world theory or view guides our actions, thereby highlighting certain data for visual perception. We see what we are looking for. When what we see does not match what we are looking for, we change our theories or modify our actions. The process is the same for teaching. Our beliefs guide and can be inferred from our teaching deci-

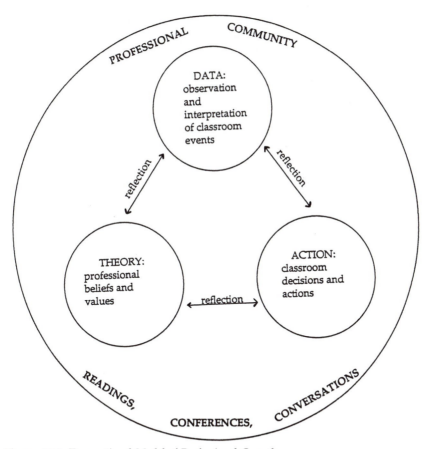

Figure 16.2 *Transactional Model of Professional Growth*

sions and actions in the classroom. These actions, in turn, highlight particular aspects of our curriculum and our learner's experiences for evaluation. Reflecting on these aspects of our classroom and our learners affects our beliefs and subsequent decisions. The entire perceptual cycle is influenced by the members and the experiences of the professional communities in which we are immersed: presentations, readings, conversations with other teachers, and so on. The model in Figure 16.2 demonstrates the process of professional transformation. At different times, we highlight one leg of the "triangle" over another, but ultimately, the entire process has been affected.

In our search for ever more effective ways of understanding and evaluating the talk in literature discussion groups, we have created, revised, and rejected various observation guides and recording forms. Because talk is the primary means available to us to evaluate what happens in literature discussions and other small group experiences, we have committed ourselves to studying the talk that occurs in these settings. Barnes (1992) reminds us that this talk embodies the curriculum that is enacted in our classrooms. To study what our students are learning, we need to find ways of looking at their small group talk with increasingly sophisticated lenses, of freeze-framing their conversations without distorting the complexity of these collaborative exchanges. The analysis of talk is a messy business. The closer we seem to come to finding a way of understanding it, the more we come to appreciate its complexity and the less we are satisfied with our current means for analysis. Our tools for observing, recording, and analyzing talk in literature discussion groups are in a continual state of change as our needs and values evolve.

The first form we used to analyze the talk in literature discussions was borrowed from another group of teachers working with literature discussion groups (Watson, 1990). We had great difficulty using this form because it was based on their beliefs and values and their definitions of the reading process rather than our own. Our next form was based on a return to the basal reading program definitions of the reading process as a series of skills to be mastered. It included a list of the basal reading skills we felt were most important and a place to note the contexts in which we observed learners demonstrating each skill: writer's workshop, literature discussion, basal end-of-unit test, and so on. We quickly rejected this form, too, because it failed to provide us with a sense of direction for our learners and because it didn't seem to match what we valued in our observations of readers in action.

As time passed, we began to realize that we needed to clarify our definitions of reading and our overriding intentions for readers—each influencing the other. To do this, we listened to tape recordings of our literature discussion groups and made note of the things we valued and the observations that troubled us. This led us to create a set of categories into which individual reader comments could be placed. The categories were grouped under two major headings: retelling and making connections (Pierce, 1990). Our form, therefore, helped us focus our attention on the types of comments we valued: retellings of portions of text for specific purposes and connections with other texts and life experiences.

Our learners continued to provide us with demonstrations of the complexity of the reading process, and we found ourselves increasingly using the "other" category on our form to record notable observations that didn't seem to fit our current category system. In addition, we found ourselves attending more to larger chunks of conversation than to individual utterances. We needed to have larger spaces on the recording form in order to demonstrate the ways the participants had built up to a particular insight (Dix, this volume). Sharing these anomalies with one another provided us with opportunities to reflect on and articulate our beliefs and values. The unexpected data along with the opportunities to examine our beliefs and values caused us to revise our theory. Our learners helped us come to value reading as a transaction (Rosenblatt, 1978) and as a means to achieve an enhanced sense of social responsibility (Freire, 1970). Our students were using reading for the personal and social ends they valued (Von Dras, this volume). Currently, we are using anecdotal records maintained in spiral journals because they provide us with the greatest flexibility in recording and reflecting on our observations of readers in a variety of contexts, particularly across areas of the curriculum and across time. Although we occasionally use a specific recording form to focus our observations on a particular aspect of the reading event, this form is always interpreted in light of the richer details available in our anecdotal records.

Creating professional growth portfolios of artifacts from our teaching enables us to celebrate the small, but important cycles in our own learning in much the same way that we have used student work portfolios to help students and teachers reflect on student growth. These records of our growth help us gain insights into the process we ask our students to use in reflecting on their own learning. These portfolios include samples of "best work" from students, "I used to . . ., but now I . . ." statements, a paper trail of evaluation instruments we have developed over time, student interviews about the effectiveness of particular strategies, notes and letters from visitors to our classrooms, and charts we have created identifying our strengths and asking questions about particular aspects of our teaching.

Reviewing these portfolios, which reflect our ongoing search for ever more effective evaluation strategies, reveals several types of experiences all of which have contributed to our professional growth. The ongoing collaboration within the group of teachers familiar with our setting and beliefs provided a supportive context within which we could explore complex and challenging concepts related to evaluation. This group further supported each member's professional study through shared readings and discussions of conference presentations. Coming to understand the value of this collaborative relationship encouraged us to seek collaborative relationships with students and their parents. In similar fashion, coming to understand the value for our students of literature group presentations and other culminating experiences encouraged us to create our own professional writings and conference presentations.

INVOLVING STUDENTS IN EVALUATION

Carolyn Burke's ideas, illustrated in a model of the processes and perspectives involved in evaluation (Short and Burke, 1991) reminded us that student input was being neglected in our continuing search for effective evaluation strategies. Initially, we relied on several student self-evaluation forms created by others because we hadn't sorted out our own questions and values in relation to student self-evaluation. We knew we *should* be doing something with student self-evaluation, and trying out the forms created by others was a place to start. A real turning point came when I talked with Tim, a sixth grader in Joan Von Dras's classroom. Tim frequently worked alone, and his teacher described him as "an outsider" in the class but someone respected by his classmates as "really bright." The following is an excerpt from our conversation, taken from the running script I made as we talked.

01 KATHRYN: How do you know if it's a really good literature discussion? What makes a good discussion?

02 TIM: If she [the teacher] needs to come in often and help us out it's not as good. I enjoy it more when we can do it ourselves. . . .

I love books where I can relate my experiences to them and my friends to them. The book I'm reading now, *Number the Stars* (Lowry, 1989), I can't relate anything to it, but it's still a good book. It's historical fiction. I like that type of book. It appeals to me. Like *Johnny Tremain* (Forbes, 1987). I know about the book. I've read different books about [World War II] often, so I *can* relate to it, come to think of it.

See, in a discussion group, the kids try to control, or conquer me in a group like the Nazi's did to Denmark. You know, kid to kid, country to country.

It's like in the Middle East right now. Iraq needed a leader and Hussein took over. He's on the warpath, taking control of other countries just like Hitler did in World War II. He does have a few allies like Hitler did. He's promised them power so they can come with him. It's kind of like that in some literature discussions, too. The ones that aren't so good.

03 KATHRYN: So what do you think makes *good* groups? What would you say are the criteria for a *good* discussion group?

04 TIM: When everybody is participating and nobody has to bring other people into the discussion. No time lapses when nobody's talking. That's boring and not as meaningful at that time. *I* help bring others into the discussion. Like slower people. They need encouragement to talk or share information.

05 KATHRYN: What do you mean, "slower people"?

06 TIM: Kids who aren't on as high a level as [names several classmates] are. It takes them a little bit longer to learn. It's not that they can't or won't learn it, they're just a bit slower than I am at learning it.

07 KATHRYN: O.K. Other criteria?

08 TIM: Well, when everyone contributes *good* thoughts, fascinating and superb things. When they soak the information in, not just saying "Oh yeah, O.K.," but really active in it. In boring or uncomfortable times, the teacher has to come in.

09 KATHRYN: How do you solve this or avoid having the teacher step in?

10 TIM: Well, people in the group try to bring them back in. Sometimes it works, sometimes it doesn't. If it doesn't, they sometimes start messing around.

My discussion with Tim reaffirmed the importance of students' involvement in the evaluation of their own learning and demonstrated their awareness of the curricular strategies they were experiencing. Listening to Tim helped me begin to understand how he was experiencing literature discussion groups, particularly his views of the social relationships among group members. I was impressed by his ability to use the literature he was reading and his knowledge of broader political relationships between countries in creating a metaphor to explain the social dynamics of classroom discussion groups. Later, we interviewed other sixth-grade students and then asked them to interview third-grade students about their perceptions of literature discussion groups.

Using a variation on "three pluses and a wish" (Mills, 1986), Joan, Tonya, and I wrote responses to the tapes of these interviews. On the left side of the paper we listed the comments that suggested the literature discussion strategy was working well. On the right side we listed the comments we heard, or didn't hear, that indicated areas in which our use of the strategy could be improved. We were pleased to hear students defining "good" literature discussion groups as those in which everyone participates and the teacher doesn't have to step in. Like Tim (04, 08), they value discussion groups in which students build on what one another has said. They also feel responsibility for bringing quiet members into a discussion, without pressuring them to participate.

At the same time, we were concerned to hear students say that good discussion groups cannot occur if the group doesn't like the book. We were most concerned, however, with the number of comments about the value of sharing personal feelings in response to the books to the exclusion of comments about using the group to work at understanding complex texts. Comparing our "results" with those of teachers in other settings helped us realize that we must be communicating to the students that we value connecting personal feelings and responses in the literature discussions but not collaborative meaning-construction. Reflecting on these tapes led us to make changes in the ways we interacted with students during discussions and in the types of information we recorded and encouraged. Eventually, student comments from interviews such as these were used to support students in creating their own self-evaluation tools for reflecting on their literature discussion experiences (Dix, this volume).

DEFINING EVALUATION AS AN EXTENSION OF THE "GETTING TO KNOW YOU" PROCESS

Teachers begin the school term with the process of getting to know their students and communicating to students their expectations and ways of operating. This "getting to know you" process is essential to building a supportive learning community, and it is ongoing: the more time teachers and students spend together, the more they come to know one another.

Evaluation is an extension of this "getting to know you" process. In order to participate in the evaluation process, teachers must come to know their students as individuals, including how they view the world, how they organize and construct meaning, and how they communicate what they have come to understand.

Evaluating, learning, and relationship-building occur continuously and simultaneously as teachers and students work together. The better teachers know their students, the more sophisticated their evaluation can be, and the more students' learning becomes visible. At times, it is difficult to separate "I know you better now" from "You didn't used to be able to do this." Evaluation always focuses on a moving target.

Teachers have the primary responsibility for supporting this relationship-building process, although both teachers and students have developed an extensive repertoire of strategies for getting to know one another. Beginning-of-the-year strategies such as letters of introduction (from parent or child to teacher), show-and-tell, sharing circles, and "me boxes" (collections of artifacts representing different aspects of the teacher's or student's life) help members of a learning community come to know one another, to perceive one another as resources, and to begin evaluating growth and change. We cannot evaluate the growth of our learners effectively until we have a sense of where they have been and where they perceive themselves as going.

EXPANDING THE INQUIRY TO INCLUDE PARENTS

Another outcome of our reflections on Burke's evaluation model was the realization that parents and the other significant adults in the lives of our students were being treated as "outsiders" in our evaluation conversations and that we had not explored the potential of collaborating with them in the creation of records of student growth. New appreciation for the value of involving students in the evaluation process led Tonya to include parents in her initial use of reading/writing portfolios to replace traditional forms of documenting literacy growth. We used what we had learned about getting to know our students in order to create strategies for getting to know the adults in their lives as partners in their education.

Through Tonya's initial experiences in attempting to create more collaborative relationships with parents, we all began to seek meaningful ways of inviting parents into our evaluation discussions. Most of the information we found on parent involvement was based on one-way communication in which the school was "teaching" or "informing" parents about ways they could support readers at home but not inviting parents to teach or inform school personnel about their own insights into their children as readers and learners.

Tonya began our inquiry into parent involvement when she chose to work with students and parents to create reader portfolios that would communicate information about student growth to both students and their parents. Tonya invited the parents of her third-grade students, Joan, and me to attend a series of informal, after-school parent meetings during which we would collaboratively create a portfolio "system." From the beginning, she wanted these sessions to be more than parent education opportunities, although her early meetings focused on teaching the parents how to interpret her current recording forms for literature discussion groups. By introducing them to her record-keeping strategies, she wanted to help parents come to appreciate what we had come to value about reading. Ironically, we expected parents to understand "current" views about the reading process in the course of a single parent curriculum night, forgetting that we had invested several years of professional inquiry in developing these views ourselves.

A real breakthrough in our work came when we identified questions that successfully invited parents to share evaluation information from their unique perspectives as parents. We had been asking them to tell us what goals or intentions they had for their children as readers, writers, and learners. Initially, the parents weren't sure what we were asking for or whether their views on the reading process and their children as readers could be useful to a reading "professional." Through our small group discussions with parents during the third parent meeting, we developed the following set of questions, which seemed to communicate both what kinds of information we were requesting *and* our belief that parent input was essential for us to truly understand their children as readers and learners.

- What evidence would you accept that your child has grown as a reader? a writer? a learner?
- What would you like your child to be able to do, or do better, or do more at the end of the school year?
- In what ways would you like this evidence communicated to you (e.g., grades, narrative reports, work samples, annotated work samples, checklists)?
- What have you observed at home that indicates to you that your child is growing as a reader? a writer? a learner?

We were surprised by many of the things the parents shared with us. For example, they were less interested in grades and test scores than in the "before and after" pictures we could create using samples of their child's work. The long-term goals they shared were similar to our own goals for their children: to read for pleasure and information, to balance reading with other recreational pursuits, and to use information learned through reading and other forms of inquiry to develop, articulate, and defend particular points of view. In addition, they shared with us and other parents examples of the ways they encourage their children to value reading: taking books on family trips, saving time for reading together at bedtime, asking older children to share books with younger siblings, giving books as gifts, and making trips to the local library fun family events. As parents shared family stories with the rest of us, we were struck by their insights about the history of their children's reading development through second grade and were ashamed that we had never before invited them to share this information.

We came to realize that we needed to get to know the parents and their interpretive schemes for reading, evaluation, and schooling in order to help them see the relationship between their schemes and our own, and to jointly establish our goals for the children. By trying to get to know parents and their beliefs, we found ourselves entering into more collaborative relationships. We also realized that the parents were getting to know us in order to find ways of sharing with us what they knew about their children as readers and learners. The initial "getting to know you process" took time and numerous informal conversations to develop and we worked to sustain our relationships with one another by continuing to share and celebrate the stories that captured children's growth. This sharing was essential in establishing mutual trust and an environment in which teachers and parents felt comfortable talking about and exploring new ideas. Through our conversations and stories, we were able to better understand our own and one another's values and beliefs as we worked to make them explicit for others.

The success of our sessions was the result of our shift in perspective from "parent as reading teacher in training" to "parent as unique informant" and potential collaborator. Later parent meetings were organized around portfolios of student work and small group discussions of parent responses to this work. Again using the "three pluses and a wish" format, parents were invited to share their perspectives on these portfolios, including the goals or wishes they had for their children's continued growth. This shift in perspective also signaled to parents that their input on all facets of the classroom was valued. Later parent meetings were organized to seek parent input into the design and implementation of the annual science fair and the culminating event of a major economics unit, the farmer's market. The following year, Joan expanded parent involvement in her classroom from parent meetings to parent-teacher study groups that focused on professional books of interest to both teachers and parents.

REFLECTING ON THE POTENTIAL OF PRESENTATIONS

Pausing throughout the journey to organize and share our information with others has been invaluable in helping us come to know our views about evaluation. Just as writing helps learners organize and reflect on what they know, presenting helps us know our work better. It is an invitation to engage in reflection and to participate in the collaborative restructuring of our prior experiences and how we have made sense of these experiences. This double cycle of creating meaning and then creating ways of presenting this meaning to others is a complex process that facilitates further learning.

Through his extensive work on talking and learning in small groups, Douglas Barnes (1992) has helped us to see the value of stopping to reflect and consider what others might think of our work.

> Now anyone who has sat on an effective committee knows how valuable it is to stop everyone now and then to ask: "Where have we got to?" in order to reach an explicit reformulation of ideas which have already been mentioned in a less explicit and organized way. It would seem to be extremely valuable for groups of children similarly to discuss work in two stages, one a less formulated and more exploratory one, and the second more planned and organised. (61)

Barnes goes on, however, to warn against classroom practices that rush learners to present the meanings they have created before they have had ample time to develop them fully. Formal presentations rarely offer opportunities to engage in exploratory talk with unfamiliar others. In our classrooms, however, we can offer students opportunities to engage in this exploratory talk, revise the information and adjust the presentation, and possibly present to the class again. While few students accept the invitation to take the process completely through to the re-presentation, they seem to find comfort and support in the opportunity to think through how they *would* do it differently next time.

Reflecting on the value of our own presentations has helped us rethink our use of literature discussions and literature projects or presentations in the classroom. Too often our learners rushed into presenting the literature and moved quickly into presentational talk without having collaboratively explored their experiences of the text in more depth and from several perspectives. Similarly, the first time we attempted to present the models of our professional growth, we focused so much on getting the models across that our presentations lacked a sense of the classrooms within which we were working. The passion of our inquiry and the sense of a real story were missing.

At other times, audience questions or comments have revealed new areas of inquiry to us. During one such presentation, a member of the audience, Adrian Peetoom, asked Tonya a question about her use of spelling words within an otherwise rich and engaging inquiry into the human body. This question forced Tonya to work through an anomaly that had been in the background of her thinking for some time. The rest of us had abandoned specific spelling lists some time ago, but we had respected Tonya's decision to retain them in her classroom. By the end of the six-hour drive home, Tonya had talked through her concerns and experiences. She had reached the decision to discontinue her use of isolated spelling lists, even of words related to the children's current inquiries. In retrospect, she realized that Adrian's question was an invitation to continued inquiry and not an evaluation of her presentation. Using our own presentations as examples, we have helped our students view their "unsuccessful" presentations, unexpected audience responses, and new questions as invitations to continue their own inquiry.

DESIGNING EVALUATION FOR LEARNING

Evaluation, primarily because it is based on values, is a highly political activity. The commercially published evaluation schemes with which we were most familiar (standardized achievement tests and end-of-unit basal tests) seemed to be based on the political process of valuing one reading performance over another. These schemes encourage teachers to compare children with one another in terms of predetermined benchmarks. This perspective establishes a powerful and dangerous caste system in schools: those who are "on grade level" or who make the mark are on one level, those who exceed our minimal standards on another, and those who do not meet our standards on still another. This perspective seems incompatible with current views about the ways children learn and the most supportive learning environments for that learning (Roderick, 1991).

Distinguishing among children on the basis of norms and standards seems less useful in our instructional decision making than recognizing children as individuals. Shifting our perspective from evaluation *of* learning to evaluation *for* learning requires us to move away from evaluation strategies that rank-order our learners along a single, linear growth continuum and to seek strategies that highlight the unique ways learners approach complex tasks. Rather than trying to untangle and straighten a child's growth in order to understand it, teachers attempt to understand unique growth patterns while protecting this complexity. To do so, teachers move away from comparing learners against rigid standards and toward recognizing patterns and trends in growth within and among particular children. They move away from evaluation strategies that sequence learners from best to worst and toward evaluation strategies that inform teachers' *and* students' classroom decisions.

Knowing that half of the students in a class have learned to identify relationships among character, action, and plot does not reveal what they will learn in the following three weeks. Some may focus on authors' strategies for developing characters while others explore use of flashbacks. Still others may appear not to have learned anything at all because they have been in the process of reorganizing prior learning in light of their new-found knowledge. Because learning is an individualized and idiosyncratic process, evaluation must move beyond narrow interpretations of what learners have already achieved.

Evaluation best serves the needs of learners when it is focused on what they can do now and what they will be able to do in the near future. Traditional achievement tests and other, similar ways of looking at students tend to focus exclusively on what students may have learned by some discrete measure. While this information is widely viewed to be useful, it does not provide a sense of perspective. It does not help us answer the question, "Where is this learner going next?"

Vygotsky (1978) helps us understand that instruction must focus on those areas where students are likely to take their next (proximal) learning steps. He defines this "zone of proximal development," as the space between what the learner can do independently and what the learner can do with the assistance of a more able peer. Vygotsky's scheme suggests that the things learners support one another in doing through a collaborative literature discussion will soon be the things these learners can think about and do on their own. In order to identify this zone of proximal development, teachers must continue the process of getting to know students as individuals, particularly the ways in which they are working at understanding new concepts and using others to support this process.

When we focus on evaluation *for* learning rather than *of* learning, we offer a sense of perspective to both teachers and learners. This perspective makes it more likely that learners will continue to "move ahead" with their learning and that our instructional efforts will be aimed at the specific needs of individuals rather than at a generalized path of learning. Studies of how learners expand proficiency in language and literacy do indicate general patterns of learning that seem to be consistent across most learners. These general patterns are most effective when perceived as ways of narrowing down the options we consider in attempting to support a particular learner's next (proximal) step.

Most of our best instructional strategies provide the information we require in order to support learners' growth. Learning logs (Pierce, 1987) invite students to take stock of what they have learned, the questions they may still have, and the ideas they wish to explore the next day. When preserved in a collection or portfolio, these logs provide a written record of conceptual growth that can support both students and teachers in evaluating that growth. Goal-setting conferences, particularly when used in conjunction with a portfolio of selected work samples, enable teachers and students to share their perspectives on the student's work and to identify the patterns that will lead to new areas of learning.

LOOKING AHEAD AND DEFINING A PERSPECTIVE

Learning, including inquiry into effective evaluation strategies, is a self-regenerating cycle. Taking time to reflect on the learning so far, learners seek to uncover the new questions and anomalies that will begin the cycle anew. As I reflect on where we are in our understanding of the evaluation of literature discussion groups and learning in general, the following questions seem to suggest the way ahead:

- How do we help learners develop and maintain a sense of perspective in their learning and continue to focus their evaluation on the new potential they have created for themselves?
- How do we develop evaluation strategies that enable us to see the connection between today's experiences and tomorrow's?
- How do we extend the "getting to know you" process to the increasing numbers of parents and children whose beliefs, cultural experiences, and values for education as well as strategies for getting to know *us* are different from ours and unfamiliar to us?
- How do we expand the potential of literature discussion groups to support children in reflecting on their out-of-school lives, thereby expanding the options they recognize for themselves and their communities?
- How do we bring the larger community into this process of defining and evaluating growth in reading relative to social responsibility?
- How do we help prospective and inservice teachers benefit from our experiences without having to relive them, or can we? How do we balance the process *and* the content of our inquiry?

As I have come to understand myself as an individual learner working at creating personal understandings of my experiences and as a member of a larger professional community working at creating community meanings, I realize that the ways in which I have grown are very similar to the ways in which my students are growing. The processes that support my learning provide insights into the ways I can support my students in their learning. At the same time, the insights I gain into their learning expand the potential for my own learning. My professional development journey and those of my students and peers are integrally related. I became a teacher in large part because I wanted to "change the world." In accepting this challenge, I must also accept the responsibility for empowering my students to do the same by supporting them in developing the tools, the feeling of responsibility, and the passion to actively pursue their own causes.

REFERENCES

Barnes, D. 1992. *From communication to curriculum.* 2nd ed. Portsmouth, NH: Boynton/Cook.

Crow Dog, M. 1990. *Lakota woman.* New York: Harper.

Dewey, J. 1963. *Experience and education.* New York: Macmillan.

Forbes, E. 1987. *Johnny Tremain.* New York: Dell.

Freire, P. 1970. *Pedagogy of the oppressed.* New York: Continuum.

Goodman, Y. 1989. "Evaluation of students: Evaluation of teachers." In *The whole language evaluation book,* edited by K. Goodman, Y. Goodman, & W. Hood. Portsmouth, NH: Heinemann.

Hanssen, E. 1990. "Planning for literature circles: Variations in focus and structure." In *Talking About Books: Creating Literate Communities,* edited by K. Short & K. Pierce. Portsmouth, NH: Heinemann.

Harste, J. and C. Burke. 1977. "A new hypothesis for reading teacher education research: Both the teaching and learning of reading are theoretically based." In *Reading: Research, theory and practice (Twenty-Sixth Yearbook of the National Reading Conference),* edited by P.D. Pearson. Minneapolis, MN: Mason.

Huck, C. 1990. "The power of children's literature in the classroom." In *Talking about books: Creating literate communities,* edited by K. Short & K. Pierce. Portsmouth, NH: Heinemann.

Lowry, L. 1989. *Number the stars.* Boston, MA: Houghton Mifflin.

Mills, H. 1986. *Writing evaluation: A transactional process.* Unpublished dissertation. Bloomington, IN: Indiana University.

Neisser, U. 1976. *Cognition and reality,* San Francisco, CA: W.H. Freeman.

Pierce, K. 1992. "Afterword." In *From communication to curriculum,* 2nd ed., by D. Barnes. Portsmouth, NH: Heinemann.

———. 1990. "Initiating literature discussion groups: Teaching like learners." In *Talking about books: Creating literate communities,* edited by K. Short & K. Pierce. Portsmouth, NH: Heinemann.

———. 1987. "Learning logs." In *Ideas and insights: Language arts in the elementary school,* edited by D. Watson. Urbana, IL: National Council of Teachers of English.

Roderick, J. A. Ed. 1991. *Context-responsive approaches to assessing children's language.* Urbana, IL: National Conference on Research in English.

Rosenblatt, L. 1978. *The reader, the text, and the poem.* Carbondale, IL: Southern Illinois University Press.

Short, K. & C. Burke. 1991. *Creating curriculum: Teachers and students as a community of learners.* Portsmouth, NH: Heinemann.

Vygotsky, L. 1978. *Mind and society.* Cambridge, MA: MIT Press.

Watson, D. (in press.) "Whole language: Why bother?" *The Reading Teacher.* Newark, DE: International Reading Association.

————. 1990. "Show me: Whole language evaluation of literature groups." In *Talking about books: Creating literate communities,* edited by K. Short & K. Pierce. Portsmouth, NH: Heinemann.

Tonya Dix has taught grades three, four, and five and is currently a fourth-grade teacher at Wren Hollow Elementary School in the Parkway School District, St. Louis, Missouri. She is working toward creating a classroom where respect for learners and their needs is inspired through her own discoveries as a learner. She also serves as a member of the Editorial Advisory Board for the "Children's Books" column in *The Reading Teacher*, published by the International Reading Association.

Chapter 17
Cycles of Professional Growth: Evaluating Literature Discussion Groups

TONYA DIX

I was once asked to draw a picture of my professional growth time line. Much discussion and many discarded pieces of paper later, my time line took on the shape of a cycle or spiral that continues to feed back on itself. My work with small group problem-solving activities in science guided my explorations of literature discussion groups and writer's groups in my classroom. These new curricular strategies led me to revise the methods I used for evaluation and later affected the ways I organized my content-area curriculum. These changes, in turn, led me back to literature discussion groups with a slightly new perspective. The questions were the same, but somehow the way I approached them had changed. My efforts to evaluate what I saw happening in my literature discussion groups and to communicate this information to others has created a series of questions that have driven my professional development over an eight-year period. This process also has affected every aspect of my curriculum as well as my own understanding of how I learn as an adult. In this chapter I describe the complex cycle of my professional growth using as an example my work with literature discussion groups. Then I demonstrate how this repeating cycle of inquiries related to literature discussion groups has sparked similar repeating cycles of inquiry in other areas of my curriculum.

In sharing my own professional growth story, I hope that others will come to value the power of teachers' classroom-based questions to guide and energize their professional development. The more I have come to value the need for my students' investment in their own inquiry questions, the more I have come to appreciate the need for staff development for teachers to begin with *their* questions rather than with questions imposed by others.

INITIATING AND EVALUATING LITERATURE DISCUSSION GROUPS

Eight years ago three colleagues—Joan Von Dras, Mary Ann Rankey, and Kathryn Mitchell Pierce—and I decided that we needed a change in our teaching. The way we had been teaching just wasn't doing enough for us. After several discussions, one of which was with our principal to secure his approval, we set the wheels of change in motion. In my case, the first step was to start using fiction literature as a systematic and essential part of my reading program. I say "in my case" because my colleagues didn't start the same way I did, although we supported one another and worked closely together throughout this change process.

Our first discussions were about how to get multiple copies of our selected books, how to get the discussions started, how to lead them, and how to evaluate the students' comprehension of what they had read (Pierce, 1990). We agreed that we couldn't begin to answer all of our questions in advance and that we needed to try the discussion groups and let the answers emerge from our explorations. Obtaining the books and getting the discussion groups started seemed relatively easy. We struggled over the selection of titles and searched out various means of acquiring multiple copies, primarily through the bonus points from our Scholastic and Trumpet book clubs. By January we had enough initial answers to our questions and enough books to begin.

Over the next few months we established a routine. There are a variety of ways to organize Literature in Discussion (L.I.D.) (Hanssen, 1990). In my classroom students self-select into discussion groups according to book titles. Students make first, second, and third choices, and groups are formed according to those choices. Then students meet to decide on what the reading assignment will be and when they will meet to have their discussions. After they have made these decisions, students read the agreed upon pages individually or with a partner. While reading, students record their responses to the literature in their journals, including things they want to discuss with the group, reactions to the story, predictions of what will come next, and so on. When the groups meet to share and discuss their responses, they deal with many elements of the literature. They may choose to talk about character development or plot interpretation, offer their opinions with reasons to support them, or clarify a point. Very often, students make connections between the literature they are discussing and other books by the same author; related books by other authors, including fellow classmates; and their own or others' life experiences. One goal I have for these discussions is that students develop an ability to interpret the literature from a more sophisticated problem-solving standpoint.

During the discussions the students may choose to share entire entries from their journals, but as time goes by, they read smaller sections as springboards for discussion. Usually the groups meet an average of three times to discuss the book and then schedule additional meetings as necessary to develop extensions of the books. These extensions take on many forms, ranging from skits to sequels, and serve as culminating activities for the books.

The dominant force that guided my revisions of the discussion group strategy during the first few years was my overriding concern with "covering the skills" from our required basal reading series. This shift to teaching the skills through the literature led to a second challenge: the question of appropriate and useful evaluation of how my students were growing as readers.

Working with my colleagues, I explored various questions about the evaluation of literature discussion groups. The first question was how to "do" evaluation of a book discussion. We decided that our initial step should be to develop an evaluation tool that would help us observe and interpret the talk in these discussions. Using examples from other teachers (Watson, 1990), we developed our first grid (Figure 17.1). Developing the tool was relatively easy, but learning to use it was considerably less so (Pierce, 1990). Many changes dealing with the uses of the grid and evaluation of discussion groups occurred over the next few years. During this time, my need to teach the skills separately diminished, particularly when I saw the impressive interpretations and connections students were making during the discussions. It was obvious to me that they were developing and using skills in a far more sophisticated way than when I was teaching the skills in isolation: skills used in context were being learned naturally.

Brian Cambourne's work (1988) encouraged me to compare the ease with which a child learns to talk with the process of learning to read and write. It suggests that left to their own rhythm and given the opportunity, children develop the basic frameworks of language as naturally as walking. Cambourne goes on to say that if a similar environment could be developed for children learning to read and write as is developed for a child learning to speak, then learning to read and write would be as natural as learning to speak. In support of his claim he makes the following statement:

> Reception, i.e., listening in the oral mode and reading in the written mode, once past the eye or ear, the sound waves (oral mode) or light waves (written mode) which set the processes of meaning construction in action are reduced to the same basic sets of neural impulses. The same neural processes are

NAME: _____   DATE(S): _____   GRADE: _____   TEACHER: _____

RETELLING	Story Elements	Characters & Plot	Character Development	Plot Interpretation
	Purpose	Opinion (like/dislike)	Prove a point	Clarification
CONNECTIONS	Lit./Writing	Books by same author	Books by other authors	Compares student authors
	Life experience	Personal:self	Others	Social issues / Relates journal

Figure 17.1 *Responses to Literature*

involved using the same neural machinery. With respect to the production of meaning (speaking/writing) the texts which are created for others to hear or read originate in the same parts of the cerebral cortex, traverse much the same kinds of neural pathways, using much the same kinds of neural processing, before the organs of production (tongue/hand) go into action. (p. 29)

Cambourne goes on to outline a list of eight conditions that are present when the child learns to speak. I share his belief that these same conditions must be present for the child to learn to read and write, or for anyone to learn at all.

1. Immersion: Learners are immersed in an environment that is saturated with meaningful, contextual language.
2. Demonstration: Within this context, learners are provided with actions or artifacts that demonstrate potential uses of language. Each learner sees the learning differently and attends to different demonstrations of the complex task of language use.
3. Engagement: To become language users, learners must engage in the demonstrations they have observed. However, they will do so only when the following conditions have been met. First, the learner must see the task as "doable." Second, the learner must see the task as furthering the purpose of his or her life. And third, the learner must believe the environment is low risk and free of negative repercussions.
4. Expectations: The learner, and respected others with whom the learner interacts, must expect that the learner will learn to use the language successfully.
5. Responsibility: The learner has responsibility for deciding how to tackle the complex process. While the learner must eventually learn the complete task, he or she must decide on which aspect to focus today.
6. Approximation: The learner does not wait until total mastery before initiating language (task). Teachers and others in the learning environment must acknowledge and praise the necessary risks taken by the learner.
7. Use: The learner requires time and opportunity to use language (task) in a variety of meaningful contexts.
8. Response: The learner requires supportive responses from others about the learning. (Cambourne, 1988; pp. 43–79)

I believe that if we can create similar conditions for children learning to read and write, then children will learn these complex language tasks as easily as they learn to speak. Obviously, the environments can't be identical, but they can be very similar. Schools could definitely create settings where reading and writing could be learned naturally, like speaking. Such environments enhance language learning as well as all other forms of learning.

As I began to use Cambourne's conditions for literacy learning in my revision of the role of skill development in discussion groups, a problem started to emerge. I began to feel that if I didn't put as much emphasis on teaching skills in isolation, then I had to be ready to present tangible proof to those outside my classroom that these skills were being addressed through the literature discussion groups or writing workshop. The evaluation grids we had developed earlier became the central focus of my attention. I saw these grids as a concrete way to demonstrate to myself and to others that the students could read and discuss the books, with some guidance from me, making use of literary elements as necessary. In addition, I believed that the examples recorded on the observation grids could prove that skills need never be taught in isolation. I began to put hours into the grids: audio- and videotaping numerous discussion groups, developing written scripts of discussion groups, analyzing student comments and recording them in various cells of the observation grid, and discussing particular examples with other teachers in order to better understand and articulate the growth I saw represented in those comments.

After some time, this intense scrutiny of the observation grids and of the literature discussions themselves led me to greater understanding of the evaluation process and the literature discussion strategy. In short, I began to outgrow the observation grid. Using an assignment in a graduate educational measurement course, I set about redesigning the observation grid to fit my current understanding of what the students were doing during their discussions. The use of this new grid was short-lived, and I soon found that I wanted to return to the original grid (Figure 17.1). I was more comfortable with the old grid now that I understood it better. For a while, the return to the original observation grid did provide the sense of security I used to find in the basal reading program: everything was neat, everything fit into a box.

But as I continued to explore literature discussion groups, reading professional literature and talking with colleagues, two further problems began to emerge: First, I began to notice more and more comments that seemed important but didn't seem to fit into any cells of the grid. Most of these comments made by the students were typical of what I had heard in the past, but they now seemed important in ways I wasn't sure I understood. Recording them in the "other" cell allowed me to save them for further consideration and for discussion with my colleagues, but it seemed that I had more comments in the "other" cell than anywhere else. The second problem centered on the use of isolated comments from an ongoing discussion. Initially, I recorded specific comments that seemed significant to me. However, as I shared these comments with my colleagues, I found that I needed to explain the context of the discussion that led up to the comment. The next step was to record the context for these comments on the grid. I labeled these "set-ups" to explain how the comment of interest was "set-up" in the preceding conversation.

I want to present an excerpt from a discussion group about *A Taste of Blackberries* by Doris Buchanan Smith (1973). The discussion, which focused on the two main characters and their actions, demonstrates my understanding of how the connections my students made ultimately lead to a high level of interpretation of meaning.

01 KELLY: I know these two kids that are exactly like these two kids, my brother and Nick.

02 ATIYAH: Who's Nick?

03 KELLY: Nick is my brother's best friend. I mean all they do is play with guns and they just get into a lot of trouble . . . dumb stuff. But my brother really doesn't matter now, it's just a comparison.

04 JAMES: [Looking at Kelly] You like to play with guns?

05 MIKE: No, how old's your brother?

06 KELLY: Oh, thirteen. O.K., we're not talking about my brother now.

07 ANDY: Yeah we are.

08 KELLY: Let's get back to the book.

09 ANDY: Did he die?

10 KELLY: I just think that the author is trying to get to you . . .

11 ANDY: About what?

12 MIKE: About dying.

13 KELLY: He is trying to tell you that, um, so far I know that if you get in a lot of trouble, he's telling 'em about friends and one of 'em dies and how the other kid goes on with his life.

14 JAMES: Yeah, that's what I was going to say.

In past years I might have looked at this section of the discussion as having two important parts to put on my grid: one, the connections made at the very beginning, and two, the interpretation of the story at the end of the conversation, which showed a great deal of understanding. However, without the rest of the dialogue in between (set-ups), which at times seemed "off" of the subject, Kelly might never have reached her understanding of the author's words.

About this time I joined the Barnes Study Group (Pierce, 1992), and began reading *From Communication to Curriculum* (Barnes, 1992). During our discussions, I listened as Carol Gilles gave an overview of a related book, *Communication and Learning in Small Groups* (Barnes and Todd, 1977). As I discussed the connections I was making between my classroom experiences and the ideas in Barnes' books, I recognized that he and I had been looking at similar phenomena: single meanings could not be attributed to individual statements made by participants in a conversation. Rather, these meanings built over time through the series of statements made by several participants.

As Carol helped us understand the significance of the work of Barnes and Todd for our studies, I came to believe that category systems could not be developed to capture the complexity of talk. "Talk produced in such a context lacks the manifestations of structure common in other situations" (Barnes and Todd, 1977, p. 16). These researchers and the discussions in our study group helped me understand why utterances couldn't be made to fit into categories on a one-to-one basis, and why I thought some utterances seemed to belong in several categories. In addition, the meaning created in a discussion group is not constructed by any one utterance but by "cycles of utterances" that may span a lengthy period of time (Gilles, 1991; Gilles, this volume; Barnes and Todd, 1977). These cycles can't be isolated because they are an integral part of the interaction of the dialogue. Therefore, to capture the significance of a statement made by one student, I needed to record it as part of a cycle of statements, one part of a cycle of meaning. I was elated when I realized I was discovering ideas in my classroom that an esteemed researcher had discussed in his work!

This shift in attention from individual statements to longer excerpts within a discussion made further revision of my observation grid necessary: larger boxes and fewer boxes (see Figure 17.2). In part, this change was the result of my having internalized many of the concepts included in earlier versions of the observation grid.

I continued to invest extended periods of time in analyzing tapes of discussion groups and recording excerpts from these tapes on the observation grid. I have since come to appreciate the value of the process and feel that the time invested has been beneficial, and I have gained greater confidence in my ability to evaluate my students as readers. I have come to understand and can apply more sophisticated ideas about literature and literary elements, having learned them with my students in ways I never learned them in high school and college English courses. I have also developed significant understandings about the evaluation process and my role in that process. Since then, however, I have decided that I can't always give this much time to the evaluation of the discussions. It is very time-consuming to listen to the tapes, transcribe them, and place the comments on the grid. Therefore, I have developed a more detailed check list (Figure 17.3) to use as I listen. At the present time, I use both the check list and the five-section grid (Figure 17.2) on an alternating basis.

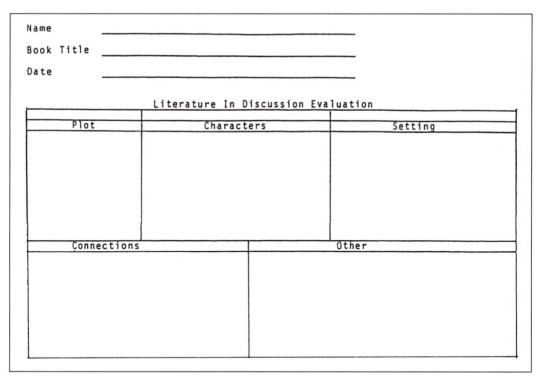

Figure 17.2 *"Literature in Discussion" Evaluation Form*

CONTINUING THE CYCLE

It seemed that every time I reached a comfortable plateau in my work with literature discussion groups, some book, person, or experience would come along and jar me into a state of discomfort again. The high point of our work in the Barnes Study Group came when Douglas and Dorothy Barnes arrived in St. Louis to work with our group over a period of several weeks. During a visit to my classroom, Douglas Barnes made an observation that challenged my comfortable, confident state.

While in my classroom, Barnes saw what I thought were two examples of good discussions in the groups. The participants had a lot to say, they made use of their knowledge of the elements of literature in the course of their discussions, and I participated as an equal member of the group. During his visit, we also managed to find time to discuss the observation grids and how they had evolved. His supportive and encouraging responses to

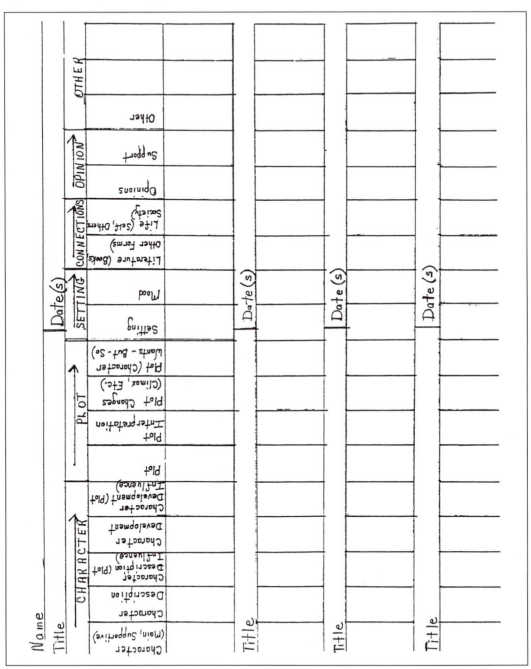

Figure 17.3 *"Elements of Literature" Evaluation Form*

everything we shared affirmed my sense of confidence in what I was doing. But then he made an important observation, "This is all very nice, but this is *your* agenda, not the children's."

As I wrestled with Barnes' observation, defensively and then excitedly as an inquirer, I set my mind to creating a comfortable answer to the question he had raised: How does the agenda in the discussion groups become *ours* (including students) rather than mine? My inquiry into this classroom-based question, like my earlier inquiries, involved me in reading professional literature and collaborating with Joan, Mary Ann, and Kathryn as well as other members of the Barnes Study Group. What is perhaps more important, I also began to involve my students actively in my inquiry. As I reflect back on this period in my professional development I realize, too, that I had ceased to be driven by concerns about communicating to and demonstrating proof for those outside my classroom. My primary concern had shifted to evaluation that was embedded within my curriculum and that informed my instruction and my students.

Creating situations where the discussion groups had a *we* agenda was challenging yet fun. I started fresh at the beginning of the school year. One of the things that bothered me was that everything I was looking for in the groups had been developed by me and my colleagues, complete with terms and definitions of those terms. If a student could talk about the characters, their changes, and how the plot affected those changes, then I accepted this as a sure sign of higher level interpretation. And for the most part, my analysis of the group discussions confirmed that students who used the terminology often understood the concept; often, but not always. And there was something about it that was stiff. As Douglas Barnes had pointed out, these terms were mine.

The students could give the terms, what they meant, and examples for them. I wanted more; I wanted it more natural and with less involvement from me in the groups. I felt that if someday the discussions were in the students' hands, they would talk about the literature using their own terms and develop their own agendas. However, I did reserve the right to join groups from time to time to ask occasional questions if I felt a certain point needed to be addressed.

Now the question was, How do I get them to the point where they can handle the groups by themselves? I wanted them to start off without me in hopes that they would develop their own ways of talking about literature and learn group dynamics naturally. I took the month of September and the first week of October to develop discussion skills. At first we started off as a whole class. I read to the class from picture books that had deeper multiple meanings. Students talked about their reactions to the books during and after the reading and then they displayed this information on a web either on the board or on butcher paper. As we discussed more books, we started categorizing our comments and naming the categories. The categories were very similar to those already developed by me and my colleagues, only this time they came from the students. When talking about the literature they used *their* terms. Later in the year they developed their own self-evaluation tools using these terms (see Figure 17.4). We learned group dynamics by using picture books in small groups: reading them, discussing them, noting the responses and then writing pluses and wishes (Mills, 1986) for the way the group functioned. These pluses and wishes were put on display to act as reminders of what was expected in the groups. The students were ready for L.I.D. using chapter books.

I couldn't have been more pleased with the results. *Students* ran the groups and discussed the literature, displaying great interpretive abilities, and I joined in from time to time. Occasionally we returned to whole-group discussion of picture books to review our categories and group behavior. As I have mentioned, students regularly self-evaluated their talk and group effectiveness. At last I felt as if the agenda had shifted from *mine* to *ours*.

INVOLVING STUDENTS AND PARENTS IN EVALUATION

A concurrent theme in my search for more effective evaluation strategies involved consideration of student self-evaluation. This theme was influenced primarily by my discovery and interpretation of an evaluation model developed by Carolyn Burke in 1985 (now included in Short and Burke, 1991). Burke's model led me to reconsider the roles of students and parents in the evaluation process. Up to the point of Barnes' visit to St. Louis, I had been exploring my evaluation of literature discussions and student self-evaluation almost as two separate issues. Barnes' challenge brought these two themes together into the same inquiry, led to significant changes in my views of literature discussion groups, and clarified the need for multiple perspectives in evaluation. I realized that I had allowed my intentions for learners to dominate and that I was excluding the learners' intentions for their own work. As I explored ways to involve students in establishing the agenda for the discussion groups, I simultaneously explored ways to involve them meaningfully in evaluating their work in those discussions—as individuals and as contributing members of a collaborative group.

Burke's evaluation model, Barnes' challenge, and the process I followed in exploring student self-evaluation have provided encouragement and support for my current exploration of parent involvement in the evaluation of their children as readers, writers, and learners. Literature discussion groups served as the initial focus for this ongoing inquiry.

NAME _____

TITLE OF THE BOOK _____

DATE _____

L.I.D. STUDENT SELF-EVALUATION

YES	NO	During discussion groups I:
		1. Talked about who was in the story
		2. Talked about what happened in the story
		3. Talked about if the characters changed
		4. Talked about how the characters changed
		5. Talked about what happened to make the characters change
		6. Talked about things I thought the author meant
		7. Told if I liked or did not like the story and WHY (didn't use words like "neat" or "bad")
		8. This book reminded me of: other books and WHY
		___ ___ ___ ___ movies and WHY
		___ ___ ___ ___ "Me" and WHY
		___ ___ ___ ___ people and WHY
		9. I took my turn talking
		10. I listened to the people in my discussion group
		11. I looked at the person talking
		12. I added on to the talking
		13. I did not always agree, but was nice when I did not agree

Figure 17.4 *"Literature in Discussion" Student Self-Evaluation Form*

EXPLORING CONTENT-AREA CURRICULUM

My focus on literature discussion groups as a curricular strategy led to another theme in my professional development. As I reached a comfortable plateau in my use of the strategy and my ability to evaluate student growth in terms of that strategy, I recognized that nonfiction materials were being neglected in my classroom. During the same year that we prepared for Barnes' visit (a very busy year), I completed the culminating curriculum project for my master's degree. For that project, I chose to take what I had learned about literature discussion groups and professional inquiry in order to explore evaluation strategies for small group discussions of nonfiction materials.

What started out as a fairly simple project developed into a major shift in the way I viewed curriculum in my classroom. In order to observe and evaluate small group discussion of nonfiction materials, I needed to initiate these discussions in my classroom. For these discussions to be successful, they needed to be embedded in a curricular context—a thematic inquiry cycle—in which print sources were used as students sought answers to questions related to their topic of inquiry. In order for their questions to be meaningful, the students needed to have a sense of ownership over the inquiry. Eventually, this inquiry into the evaluation of literature discussion of nonfiction materials led to my development of an overall curricular framework based on collaborative, inquiry-oriented theme cycles.

The master's degree project provided another unanticipated outcome. Shifting my attention to the ways students were discussing and using nonfiction materials, I began to be less concerned than I had been with the actual dynamics of the discussions and more focused than I had ever been on the outcomes of those discussions. I now viewed the literature discussion groups of fiction, nonfiction, or combined literature as means to curricular ends, not as ends in and of themselves. My values in relation to evaluation had shifted, creating yet again the need for change in my evaluation strategies.

Throughout this evolution of my understanding of literature discussion groups, I learned about my own inquiry process, discovered how to support and understand the inquiry process of my students, and came to value the unique power of collaborative inquiry. I reflected upon my collaborative inquiry with teaching colleagues, upon my collaborative construction of curriculum with my students, and upon the collaborative meaning-making among my students during literature discussions and other curricular strategies. I learned that identifying a driving question in an inquiry cycle is the first—and most difficult—step for any inquirer, that fiction, nonfiction, poetry, people, and life experiences are valuable resources in the search for answers to significant questions, and that presenting the results of an inquiry leads to further insights and new questions. I also learned that some questions will not be answered in the course of one inquiry cycle, and that some questions will never be answered because in the search for the answer we continue to redefine the question. Perhaps most important for my own professional development, I learned that the seductive comfort I found in my early use of the neat, all-enclosed basal program and in the neat boxes of my early grids was not conducive to my professional development or to the learning of my students. Rather, my goal is learning to manage the "messy" and uncomfortable parts of learning and evaluation—to be comfortable with the excitingly uncomfortable inquiry process.

REFERENCES

Barnes, D. 1992. *From communication to curriculum.* 2nd ed. Portsmouth, NH: Boynton/ Cook.

Barnes, D. and F. Todd. 1977. *Communication and learning in small groups.* London: Routledge & Kegan Paul.

Cambourne, B. 1988. *The whole story: Natural learning and the acquisition of literacy in the classroom.* New York: Ashton Scholastic.

Gilles, C. 1991. *Uses of talk in literature study by adolescents labeled learning disabled.* Unpublished dissertation. Columbia, MO: University of Missouri.

Hanssen, E. 1990. "Planning for literature circles: Variations in focus and structure." In *Talking about books: Creating literate communities,* edited by K. Short and K. Pierce. Portsmouth, NH: Heinemann.

Mills, H. 1986. *Writing evaluation: A transactional process.* Unpublished doctoral dissertation. Bloomington, IN: Indiana University.

Pierce, K. 1992. "Afterword." In *From communication to curriculum,* 2nd ed., by D. Barnes. Portsmouth, NH: Boynton/Cook.

———. 1990. "Initiating literature discussion groups: Teaching like learners." In *Talking about books: Creating literate communities,* edited by K. Short & K. Pierce. Portsmouth, NH: Heinemann.

Short, K. and C. Burke. 1991. *Creating curriculum: Teachers and students as a community of learners.* Portsmouth, NH: Heinemann.

Short K. and K. Pierce. Eds. 1990. *Talking about books: Creating literate communities.* Portsmouth, NH: Heinemann.

Smith, D. B. 1973. *A Taste of Blackberries.* New York: Harper and Row.

Watson, D. 1990. "Show me: Whole language evaluation of literature groups." In *Talking about books: Creating literate communities,* edited by K. Short & K. Pierce. Portsmouth, NH: Heinemann.

Camille Fried has taught children in grades 5–8 reading and literature for the past ten years. She currently teaches seventh- and eighth-grade reading at Brittany Woods Middle School in St. Louis, Missouri, where she continues to explore literature discussion with children. In addition, Camille participates in an action research group in her school, which is focused on supporting middle school writers-at-risk.

Chapter 18
Evaluation, Reflection, Revision: Using Literature Discussion Groups in Middle School

CAMILLE S. FRIED

"Shh! No talking!" This demand is one that almost everyone has heard before in the classroom. Students are to be quiet while the teacher gives directions, teaches, or just talks to the students. The teacher controls the classroom and the learning by dominating what is said during the class. This is the traditional classroom pattern of communication that is familiar to most people.

But this is not what is happening in today's whole language classrooms. The trend today is to allow students to use oral expression as much as possible because in doing so they become more involved in their learning. As Douglas Barnes explains, "The more a learner controls his own language strategies, and the more he is enabled to think aloud, the more he can take responsibility for formulating explanatory hypotheses and evaluating them" (1992, p. 29). In addition, by observing students using these oral language strategies, teachers can determine the effectiveness of their curriculum. "Only by using children as our curricular informants—by studying the mental trips they take as a function of the curricular experiences we provide—can we judge whether a set of instructional activities has achieved what we hoped" (Harste, Short, and Burke, 1988, pp. 4–5).

These two ideas—allowing children to talk as a way of making meaning from what they read and observing how they do so—have been the basis for my own exploration into the way children discuss novels. For the last three semesters I have used literature discussion in my classroom. I wanted to discover for myself the value of student-to-student discussion and decide whether it should be a regular part of my curriculum. Each semester I modified the way I supported discussions and response journals in an effort to find the best method. I began by encouraging my seventh- and eighth-grade reading/literature students to talk about the books they read. By observing my students, inviting them to self-evaluate, listening to their discussions, and self-evaluating my own teaching, I learned much about my students, myself, and the teaching/learning process.

The first semester I used group literature discussion, students self-selected their discussion groups but I assigned the book to be read. My students read the novel, *Julie of the Wolves* (George, 1972). Julie/Miyax is a thirteen-year-old Eskimo girl who has been forced into an arranged marriage. She is unhappy in the marriage and runs away. Alone and on foot in the tundra region of northern Alaska, Julie/Miyax becomes lost and must use her wits and the help of a wolf pack to survive.

When I began using group literature discussions in my classroom, my hope was that group discussion would affect the length of students' written responses. I also assumed that allowing students to listen to their tape-recorded conversations would serve as a review of the discussion and make writing a journal entry or response letter easier.

Most of my students are reluctant writers, and when I assign a piece of writing I am usually asked, "How long does it have to be?" They are preoccupied with writing a specific amount, so I hoped that having them participate in literature discussions would somehow make journal writing easier.

To aid the discussion process, I decided to use a modified version of a procedure called "Save the Last Word for Me" (Harste, Short, and Burke, 1988). This is a discussion technique whereby group members identify topics of discussion from their reading. They may want to discuss characters' decisions and motivation, plot situations, dialogue, or quotations from the book. Each student individually presents a topic, then listens to what the other group members have to say. After all members have shared their ideas and feelings about the subject, the person who originally presented the topic has the last word about why that topic was chosen and what he or she thought or now thinks about it after listening to the other members' ideas. I explained to my students that they were to listen to each group member's comment or question about Part I of *Julie of the Wolves.* When that individual had finished speaking, they could then respond by stating their opinions, answering the individual's question, or questioning the individual. Once they had exhausted that topic of conversation, they were to repeat the procedure with the next group member. I wanted the groups to function as Literature Circles (Harste, Short, and Burke 1988) and to feel comfortable thinking aloud and expressing their own ideas, not something they had heard me say. I hoped the freedom of this environment and the learning that would take place would facilitate their writing.

Groups were organized according to whoever had completed the reading of Part I, so they varied in size. Over a three-day taping period, I recorded seven groups of students ranging in size from one to six members (the smallest consisted of one student and me).

The groups were isolated as much as they could be in the hallway outside my classroom. They could use their paperback novels and the cassette tape recorder. After I had explained how to conduct their discussion by using "Save the Last Word for Me," I left them alone. I checked on them periodically, allowing them as much discussion time as they desired. No group used longer than my forty-two-minute class period.

I wrote a rough draft summary while listening to the cassette recordings of each group discussion. These summaries helped me to evaluate each recording and determine those most useful for my purposes. Each tape gave me insight into the individual groups, but one of the tapes (with five members) was particularly interesting. I transcribed the discussion from that tape (Group G). Although this group strayed from the format of "Save the Last Word for Me," so that one member tended to control the group, their discussion was the most intriguing.

In the following example, Group G compared the hierarchy within the wolf pack to the traditional male-female roles still prevalent in society.

01 MIA: And I didn't like the point where they said the Alpha Male is higher . . .

02 CINDY: Yeah . . . Yeah . . . but you know what . . . I think that the Alpha Female should be higher because she tells them where to camp. She tells them how to food [sic] . . .

03 LATRELL: But the Alpha Male protects their territory for them.

04 CINDY: Yeah . . . but the female could do just that too. I mean she just don't have the babies and cook food . . . (inaudible) . . . she wears the pants too. Like you know how it use to be when the women usually didn't get no job cause of discrimination. Well, you know women was just the same as men. They can do anything a man can do. And probably better 'cause you don't see no man out there uh . . .

05 MIA: You know it was O.K. It was confusing and strange. It was different. I didn't understand Part I.

06 OTHERS: Yeah.

07 CINDY: Wait a minute. It seemed like the wolves ain't no different than us. Yeah, they're wild animals. Yeah, that's the only thing that's different. But you know the way it is like the Alpha Male and the Alpha Female. They is like that at home.

This excerpt was significant to me because it showed how my students were able to make connections between the book and their own lives. Cindy (07) was particularly good at seeing the similarities between the wolf hierarchy and the roles of men and women today. In doing so, she was able to introduce ideas into the discussion that other group members had not considered, and these ideas helped the discussion to move to a higher level of thinking.

In this second selection from the tape of Group G, group members discussed the issue of arranged marriages and applied their prior knowledge to Julie/Miyax's situation in the novel. At the same time, they were able to empathize with her.

08   LATRELL: It's strange. She isn't old enough. She can't even . . .

09   CINDY: I mean she shouldn't of got married.

10   MIA: If she did not want to marry him . . . I think it's like tradition or something.

11   CINDY: It's just something you're supposed to do—like a law.

12   MIA: Y'all, it's like you ever watch *The Color Purple*. Y'all remember that girl had to marry that boy, but see you know they couldn't say no. 'Cause it's a tradition. I don't want to get married.

13   CINDY: Mia, nobody would dare to say they didn't want to get married, but when she said that she didn't want to get married . . .

14   MIA: But you gotta understand she was by herself when she said it. She couldn't have said that to her father or whoever wanted her to get married.

15   LATRELL: When she was first born they had already arranged it.

16   MIA: But she didn't like it. She was brave.

What I found significant in this selection was the way the students helped each other make sense of what they did not understand. Latrell states his confusion and disbelief that the character Julie/Miyax would get married at such a young age (08). In the next lines Cindy and Mia help to resolve that confusion. The group discussion allowed the students to make sense of unfamiliar cultural norms regarding marriage.

In this third example, the group makes two comparisons. They discuss the similarities of the characters and draw a parallel between the story and the plot of a movie (one of the Alpha Female's jobs is to locate the den for the pack).

17   MIA: She remind me of that Arnold Schwarzenegger.

18   OTHERS: Yeah.

19   MIA: He was trying to get to that castle from a long way from where he was.

20   CINDY: Have you ever seen that movie "A Never-Ending Story"?

21   MIA: Well, O.K. He was trying to help somebody. O.K. In which the wolves are trying to help Julie, but he did it by himself. You know he was traveling by himself and he was already trying to get to the castle.

But, he needed someone to help him, which she needs the wolves to help her get through her journey. And . . . but think about it, though. She needs food and, I mean, the wolves are the only things, living things, roaming around on this land who know where the food is.

22 CINDY: Yeah, yeah.

23 MIA: And Arnold S . . . he needed rest or he wouldn't be able to get there. So I think it's just like *Julie of the Wolves.*

24 CINDY: Yep, cause he's the Alpha Female. [Laughter from the group]

My students' comprehension of their reading assignment was quite extensive. They were able to compare incidents in the plot of *Julie of the Wolves* to those in movies with similar plot situations, and they were able to connect their thoughts and ideas about the book to other story plots while at the same time enjoying themselves.

Although my goal was twofold—to determine if group conversation would improve written responses and whether having the students listen to their discussions would affect their writing—I gained additional useful information without actively seeking it. I found that students' discussions alone are valuable and that I needed to adapt my curriculum to allow more time for student talk. Until this realization, I had been viewing the discussions primarily as preparation for writing.

Initially, allowing students to discuss their novel in Literature Circles seemed successful. I found that my students' group discussions were similar to those reported by other teachers. "They are learning the joy of exchanging interpretations, of expressing them in writing and speaking, of respecting what they have to say as well as what others may offer" (Horton, 1986, p. 57). My students were more cooperative and on task and enjoyed their learning more than when I have conducted whole-class discussions. I believe groups of around five members are necessary to get a variety of responses. Diversity makes for a better group discussion.

I found that students still felt confused about some issues in the novel even after discussion. Group discussion is not a substitute for teacher-pupil interaction, but it does allow students to clarify their thoughts about the book. In addition, it is an effective way to determine what they need to have explained.

After the taping, I asked my students to complete a questionnaire (see Figure 18.1) to find out how they felt about what they had done. Most students thought the activity would help them write a longer journal entry. When I read the various group members' journal responses, they did seem to be longer, and included many of the topics students had discussed. I was especially pleased with the content, because I did not get boring summaries of the story. Instead, I read students' reflections, opinions, and criticisms about the characters' actions and the events in the story.

Dear _____,

     Please take a couple of minutes to tell me what you thought of your group's literature discussion over Part I of <u>Julie of the Wolves</u>. This information will help guide future discussion groups. Be honest and really tell me what you think.

                     Thanks a bunch,

                     Mrs. Fried

1. What did you like about your group's discussion?

2. What didn't you like about your group's discussion?

3. Do you think that discussing the story with other students will help you to write your letter to me about Part I? If yes, explain why this helped you.

4. How will the content of your letter be different now that you have discussed the story in group?

5. Will the length of your letter be different from what you would normally have written?

6. Give me your overall impression of this experience. Would you like to do this again? Explain why or why not.

7. Did listening to the tape help you in any way? If it did not, do you think it ever would?

8. Please give me suggestions about this group activity that will help me in planning future literature discussions.

Figure 18.1 *Literature Discussion Group Evaluation Form*

According to their responses to the questionnaire, most students thought listening to the tape was beneficial. Although they seemed to feel a sense of pride as they listened to themselves, I do not think there was any significant learning or usefulness in their listening to the tape. I believe they confused their enjoyment in listening to themselves with actual learning. I suspect that the reason their journal entries and letters to me were longer was because they had had the opportunity to verbalize their ideas and expand their thoughts as they discussed the novel with their peers. It was this opportunity for "exploratory talk" (Barnes, 1992) with peers that helped students prepare for their writing.

During the second and third semesters of my exploration of literature discussion groups, I focused less on how the discussion would affect students' writing and more on the benefits of students talking about their books. I centered my investigation on different ways of having students use their journal before meeting in their discussion groups. I also tried to incorporate the reading skills that are emphasized on my students' standardized tests by asking them to apply those skills to reading their books. In addition, during the second semester I read Nancie Atwell's. *In the Middle: Writing, Reading and Learning with Adolescents* (1987) and tried to incorporate her idea of "mini-lessons" in teaching my reading and literature lessons to my classes.

Atwell begins her reading classes with short lessons: "In literature mini-lessons I do one of three things. I read aloud and talk about a short work—a poem, essay, scene, myth, or short story. I tell about an author and read an excerpt from the author's work. Or I present information or ask kids to gather information about literature and how it works" (p. 204). I was interested in Atwell's approach to presenting information to students—in small doses—but I was reluctant to give up my old ways of teaching. I was concerned that my students would not grasp the concepts unless I presented them over many days and in many ways. In an effort to make sure my students knew the required concept or skill, I assigned specific journal entries.

At the beginning of each thematic unit, I gave my students a sheet with the topic they were to address for each journal entry. For example, after teaching the idea of conflict in a story, I asked students to identify and describe the conflicts in the books they were reading. I then expected them to meet in their discussion groups to discuss the conflicts they had identified.

The resulting discussions were stilted and boring. The children discussed exactly what I asked them to think about, and they expressed no spontaneity or original thought. They still enjoyed talking with their peers, but their discussions were contrived, short, and uneventful. Instead of encouraging extensive or in-depth conversation, the discussions seemed more presentational. After observing this result time and again in my classes, I decided to modify my use of the journals and see if more interesting discussions would result.

During the third semester, I decided not to assign specific journal entry topics. Instead, I tried Nancie Atwell's dialogue journal approach and had my students write letters telling me anything they wanted about their books. I was surprised and pleased when I read the letters my students wrote, and I replied to them in different ways. Sometimes I would agree with what they had to say about their books and other times I would ask them questions in an attempt to get them to think about another aspect of the book or character.

Eliminating the required journal topics of the previous semester freed my students to write what they really felt about their books. These letters had no parameters, so their content varied widely. Students went beyond simple summarization, exhibiting evidence of comprehension and higher level thinking. The next step was to have my students use their letters to really talk about their books. Some groups began their discussions by sharing their letters, using the content as conversation starters. While other groups never referred to their letters directly, I believe they were helpful in supporting the discussions.

During my exploration into literature discussions, one of the thematic units we covered focused on the Holocaust. The letters the students wrote to me and their subsequent discussions were interesting because many of them had intense reactions to the books they read. What follows are selections from some of the group discussions.

In this transcript of a group discussing the book *I Am Rosemarie* (Moskin, 1972), the true story of a young girl's survival in the concentration camps, the group members confirmed their comprehension of the story and contemplated luck as a factor in Rosemarie's survival.

25 SEAN: I pretty much think you almost had to be lucky to like survive because . . .

26 NICOLE: I know. I know, but she was that lucky. She had her whole family . . .

27 REBECCA: And she was just one person out of millions of people.

28 SEAN: It didn't make any sense how her whole family kept getting away like scott free.

29 REBECCA: And like how her mom knew that she had to take both of them. How she had to take both of them, Rosemarie and her father, even though they were both sick.

30 SEAN: Yeah.

I was pleased with the way the students in this group responded to one another's comments, exploring the ideas in greater depth than I was accustomed to seeing.

At about this time I had instituted the use of a discussion form (see Figure 18.2). I found that the groups that used the tape recorder took their discussions much more seriously than the groups that did not, and since I had a limited number of tape recorders and wanted students to take a more serious attitude toward their discussions, I began having them keep written

Grading Criteria:
    1. Participation   1 2 3
    2. Stayed on task   1 2 3
    3. Completion of form   1 2 3
    4. Appropriate volume   1 2 3   Period_____
    5. Coverage of topics   1 2 3

NOVEL DISCUSSION FORM

Group members: _____   _____

                _____   _____

                _____   _____

Date_____

Discussion number_____

Book title_____

Pages discussed_____

Time discussion began____ Time discussion ended____

Topics discussed/Questions we had   Comments

Figure 18.2 *Novel Discussion Form*

records of their talk. This seemed to help keep playful students on task and hold groups accountable for their discussion.

The following transcript records a group that chose to read aloud the letters they wrote before discussing their novel, *Alan and Naomi* (Levoy, 1977). The novel, set in 1944 in New York City, tells of a friendship between a young boy, Alan Silverman, and Naomi Kirshenbaum, a twelve-year-old war refugee from France. Naomi is so traumatized by the death of her father at the hands of the Nazis that she cannot speak. With Alan's help and understanding, Naomi begins to open up. Although this discussion was more formal than the others,

341

perhaps because of the use of the recording form, students nevertheless reached a consensus and explored the similarities in their letters.

30   KIM: O.K., what do you think we discussed? What was the main thing that we discussed about our book?

31   CONNIE: I think we discussed on how Alan and Naomi's friendship has increased into a little sister friendship.

32   TASHA: They're not afraid to go outside with each other. Alan's not afraid anymore about his friends outside and he'll take up for her more. I think he's taken up for her and standin' up and not bein' afraid to show that they're going to be friends. And I think she's showed progress to be able to start school now. And that will be an improvement, and the doctor couldn't even do that, so Alan should be very proud of himself.

33   CONNIE: Another thing that we wrote about is how she was intelligent by learning the American (unintelligible).

34   TASHA: Yeah, it didn't seem like she would be that smart coming from England and everything. But she's not afraid to speak. She's more Naomi now than she was in spirit at first.

35   CONNIE: She's more like a normal girl.

36   JAYNA: She was scared at the beginning of the book and now she's becoming more and more nonscared and she's starting to get along with other people.

37   CONNIE: Another one could be that, Naomi, she is talking a lot for herself and not using Yvette and Charlie as her characters as Alan and Naomi. She's got her own mind and her own way of feeling about things.

38   TASHA: About Shawn, I think that was because he said that Alan did not tell him what he wanted to do. At first, it was that he was going to help Naomi.

39   CONNIE: I think that Alan brought that on himself though, because he should have told him from the beginning. If that was your true friend he should have been able to tell him.

In this discussion, group members were able to analyze, interpret, and understand the characters' behavior. I also found the way this group approached their discussion to be interesting. Each member read her letter to the group before beginning to talk about the book. Group members found that their letters had common themes. Although it was not directly stated, the students appeared reassured that others shared their feelings about the book.

I am now in my fourth semester of using literature discussion groups with my students and, of course, I am still exploring variations in the strategy. I now teach both seventh- and eighth-grade classes. My seventh graders are using letter journals, while the eighth graders are using double-entry journals. The double-entry journal (summary or questions on one side and responses on the other) has so far been a better format for students who have specific questions they wish to discuss with their group. It also serves to help students remember the particulars of the story. The letter format journals, on the other hand, support more general discussions of the books.

I have also noticed that I have shifted my original focus on having students discuss before writing in their journals to having them write before meeting in their groups. I am less concerned about how much students write, and more attentive to how much they think. Not surprisingly, as students become more comfortable with the literature discussion process, they tend to write lengthier, more thoughtful entries in their journals.

My students look forward to their group discussions and ask me to allow more time for these groups in class. I am currently organizing my class periods so that all groups are discussing simultaneously. However, I am moving toward allowing groups to set their own discussion schedules. I look forward to the day when all the discussion groups will be able to function independently.

My tapes affirmed the ideas of both Douglas Barnes and Jerome Harste: Allowing students to interact in small group discussions empowers and motivates them to seek knowledge for themselves. Giving students the opportunity to discuss helps to instill responsibility for their own learning. It also provides the teacher with opportunities to observe and evaluate student's learning in ways paper and pencil tasks cannot. Observation also allows the teacher to determine the effectiveness of the curriculum, making changes when necessary. My efforts to evaluate students' use of one curricular strategy—literature discussion groups—have helped me gain a better understanding of students' learning while simultaneously contributing to my own professional development.

REFERENCES

Atwell, N. 1987. *In the middle: Writing, reading and learning with adolescents.* Portsmouth, NH: Boynton/Cook.

Barnes, D. 1992. *From communication to curriculum.* 2nd ed. Portsmouth, NH: Boynton/Cook.

George. J. C. 1972. *Julie of the wolves.* New York: Harper & Row.

Harste, J., K. Short, and C. Burke. 1988. *Creating classrooms for authors.* Portsmouth, NH: Heinemann.

Horton, L. G. 1986. "A whole language unit for ninth graders." *English Journal* 75(8):56–57.

Levoy, M. 1977. *Alan and Naomi.* New York: HarperTrophy.

Moskin, M. 1972. *I am Rosemarie.* New York: Dell.

Afterword:
The Way Ahead

DOUGLAS BARNES

This book is an impressive report of what has been achieved by teachers through mutually supportive self-development. I have been asked in this Afterword to identify the major themes of the book and to suggest further directions that groups of teachers might take in developing their understanding of the place of talk in learning. The themes discussed are:

- The place of talk in children's learning.
- How to recognize good talk for learning. —
- The changing role of the teacher.
- The class as a learning community.
- The nature of knowing.
- Reflection as part of learning.
- The professional development of teachers.

THE PLACE OF TALK IN CHILDREN'S LEARNING

During the last twenty years, the processes by which young children learn their native tongue have been given a different perspective by those researchers who have investigated it (Cazden, 1972; Halliday, 1975; Wells et al., 1981; Bruner, 1983; Heath, 1983; Tizard and Hughes, 1984; Lindfors, 1987). The emphasis has turned away from the child's ability to construct acceptable sentences toward the purposes that early language serves for the child. The infant strives to join in the life about him or her, to influence and to understand the world, and does so increasingly through talk. Through talk we first enter into our cultural inheritance. Speech first appears as a crucial element in this struggle to join in, to belong first to the family and then to peer and other groups. Children learn to talk in order to satisfy their needs and desires by joining in the life around them: thus, early language learning is *interactive* and *purposive*. And when we turn to the further development of language up to and including adulthood the same principles apply: we develop our ability to use language when our aims and interests engage us in interaction with others.

This way of understanding language acquisition goes far to explain why the teaching of the mother tongue through exercises out of context is so often ineffective: such exercises deprive the learner of the advantages of using language for his or her own purposes in communication with an audience who will respond with interest. The development of students' language is more likely when they are using it for purposes that have arisen elsewhere in their lives or in the curriculum, and doing so in an interactive context. The contributors to this book have all emphasized the importance of talk in classroom learning in a range of curricular subjects; science, social studies, literature, moral education, and English as a second language are all represented. The struggle to communicate with someone who only half understands can contribute to the clarification of the speaker's own thinking, and this is why so many of the contributions to this book deal with collaborative talk between peers. In struggling to explain to one another, some groups of students achieve what can be called "collaborative explicitness." The various contributors to this volume all share the conviction, based upon careful observation in classrooms, that students' own efforts to express their understanding are a major means of enhancing learning.

HOW TO RECOGNIZE GOOD TALK FOR LEARNING

As the British National Oracy Project found, for many teachers the excitement of finding that their students could and would talk with serious interest about school topics often discouraged them initially from looking critically at the nature and value of that talk. Teachers wrote articles quoting lively exchanges between their students but hesitated to explain why they valued the exchanges quoted except as evidence that their students were enthusiastic and taking a more lively part in their learning. Many of the teachers who have written in this book identify particular occasions when they recognized valuable talk. Enlightening as these examples will be to teachers, there is a case for developing the perceptions into an inclusive system.

When a group of teachers first sets out to inquire into classroom talk they frequently commence by "trying out" new activities in their own classrooms so that they can share and discuss the talk that occurs. As in this book, this leads them to formulate in more general terms what they have learned about the relationship between classroom procedures, children's talk, and their learning. As a further step they can usefully set themselves the task of producing a more systematic analysis of the kinds of talk that prove valuable, how these can be recognized, and the contexts and tasks that are likely to elicit them. The purpose would not be to set up an abstract and idealized picture of "good talk" but to sharpen their perceptions of when talk was contributing to their students' learning. Such an account would be extremely valuable, because it would help teachers to discuss more explicitly what they value in the classroom conversation, not only to clarify and sharpen their own thinking, but also as a first step toward making the insights available to their students in some suitable form. If students discuss and understand the purposes of talk, they are more likely to use it constructively.

THE CHANGING ROLE OF THE TEACHER

This book is premised on the conviction that most learning depends upon the learner's active and deliberate participation in his or her own learning. It is not uncommon for teachers, especially those who are inexperienced, to become overanxious when they observe their students' difficulties and misunderstandings, and therefore to try to do too much for them. The teacher who tries to predigest and overteach is not unlikely to impede his or her students, partly by failing to give them time to make the journey of learning, but even more by unintentionally transmitting to them too passive a version of their role. That is why the discussion in foregoing chapters of how to help students to reflect upon and reconsider their roles as learners is so important, a topic to which I will return in a later section.

The teacher's contribution to talking for learning is of two kinds, immediate participation in the talk and longer-term influence through the establishment of taken-for-granted priorities, values, and ways of going about classroom activities. Teachers' long-term responsibilities will be discussed later; here we are concerned with their participation in the moment to moment exchanges of lessons. It is useful to think of talk in the classroom as a continuing conversation; reading, films, practical work, visits, and teachers' presentations are both contributions to it and definers of its nature and purposes. Contributors to this book have identified teaching strategies that profoundly influence talking to learn; these include asking questions to enable students to discover what they already know, giving students time to respond, avoiding right/wrong evaluations that might short-circuit inquiry, helping students to use evidence (such as the clues in a story about where it takes place), to form hypotheses, to monitor progress, and so on. The good teacher is participant in conversation as well as observer, though she may sometimes find that silence provides the best encouragement to children to talk their way into understanding.

The role played by the teacher is crucial, not so much for transmitting knowledge as for its effect in defining the student's role as learner. This volume contains many quotations from classroom talk, and a very large proportion of them illustrate events in small group talk for learning. However, as has been made plain, this is in no sense a recipe for teacher inactivity; indeed, enabling students of any age to take responsibility for their own learning takes more skill—and possibly more effort—than didactic teaching. Moreover, what goes on in small groups is crucially affected by the norms set up by the teacher in the activities that he or she has under more direct control. If the teaching in a particular classroom appears to imply that what the students already know is of little importance, if it implies that their contributions are not worthy of a serious response, if it implies that they cannot contribute to learning, and if it implies that wisdom is merely a matter of information and skills that can be judged right or wrong, then these messages will be received and acted on by the students when they are working individually or in groups.

In the foregoing chapters, examples of children's talk have been accompanied by valuable accounts of the teaching that has brought it about. It is to be hoped that this can in the future be developed into a systematic analysis of what teachers can do to support talking for learning and of ways of teaching that impede it. In Chapter 7, Short and Armstrong formulate a picture of classroom talk in terms of "inquiry," suggesting that teachers should shift their attention away from a view of learning that places product (received information and skills) at the center to one that directs attention to the processes by which learning is carried out. This is in line with the results of the ORACLE study (Galton and Simon, 1980), which found that the most effective learning arose when the teacher involved the class in joint inquiry. In parallel with the analysis of students' talk already suggested we need further study of the nature and characteristics of the teaching that supports it. How do teachers set up contexts in which students' own talk and writing play a full part, and how do they at times unintentionally prevent it? This task is particularly important, because successful teachers are often very vague when they talk about their work, falling back upon such phrases as, "the class decided that . . ." or "the students chose the things they were interested in." Such expressions fail to indicate to the inexperienced teacher the complex skills involved in focusing students' interest on a topic, eliciting suggestions, encouraging students to elaborate on their existing ideas, tactfully discouraging unpromising lines of thought, and managing the eventual choice so that the students experience it as consensus. As with the analysis of good student talk, the more such skills can be described and illustrated, the closer the teaching profession will come to giving an explicit account of its work to one another, to teachers in training, and to the public.

The analysis I envisage would have to treat separately the various "task situations" that constitute classroom activity. At one moment a teacher is setting up a new topic, engaging students' interest, and opening possible questions; a few minutes later she may be eliciting from them what they already know and helping them to relate the issue to their personal experience. At other times the focus is likely to be on providing experience and information, which may be through various media, including the teacher's own demonstrations and explanations. Other essential task situations are the organizing of learning activities (including helping the children to see tasks that they can undertake and negotiating choices), engaging with groups while they work, setting up occasions for public display of work done, and encouraging reflection upon what has been learned. It would be possible to collect examples of each task situation in turn and to examine in each case what options and strategies were available to teachers and the likely effects of each. Few teachers ever make these options and strategies explicit, even to themselves: analysis of the basis for choosing them would be likely to help the teachers themselves as well as others. However, it is clear that the analysis would need to deal not only with concerns and strategies appropriate to each of the task situations (and there are others not mentioned here), but would develop further the account of the inquiring community that appears in foregoing chapters, thus providing the principles underlying all the situations.

THE CLASS AS A LEARNING COMMUNITY

Several contributors discuss social relationships in classrooms under the rubric of "the learning community." There is no doubt that building the trust on which collaborative inquiry depends takes time and care: it does not appear of itself and may need constant renewal. Communities, however, can be good or bad, their cultures supportive or oppressive. In this book the concept of "community" has been used entirely positively to represent a classroom culture that provides trust and mutual support for all its members, tolerance of subcultural differences while seeking common ground, and collaboration in learning and understanding. This ideal, a very attractive one, is not intrinsically in contradiction to the parallel emphasis upon inquiry that appears in other chapters, yet there is some tension between the two that deserves discussion.

There is a danger that too heavy an emphasis upon community might in some teachers' hands allow the social goals (important as they are) to outweigh the other kinds of learning that are the responsibility of schooling. During the 1960s, when "child-centered" was the watchword for liberal-minded teachers in Britain, it became all too clear that some teachers were interpreting it to mean that any activity that interested the students was acceptable, with the result that some of the essential cognitive purposes of schooling were underemphasized or even ignored.

Alongside the creation of a cultural community in a classroom, teachers and students need a changed view of what constitutes schoolwork. Talking to learn cannot be imposed as a mere matter of classroom management, since everything a teacher does sends messages to students. This is the reason why teachers who wish to change often need to undertake a long period of reflection and reshaping of their preconceptions about children, about learning, about knowledge, and about what is possible and useful in the classroom, since they need to "reframe" their perceptions (Schön, 1983). In the creation of an inquiring community it makes little sense to separate the establishment of a supportive social order from the creation of collaborative patterns of learning.

Learning to engage in critical inquiry may generate disagreements and uncertainties that will ruffle the social surface of the classroom conversation. At times, even students value consensus at the expense of critical discussion. I have noticed when group work has been in progress that some students are so eager to avoid disputes among themselves that they fail to challenge the views of other students even when their proposals are likely to spoil the work of the group. Much learning is not a matter of accepting received knowledge; uncertainty and disagreement are a normal part of life. Since most people become anxious in the face of uncertainty, students need support in looking at alternative explanations and actions. The necessary learning includes finding out how to disagree with another student without making it a personal attack and how to receive criticism without feeling rejected. This is indeed social learning, but it is social learning in the service of the topic under discussion.

What is needed is a mutual trust that nevertheless has a critical edge; consensus is not enough. If we value students' active involvement in learning, this must include the negotiation of topics and the exercise of judgment when they choose between alternatives. Both of these require critical acumen. There is no contradiction between the principles of community and inquiry, but there needs to be a balance between consensus and criticism.

THE NATURE OF KNOWING

Our thinking about children's learning should include adequate models of what constitutes valued knowledge, since this can help to shape teaching. These models need to deal both with the formation of knowledge structures and with the personal meaning of these structures to the learner. It is possible to represent what we know as a series of more or less interlinked systems, perhaps organized in a multidimensional universe (Kelly, 1963; Minsky, 1975; Marton, 1975; Novak and Gowin, 1984; Wyer and Srull, 1984; Strike and Posner, 1985). How are these systems formed? Baird and White (1982) suggested in a study of adults that the most effective learners do not isolate their learning but make links with many aspects of what they know already, even with parts of their lives that seem entirely irrelevant. For example, a person learning about the strength of biological structures might make links with a whole range of firsthand experiences of humans and animals, with things in the home and elsewhere that collapse under pressure, and even with ideas about psychological strength or weakness. John Baird and his associates in Australia have tried to build this insight into teaching. They set out to find out how students can be encouraged to take more responsibility for their learning, monitoring what they understood, identifying the next task, making links so as to embed their school learning in firsthand experiences and understandings (Baird and Mitchell, 1986; Baird and Northfield, 1992). There seems to be every reason why these ideas should be brought to bear upon future thinking about the role of talk in learning, since the students' own talk plays a central part in setting up relationships between new ideas and existing knowledge structures.

Several of the contributions to this book mention the importance of the personal meaning of knowledge. This might appear to refer to the matter discussed in the previous paragraph: each of us indeed needs to relate new experiences and ideas to our existing pictures of how the world is. But in fact, "personal meaning" raises further important issues. All knowledge is potentially value-laden: some new ideas are threatening or frightening, others are exciting because they open new possibilities in our lives. School knowledge that seems entirely neutral will soon be lost to the learner because there is little reason to make connections. Indeed, much of what is taught in school is threatening to unsure students precisely because they do not see it as relevant to their concerns. If students are to find personal significance in what they learn, this carries two implications: first, they need opportunities to make choices and negotiate what and how they learn, for only they know where significant links are to be made; and second, the classroom must display those characteristics that have here been associated with the concept "community," since it is in a supportive milieu that young people are able to come out into the open about those aspects of experience that affect them deeply. The classroom implications of "personal meaning" deserve further investigation.

Schooling by its very nature is removed from the everyday pressures of life, since thereby children's learning can be simplified and controlled and children can be protected from any exploitative forces that might threaten them. But this also carries limitations; much of what students do in school has no obvious effect on their lives elsewhere, parts of which may be considerably more urgent than anything that happens in class. Students need help in making links between school and the world outside, so that they perceive the social topics discussed in class, such as violence or the plight of disadvantaged ethnic groups, as relevant to their own lives, present or future. When children talk about a story, too, they are not merely decoding the text but using their knowledge of the real world to give substance to what they read, so that ideally there is a dialectical interplay between what they read and those aspects of their lives that seem relevant. Moreover, when adults write or make something they do so for a purpose: a document makes a social contact or attempts to persuade, while an artifact is for use. But what children write and make in school often has little or no function in the world of action. Indeed, what they are asked to do in some classes is oversimplified and predigested, very unlike the complex choices and decisions that they are already having to make in their lives outside school. Can learning genuinely be "active" when this is the case? Much schooling is inevitably a preparation; yet, as Freire (1972) pointed out, we are all most likely to learn from actions that are intended to influence our own lives. How far can this be reconciled with the protective function of schooling?

REFLECTION AS PART OF LEARNING

Several contributors have highlighted the importance of the learner's reflection upon what is being learned. Some learners adopt much more effective learning strategies than others, and a tradition of research has developed in what is often called "metacognition," the learner's perception of the experiences and activities that constitute learning. Jones' study (1988) showed that even many older students were making poor use of opportunities for group discussion because they were trapped by their belief that learning was concerned with right answers about facts, and they therefore saw no point in deepening their understanding. Similar misconceptions were reported by Baird and Mitchell (1986). This is why some teachers try to help their students reach conscious awareness of their own learning strategies in the hope of thereby improving the effectiveness of these strategies. Indeed, the earlier chapters of this book describe some ways of encouraging reflection, including introducing journals and notebooks, discussing tape recordings of the students' own discussions, and explicitly negotiating with students of "the social parameters of their discussions." A further extension of this would be to involve the students themselves in investigating their own spoken learning behavior, for they have the advantage of being able to speak authoritatively about their perception of what was going on and why they said what they did. At first students find it difficult to think abstractly about what was said and why, but the more they can be encouraged to understand the role of talk in learning, the better use they will make of opportunities for it.

THE PROFESSIONAL DEVELOPMENT OF TEACHERS

The contributions to this book provide an extensive program of possible changes that teachers can make in an experimental frame of mind in order to observe how learning can be improved. These changes go far beyond surface "teaching methods." Any teacher who sets up group discussion, for example, without understanding the meaning of the change is all too likely to report that "it doesn't work with my children." Teachers are unlikely to make radical changes in their perceptions of what is possible and valuable in their classes merely in the light of what they read. Professional change is an exciting but demanding process. Trying out new ways of shaping classroom work can make an experienced teacher feel all the uncertainty of a beginner. Nearly all the teachers and academics who have written chapters for this volume have had the support provided by working in a group or network of others attempting similar changes: this has enabled them to discuss with other innovators the effects of the changes they are making, and to share both the problems and successes. As Pierce argues in Chapter 16, this process of evaluating and reevaluating what happens in lessons is an essential part of any curricular alterations that require teachers as well as students to change their perception and understanding of classroom learning. After each meeting teachers return to their classes refreshed to try out new possibilities and to collect further material that will help them to understand what is happening in their lessons.

The teachers who have written this book found great value in learning to listen to what their students said, not in order to judge it right or wrong but to understand how it contributed to their current learning. Study groups sometimes first choose the less threatening task of looking at students' writing, and later move to recording their talk in groups. Eventually most of them pluck up courage to record their own part in the classroom conversation, sometimes talking to one student, to a group, or to the whole class. Through reflecting on this in the support and safety of a sympathetic group, they come to understand what aspects of their students' talk and writing contribute most to learning. Equally important, however, is understanding how the cultural expectations of the classroom, for which they themselves are largely responsible, tend to shape how their students take part in lessons.

The British National Oracy Project shows one way in which teachers' professional development can be supported. Though set up with government funding, the project chose to work through local authorities which provided further funding. The national aims for the project included "to enhance the role of speech in the learning process . . . by encouraging active learning," "to improve pupils' performance across the curriculum," and "to enhance teachers' skills and practice." Policies for local projects were negotiated to ensure diversity, so that across the national project all the phases of education and a wide range of curricular subjects were involved, and proper attention was paid to issues such as continuity and the effects of gender and ethnic identity upon children's talk. Local projects identified groups of schools that would be active in the development work, and these in turn nominated two or three teachers as leaders of the work in the school. Each local project was led by a teacher released from classroom duties to act as coordinator, organizing and supporting the work of the participating teachers. Each coordinator was in turn supported not only by visits from a member of the national team but also by a sequence of meetings, conferences, and publications. Thus, the direction of local development was chosen by the teachers themselves within a national framework; they decided what new practices were to be tried out, they collected and evaluated evidence of their effects, and they reported their discoveries in writing and at conferences. As a result, perhaps a thousand teachers had the benefit of actively investigating and reinterpreting the role of talk in learning and of passing on these insights to their colleagues in their own and nearby schools.

The chapters in this book offer many ideas that can be used by teachers who read it; many will find that they can engage in similar teaching and study. Through teacher groups, teachers begin to realize that they are not only implementors of other people's theories but are able to develop and test their own. Such groups generate new insights through the sharing and critical evaluation of one another's findings. A new awareness of the importance of talk in learning is spreading throughout the English-speaking world. What is needed are networks of teachers carrying out parallel inquiries in their own classrooms, for this will both enhance their teaching and prepare them in the future to make their own the advances made by others. Some groups arise voluntarily, perhaps around someone who has already been made enthusiastic by earlier discoveries; others may be linked to advanced courses in which the professor is enlightened enough to realize the value to teachers of informal investigations; still other groups may be encouraged by a funded project like that in Britain. Whatever the structure, it is essential that, like those who have written this book, the teachers are active creators of new insights through their own inquiries.

REFERENCES

Baird, J. R. and I. J. Mitchell. 1986. *Improving the quality of teaching.* Melbourne: Monash University.

Baird, J. R. and J. R. Northfield. 1992. *Learning from the PEEL experience.* Melbourne: Monash University.

Baird, J. R. and R. T. White. 1982. "A case study of learning styles in biology." *European Journal of Science Education.* 4:325–37.

Bruner, J. 1983. *Child's talk: Learning to use language.* London: Oxford University Press.

Cazden, C. B. 1972. *Child language and education.* New York: Holt, Rinehart and Winston.

Freire, P. 1972. *Pedagogy of the oppressed.* Harmondsworth: Penguin Books.

Galton, M. and B. Simon. 1980. *Progress and performance in the primary classroom.* London: Routledge and Kegan Paul.

Halliday, M. A. K. 1975. *Learning how to mean: Explorations in the development of language.* London: Edward Arnold.

Heath, S. B. 1983. *Ways with words.* Cambridge: Cambridge University Press.

Jones, P. 1988. *Lip service.* Milton Keynes: Open University Press.

Kelly, G. A. 1963. *A Theory of personality.* New York: Norton.

Lindfors, J. W. 1987. *Children's language and learning.* Englewood Cliffs, NJ: Prentice-Hall.

Marton, F. 1975. "What does it take to learn?" In *How Students Learn,* edited by N. Entwistle & D. Hounsell. Lancaster: University of Lancaster.

Minsky, M. 1975. "A framework for representing knowledge." In *The psychology of computer vision,* edited by P. Winston. New York: McGraw-Hill.

Novak, J. D. and D. B. Gowin. 1984. *Learning how to learn.* Cambridge: Cambridge University Press.

Schon, D. A. 1983. *The reflective practitioner.* London: Temple Smith.

Strike, K. A. and G. J. Posner. 1985. "A conceptual change view of knowledge." In *Cognitive structure and conceptual change,* edited by L. West & A. Pines. New York: Academic Press.

Tizard, B. & M. Hughes. 1984. *Young children learning.* London: Fontana Books.

Wells, G. et al. 1981. *Learning through interaction.* Cambridge: Cambridge University Press.

Wyer, R. S. and T. K. Srull. Eds. 1984. *Handbook of social cognition.* Hillsdale, NJ: Lawrence Erlbaum.

Also available from Heinemann. . .

Talking About Books
Creating Literate Communities
Edited by **Kathy Gnagey Short** and **Kathryn Mitchell Pierce**

Talking About Books brings together the ideas of teachers who have been exploring collaborative strategies for encouraging talk about literature. The 14 authors share the belief in the power of literature and the power of interaction within collaborative communities, but they realize this belief in a variety of ways. From Charlotte Huck's opening essay on the power of children's literature through Dorothy Watson's closing paper on whole language evaluation, the writers underscore their common goal to create classrooms in which students become members of a literate community using reading as a way to learn. Thus, the dual focus of the book is on learning communities which support readers as they learn and interact, and on encouraging literate talk about literature. The types of classroom experiences that are particularly highlighted are read-aloud time with a whole class and discussions of literature in small groups.

0-435-08526-3   1990   224pp

Listening In
Children Talk About Books (and other things)
Thomas Newkirk with **Patricia McLure**

Joyce: *If you had a magic wand* [like one of the characters in the story], *what do you think you would do with it? To get rid of. . .*

Cindy: *I would try to get rid of maybe my brother sometimes. If he's bothering me. But if he's being nice I wouldn't.*
                          —From *Listening In*

In *Listening In*, Thomas Newkirk invites the reader to eavesdrop on the student readers in Patricia McLure's first/second-grade classroom in Lee, New Hampshire. As the children joke, tell stories, and exaggerate during discussions of the books they read, it becomes clear that these "digressions" are an integral part of the learning process, essential for reading groups to work effectively. Understanding occurs only when the children "speak over" the words of the author, interpreting the text in their own language, through their own culture, connecting literature with their everyday lives.

By examining the rich oral culture of children, *Listening In* challenges the narrow, text-dominated, question-controlled "on-task" model that passes for discussion in most U.S. classrooms. Filled with transcripts of student dialogue, the book asks readers to consider this talk as a meeting of cultures — the adult culture of the teacher and the oral culture of the children, which must be recognized and validated by the teacher for learning and sharing to begin.

Celebrating the wit, humor, and intelligence of these children, *Listening In* is an invitation to teachers to be more aware of the opportunities for talk in their own classrooms.

0-435-08713-4   1992   176pp

*These and other fine texts available through
your local supplier or favorite bookstore.*

Heinemann
361 Hanover Street
Portsmouth, NH 03801-3912
1-800-541-2086